TESTING THE LIMIT

Cultural Memory
in
the
Present

Mieke Bal and Hent de Vries, Editors

TESTING THE LIMIT

Derrida, Henry, Levinas, and the
Phenomenological Tradition

François-David Sebbah
Translated by Stephen Barker

STANFORD UNIVERSITY PRESS

STANFORD, CALIFORNIA

Stanford University Press
Stanford, California

Testing the Limit was originally published in French under the title *L'épreuve de
la limite: Derrida, Henry, Levinas et la phénoménologie* © Presses Universitaires de
France, 2001.

This book was published with the assistance of the Edgar M. Kahn Memorial
Fund and the University of Technology of Compiègne (UTC).

Cet ouvrage a bénéficié du soutien des Programmes d'aide à la publication de
l'Institut français / ministère français des affaires étrangères et européennes. / This
work was provided support by the Publication Assistance Program of the Institut
Français / French Ministry of Foreign and European Affairs.

Library of Congress Cataloging-in-Publication Data

Sebbah, François-David, author.
  [Épreuve de la limite. English]
  Testing the limit : Derrida, Henry, Levinas, and the phenomenological tradition
/ François-David Sebbah ; translated by Stephen Barker.
    pages cm. — (Cultural memory in the present)
  "Originally published in French under the title L'Épreuve de la limite."
  Includes bibliographical references.
  ISBN 978-0-8047-7274-7 (cloth : alk. paper)
  ISBN 978-0-8047-7275-4 (pbk : alk. paper)
  1. Phenomenology.   2. Philosophy, French—20th century.   3. Derrida,
Jacques.   4. Henry, Michel, 1922–2002.   5. Levinas, Emmanuel.   6. Intention-
ality (Philosophy)   7. Subjectivity.   I. Title.   II. Series: Cultural memory in
the present.
  B829.5.S4313   2012
  142'.7—dc23

                                                        2011032773

Contents

Acknowledgments   *ix*

Introduction   1

PART I: TOWARD A CRITIQUE OF
PHENOMENOLOGICAL RATIONALITY   15

 1 Research   17

 2 Intentionality and Non-Givenness   34

 3 The Question of the Limit   58

PART II: THE FRONTIER OF TIME   67

 1 At the Limits of Intentionality: Michel Henry and
    Emmanuel Levinas as Readers of *On the Phenomenology
    of the Consciousness of Internal Time*   75

 2 Anticipating Phenomenology: Jacques Derrida and
    Jean-Luc Marion, the Impossible and Possibility   88

    *1: The Time of Ordinary Phenomena and Phantoms
    (Jean-Toussaint Desanti; Jacques Derrida)   88
    2: The Impossibility of the Gift: Within the Extreme
    Possibility of Givenness (Jacques Derrida; Jean-Luc Marion)   104*

PART III: THE TEST OF SUBJECTIVITY   123

 1 Subjectivity in Contemporary French Phenomenology   127

 2 The Birth of Subjectivity in Levinas   142

3   Born to Life, Born to Oneself: The Birth of Subjectivity
in Michel Henry   156

4   Spectral Subjectivity According to Jacques Derrida   174

PART IV: PHENOMENOLOGICAL DISCOURSE
AND SUBJECTIFICATION   191

1   The Rhythm of *Otherwise Than Being*
According to Levinas   202

    1: Reading Levinas and Thinking Entirely Otherwise   202
    2: Rhythm as the Question of Intentionality in Levinas   212

2   The Rhythm of Life According to Michel Henry   219

    Conclusion   243

    Abbreviations   257

    Notes   261

    Bibliography   313

Acknowledgments

This book is the result of many years of research. I want especially to thank Jacques Colette for having made me the beneficiary of his expertise along the way. I offer deep thanks as well to Françoise Dastur not only for the generous attention she gave to these pages, but also for the ceaseless encouragement she showed me over long years. In addition to Jacques Colette and Françoise Dastur, Rudolph Bernet, Jean-Toussaint Desanti, and Jean-Michel Salanskis gave invaluable advice; I thank them for their commentary, of which this text, I hope, carries many traces.

I want to express my profound gratitude to Jacques Derrida, Jean-Toussaint Desanti, and Michel Henry, who read certain passages addressing their work and who always encouraged me to proceed in my own direction.

Thanks as well to Alain Cugno, Anne Montavont, Jacob Rogozinski, and François Roussel, who offered editorial assistance in the final stages. Special thanks to Mireille Séguy, who assisted in the book's development.

Warm thanks as well to Elisabeth Lemirre for her manuscript editing.

The solitary work of reading texts must be perpetually stimulated, at least for me, by discussion; I want therefore to thank all those involved in the various spaces for philosophic discussion in which I worked for seven years. I think particularly of the fruitful exchanges I was able to have at the revue *Alter*, in the TSH Department at the University of Compiègne, and at the International College of Philosophy, which published the original French version of this book in one of its series.

Introduction

This work originated, or at least received its impetus, in my encounter with certain texts of Emmanuel Levinas, Michel Henry, and Jacques Derrida.

The encounter was traumatic, so my pleasure in reading philosophy is now never free of a certain imposed discomfort. I had numerous startling surprises. First, it seemed that these texts were, at least in significant part, literary texts—which certainly does not mean that this accounts for their "essence" or that they should therefore be denied the status of philosophical texts—or, on the other hand, that we should argue in favor of a *confusion* between the philosophic and the literary. It simply means, in the first place, that the philosophical necessity for the unveiling of what *is*, *as* it is, is not in these texts separable from the work of language—language considered as something that must be "worked"—or from any specific style.

Additionally (and this is an indication of their traumatic power), one of the significant stylistic traits shared by these texts is *violence*, a violence done to the *logos* itself in its apophantic exigency as manifested, for example, in its persistent practice of paradox, metaphor, oxymoron, and parataxis.[1] And the reader is the first to be exposed to this violence, if reading a text entails re-creating for oneself the acts of thought it suggests.

These works clearly produce meaning, but do they not also dangerously deviate from the standards of evidence and the transparency of language characterizing the Husserlian idea of phenomenology as, precisely, a "rigorous science"? These are necessary questions, since they relate to phe-nomenology, and in each case this relationship concerns its very essence. My attempt here will be to demonstrate that the opposite is also true: that phenomenology is concerned, in *its* very essence, with its relationship to itself and to these questions. It must be understood, however—and this is vitally important—that none of the texts examined here is inscribed exactly on the "axis" of the phenomenology preceding them: all claim in one way or another to exceed it.

In any case, if it is true that for Adjukiewicz philosophy belongs to the evolution of logical positivism, and Husserlian *Wesensschau* was already an example of metaphoric usage and was simply suggestive of language in its conflict with direct, literal, univocal expression (a conflict necessary to the explicit argumentation required for a true scientific philosophy), then we can easily glimpse the kind of judgment to which we could submit Levinas's, Henry's, and Derrida's works on the basis of such criteria.

I am certainly not holding to these criteria: to do so would simply render the specific readings of the authors I am interested in here impossi-ble. The fact remains, however, that they do put to the crudest of tests any requirement of clarity and explicit argumentation that apparently needs to be maintained in order for philosophy to be philosophy. Yet an essential aspect of this requirement is the courage to venture into regions in which it tests the *limit* of its own power: the texts we will examine will bring us to this limit—one of the essential aspects of their traumatic nature.

The issue of this limit can be made clearer if we concentrate on the related question of the practice of phenomenological method. In fact, it seems that these texts' stylistic violence can be more precisely described as the fact of an "excessive" style. This in turn means that inseparable from any writing style a mode of phenomenological description is also brought into question.

But do these authors not, paradoxically enough, test out the idea that adhering to radicality can be pushed too far? That the discourse of radicality can be inverted into merely excessive discourse doing violence to the constraints of its own proper coherence and pertinence? Thus, it is in fact the fundamental operation of the phenomenological reduction itself that is in play: the phenomenological reduction as renewal [*reconduction*] of the phenomenological gaze, as what appears to the how? and the where?

of what appears; that is, to pure appearance? And is the phenomenological reduction not itself susceptible to being betrayed in the very act of wanting to be *too* radical?

Could there be a reading of Michel Henry, Emmanuel Levinas, and Jacques Derrida that does *not* confront their excessive application of the phenomenological method? Indeed, a phenomenology *of* excess necessarily understanding the genitive as objective as well as subjective; a phenomenological practice having lost all sense of proportion and of critical stresses, as it moves toward a description of excess itself; a phenomenology that is the victim of immoderation, since its focus on the originary would lead ineluctably and in perverse ways to its being moved ever closer toward that which *exceeds* the field of appearance; a phenomenology characterized by what might be called an *escalation of the originary*. In conventional terms we might connect a charge of phenomenology's "poetization" to that of its "theologization"; in the following I will try to demonstrate that if the latter actually means posing a quite necessary question to phenomenological practice, it still obscures the complexity and richness of that practice: by *identifying* phenomenology as a simple repetition of the theological project, do we not risk sidestepping—or even seeking to evade—this specific test? Is not every excessive practice naturally theological? We must ask this last question, however, taking care not to expand another one: has not *all* excessive practice, even when not identifying itself as "theologizing," always had to confront this risk, this temptation?

We must not allow the question of the "theological turn" to be our investigation's foundation,[2] yet we must equally attempt not to evade its problematic charge, or even to achieve its resolution, by addressing the question underlying this entire reading: what is it that we can expect, in phenomenology, from a practice of excess?

This question, then, at least up to a certain point, is manifestly of the Kantian type: with regard to the practice of the phenomenological method we can sense the risk of what Kant calls the dialectic of the "logic of appearance" of knowledge in general: the movement of that which is conveyed toward what exceeds the domain of the given. We know that for Kant this movement is illegitimate and the producer of illusions; it is the ineluctable perversion of a human characteristic that is nonetheless essential and even "positive" within the mind: our desire for the absolute and for totality (a desire replayed in phenomenology as the desire for originarity).

To be interested in the practice of excess is thus, precisely, to be interested in the practice of the *limit*, the limit through whose transgression alone excess can be what it is. In fact, in the case of phenomenology, the legitimate limit—the limit as legitimizing norm—is the limit of the domain of what appears *as* it appears, the limit of the *given*. Our interrogation here, then, continues to be inspired by Kant, but it will become clear that our interpretation of this limit's signification—and of the use we intend to make of it—is not Kantian.

The first part of this study attempts to deepen, to clarify, and to support this problematic. Its particular orientation, however, will be laid out as follows: if an excessive practice of the phenomenological method tends to destroy the constraints proper to it, then the question becomes one of knowing if such a violence can be converted into something fruitful. Such an eventual fecundity can only be instigated immediately, from the very start, since it is and must be a matter of *initial* violence. But what would be, in general, a *good usage* for the limit, and for excess, in and of phenomenology? Do the texts we will address present a useful manner of utilizing excess within phenomenology? Or are they rather entirely excessive texts whose eventual fruitfulness depends from the outset, perhaps exclusively, on the use the reader makes of them?

The present interrogation is formulated according to two irreducibly intertwined dimensional questions: Is there an inherent fecundity of these phenomenological practices within a description of appearance as such? Is the traumatism inflicted by these texts' excesses, paradoxically, capable of engendering its addressee, or at least its receiver, as a philosophizing subject?

It should be understood that the impression of the reading being laid out here—this traumatism in encountering these texts—is not simply the most immediate access to the problem, and certainly not the most superficial. If these works pose the question of the correct usage or the correct regulating of this excess, then this questioning (which might be called an ethics) is indissociable from an aesthetics of reception: as the reader of these texts, I must accept the responsibility for their usage in the very gesture by which I nonetheless expose myself integrally to their traumatic power, and this is just as much a matter of their phenomenological fecundity as of my emergence as a philosophizing subject.

My effort will be to show that this practice of the limit, of excess, is exemplarily brought into play in the confrontation with temporality (Part 2).

I will then work to characterize more clearly the test (*as* a test) from which the Self emerges, or more precisely that experiences it as always already there (Part 3). In fact, if excess is always the threat of destruction, could it be brought to life in any way other than through a test? And is it not through such a test that I am *myself*, in the sense in which I "prove" myself *to be* myself? And further, is the test of the limit not always already in the same gesture the test of the Self *by* itself—that is, of the Self emerging from the test *of* the Self?

The idea of "the test of subjectivity" is explicitly thematized by Michel Henry. I will attempt in what follows to show that the Levinasian notion of "traumatism" from which the Self emerges and the Derridean notion of the "endurance" of the limit at which one encounters oneself also allow for the formulation, in a clear and precise manner, of the expression "test of subjectivity." For these three thinkers, this process is a matter of indicating an experience *that is not one*, since it is not constituted by a subject, and that consequently precedes both all activity of the subject and all objectivizing knowledge. But it thus also presupposes a connection to a self from which the Self arises, in the obscurity and passivity of auto-affection: this is precisely the question of "self-testing [*s'éprouver*]."

It is therefore a powerful characteristic of the works we will examine to make subjectivity, in its differing configurations, originary in its own manner, even though they will have stripped it of the prerogatives and privileges that have accrued to it in the modern world and relegated it to a radical passivity, to the pure self-immanence of a subjectivity "driven back on itself" in an expression as Levinasian as it is Henrian. And this is accomplished in the same gesture through which they have shown that this subjectivity is engendered by an injunction older than itself. I will try to describe, without becoming absurd, how subjectivity can *simultaneously* be in some sense originary to itself, caught in advance in the immanence of the test of its auto-affection, so to speak, *and* arise despite the risks of being "older than itself."

In other words, I want to suggest that in their practice—their test-ing—of phenomenology, these three writers have all exceeded intentional-ity (the Husserlian term for the milieu of everything that appears insofar as it appears and, more radically, of the power to give itself everything that is given) in the direction (a direction no doubt not exclusive for all, but always decisive) of a Self, a Self older than the knowledge of intentionality. And it is, moreover, an idea common to all three that they have made their texts just as much a witness to this test as its thematic description.

We must understand that it is essential that these philosophies have for their common theme a problematic of originary subjectivity in its con-nection with an address older than itself, and, at the same time, that it consists in a sense entirely of *one* address: they appear to their addressee through a traumatism under the ambivalent sign both of destruction and of the engendering of a philosophizing subjectivity.

The fourth part of my inquiry will shed light on what might provi-sionally and somewhat awkwardly be understood as the *mise en abyme* of these works' thematic form.

Before plunging into the heart of the matter, it is necessary to point out some supplementary aspects of the nature of the project at hand and its methodology.

Our focus here will not be the presentation of a *panorama* of con-temporary French phenomenology, for several related reasons.

First, many eminent representatives of contemporary French phe-nomenology are not evoked here, not even allusively or indirectly. My project is a more modest one, interested only in a particular *family* of contemporary French phenomenology. What do I mean by this? A fam-ily is characterized by a "family likeness"; that is, by a resemblance. And a "resemblance" is a characteristic that can never be completely clarified and formalized, even though it gives the impression of being meaning-ful. It can never be formalized because by definition it is not an *exact* resemblance: if it were, it would be an *identity*. All resemblance contains a difference, and, conversely, in it difference is present as such only on the basis of a commonality. Wittgenstein thematizes the idea of a "fam-ily" as being freed from a purely formal characteristic of language,[3] and he does this in the following way: for him it is a question of marking the fact that there can be a complicated network of linked significant and irreducible resemblances uniting differing elements; a network never integrally formalizable yet that can nonetheless permit the inscription of these different elements in a single and unique "family," even while they do not share a group of commonly articulable properties. These elements share a "family resemblance." Just as there is thus no "essential" common denominator for the different elements composing a "family," the *borders* of a family are not clean ones: they are susceptible to modification from other adopted perspectives. The intrinsic haziness of the "family" frontier means that this frontier can be refigured relative to the specific stakes of one or another moment of reflection.

I want to demonstrate here a particular kind of relation that is comparable to Wittgenstein's "family resemblance." I will thus try to show that if no common denominator essential to each can be found in the works addressed—such a reading would be simply reductive—these works still remain in not always explicit relationships that can determine and open out a specifically thinkable field.

It would be unnecessary to acknowledge the need for an interest in "family resemblance" if we did not want to renounce our ordinary understanding of the richness of meaning overflowing the domain of exactitude. Since the "border" of a family is by definition unclear, it will always be important to indicate the resemblance of this or that thinker to the family being explored even when it is not apparent at first glance. Such a resemblance emerges from a specific viewpoint. Rendering the resultant frontier even more complex will in no case alter the power of analysis and determination; on the contrary, it is precisely in the varying of the angles of attack, in the play of resemblances and differences, that a family resemblance can be incrementally affirmed. The progress of this exploration will thus proceed less by linear accumulation than by variations in those angles of attack on the problematic at hand. We must, however, guard against a possible default. There must be no question of throwing oneself into an endless quest for resemblances and differences; a great deal of insipidity and coarseness would inevitably result from any attempt to demonstrate that in some sense Levinas, Henry, and Derrida are saying the same thing; immense naïveté would be required to make such a claim despite their many differences. My task is thus the following: while laying out a "family resemblance," to open out a field of thought in its own properly problematic configuration, to assist in bringing it to light. And also, doubtless, to see that the link uniting the different works in this family is all the stronger in that they do *not* conjoin integrally—do not melt together—their discrete differences into a singularity, as Wittgenstein says, in the same way that a cable's separate strands conjoin to augment the cable's strength.

In one sense, this work can be read as an attempt at the rigorous description of this kind of family within contemporary French phenomenology. A too-great dissimilarity within this or that trait constitutive of the given family would mean that a particular work, or even a particular writer's oeuvre, could not properly be a focus of our concerns, though we might refer to it in order to mark a particular affinity or, contrarily, a counterpoint.

Thus, we will not focus on the work of Paul Ricoeur, since I have retained the violent and excessive nature of the gesture of thought as a constitutive trait of the family resemblance I am exploring; as is well known, Ricoeur locates his philosophical practice under the sign of a respectful hermeneutic whose generosity makes a powerful case precisely *against* a concentration on the violence in these texts.

As another example, though we will refer to the work of Jean-Toussaint Desanti on certain vital points, we can still not fully integrate him into the family: Desanti might be suspected of wanting to exceed the field of appearance; his phenomenology, far from making subjectivity originary, tends in a structuralist gesture toward reading it out of a system of *formal* configurations. Although he can be quite instructive, I will refer to him in order to bring out and to amplify a resemblance between Desantian and Derridean descriptions of temporality.

As a final example, I will frequently characterize the family on which I focus by contrasting it with another family—one that will, however, be approached only at an angle, not through its own problematics. The principal members of this other family are, chronologically, Henri Maldiney, Jacques Garelli, and Marc Richir. This family shares the constitutive trait of drawing its inspiration from Merleau-Pontian phenomenology; it thus also tends to concentrate on what exceeds and what is prior to intentionality, but this gesture, far from leading it toward an originary subjectivity, in fact leads it toward an originary anonymity. The importance of this

Merleau-Pontian influence means that Marc Richir's work cannot be integrated into the family on which I will be focusing here even though Richir has thematized a phenomenology of excess that is in some respects close to Levinas's.

Concentrating, thus, on a certain restricted family of contemporary French phenomenology will mean that the "family portrait" I construct here will necessarily be limited, incomplete.

One further possible misunderstanding must be prevented: in what follows I will absolutely not be constructing a map: the work at hand is not that of mapping, in any strict sense, the home territory of contemporary French phenomenology—or even of one of its constituent families. My aim is more modest, and not simply because it is not exhaustive: it consists simply in relating the development that has occurred within a particular area of contemporary French phenomenology, all the more since we have approached it as a landscape and not as a space, to recall Maldiney's distinction reading Erwin Straus. The changing, always unfinished, nature of this field constrains me to adopt the only position possible relative to works of thought: immersion in an *Umwelt* rather than taking the position of a spectator before what would then be merely an object. To think *within* works is to be a stroller in a particular countryside, not a spectator before a map representing a space of thought.

This characterization is not without implications: such a countryside is what it is because it is focused by a consciousness situated within it, which then becomes the absolute focus of that consciousness, disconnected from any integration into a larger space of which it might be part: "We are immersed in it: our 'here' refers only to itself. Wherever we step, our horizon moves with us. We are always at the origin. We are lost," as Maldiney writes,[4] which means that the landscape and the singular consciousness moving through it are dedicated to each other, and that it is this co-originary relationship that gives each its identity just as much as it relates them to each other. It would thus be a gross error to conclude that though one is strolling through this landscape but does not entirely traverse it, therefore this landscape has no other value than the entirely relative and arbitrary one of painting private impressions lacking all objectivity. If it is true that without a strolling figure there is no countryside, no landscape, the still-inchoate countryside nonetheless limits the perspective that gives birth to it, orienting the work of the very gestures that manifest it.[5] In order to recall the nature of phenomenological practice, we should quickly recall a comparison made by Desanti: like the carpenter, the phenomenologist must in certain respects "work"—"open up"—his material; he must separate it from its surface in order to *make it appear*—but this action is by then already guided by the limitations and constraints of the thing itself, such as the wood's grain and knots.

The glance I want to cast "into" the countryside rather than "onto" it constitutes the composting soil in which it is rooted and that conceals the position of the overview that produces the object. The phenomenologist attempts to connect to this model in life just as in texts, even while the latter operate as frames for the former. According to Maldiney, we can learn only through rigorous paradoxes, *orienting* ourselves within a landscape of thought as though in a landscape as such; we must know how to "lose ourselves"; that is, precisely, to "throw ourselves out the window" *into* it, letting ourselves be traversed by it, seized in its always-prior *rhythm*, constantly renewing it.[6]

In this sense, *description* of the field is indissociable from *intervention* in the field. The description proposed here intends to be neither arbitrary nor "objective." This strategy is of interest to philosophy in that as it constructs itself, by definition it cannot be the determination of an object, since objectification implies distancing as well as rupture from the object and thus its successful completion. If "history" consists of a practice of, so to speak, separating oneself from the dead in order to certify and even to perfect the dead in one's act of distancing them through objectification,[7] then our work here arises in no sense from the genre of the history of philosophy.[8]

It would be equally erroneous, however, to deduce from this that we will not be concerned with filiation. Rather, we will be preoccupied with it in one specific sense: the familial texts being read here could be considered to be an attempt at receiving, and witnessing, a transmission. This can occur only on the condition that we take these texts into consideration as living things (whether their authors are still living or long dead), that is, as capable of engendering and being engendered, at the potential cost, no doubt, of always-new displacements, since the life of thought, like life in general, never repeats itself.[9]

The project I am describing here promulgates a way of reading that allows us to take precautions against the risk of being dissipated among various works and themes. This is precisely why I am certainly not proposing any synthesis of the philosophical content of Derrida, Henry, and Levinas as accompanied by a "glimpse" at some other works: such an effort is hardly philosophical. Nor will I engage here, in the manner of a historian of philosophy, in a genetic and structural study of these works in a step-by-step constitution of their problematics: such an effort exceeds my competence as much as the proportions of my intent; in any case, it presupposes a constituted object that, as I have already insisted, is not relevant here. Let me simply say from the outset that the specificity of this connection with the corpus addressed here is clearly marked by the contamination at work between my discourse and its own, even while I will make operational such notions as "diachrony" and "double bind," borrowed from Levinas and Derrida, respectively. This undoubtedly poses some methodological problems, the price to be paid for approaching philosophical texts in the only appropriate manner: not to summarize doctrinal content, not to analyze a particular argument or system, not to locate principal concepts, not even to ask questions *of* a text, but rather to think *within* a text, to take it as a *medium* allowing for the possibility of a thought that no other has ever made or will ever make possible. That is, it is a matter of becoming permeable not to contents, and not even to questions, but to a "gesture of thought," to a certain way of posing questions in order to revitalize them, which implies simultaneously letting them take possession of us, since properly seen, they are a field of forces, and to dislodge them from any particular teleology, just as a navigator is simultaneously carried along by water and wind and is oriented there.

Our two chief instructors here, though they might initially seem to be antithetical to each other, are Bergson and Derrida, Bergson because he engages in raising himself beyond the extension of doctrine toward the intensity of intuition as a living force deployed in it, but that is also diluted and masked there.[10] That is, he invites us to seize what we might freely call a writer's "diacritical posture," as inscribed in the field of philosophy through the production of (a) difference. Bergson also invites us less to locate constituted notions than the matrix of their constitution, the style—in Leo Spitzer's sense—of a thought.

But from another perspective, must we not be on guard against—or at least question—what might be the full presence to itself of an intuition, and henceforth to return to text(s) less as faithful guardian(s) of well-argued thought than as marginal, perhaps even originarily, distancing us from the senses and eroding presence? This working hypothesis is clearly Derridean, and the addressing of texts to which we will invite Derrida does not consist of following a well-mastered argumentation but rather of suspending it, forcing it toward the nonmasterful—deconstructing it. Faced with adopting such a method, one must have an obvious reticence: paradoxically, does not forcing textual mastery on oneself present itself as an effect of mastery? And does deconstructing mastery not manifest itself as an attitude of overarching with regard to a text? It is certainly not a question of foreclosing it but of opening it out—but immediately the spectre of mastery reappears, insofar as even if the figure of the master is no longer there to question everything, its ironic spectre questions from "nowhere." To make such a claim would be to do justice to Derridean deconstruction. We must never forget that it is not a matter of taking the text unaware but, in a motivation more originary, to let it take itself by surprise. Deconstruction is not a gesture of negation; to deconstruct is to say "yes," as Derrida says, to invent: to allow "a field of forces" to take possession of us, which can occur only through taking maximal risk, consisting of having the strength to renounce all calculation and all predetermined meaning. Clearly, regarding deconstruction and the force of intuition, even if they are opposites, they are not contradictory. Deconstruction liberates the force of a thought, its "unthought" being itself not an instance of mastery but the very thing that defeats all mastery, including (before all else, if one plays its game) that of the deconstructive gesture itself.

Such a manner of being inserted into texts and of being mobile in them implies certain things, certain insistences, or, on the contrary, certain attenuations. Thus, for example, nearly nothing will appear here on the question of "the face of the other" in Levinas, though that is, so to speak, a "star" issue for him. On the contrary, I will propose an analysis of Derrida's notion of subjectivity, although the notion appears very seldom in his work other than in some critical confrontations, and, once again, I will approach it without stopping preferentially at the part of the Derridean corpus in which it seems to be imposed "naturally," the texts interrogating the proper name and the signature. I hope to be given credit for the fact that this is neither a matter of ignorance nor of excessive frivolity, nor some arbitrary, "subjective" choice; these perspectives have been dictated, as it were, by the global configuration of the phenomenological family under consideration. Describing this configuration should imply undoing certain "false likenesses" of the family, certain superficial resemblances, or alternatively "forcing" certain traits and certain contrasts in order to uncover an affinity at first hardly manifest.

The work of reading I propose here, then, is a mode of reception and transmission attempting to test out constraints determining a family of contemporary French phenomenology in order to offer an account—a singular one—of the opening out of a field of thought—one that everyone can experience and experiment with.

PART I

TOWARD A CRITIQUE OF
PHENOMENOLOGICAL RATIONALITY

1

Research

The field and focus of research

Husserlian phenomenological methodology has many descendants. And the current phenomenological landscape is not merely diverse but at the very least full of tensions. It is astonishing to see, for example, the many different—if not contradictory—claims, such as those of Hubert L. Dreyfus, who claims Husserl—though unrecognizable in his immediate offspring—as a father figure for classical cognitivism,[1] and that of Levinas, who claims to radicalize Husserl's insistence on originarity by designating Alterity as the unconstitutable underlying all appearance, all appealing to the same ancestor, by the same name, in the same space. Looking closer, we are encouraged to see that each of these descendants appears to be an absolutely legitimate—and an absolutely monstrous—heir, following the adopted perspective—and is that not the law of all filiation? The legitimate Levinas refuses all naturalization of thought and of consciousness in general, continuing work begun by Husserl and Heidegger but separating himself from all models of an ontic understanding of being. Highly suspect in the eyes of "phenomenology as a rigorous science," he meditates on a transcendence exceeding all thought, *sometimes* manifested in a style that could be called poetic or even "laudatory." Dreyfus's reading of Husserl is also, doubtless, "legitimate," relying on the Husserlian description of the *noëme* as a hierarchized group of formal rules, which thus perpetuates the rigorous necessity for a mathesis of lived experience. This is no less "monstrous," in that it naturalizes consciousness and perhaps thus confuses rigor and exactitude.

As exemplars of the current state of phenomenology, these progeny seem to have no possibility of communication between them: their fundamental differences result from a chiasmic connection to their common source.

It seems hardly necessary to ask here who respects and who betrays phenomenology: this would imply asking oneself to be the executor of what phenomenology actually is; one would then necessarily have to ask if such a position could in any simple way be philosophical. Fairly prejudicially, it would be a matter of asking if this formative power over phenomenology is a sign of its vigor and fecundity or contrarily a sign of its weakness, a weakness that would render it colonizable and manipulable by other, radically diverse, projects: "theological spiritualism" or "formalist naturalism"—the name "phenomenology" could only be shared in and as an empty set.[2]

If it is striking from a viewpoint one might call diachronic, this diversity is also marked out from a synchronic viewpoint: one can only marvel at the extraordinary capacity of phenomenology, as first and foremost a method, to invest in different fields. Ethics, aesthetics, politics, sociology, ethnology, psychiatry, psychology: all these fields find a way of approaching phenomenology, but in none of them—and this can fairly be stated from a strictly factual point of view—does phenomenology impose itself as a dominant methodology. From this viewpoint, too, the question arises of knowing whether such diversity is a sign of fecundity or of weakness.

Having this question regarding the fruitfulness of the phenomenological method in mind at and as the very heart of phenomenological diversity, we are inducted into a family.

Thanks to geographical and chronological criteria, this family can be characterized: we concern ourselves here with the most contemporary French phenomenology, after Sartre and Merleau-Ponty, which is still *in the making*. The principal works we have in view are those of Emmanuel Levinas, Michel Henry, and Jacques Derrida, but in our attempt to lay out a "family resemblance," we will also be led to consider other works, such as those of Henri Maldiney, Jacques Garelli, and Marc Richir, who, so to speak, "swim in the same water," Merleau-Pontian "water"—or rather, that of Jean-Toussaint Desanti, Gérard Granel, and (seen from a different perspective) Jean-Luc Marion, as one who should be seen as in close proximity to the "family" being studied. This project will be a matter of marking out contrasts; these contrasts are sometimes explicit, even mandatory; sometimes, however, they must be shown to have, at their very core, what amounts to a strong resemblance.

Preliminarily, it is important to acknowledge that any such "family resemblance" is not self-generated: on the contrary, it would be entirely possible to spotlight, within this field of linked affinities, differences and even hostilities that separate and reconfigure them, according to one's angle of approach. Yet I still maintain that the "divisions" put forward here do not rest on some arbitrary chronology. Were it possible to speak validly here of a "generation," in one sense it would simply not be factual; to be even more lapidary and allusive, however, my hypothesis is that all of these thinkers/writers could validly lay claim to Jacques Derrida's assertion with regard to phenomenology: "I still see it today, in different ways, as a discipline of incomparable rigor. Not, certainly not in the Sartrean or Merleau-Pontian version that was then dominant [during the 1950s], but rather contrary to it or without it."[3] The texts on which we will focus will have in common at the very least this whole negative factor: they all attempt to initiate a phenomenology that is neither Sartrean nor Merleau-Pontian.

This criterion for grouping them together seems pertinent if we remember not their attitude of rejection, but rather—beyond any thematic affinities—that they mark a rupture in phenomenological *practice* and *methodology*.

In fact, phenomenology must be a method from the outset,[4] before being a "theorizing" of that method (as "the idea of phenomenology") and a constituted, embodied doctrine. Heidegger, fully agreeing with Husserl, writes that "phenomenology, if it is understood correctly, is a concept of method. Immediately excluded is thus that it could assert theses, or a determined continuity, regarding a being, or that it could defend a self-declared 'point of view.'"[5] This method is clearly to be determined in contrast to that of the positive sciences: far from being supported by a positive given, through an exigent radicality absent of all presupposition, it is essentially enacted through an operation consisting of attaching itself to a "natural" position (one engendered through the positive sciences). This operation neutralizes all belief and all theses of existence (to neutralize is not to repudiate).

We must recall this canonical definition of the phenomenological reduction without misunderstanding its simply indicative nature: entirely a posture, the phenomenological reduction, as the conversion of the Platonic gaze, can only truly be produced in being implemented, even if, through various philosophical temperaments, one vacillates between two modes of association with it: one must opt either for the certitude of the reduction's completion or for the disquiet of its intrinsic *in*completion. These two options define the intrinsically obscure nature, unmasterable through any theoretical protocol, of the *point of passage* from the natural to the phenomenological posture. And phenomenological texts, not being able directly and fully to accord with phenomena, in some sense arise protreptically, from incitement, to engage in an operation existing nowhere other than in its implementation in the first person, through an effort and a risk that must be tested out individually and that cannot be preserved in the reported "results" arrived at by others. It is for this reason that the phenomenological method is not a technique, if we understand by that a set of rules governing a procedure that could be mechanically applied. This is all the less possible since, as Heidegger notes, "the phenomenological method, like all scientific methods, is developed and transformed as a function of the progress it allows to be accomplished regarding access to things. The scientific method is never a simple technique. As soon as it becomes such, it is deprived of its proper essence" (*BPP*, 39). This should in turn remind us of what Descartes taught us: method is "an art of inventing"; that is, it does not preexist as knowledge of itself, with the singularity of the path it traces when confronted with the specifics of its objective; it is always *at risk*.

Yet when we look at the French phenomenologists' investment in the phenomenological method, we can see that

- if Sartre operates within Husserlian phenomenology while pretending to massively radicalize it, it is in the sense in which he "completes" it as a philosophy of consciousness—of the absolute originarity of consciousness as self-presence that produces all appearance.[6]

- Merleau-Ponty, closer to contemporary French phenomenologists and more widely read by them, pays meticulous attention to the world's exceeding of consciousness, and to the ambiguity of this interlacing that is hardly recognizable in the instability of its endless reversibility, in the work. In this sense, Merleau-Ponty locates himself at the limit of the powers of elucidation of the phenomenological method (he marks, for example, the obscurity of its "open sesame," reduction, by insisting on its unachievable nature). As a thinker of the limit, however, Merleau-Ponty is not a thinker of *rupture* but, on the contrary, of *encroachment*.

- the figures in whom we are interested here—such is at least our working hypothesis—are characterized (1) by practicing phenomenology *at the limit*; (2) by a practice of the limit that engenders more of the violence of *excessive*[7] movement than of the nuance required to describe ambiguity.[8] That is, they attempt to radicalize the fundamental concepts, and thus the proper constraints, of the phenomenological method, to the extent that it becomes legitimate to ask whether, paradoxically, that radicality does not turn into an excess that, far from sharpening the method's edge, would in fact explode it. This question, then, is what leads to the perhaps astonishing relationship between these phenomenologists, beyond the simple, empirical generational effect:[9] they seem to adhere to the focal point of the phenomenological movement, the point of its highest intensity, *and/or* beyond it, to have exploded it.

At its base, my project here—which will not concern itself with the history of philosophy since that would require being installed within philosophies in the course of so doing, in the space where thinkable fields open out—refers to navigation: how is one to *orient* oneself within this "galaxy" that is contemporary French phenomenology? This question has particular importance if one forms the hypothesis that the phenomenological method is pushed here to its limit, to the very edge of its fruitfulness, but also to the point of its defeat or its disaster: being installed in this field, what can one expect *today* from the phenomenological method?

A guiding thread: The notion of intentionality

Although our research proposes to explore many diverse thematic bodies and fields of work, it should not focus its initial attention on the contents of thought lest it dissipate itself. Its primary interest, above all else, should be the different ways of being invested in the phenomenological method. That is, it should focus on *postures and styles* (see Introduction). To approach a posture is to approach that which, in a thought, precedes all thematization (and thus all thematization of itself) and determines it, by an originary determination in which the arbitrary inaugural and the necessity always imposed by the thing itself are not allowed to disentangle. This means being brought toward the astonishment in which even the traumatism that inaugurates all thought that could be called philosophical, which is not even what *should be* of a/the being (or not) but as phenomenology, reveals being to us, more precisely and more originarily than "that which is given" (or not). Every posture of thought is an attempt to control this event, the first *gesture* turned toward it: a posture of avoidance or of encounter.

For this reason the guiding thread of our research, the Ariadne's thread among many styles of thought and regions of objects, will from the outset be the notion of *intentionality*, which, as Husserl says, is the crowning theme of phenomenology.[10] In fact, as we must remember, intentionality is the technical name that in Husserl conceals the mysterious aura in which the gift of all being as a sense of being is at play. Intentionality is the crowning theme of phenomenological discourse, that to which it is "reduced" (i.e., "brought back"), only because it is so more fundamentally, though in a manner initially not itself manifest (since it is operational and thus not thematized), as the medium of its practice. And if it is this, it is so because more fundamentally still, it is the constituting power of all sense of being. This is the manner in which it is presented by Husserl.[11] And even if one does not immerse oneself from the start in the Husserlian confidence in intentionality, one will remark at the very least that in its link—whose resistance must be tested—to the (transcendental) deduction is the central operational concept of phenomenological practice.

After presenting our field of research and its various engagements, focusing on the "wide" picture, we will then concentrate our work on narrower questions: Why move toward limited practices of intentionality? And why choose those particular ones?

As precise as it may be in Husserl's work both generally and specifically, a philosophical work must be supported by one of these great questions—to which any definitive response is not possible. It is this fundamental questioning that I propose to engage in first of all, in order to demonstrate by so doing how it condenses and specifies the study of a course of contemporary French phenomenology and gives it its meaning.

Perhaps no one more than Husserl in *The Crisis of European Sciences* has taken the measure of the fragility of modern rationality; it is as if, fortifying itself as mathematical *ratio*, reason saw its field of inquiry reduced to a tattered remnant. The more precise it became, the more narrow, abandoning whole aspects of human experience and thus delivering them up to a functional irrationalism whose practical effects are all too well known. We are living in a period of thought in which a rationality such as that at work in the exact sciences is not precluded from sharing space with irrational conduct, since it draws its productiveness from being confined within the narrow field that it delimits.

Consequently, we are faced with the problem of the invention of a rationality that would itself be "wide" yet pervasively rigorous, less calculating than the producer of meaning.

This has been, since 1911, the very necessity to which Husserl gave the name of phenomenology. Phenomenology as rigorous science must escape the hegemony of exactitude reigning in the natural sciences, losing sight of the specificity of mind [*esprit*] as well as the obscurity that seems to invade the idea of *Geist* central to the sciences of the mind since Dilthey.[12] In the same movement, phenomenology is constituted in the need to short-circuit the following alternative: to choose between a positivism that has never ceased to naturalize all givens and to exclude all questioning in the direction of the roots of the living being, and a caricature of metaphysics that is tempted to abandon the given in favor of a world of smoke and mirrors. Husserl could write that "we are the true positivists (or empiricists)" because he had liberated the given from its physico-mathematical interpretation, thus revitalizing the "metaphysical" question—"metaphysical" here signifying the *radicality* of questioning what is, questioning the engendering of *origin* itself. A metaphysical project such as this paradoxically (but quite rigorously) implies a return to things themselves. This is, moreover, why Husserl does not use the term "metaphysical," given its risk of evoking in us "numerous varied sediments deposited by historical tradition, which co-mix confusingly within the vague concept of metaphysics memories of diverse metaphysical systems from the past,"[13] but prefers, following the moments of his itinerary, the expressions "first philosophy" or "transcendental philosophy."[14] Phenomenology is thus reactivated and even, in the end, revealed to itself, in the radicality of "metaphysical" exigency, at the very point of the end of metaphysics as historically constituted—through participating in this execution, this death struggle.[15]

The decisive invention that Husserl implements in order to adhere to requirements of this exigency and to confront the aporias it implies is intentionality. This idea has a double value: ontological and gnoseological, these two perspectives being closely interlinked. In fact, in order to be understood as intentionality, consciousness must be freed of all "realizing" understanding; must be recognized as being the source of the entire constitution of the sense of being. It is also the power of elucidating all meaning, and finally the decisive operatory concept within the phenomenological discourse itself.

Yet the reader of phenomenological texts cannot fail to be astonished by what the idea of intentionality becomes for the post-Husserlian phenomenologists in whom we are interested here: it is subjected to crude proofs, its radicalization signifying its transcendence rather than its deployment. And this transcendence is hardly Hegelian, its negation neither preserving nor elevating the truth: the first it disrupts and inverts; the second it decapitates.[16] It is presented by many of these writers as the very task of a phenomenology to come.

If we look at this more closely, we see that the target of Husserlian phenomenology's inheritors, in their critique of intentionality, is what still attaches it—despite everything—to the modern space opened out, at least "symbolically," by Descartes: egological subjectivity and representation. In all of them, and in absolutely different ways, there is displayed a will to release an originary more originary than the ego in which this last would be rooted: that it would be necessary to designate an absolute presence, or even a space of "Urpresence" or "over-presence" (respectively, Henry,

Marion), or on the contrary, to state that at the origin, there was no origin but rather an irreducible absence (exemplarily, though in different senses, Levinas and Derrida, to whom, from this point of view, we could add Richir). What from a gnoseological point of view seems to imply *at the very least* an attempt to define a "place" in which consciousness is over-mastered in the *form* of its refocusing on the self—the (pure) Ego—and, perhaps, even more radically, an attempt to approach the powers of elucidation of consciousness, and even an ability to synthesize consciousness.

Consequently, the need for radicality, which was for Husserl rigor itself, seems paradoxically to lead to a transcendence of the limits of the knowable and to risk being transformed into what Kant calls the *Schwärmerei*. This necessary rigor seems to be silenced in its opposite.

It is appropriate here to bring up a supplementary detail: many different styles can be located among the gestures of radicalization claiming to exceed intentionality.

- Sartre, as I have said, claims to radicalize the notion of intentionality by "purifying" it, "purging" it, so to speak, of ego. For Sartre this is to be accomplished through the liberating of the ego that remains, in the last analysis, irreducibly attached to Husserl in order to better assure its absolute status as *consciousness*, since the ipseity he describes, having been hollowed out by its own self-destruction as for-self, is no less—and may even be only this—presence *to-self*; that is, more consciousness than ever.[17] Sartre is not part of our field of investigation.

- Heidegger and Merleau-Ponty each seem in his own way to *derive* intentionality out of something more originary: for Heidegger, ontological difference; for Merleau-Ponty, the world's interlacing. For both, then, intentionality is but a foretaste masking rather than revealing the fundamental structure from which it is derived.

- Finally, and it is to this last that I relate our study here, one might try to exceed intentionality without dissolving it in a structure other than itself, without deriving it integrally out of something more originary than itself, but still disturbing it not only in its egoity but even more radically as consciousness, making it attentive to what escapes its constitutive powers and seems even more originary than it is, "giving" it to itself. This undertaking would mean accounting for the manner in which intentionality is related to what will always have preceded it. Such a connection cannot fail to be paradoxical so long as intentionality, recognizing an origin in some sense older than itself, could nonetheless be apprehended as causally derived from this origin, not pretending to make itself prior to that separate origin. It is *born*. And since, by definition, one cannot assist in the event of one's own birth, which always already has its own perspective, it is caught in an irreducible originary delay.

This then would be the central question: how to examine the limits of intentionality apart from its own internal border? It is certainly this internal border that must be maintained at the risk of no longer respecting the rigor of intentional constraints. The writers on whom the focus falls here either explicitly insist on practicing this gesture (Levinas, Derrida, Marion) or place themselves *elsewhere* (essentially, the magnificently solitary gesture of Michel Henry, who neither respects nor transgresses the limit of intentionality—he pays it no attention—since he identifies his own constraint in the capacity to be located within an originarity that is always already unintentional). In all these cases, whether intentionality's limit is respected or not, whether asserted or not—remembering that those who assert it do not necessarily implement it, and that those who ignore it sometimes do implement it—it is the relevant reference mark for orientation within the field; at least, this is my hypothesis here.

The test of subjectivity

In other words, and more precisely, the family we have identified regarding the violence of its thought-gesture, that is, by asking ourselves the question of going beyond *the powers of rationality*, "rediscovers itself," and this is not by chance—it will be my task to demonstrate this—from another angle of attack: that of the question of *subjectivity*.

In fact, the themes of rationality and subjectivity are intimately interwoven in intentionality, the latter being the place of ontological anchoring of the gnoseological power of the former. Subjectivity is above all else the pole of synthesis, identification, of what would thus necessarily

be called meaning. And we must remember that subjectivity is the principal focus of Husserlian phenomenologists insofar as it is the residue of
a realizing ontic understanding of being: it is nothing but a construction.
However, while the Heideggerian gesture—or, still more obviously, Merleau-Ponty's—attempts to denounce subjectivity as being but the cover of
a more fundamental structure (if not its simple surface effect), the writers
in whom we are interested here discover subjectivity as opposing a "resistance" to the critique (albeit legitimate and radical) that must be opposed
to it. "Denuded" of egoistic form from the outset, and then more radically of the undivided power of consciousness, subjectivity persists: what
remains is the originality of the *self*. If this is a question of the ultimate
resistance of what would be merely a "Cartesian phantasm"—and even of
its "return" following the Heideggerian *Abbau*—or of an "irreducible," it
is certainly not in the sense of a fundamental instance but in that in which
all views, in order to be overcome, could only be seen from the viewpoint
of, could only be assigned to, a self. Consequently, and here we might agree
with Jocelyn Benoist[18] rather than Rudolf Bernet,[19] the meager powers of
subjectivity never show themselves more than when they are radically in
danger, overflowing and taken to their limit: they *still* appear—and more
than ever—in that it is only from them that "one" can, that *I* can, assist
in their defeat. Subjectivity resides in the vestiges of the triumphant subject of modernity—that subject spewing forth its last fire and undergoing
its first shocks with Husserl. This remainder, given that subjectivity is
essentially only a remainder or a debris, would therefore not be the metaphysical *remaining* that its irreducibility promotes at a fundamental level
within a plenitude that is in itself ontological (as in Descartes) but, on the
contrary, a scrap that is already breached yet seemingly unsinkable; that
might, so to speak, "float" and *re*surface. Is there any subjectivity other
than one that is exploding, since it could have intentionality only through
the exploding of intentionality? Does only that which flies into pieces, is
"shattered," finally appear; does it make the phenomenon?

Vital differences are apparent within these hypotheses. But whatever
they may be, bursting subjectivity (Levinas, Marion), revenant (Derrida),
or else, as another possibility far from the basic initiative, crushed against
itself (Henry, Levinas again), subjectivity survives in *and through* the ruin
of the pride of the subject. Consequently, it is properly the place in which

the need for rationality is at once reaffirmed (see Husserlian subjectivity as a centering pole, or as identification) and risks molting into its opposite (as finitude—or the absoluteness—of pure passivity, or still better, as pure differentiation, pure relativity).

Elements for a critique of rational phenomenology

Now that we have determined the phenomenological "family" in which we are interested, and clarified the reasons for this choice, it still remains to specify the kind of questioning one might address to it, such as the posture of thought through which it is legitimate to approach it.

We have been incrementally brought toward phenomenology in order to discover this rationality that is rigorous beyond all exactitude, capable of short-circuiting the alternatives between a narrow, physico-mathematical rationality and an irrationalism: at its core the spectre of the absence of rigor stands out against it and is even made exemplarily menacing.

The typical—even paradigmatic—reproach made against contemporary French phenomenology is a familiar one: it betrays the requirements of philosophical rigor in its tendency to bring together an originarity outside, beyond consciousness.[20]

This is the essence of Janicaud's attack in *Phenomenology and the "Theological Turn"*:[21] since *Philosophy as a Rigorous Science*, for Husserl "rigor" meant the need for radicality: for reorienting the given toward the originary field that will be revealed as "being" the source of the constituted meaning that will have been precipitated through a return to its roots. And the stance of the great majority of phenomenologists is to reiterate—following Husserl—his attitude toward the philosophers he recognizes as having opened the rupture in phenomenology; that is, to demonstrate how they should have foreseen what was clearly visible but did not see, would not have supported it had they seen it, and would indeed have reconcealed it: how, in short, they could not go far enough. Janicaud sees this as a heightening of what is at stake in the idea of the originary transforming radicality into its opposite. Thus, reduction would no longer be the means to an end [*un but*]: precisely to confront [*buter*] the apodictic evidence of the clear presence of the self in consciousness.[22] On

the contrary, it would apply to itself the pure movement of the very reduction that would allow it to be satisfied—on principle—with no principle,
that would allow it to come to rest at any evidentiary base. The quest
for the originary, the quest to be radicalized, would be transformed into
the originarity of a quest whose ceaseless, atemporal movement would
be perpetually reinitiated (something like the spectre of skeptical doubt
hovers over Cartesian methodological doubt). Thus, Levinas asserts the
"emphasis," the "exasperation," and the "hyperbolic" as a philosophical
method.[23] The double suspicion to which these writers would thus expose
themselves would be the following:

1. Brought toward what, through the same movement, exceeds the
   powers of elucidation of consciousness and of phenomenology, they
   clearly risk distancing themselves from the *logos* that "gathers" in
   order precisely to be brought to light, the apophantic *logos*, replacing
   it with poetic suggestion.

2. They also risk allowing themselves to be mesmerized by a transcendence, and thus to be manipulated by a theological discourse. In fact,
   the sole means of giving a final meaning—and in a single direction—
   to this quest, endless because it is foundationless—to this quest with
   its rigorous, anarchic terms, is to make this "principle of anarchy" no
   longer an engine of ceaseless searching but rather that before which I
   must abdicate all my powers of research, not that I would then have
   encountered the solidity of the base against which they had argued
   but what has protected and thus concealed them, being *given* precisely
   as that which is concealed.[24] What is at play here, to be more precise,
   is *faith* rather than the theology about which Janicaud speaks (rather
   vaguely). We must remember that this second reproach does not apply
   to all members of the family in which we are interested but only to
   those who interpret the absence of what is ineluctably hidden as the
   sign and even the gift of an "Urpresence," of a "being" beyond the
   ontic and even beyond the ontological.

We must therefore distinguish two "subfamilies": facing the thinkers of
absence as the originary divergence from the presence of what is given
(Derrida and Levinas are close to this viewpoint as much as Desanti
and Granel, as Maldiney and Richir) are the thinkers of the "full gift"

or of "ur-giving" (Henry, Marion). It cannot be emphasized enough that the frontier between phenomenological "theologians" and "non-theologians"[25] exactly recapitulates the frontier between those who locate themselves relative to the description of full presence and those who associate themselves with description as the originary of temporalization (temporal dissociation): and if the aporias of these two tasks are somehow *resemblances* at the same time that they are present from opposite—contradictory?—poles, this proximity must be further elucidated.[26] This elucidation, to be precise, will have to grant a certain *trembling* at the very heart of the need to draw a frontier (for example, Michel Henry, the thinker of the originary *revelation* as representative structure, is *also* the thinker who insists on *immanence*; more obviously, is not Levinas— whom Janicaud "classes" as unique among the "theological" phenomenologists, *above all* the thinker who claims philosophy as atheism,[27] the thinker of the radical temporal gap *grasped apart from* immanence in what he calls dichrony?).

Whatever the details of this interrogation might be, the spectre of an absence of rigor stands out in high relief—its signs are abundant—within contemporary French phenomenology. And it is intentionality that is the most exemplary test of this paradoxical reversal of rigor in *Schwärmerei* under the impulsion of a radicalization that becomes excess, since it is the place in which the necessary rationality simultaneously reaffirms itself and attempts a metamorphosis that would allow it to escape the limitations or calculating reason.

A *critique* (in the Kantian sense) of phenomenology thus arises. It becomes necessary to try to trace the limits of the phenomenological field beyond which the radical nature of the quest for the originary suddenly and excessively reverses. A critique such as this must be on guard against two major concerns. It would be a mistake to focus on deciding who respects and does not respect phenomenological "orthodoxy," or of distributing labels of phenomenological purity. As Husserl never ceases to repeat, phenomenology is not a doctrine or a dogma: it contains no orthodoxy. This also means that the need to trace the limits of the phenomenological field must not be confused with the temptation to close this field in on itself. If to free phenomenology from all constraints of rigor by letting it digress beyond the domain of the given is an/in excess, to sensitively close it in on itself is to risk denaturing it by folding it back on a positivist project that creates a symmetrical excess.

Our task must thus consist simultaneously in *opening* the phenomenological field onto its exterior—if phenomenology declares itself to be nowhere but at its limit—and to *circumscribe* it—if through a similar process to the one at work in the rapport between reason and the idea in Kant it is in the nature of phenomenological meditation to want ceaselessly to exceed its limits. And we must ask if our questioning of the Kantian project manages to escape from what might seem a residual naïveté of the critical gesture, which is grounded—unquestioningly?—in the possibility of separating the pure from the impure. Yet it is necessary at the same time to remember the need to trace boundaries and frontiers. This task seems in many respects to be contradictory. In our attempt to rise above the inconsistency of this contradiction and far from the weakness of the compromise required to maintain us at the height of paradox in its strongest sense, Derrida will be our guide. This will, in fact, confront us with the need to think an *originary mixture* in a mode of *contamination*, which does not signify our first installation in the indistinct and in indetermination but that nonetheless destabilizes the position of an inaugural differentiation between the "one" and the "other," the pure and the impure. And this is the reading that introduces the *double bind*,[28] which permits the short-circuiting of the opposition between the indetermination of what has been mixed together, on the one hand, and the position of an inaugural separation, on the other, without condemning ourselves to incoherence. We must think what is at once entirely and "purely" the one, and entirely and "purely" the other, the one being the one only *through* the other, and inversely; that is, what is never pure, never intact, and yet never the simple result of the mixing of two elements supposedly already pure. Within the frame of our project here, the hypothesis will be that the contemporary French phenomenology that interests us is exposed in exemplary fashion to the *double bind* that wants to be in excess of itself in order to be clearly itself, in the contradictory act of having to be ceaselessly "exasperated," in Levinas's expression, while in the process of re-turning on and to itself, while "originating" itself again. In other words, this is a matter of infidelity to the self, of a self-interruption to which phenomenology must consent in order to be true to itself, and such a formulation is legitimate if it means that it is what is most intimate *within it* that requires the "ex-cessing" movement toward a beyond.[29] The "pendulum movement," the oscillation, is thus ineluctable, since for phenomenological meditation to solidify in one of these two poles is to engage in treason. They are clearly themselves only through each other; leave one to itself and they are both lost, in the absence of rigor for the one and positivism for the other. Put-ting forward the metaphor—intended as the model of intelligibility—of the "pendulum movement" to account for the impossibility of articulating the *double bind* in question here, is to say that the contradiction is man-ageable only if it is inscribed in time; more exactly and more radically, if one recognizes it as being in some sense temporalization itself. We are in agreement with Levinas when he suggests, in *Otherwise Than Being*, that philosophic discourse "is" one "of" temporalization—and perhaps even the inverse, that all temporalization is discourse. More precisely, Levinas says that all temporalization is the event of a Saying [*Dire*], precisely as its echo or its trace at the heart of a Said of which philosophic discourse would be exemplary. Levinas calls to the diachrony that is thereby put into play: diachrony as articulation and the inarticulatable.[30] There would be, in Levinas's[31] (and Richir's[32]) terms, an oscillation, or more precisely a "blinking," between the phases of excessivity and the phases immanent to the constraints proper to the phenomenological field. These two types of phases "render each other possible," mutually. The "to render possible" in question here is certainly not to be understood in the Kantian sense, since it is necessary to be situated outside all powers of transcendental synthe-sis. And since diachrony conceals neither an inconsistency nor a delusion, since it is at once divergence and hinge, it must be—and this does not cancel out the aporetic burden invested in it—that it is temporality itself.

The hypothesis that I propose here certainly requires being put to the test: the following is nothing other than this work. In any case, it will allow our research to take a fresh look at the questions with which we are starting out. Certain of them will reveal their naïveté, while others will become more complex.

    1. We will see that the question "what is and what is not phenomenol-ogy?" is fundamentally very naïve if, within a given work, a flicker-ing between phases of excess and phases immanent to constraints proper to a phenomenological method can be detected.

2. It is thus necessary to prevent any belief in textual homogeneity and to renounce not the figure of the author as such—are not texts always the place in which subjectivity is tested out?—but the idea of an author as the master of the work. And the question becomes even more complex when its philosophical audacity remains concealed, incognito. Where is its courage? Does it consist of remaining within the constraints of the phenomenological field, or of exceeding them? Does its weakness consist of allowing for digressions beyond those frontiers, or to remain cautiously inside them, without (in Derrida's expression) running the risk of invention? Is weakness, for a phenomenological method, not fundamentally to congeal at one of the two poles just described? Is it not to lack the force to ceaselessly demolish itself precisely in order, according to Husserl's formulation (now more than ever appropriate), to ceaselessly begin again?

This is the kind of questioning that will orient our *use* of texts in the following investigation. It will involve the juxtaposition of both an epigonal genre and a genre of invective. In a sense, there is nothing to anticipate of these texts other than that they perpetually begin again and that we allow them to do so.

Must we not learn to read, at the heart of the disaster of intentionality, in a fugitive flickering, the greatest success?

2

Intentionality and Non-Givenness

In an effort to be as little deceived as possible in our investigation of the possibility of identifying an origin, it is appropriate here to revisit at its "source" the aporia inherited by contemporary French phenomenologists, and thus, from a viewpoint one might define as genetic or genealogical, to characterize the *manner* in which they put it to the test.[1]

Husserl

The hypothesis lying beneath this work claims that contemporary French phenomenology is like a territory in which one must orient oneself; like a solar system, whose center of gravity—controlling, from a great distance, the positions of various stars in their relations to others given that in the first place they are all related internally—is Husserl. These planetary objects have names like Derrida, Desanti, Henry, Levinas, Marion. They are situated as much in their proximal relations—sometimes their trajectories even cross—as in their "nonrelations" of indifference. In the latter case, it is possible to think that these parallel routes, all invisible, are nonetheless even in their reciprocal misunderstandings oriented through some kind of connection they have established with Husserl (for example Desanti, among others, searches in Husserl for a self-definition of a textured intentionality for immanence and refuses the help of all resources from elsewhere, searches for a transcendental subjectivity or, which is worse from the viewpoint of his own requirements, a theological one—such a requirement orienting Desanti's reading, which means that he cannot address Marion, makes the case for indifference a flagrant one. The opposite could also easily be constructed.)

Working within the phenomenological concern for a rigorous description of what is given when it is given, Husserl insists on the inadequation that necessarily affects the results of perceptual relations: the sensory can be given only through "sketches," "adumbrations" (*Abschattungen*).[2] Husserl's close attention to the distinguishing of adequation from originarity is well known. Even if representational perception can merely show one side of a thing, its silhouette, it is nonetheless the thing itself that is given to me "in flesh and bone," in person, originarily: the object is given to me as phenomenon, in its fullness and entirety, in the glance I cast on it, appearing precisely as such, as phenomenon, as a correlate of my glance. And this is true even if its being given in all its facets must escape me.

Adequation and givenness are therefore clearly to be distinguished: they are not on the same plane. Adequation is a mode of givenness: there can be no adequation without givenness—but a givenness is possible without adequation.

However, as Ricoeur seems to suggest,[3] it is the radical adequation of consciousness with itself that will define absoluteness, in contrast with the given of external worldly reality: the perceptions through which consciousness envisages itself can be fulfilled only in a fully adequate fashion, as if when it is receptive to being linked to it, the criterion of adequation could approximate the given's originarity, and even be confused with it.

The distinction between the two, to be quite clear, is thus not without ambiguity. Ambiguity is not incoherence; on the contrary, it signals that if Husserl can so easily distinguish, at the perceptual level, the capacity of the perceptions, of the inadequation of their fulfillment, it is givenness that is always at play somewhere other than in the encounter with the object. If the inadequation of perceptual representation can but disturb the power of givenness, this is because all representation—perceptual or not—can give its correlate only insofar as it gives it *itself*, and it can give itself only to the precise degree that it is auto-revealed as the power to be given all phenomena precisely based on the absoluteness of its auto-givenness; that is, as being absolutely adequate to itself.

The inadequate is best given in person; it is quite simply in another mode from adequation. It is vital to emphasize that Husserl would not know how to juxtapose non-givenness with phenomenology, perceptive inadequation being for him always caught within the horizon of a full adequation functioning as a regulatory idea for perception, as a witnessing. Certain intuition, unlike perception, is not given in person, does not give originarily. The remainder is less than the given; they give the difference, or at least the "shifted" as such: these are what Husserl calls "presentifications" (*Vergegenwärtigungen*).[4] As opposed to intuitive representations, signative representations are empty. But according to Husserl "empty" does not mean radically and absolutely without any present given: signative intention gives the object, but gives it as an object simply represented. The fact that signative representations are "empty" thus simply means that they are waiting for completion, even if this completion, in terms of its specifics, is structurally precluded. This means that more than ever they draw their meaning and their being from the full presence toward which they are entirely directed, and that must be their proper promise.

As cannot be overestimated, the practice of phenomenological description, this "practicing of phenomenology on the job," as Desanti has it, works ceaselessly to destabilize the sovereignty of the consciousness donor who is given all phenomena all the more fundamentally only insofar as she gives it to herself. Husserl, and even more the "second" Husserl, never ceases to explain thematically that consciousness is the absolute *Ur-region* toward which reduction is headed, and that reduction reveals as such. Yet the reading of minute phenomenological descriptions by that same Husserl gives rise to a certain suspicion: less than to an originary toward which the constraints proper to the phenomenological method lead, would this not concern a secret decision, unquestionable in itself, that would inaugurate the practice of phenomenology and would be, paradoxically, implicated by the very thing that makes it possible? Is that not the very tension haunting a Husserlianism that never ceases now to leave level through descriptive probity, now to recover, to conjure while reaffirming precisely as in extremis the absolute character of donor consciousness? Such would be the movement of the pendulum on which Husserl is caught, between two irreconcilable yet indispensable poles. From the perspective of phenomenology, all-enclosing absoluteness of consciousness must have the last word. But from the viewpoint of phenomenological *description*, it is the thing itself that in always escaping, ceaselessly reopens the descriptive field and the text that pretends to saturate it.[5]

The mark of Husserl is clear in this tension. It will have to suffice to recall briefly here Husserl's problems managing the phenomenological descriptions of the other/others and of time.

1. The other/others are never addressed, as an *originary given*. And we must concur with Françoise Dastur regarding "the perception through originary interpretation of the otherness of irreducibly indicative structure": "We can clearly see here that in terms of the perceptive impossibility, that is, presentation, Husserl preferred perception as the experience of an impossibility, that is, of the unpresentable."[6]

2. The past, for Husserl, is given to me originarily, but not in "flesh and bone."[7] In a sense, the implied gap is less radical than that in the experience of the other/others since for the latter, according to Husserl, the originarity of givenness subsists, What remains of it is nothing less than its difference from retention, since re-remembering [*re-souvenir*] requires the unifying role of a pure "I" while the flux of consciousness, at its own level, is compromised in its continuity. More fundamentally, if retention is in a sense radically contiguous with impression (since it is nothing other than impression that destroys it), there remains of it only the impression as pure appearance that can be apprehended only *through* retention; that is, through a delay, an irreducibly originary gap.[8] In the face of the time that is revealed as being less its object than its secret habitat, intentional consciousness is confronted by the significant requirement of having to elucidate the risk of its own dispossession of itself.

These are but some of the symptoms leading to the suspicion that the absoluteness of consciousness and its mastery of the phenomenon are not without weaknesses. And we can thus take a fresh look at perceptual inadequation itself. Perhaps it is not as offensive as all that, and in fact concerns itself—despite what Husserl says explicitly—with the power of givenness itself. Is it actually disturbing in its originarity and absoluteness?

Let us examine it more closely.

If the sensory thing is given only by a "sketch," for Husserl that means that neither our power of understanding in general (and of sensing in particular) is finite, nor—and this is the usual logic of the opposition—that the thing exists outside of its appearance, concealed just as much as revealed by it. The notion of intentionality, as a priori to correlation, seeks precisely to short-circuit this aporetic configuration that is only imposed as a subjectivity from the outset closed in on itself and thus not confronting the difficulties of joining with an "outside."

Consequently, we must see the following consequences in the discovery of intentionality:

1. The "sketch," as the absenting of the thing from the glance is irreducible, and irreducibly the recipient of an already-existent alliance between the glance and the phenomenon.

2. Since this is not simply a matter of flushing out a transcendence of the thing as a "presence beyond" (the perceptive glance): a *nothing* (of the existent itself) always already inhabits both immanence and perception. It would then be a matter of an absolutely radical absence, of a nothing, since it is "being" the nothing of an absent presence.[9] This nothing of the phenomenon, which is not a "phenomenon beyond," invites us to consider an originary collusion between perception and temporality, if time is precisely the possibility of the collapse of consciousness into itself, along with its characteristic immanence. The perceptive gap, which is immediately spatial, is also profoundly temporal; it is in complete accord with Rudolf Barbaras when he says "the sketch can only be understood from the point of view of time.[10]

Yet Husserl never drew out these consequences; even when he began to do so, it was only to cover them over again. This re-covering is marked by its very terminology: we can see this when, in saying that perceptive representations are inadequately fulfilled, we still conceive of them within the horizon of adequation; the correlative notions of *Mehrmeinung* and of "horizon" connote less the irreducibility of that which escapes the glance than the idea according to which gradually, through contiguity, everything that escapes the glance inexorably returns to it. More radically still, to conceptualize perception—that is, all representation—in terms of "empty" and "full" is to indicate that the unquestioned originary of Husserlian phenomenology, the connection designating what is thinkable—is *presence*. This is what is always, in advance, at play in phenomenological theory, and what informs and inflects all descriptive practice.

In the final analysis, if Husserl knew how to take advantage of the invention of intentionality for the problematic trapping of theories of consciousness (essentially solipsism and the related problem of the objective value of representation), there would still be another problem that would remain despite all his efforts, precisely *in* any theory of consciousness based on a model of presence-to-self valuing notions of subject and object.[11] And in terms of the question of perception, Husserl's "retreat" from the audacity that also characterizes him is telling: he finds it *necessary* that absolute consciousness reign supreme, in a full presence shown to be one's own. In extremis, Husserl must reestablish the preeminence of absolute consciousness, of presence over absence; must reestablish that intentionality is clearly in a sense an unalloyed bursting forth, pure divergence from self revealing pure self-presence; pure, absolute immanence. This also means that theoretical decisions, destabilized by description itself, have the last word.

We must recall the privileged place of perception for Husserl: all other intuitive acts are either grounded on it (categorical intuition) or are the results of modifications made on it or on the acts it grounds (presentifications); non-objectivizing acts accordingly presuppose objectivizing acts that all owe something, in one way or another, to perception. With this privileging of perception in mind, what one might almost dare to call Husserlian denial (or in some indeterminate way "non-givenness") should not be underestimated.

Within the theoretical constraints of Husserlian phenomenology, non-givenness has the status of a risk that has already been avoided: it must always be (re)established at its proper level, even if it is sometimes necessary to work all the way back to its originary nature.[12]

However, the question is whether the risk of non-givenness is truly intentionality's disaster. Is it not—and this is but the appearance of paradox—rather what *saves* it and even brings it into being?

We must look more closely at the formal constraints of all intentionality.

What is it that causes intentionality if not the lack, for Husserl the "void" or "emptiness," that inhabits it? Since non-givenness is nothing other than the movement of "turning toward," what *sense* has—what *is*—intentionality since it is fully satisfied, filled up? In a sense, intentionality "is" thoroughly contradictory: if it succeeds, it dies. An absolute givenness implies the reduction of all distance between seeing and seen. But seeing and seen exist only because of the division that in separating them places them in relation to each other and thus "gives" them to each other. The abolition of the gap would abolish the two poles, seeing and seen: to give too perfectly would mean losing authentic givenness [*l'instance donatrice*], but also losing the gift—that is, givenness as well as the gift—and finally authentic receiving as such. An intentionality fully giving the phenomenon would proclaim its self-dissolution, the accomplishment of its own suicide.

In this sense, Michel Henry correctly lays claim—and in an absolutely logical way—to the most radical phenomenology by proposing to define the phenomenality of the phenomenon through the revelation, absolutely without distance from itself, of what is defined within this very absence of distance of self from itself—constituting as such the connection of self to itself—life and/or affectivity.

And is, then, a phenomenology requiring the plenitude of givenness and thus from the outset placing intentionality on the pedestal of absoluteness—and consequently attempting to reabsorb dynamic, Ek-static movement by attaching it to an egoic, transcendental, and self-centered pole—not consequently required to expel it from its own field (in the movement from Husserl to Henry)?[13]

Attempts such as Michel Henry's must be taken very seriously, given their audacity grounded in a necessity whose rigor is flawless in its Husserlian filiation. Also clear, however, are the aporias to which they expose themselves, most prominently (if the paradox that authentic phenomenology resides in the invisible, in the non-intentional, is thoroughly tenable and productive) the problem of the implementation of a philosophy requiring being itself located beneath—rather than beyond—the collusion of seeing and saying inaugurating philosophy in its Greek origins.

I will not stop to explore Michel Henry's route, which disunites the revelation of phenomenon and intentionality. By contrast, we will attend to the fact that in maintaining intentionality as a fundamental phenomenological theme, it is perhaps appropriate to reexamine the notion of non-donation.

It is not necessary to give too much weight to intentionality, let alone to give it everything: all that is necessary is for something of the phenomenon to escape, as it were at first speculation.

But if at the perceptual level Husserl simultaneously both indicates non-givenness and recovers his radicality in the notion of the "perceptive sketch," it is because in his concern with *categories* he goes further, accounting for what can only exceed the glance as such. Jacques Taminiaux, in *Le regard et l'excédent* reading Husserl's *Logical Investigation VI* in the wake of Heidegger,[14] shows how much categorizing, not being a given anywhere in the sensory, thus gives the sensory to perceptive representation, precisely by inexorably exceeding the sensory; that is, by exceeding representation directed at the sensuous. The categorical gives the sensuous to irreducible excess. Inversely, the categorical's mode of givenness resides at the heart of the sensuous in the very movement that absolutely refuses it. Categories rigorously give themselves as *not being* (there) by giving the "what is there" (the ontic) of the not-being-given.

Three comments need to be made here:

1. The excessive gives itself a constitutive role in the structural economy of intentionality.

2. Non-givenness cannot be absolute: the sensuous and the category play hide-and-seek with each other. The phenomenon must allow itself to be foreseen; if it is not, it cannot incite the intentional movement that is its deepest desire. Radical non-givenness creates a circularity nothing can escape, not an arrow nor representation itself. The structure's formal constraint is thus doubled: necessarily, neither nothing nor everything can be given.[15]

3. Most important, accounting for the *surplus* in the glance absolutely does not direct the Husserlian problematic toward a glance that is exceeded or excessive, relative to itself. On the contrary, according to a gesture already mentioned, Husserl addresses the risk of unforeseen non-donation, twisting the problematic in the other direction in order to compensate for the higher stakes of presence. As Taminiaux

explains, not only the excessive can be thought as given, even if it is given as other than the sensuous. In a reversal, what exceeds the sensuous representation reveals itself as presence that is fullest as "the most perfect phenomenon," the originary phenomenon. Thus, since it is installed within the Kantian dichotomy of category and sensuous, Husserl places it in crisis by describing a categorical *intuition*, and one with the dignity of a donor more important than sensuous intuition—which is even maximal since it is characterized by a givenness that is not merely sketched but full, remainderless.

From a perspective exterior to Husserl's, the reversal that has taken place here is surprising: what exceeds givenness at a certain level (that of sensible perception) is revealed—can only be revealed—as better given at another level.

On this point we must look again at Desanti's analysis according to which intentional representation for Husserl exemplarily runs the double (at least) risk of being overrun by its correlates, both when it is faced in *Leçons sur le temps* with the threat to make it a lower limit, and when it is confronted by the category in *Logical Investigation VI*, which threatens to make it a higher limit. Heidegger's reading of the *Investigation VI* is a familiar one: it is the maximal investigation of Husserl's most emphatic Ek-static opening of intentionality, indicating the excessiveness of the glance—thus presenting ontological difference—before again "falling into" immanence and the determined presence of the long, serious face of the ontic in the figure of an absolute, egoistic consciousness such as that in *Ideas I*.[16] Beside this reading, and in no contradiction with it, we might present another: this one would assert that in the *Logical Investigations*, even though subjectivity is not thematized as such, it operates there nonetheless, as the power of "immanentization." All sense data is what it is insofar as *I* see it. This is endemic to the formulas Husserl employs: all representations are what they are only insofar as they proceed from an "*I* can" of reiteration that, diverging from the Kantian "I can," has the singularity of (a) lived experience. While opposing the *Ideas* from this perspective, *Logical Investigation VI* prepares the way for it: from the first to the second of these texts, the "diachronization" of this tension is at play, from the pendulum movement between immanence of consciousness in its absoluteness and Ek-static transcendence of the glance. And, as can never be emphasized enough, this tension can be regulated—at least explicitly and thematically—only with respect to the first of these poles; in fact, within the duality at play here the other pole has a certain advantage, that of having the capacity to regulate the aporia, the tension, as the power of immanentization. As a result, explicitly and thematically, the advantage must return to the absoluteness of transcendental consciousness in the apodicticity of its lived experience of immanence: § 49 of *Ideas I*, which celebrates this absoluteness, is adumbrated subliminally in *Logical Investigation VI*. For reasons we have already begun to see, this clandestine quality can return triumphantly. Inversely, since the last word was thematically recognized within absolute consciousness, the opening through which the glance *exceeds* never ceases to open subliminally.

In other words non-givenness, as Husserl foresees, cannot be thematized as radical, first because from a noematic point of view, if nothing is given then the intentional glance cannot be born. But above all and more radically (because even though one inscribes, from a noetic and even hyletic point of view, a fracture in the very heart of the representation) this fracture can only be seen as radical: caught in an economy of the intentional structure, it is the engine of its own reabsorption.

More precisely, rather than a "dialectical movement" one is dealing here with a double regime of intentionality:[17] if the glance is endlessly gliding among things, if it is "open to" and "provoked by" them, it will sustain this Ek-stasy, this transcendence, only to the extent that it plays elsewhere and at the same time with the absoluteness of pure immanence to itself: this is its blind task, the source of all vision, its immanence the source of all intentional transcendence.

I have mentioned the aporia at the heart of Husserl's notion of intentionality, which produces the very traumatism that underpins the phenomenologies addressed here. We must be clear from the start that we can add but a variant, which is not without its posterity, to Husserl's rich work.

Now we turn to the non-real nature of intentionality, the non-reality of the interdependent representation of the non-reality of the *eidos*, since after Husserl all representation is eidetic representation perceived only through an *eidos* that can be neither here nor elsewhere in endlessly opening up intentionality so that it is nothing other than the pure power of opening, never reducible to any worldly reality. In the play of representation and *eidos*, it is the game that is first and always preventing both of them from ever being stabilized in any thing as a subsistent, whose model would be inevitably ontic. Among the *eidē*, as we have already seen, certain are (un)knowable at the very heart of the sensuous, opening and thus giving the sensuous *as such*—and being inscribed in it in a paradoxical, phantomic mode, a regulating telos. *Others* are pure idealities, given as not sensuous and, as a consequence, are characterized by their phantomic nature, what Husserl calls their *Geistlichkeit*. Thus they exist entirely— and this is a paradoxical mode of sustenance—within the interference, the white noise, of worldly reality: they "are" in being neither here nor elsewhere; they presuppose a here and elsewhere *in order to* already have evaded them, to have always disrupted their location (Derrida comments on this in his analysis of linked idealities[18]). All ideality, in its non-reality, presupposes a worldly reality any passage to which has always already been disturbed. It is phantomic if the phantom always returns to the worldly without ever being reduced to it, if the phantom is connected to itself— always being only itself—in terms of what it has always already affected.

This phantomic reality characterizes all representations of consciousness and all being it is given: being precisely phantomized as meaning, it is the element, the medium, of phenomenology.

Two comments:

1. Clearly recognizable here is the central aporia of transcendence and immanence, of non-givenness and the given, but managed differently. We must here emphasize the oxymoronic nature of a non-dialectizable and non-reabsorbable tension in Husserl. We can also see in Husserlian texts, in the theme of non-reality and in the phantomic, another model of comprehension that blurs the edges of this oxymoronic tension by presenting it as what at once characterizes and *makes possible* this properly intentional "transcendence within immanence."

   All that remains of it is this non-reality, if it is not a simple mixture of real and non-real, if it is not a simple compromise—and it would not know being—remaining in many ways the determination of a problem.

- Like *Geist*, it still presupposes the worldly, the body, to affect it, and to spectralize it as flesh.

- In a more embarrassing way, it risks only functioning as a negative theology within Husserlian discourse: it is enough for opening, for giving, the realm of intentionality (as its "coefficient," through the term "intentional") of inherited notions of the worldly. Is it sufficient—as Husserl shows in *Logical Investigation V*, to return the triad subject/representation/object (which modern philosophy has petrified as static substances whose connections were thus enigmatic) to its original fusion as intentionality—to describe what consciousness is not? (Might one say that consciousness *is not* a substance to be apprehended in any ontic model; that representation revealed phenomenologically to itself *is not* a tableau static to itself in the consciousness of the thing in the world?)

- Finally, why must intentionality's non-reality be rooted in a mode of pure presence, detached from any diurnal model, as living-present, as *Impression*? (In other words, why is reduction to the real not supported as non-reality and a return to itself, as it is in the *Logical Investigations*—and movement will continue to accentuate this—as *real*?)

Clearly, phantomicity (of the *eidos*, of intentionality, of *Geist*), if it is not simply a mixture, in the most banal sense of the term, of real and non-real (which is itself absolutely undetermined outside its reference to the real), nor a simple negative theology of the worldly, is a model of understanding just as aporetic as the oxymoronic tension between transcendence and immanence, regarding the link between given and non-given.

But equally clearly we must never stop coming back to this point, since the thinkers on whom we are focusing themselves focus on these aporetic models (bequeathed to them by Husserl, without recognizing them as such): Henry, Marion, Levinas, and Derrida in his own way, all concentrate on this tension to the point that they threaten to make it yield or until they indeed accomplish it, Derrida and Levinas—and we must explore this double-sharing—working on the side of the phantom and the trace.

2. A central focus on the question of subjectivity is consequential if since Husserl it is the point at which this tension is clearest to the senses, the point at which transcendence and immanence are sutured together, and not in just any manner, since subjectivity as living-present or as the pure immanence of hyletic lived experience within this tension seems closer to transcendence and opening. It is at least possible to say that subjectivity is more "immanentization" than immanence, more identification than identity, and that transcendence (and even intentionality), as opening through nongivenness, thus constitutes it originarily: it is the paradoxical movement of an immanence that always already reverts to the Ek-static opening that it also is; it is one against the other, as much as one through the other.

Heidegger

Within our solar system metaphor for the field of contemporary French phenomenology, there are two suns, the second (Heidegger) tending to eclipse the first (Husserl). Yet despite this it is only through the first that the second can be seen as his distorted image.[19]

I am not concerned with the question of deciding where the greatest debt lies.[20] It is fair to say, however, that it is Heidegger who liberates the force of the Husserlian text, and who also represses it.

- From a gnoseological point of view, this puts a definitive end to the primacy of representation, despite everything Husserl maintains, and more generally to the primacy of the theoretical. Significantly, the Husserlian idea of intentionality is devoid of the entirety of Heidegger's vocabulary, and from within the Heideggerian frame of thought, intentionality can no longer be described only as a derivative phenomenon: they are originary behaviors and affective tonalities. In other words, intentionality is revealed to itself in the dissolution of what it thought it was.

- Even more profoundly, on the ontological level itself, Husserlian transcendence is radicalized when it is divested of the burden of the primacy of the living-present's pure immanence: transcendence is assumed as such; that is, as no part of being but also and more significantly as nothing of the present (and consequently as no part of a presence to self, of consciousness). If the Husserlian language of transcendence is retranslated into Ek-static Heideggerian language, it would be possible to speak, with Rudolf Bernet, of an "intentionality without reserve" (see RB, 63). Nothingness, as the pure event of opening, is no longer subordinated to presence (though it seems to remain in one sense or another; we must return to this). From the viewpoint of the question of subjectivity that forms the center, or at least the best symptom, of the aporetic intensity in the play of transcendence and immanence, of given and non-given, it is quite natural to participate in the radical destruction of all subjectivity as a "reserve of presence."[21]

Again, two comments:

1. Here we must insist on the "horizontal" nature of Heideggerian Ek-stasy: nothingness is at the horizon of being, on the same plane and not "elsewhere" or "beyond." Nothingness *is* being; the phrase "being and nothingness" has meaning if being is nowhere other than in its own event. Being and the nothing are the obverse and the reverse of the same process of possibilization, which cannot have a remainder. Horizontal Ek-static transcendence is thinkable only through abandoning all substantiality (such as that still inhabiting, despite everything and in a sense more than ever—at least according to Heidegger—the Husserlian living-present) in favor of an originary "possible," a pure power of opening, a pure projection as the possibility of the self; it "is" precisely that.

   French phenomenologists, especially Merleau-Ponty, have continuously held fast to this non-transcendence (in the traditional hypostatic sense of the term) of Heideggerian transcendence—to its non-verticality, so to speak. And as for those who seem doubtful of so doing—Levinas, who might be thought to rehabilitate verticality given that he explicitly reclaims "height," and J.-L. Marion even more, who insists on a givenness beyond being—are never content simply to reject or cancel the horizontal Ek-static nature of transcendence. Their connection to Heidegger is much more complex, given that they emphasize the originary Husserlian gesture of "desubstantialization" even more than Heidegger does.

2. The phenomenological reproach par excellence might still be addressed to Heidegger: that of not having gone far enough, in this case in the direction of the "nothing," even though he pierced much further than Husserl beyond presence, at least in his explicit texts. In fact, for Heidegger nothingness is the nothing of *the* being, but not the nothing *of* being, which is to say that it is not the nothing of nothing. The retreat of being never occurs as the nothing of being: absence of being is always its very promise. Nothingness is basically only the power of being. It is full of being. This absence, as gestation of being, so to speak, paradoxically sharing Heideggerian nothingness with Husserlian living-presence that it too—one must be careful here—does not have the compactness of presence but is rather wrought from absence, a paradoxical absence as the promise of presence, virtuality, gestation of what is retained in order better to come into the world: maternity.

Consequently, even though one might wonder if Levinas is not risking yielding on something like the Heideggerian requirement of horizontality in designating transcendence as height, one might on the other hand find support in his texts for asking if Heidegger,[22] for his part, does not remain on this side of what he has seen—the radicality of the nothing—in always subordinating it to being. Inversely, Merleau-Ponty holds fast to the idea that the invisible is not beyond the visible, not other than the visible; that is, that the nothing is never only lodged in the interstices of being, is never only its very interstices. But does not requiring this immanence of the nothing to being not risk its disappearance through a too-great transience, the nothing being no more than a positive nothingness—which comes in a certain manner to respect it—at the point that, as "not nothing," it is no longer only the labile fold where the world produces the perpetual genesis of itself? We must think through this curious, chiasmic confusion in which Levinas, who *risks* the loss of "the immanence of transcendence," maintains and even radicalizes the irreducibility of the nothing,[23] when the one who radicalizes "the immanence of transcendence," Merleau-Ponty, *risks* the loss of the "nothing of nothing's" irreducibility in favor of a world enshadowed and profound, but that in its non-substantiality is more than ever generosity of presence; a presence that is never given fully except insofar as it is always promise. Remaining steadfastly on "this side," Merleau-Ponty—over-radicalizing this phenomenologically absolutely legitimate need—risks separation from the requirement of the irreducibility of transcendence as the "nothing of nothing."

At play once again here, illuminated in others of its potentialities through its inscription in a Heideggerian context, is the very aporia of the non-dialectizable tension between transcendence and immanence, between non-givenness and givenness, that we have read in Husserl as a delegated need, one that is immediately the risk of yielding before the unmanageable that requires being well managed, either in reconcealing the tension or in breaking it in order to be ensconced, in rediscovered comfort, within the priority of one of the two elements composing it.

Such is the state of the question of non-givenness we are bequeathed by Husserl and Heidegger: between the theoretical impossibility of clarifying and tackling it head-on (which despite everything still matters to Heidegger), and subterranean testing and insistence that they cannot fail to take it. The very *possibility* of intentionality depends on this *impossible* management of non-givenness.[24]

It is even clear that the idea of intentionality is at base merely the technical term within the phenomenological vocabulary that can recover—and thus render manipulable—the blind task of all phenomenology, its ineluctably operatory concept for speaking like Fink: givenness.[25] More exactly, it would be necessary to speak of the constellation of givenness (*Gegebenheit*, but also *Gabe, Gebung*). This "constellatory" quality of the notion signals precisely the difficulty, if not the impossibility, of its thematization. This constellation "irrigates," deep below the surface, all phenomenology, just like what underlies it and supports it, and that toward which it tends in a nostalgia for origin. Tempted to dig even deeper than representation and its correlate, objectness, which masks more than it shows, deeper than the opposition between activity and passivity, the closer one gets the more givenness seems to shed its covers. And does the givenness that gives (gives all being and all sense of being) allow itself to give? In a significant way, is the term "givenness" (or more exactly the semantic register of givenness in general) not worth more through what it refuses to say (*Vorstellung, Repräsentation, Objekt* . . .) than through what it succeeds in saying positively? And does this term, which wants to designate the very process of presence's completion, in its examination of all technicity, but in its unheard-of extension, not risk shining forth like a word on a marquee?[26]

This is the problematic frame within which contemporary French phenomenology is inscribed, in particular the three thinkers we are examining here. Let us see how this is so.

A number of avenues have opened up that were and are today clearly at work; briefly, as though they are characters in a play about to be presented:

A. We might *untie* the intricate knots in the thread, the one affirming the primacy of the immanence of consciousness and the one ceaselessly recalling non-givenness as a principle of opening, in a manner in some sense following on from Husserlian requisites but conserving the first thread and denouncing the second as a weakness, a concession to Ek-stasis produced through an immanence that cannot support its own immanent weight. This is the avenue taken by Michel Henry that abandons the noematic pole, so to speak, left with its non-reality, a non-reality that for Henry has a negative connotation, in order to recede toward the lived experience of consciousness. More precisely, to abandon the *noēme* is simultaneously to abandon the glance itself, in favor of a *hylē* deeper and more authentic than the glance and its correlate, the phenomenon. But what is thus revealed is neither an anti-phenomenon nor a non-phenomenon but the very authenticity of the phenomenon and the glance, the pinnacle of seeing and seen, the full presence of the one and the other in a pure coincidence in which they have both, always already, been reabsorbed. The phenomenology of the visible—that is, intentionality—is left behind in favor of an invisible that is neither a visible that is no longer given nor a beyond of the visible, but an infravisible, an auto-revelation. Having left the surface, this patina that is the glance; one thus leaves behind what it is authentically as the inauthentic, and what is given—form—in order to explore what Husserl raised as a possibility in *Ideas I* without ever implementing it, as if everything in these theoretical requisites had blocked it: a material phenomenology autonomous, and for Henry, the sole truly phenomenological one.

In order to establish a more precise filiation with Husserl and to take into account that the different periods cut from the Husserlian itinerary are not supplemented any more than they are contradicted but reveal and are revealed by his work as a field of tensions, we must admit regarding this gesture that it is simultaneously true and untrue to Husserl's *Ideas I* and to the later Husserl. It is true to the Husserl of *Ideas I* in that it radicalizes the absoluteness of consciousness, and heretical to it in that it just as radically reabsorbs form and transcendental movement. This gesture perpetuates that of the later Husserl in taking a step back from a noematic phenomenology beyond all noetic phenomenology toward the depths of hyletic phenomenology—but remaining radically distinct from it in that far from being accompanied by a genetic step, it *seems* to condemn all temporalization. More precisely, Henry denounces the inauthenticity of temporality thought as Ek-static, but in his most recent texts this is in order to better describe the "transcendental Time" that is the very movement through which Life becomes itself. In this sense, his phenomenology of Life actually is "genetic"; we will return to this.

B. Jean-Luc Marion's gesture is situated within an explicit relationship with the first gesture above: he also holds to the Husserlian thread of the presence of givenness. But the *manner* in which Marion holds to that thread, and his *goal* in so doing, is different.

Far from diverting the analysis of this phenomenological pole from its Ek-static inauthenticity, Marion's problematic carries him toward it, in order to reveal it as prioritary within the intentional correlation, thus inverting the Husserlian priority and relieving consciousness of its absoluteness.[27] This phenomenon, which gives all representation to itself, is said to be "saturated" in that its presence to itself is without any failure at the point at which it is drawn to itself and to the glance holding it in its view. Consequently, and even though Marion does not use this expression, the phenomenon is initially for the representation seeing it, "saturating" it, in the sense that the representation fills it adequately, until it is constrained and, even further, until it makes the representation fail, giving it to being in its failure. This is to say consequently that the saturated phenomenon is properly of the order of the excessive:[28] it overflows my (any) representation. This is why its presence can no longer allow itself to be described within the determination of intuition, if intuition—as givenness—does not fill the glance since from the outset it was brought about and constrained *by* this glance—as intuition. It is omnipotence and super-presence. Manifested apart from itself and provoking my glance at the very movement in which it forces its own abdication, making me see in making me lower my eyes, the saturated phenomenon *is* the originary representation. In the same movement, it is the fullest presence, overflowing the finitude of my representation, what *with regard to the ego* is super-presence. It is true that one must not understand this super-presence as the highest degree of a presence laid out hierarchically like a scale, from ego to super-presence as its pinnacle. This presence is not comparable to my sense of it:[29] it can no longer be measured; excess and plenitude coincide in it. It is clear, however, since it is where the difference between Marion and Henry lies, that in reversing its priority and even its attributes, Marion *conserves* the duality of the glance and the seen; he thinks a *super-presence* while Henry thinks *the absolute of presence*. In fact, in the full presence of immanence to itself, vision and the viewed are abolished prior to all intentionality, while the excess of the presence of the saturated phenomenon reverses but does not cancel intentionality—on the contrary. If Marion plays out the Husserlian thread of presence and of givenness, and is thus close to Henry, from another perspective the excess of presence, since it overflows representation, brings it about: in this respect, Marion diverges from Henry. The more "the everyday phenomenon," in Marion's expression, has the same effect of non-givenness, the less it is a phenomenon. Too-full presence is refused just as much as absence, and as it calls the Ek-static. As the thought of a transcendence of representation passively provoked by a transcendent, Marion's gesture is clearly related to Levinas's. This is its proper chiasm that, in order to exceed a thought of the pure immanence of presence (Henry's), carries it toward Levinasian transcendence, but as grasped by the other pole—not that of the default of being but of being's too-fullness.

    C. The other gesture possible for the theoretical matrix inherited from Husserl is the thread of non-givenness, of the default of presence.[30]

    Levinas's phenomenology is the exemplary incarnation of this step. The central intuition guiding him is well known: if intentionality, in its Ek-static movement, is itself truly nothing other than an identification exercise, a capturing by the Same and a reverting to it, then such a gesture is thoroughly contradictory: its success cancels it, causes it to kill its own properly intentional nature, since it can depart from itself only in better reentering itself. Also, "one cannot not think" that it was originarily and always already opened by what can then be characterized as a power of opening that escapes every constraint, first of all the definitional constraint: the alterity of the Other. More precisely, the defeat of my intentionality brings it into being. In Levinasian terms: the Other *gives* the Same; the "Otherwise-than-being" gives (to) being. This passive resistance of the Other, which resists not in the manner of inertia of matter but, on the contrary, as an escaping current of air—not by its ontological weight but as ontological depletion [*déperdition*], reverses itself in the most intense of its activities, not of a representation but of *the* representation that in its transcendence embeds itself at the very heart of each consciousness in order to open its immanence and thus to bring it to being. What is witnessed here is an *inversion*[31]—of the Husserlian schema of intentionality: a more originary representation is embedded at the heart of consciousness, an intentionless representation that is hardly any longer intentional in that it defeats rather than synthesizes and identifies,[32] and in that it gives being only in order to have it paradoxically but originarily already fractured, thus assigning it to the most primordial of passivities. If my egoic consciousness sees itself deprived of its transcendental dignity, it does not mean that this dignity would be entrusted to another intentionality but that the Other as Other does not identify itself (in the double sense that it is not auto-constituted and that it is the unconstitutable par excellence for me) and identifies nothing, but paradoxically becomes fruitful in altering. It thus assigns me to the originary non-intentional heart inhabiting all my intentional representations. However, it is necessary to note that Levinas never ceases to emphasize that Alterity can be shown only at the heart of the Same, the only place where it appears to remain, though only fleetingly. Altering transcendence, paradoxically, exists only in borrowing from what it *is not*, from the immanence of being and what resembles it, the *logos*. That is, it can be manifested only in the paradoxical mode of the *trace*. And this notion of the trace is therefore nodal in Levinas's philosophy.[33] From an ontological point of view it signifies an absence that is *the same as* presence, an Otherwise-than-being *within* being. It also signifies the initial linguistic nature of the problematic: if the trace is the very thing demanding to be read, then what is at play between being and Otherwise-than-being in the *de*phenomenalization proper to all phenomena is by the same token an appeal to interpretation. Finally, because it is temporal through and through, the notion of trace indicates that this "play" (in the sense that one might say there is play in any articulation), between being and Otherwise-than-being, between visible and invisible, is also thoroughly temporal, is temporalization itself: what is in play, what is play itself, as we have already begun to indicate, is what Levinas calls *diachrony*. Diachrony "makes" time and "makes" language—the latter thus revealed as thoroughly temporal—by unmaking them. The radical, inverting interruption of which it "consists," can escape only by disappearing in the inefficacy and the non-sense that "resounds"—to use another Levinasian term—in the trace in which it will leave itself without, however, identifying itself.

Rapidly situating Levinas's philosophy relative to Husserl's from a methodological point of view, and even though Levinas himself hardly proceeds from this kind of positioning, we might say that like Michel Henry's it is engulfed in the hyletic, in order to attack the originary at the heart of lived experience, but this time by giving it an entirely genetic twist. The very radicalization of the problematic of genesis is at issue here. Levinas accentuates the dimension of passivity and the temporal divergence within phenomenology that is consequently, properly speaking, a "phenomenology of birth."

D. Derrida's work is inscribed within close proximity to, and closely follows, Levinas's; it is not Levinas the commentator on Husserl who demands the greatest attention from Derrida the commentator on Husserl, but rather the Derridean philosophical practice holding it in a decisive complicity with certain phenomenological motifs at work in Levinas's texts; no doubt, their goals and methods differ, but it remains that for both the motif of *absence of origin* is at work—or rather, works.

One cannot refer to "Derrida the phenomenologist" without some misgiving, inasmuch as Derrida himself does not inscribe his work in Husserl's footsteps without remainder; he breaks with the requirement—shared by all post-Husserlian phenomenologists—to go even further than Husserl down the path he opens but then reconceals: that of being "more phenomenological than the phenomenologist." Derrida, rather, takes "Derrida *and* phenomenology" as his thematic, or "phenomenology *and* Derrida"; the ties between Derrida's work and phenomenology seem to have developed in parallel without ever having coincided, and for that very reason.

Derrida's famous reading of *Logical Investigation I*,[34] along with his *Origin of Geometry*, both grounded (though in differing ways) via Heideggerian motifs on the hypothesis that Husserl took the metaphysics of presence to its highest point while simultaneously testing out—counterintuitively, and in any case non-thematizably—its impossibility. That is, the axiomatics of presence were for Husserl theoretically thematized and, insofar as it is the medium of Husserlian research and as the fundamental notions of this research are formulated in it, unperceived as such:[35] Husserl could not see himself as "the last representative of a metaphysics of presence" and very strongly wished to say so. As the basis for all philosophy, the axiomatic of presence could certainly not be seen as the prejudice of a particular age of thought. According to it, the originarity of non-presence would be conjured up, then even denied, yet could be maintained only as that which alone would render all presence possible. It would be, in the Heideggerian sense, this philosophy's unthought; that is, what is at once contained within it and what could only escape it as the very force making it possible, and making it possible as its very impossibility. Derrida's lesson is precisely that the metaphysics of presence can never exist except as its impossibility; he also shows us—and this is his irony—that it is always only *out of* the axiomatics of presence that originary difference can be glimpsed, since by the gap's very "nature" it can never, without betraying itself, give itself without concealing itself. For Derrida, originary *delay* can be given only in a *supplement* that is absolutely originary. This is an "impossible" thesis—impossible in the sense that it enacts the collapse of all presence—that nonetheless does not recapitulate a radical skeptical doubt, since it holds that the gap is given in a presence that is consequently "spectral." This "impossible" thesis of deconstruction proceeds through the same gesture to draw out its consequences and to implement all its applications. In a paradoxical *mise en abyme*,[36] it implements what it discovers, what it invents, in the Derridean sense of "invent," exposing the unthought of a thought. It discovers both the "consubstantial" impossibility of a pure presence already inhabited by a gap, a difference, and the impossibility of the givenness of this gap, or rather that the givenness of the gap is maintained entirely within the impossibility of its originary gift. This clearly means that one cannot dismiss the metaphysics of presence, since one will be able to grasp difference only as difference *apart from* it; rather, one can only—and this is already enough—make it understand that it is not what it thinks it is: pure presence to itself. Yet, and this is mark of irony that must be received with humor, one can only tell it this outside of itself. This is the process that deconstruction both defines and tests. Consequently, the connection it maintains with the phenomenological reduction is real: if deconstruction does not actually coincide with the reduction, in a sense it is not autonomous with regard to it, and this link is not one of the incomprehension, opposition, contradiction, or even disfiguration of the phenomenological project, as it has sometimes been read. Deconstruction manifests the impossibility of "reduction," as access of full presence to itself, of constitutive consciousness; one way of doing this is to find support in texts taking the irreducible detour of eroding the immediateness of sensory experience, obliterating as much as manifesting them and thus preventing access to sense in that they hollow out a gap within its full presence. But deconstruction also demonstrates that this gap can be given only within a presence, however "eroded" it may be, even in a "spiritual" object, a text. Whence the ambivalence of the text as spiritual object: as worldly materiality, the text betrays pure presence to itself of both meaning and consciousness; it *distances itself* from them in a salutary and necessary betrayal, though from another vantage point this is not a *pure* gap but still a mode of presence, however weak it may be, however pervaded by non-presence. Yet Derrida remains close to Levinas in claiming that all gifts must be seen along with the trace, and with the text—the text precisely as the trace.[37]

Deconstruction is thus both the impossibility of the phenomenological reduction and the impossibility of not *desiring* the reduction; it is the very gesture recognizing that one can declare the impossibility of the reduction *only* in desiring it:[38] this is the core of the ultimate meaning that might be called the need to liberate the unthought of all meaning. The deconstruction of the naïveté of all presence to self, of all meaning, must always in the same gesture *also* manifest the naïveté that ineluctably still inhabits it. This is the link between deconstruction and the phenomenological reduction: it is double and contradictory; it is a double bind. Deconstruction is both the effacement of and nostalgia for the reduction, consisting of "falling out of love with" the reduction *in continuing to be taken* by it. And if the phenomenological reduction redirects itself toward intentionality, then what produces Derridean thought is at once

deconstruction of intentionality and—non-dialectical—conservation of
intentionality at the heart of the movement that can never be a simple
destruction. Therefore, in tacking toward other bodies of work than that
of the father of phenomenology, Derrida says of phenomenology that it
was like a regret for him. We must ascribe significant value to this remark,
a value surpassing any simple biographical and psychological framework.
Such remorse seems to haunt him and us like a ghost.[39] And we want to
escape from what haunts us just as we want to do so from what is *not us*,
while making it the experience we have not had—though it is, on the contrary, precisely what inhabits us and is speaking in us, permitting us to be
ourselves in forcing us to let go. As a result, if our description of the connection between Derrida's work and phenomenology is accurate, we could
say that they are reciprocally haunted. And this connection (re)produces
the very thing Derrida talks about: that there is no pure presence, that
presence is always already differed and deferred, but that the gap itself can
never be itself given fully as such, can be divined only through its trace, as
an aftertaste, a remorse, a phantom.

These are thus the principal protagonists in the play currently being
presented under the title "phenomenology"; that is, these are the principal fields of the thinkable on which the tensions inhabiting the phenomenological method are deployed. What relations are woven among
these "characters"? Do they present a tragic configuration in which excess
engenders the eruption of the field of constraints proper to phenomenology,[40] or an open dramatic structure in which excess ceaselessly regenerates the possibilities of phenomenological description?

In the final analysis, we are here chiefly interested in overcoming
the limits of phenomenological axiomatics, of the "principle of principles"
that is the full presence of intuition,[41] of which intentionality is the emphatic guardian and manager. There are two ways of risking this that,
while not symmetrical, are equivalent—at least hypothetically: the tenets
of a default of origin and those of (too) full presence at the origin; each
is like a rupture in a great tragic family that remains problematically together in the midst of their conflict. This is the most elemental sharing,
the grounding frontier that, however complicated and confused it might
be—and even if we could trace other frontiers[42]—would be decisive.

3

The Question of the Limit

Whatever it may be, this internal limit is of interest here only insofar as what is at stake in it is the very limit of phenomenology. It is thus appropriate to lay out the conceptual tools we are using here in an attempt to *work at the limit.*

First, Husserl himself employs two explicit methodological senses of the limit. As Denise Souche-Dagues shows, presiding over the *Logical Investigations* and beyond, and extending to Husserl's entire phenomenological itinerary, is the principle of the absence of limits for objective reason, the very definition of "understanding" or of thought: "Everything that is knowable 'in itself' and in its being is determined according to its content."[1] For Souche-Dagues this is a question of a means of recalling the requisite fundamental theoretics of Husserlian phenomenology that we have already begun to address: there is no subjective finitude in the power to understand; the brink of the understandable is precisely the very movement by which I carry myself toward it; consequently, nothing escapes this movement, since there is a given only insofar as I give it to myself. Certainly, there is a not-filled, and even a *structurally* not-filled, but as we remember, this not-given-there, the only one to which Husserl grants a status, can be recognized and mastered as such precisely because it is measured at the brink of fullness.

From this principle—which the "principle of principles" in *Ideas I* redoubles or, more precisely, expresses differently, just as each formulation of the Kantian categorical imperative brings to light another of its aspects—emerge at least two important elements: first, that authentic thought operates in ideal objectivity appearing as apodicticity, since the encounter of "subjective" representation with its fullness is objectivity itself, thus relegating the contingency of psychological representation to the status of inessential; second and more important, this principle describes the a priori nature of co-relation as the uniquely authentic. This is a way of saying that "all consciousness is consciousness of . . . ," and moreover that "all phenomena are phenomena of . . . ," given the primacy here of the "of." Clearly, then, with Souche-Dagues it must be said that this principle "is intentionality itself: in it the essence of consciousness as consciousness-of unfolds" (DSD, 22).

In my view, for those of us interested in the limit-practices of intentionality, it is vitally important to understand that since the *Logical Investigations* intentionality has been related to the notion of the limit whenever intentionality has had to reveal its essence; but—and this is decisive—it is equally essential to assert the *absence of limits*. For Husserl, intentionality is itself only in being limitless; and it is necessary and even urgent for it to declare itself as such.

Let us turn to the later Husserl, indeed to the final one, the Husserl of the Group C texts on time. Though his interest diverts from noetico-noematic structure and from the exemplary motivating object that is the objective ideal, focusing rather on a description of a life-grounding description of consciousness as *Urhyle*, the absoluteness of consciousness still commands Husserl's attention. But from another angle this time: when he searches into its depths, he finds that the transparency of the pure immanence of consciousness to itself, in its absoluteness, is disrupted, even while it remains necessary (we must return to this disruption, which is time itself in its originarity). In any event, in another form, more insecure than that of the *Logical Investigations* or even the *Ideas*, the principle of "absence of limits" nonetheless returns, or rather remains. Succeeding the absolute of the rationalist mathematician's objectivity, then, is its near neighbor, the speculative Absolute of German Idealism.[2] Husserl is thus caught in the tension of being attracted by its need for originarity relative to the "deep seas" in which its rational requirements, despite all its efforts and despite its resistance to all forms of mysticism, risk dissolution: such are the disruptive surprises of the *Grund*, when it is all too necessary that one confront the *Urgrund*. In any case, Husserl always asserts the absence of limits even if that absence assumes the disquieting face of the abyssal. Eugen Fink characterizes Husserl's final task thus: "Husserl wants to return to the informal base from which formations emerge; he wants to grasp the *apeiron*, the *boundless*, not by being mystically destroyed in the night within which, according to Hegel's ironic formula, 'all cows are black'; he wants to seize it in its originary leap (*Ursprung*)."[3]

However, we also see mentioned in those late manuscripts a notion of a limit that is not privatized: envisaged there is a limit to powers of consciousness that is as much constitutive as gnoseological, and it is precisely temporality that is in play. Husserl addresses, centrally with regard to birth and death—and this itself is significant—the *Grenz-phänomen*. But it is imperative to note that Husserl characterizes this limit not as *Grenz* but as *Limes*. The mathematician in Husserl recalls that in mathematics what is properly called *Limes* is never known in itself, since it is that out of which one can know anything at all. It can thus be known only as having this function; the *Limes* is that toward which consciousness *infinitely tends*,[4] a point of convergence, an asymptote. Yet on the contrary, it functions less as a principle of closure than as one of opening:[5] for Husserl birth and death, far from signifying the irreducible finitude of existence and of thought, far from limiting, ceaselessly reinitiate the infinite force of thought toward the absolute.

Derrida's proposed analysis of the connection that philosophy as such—and especially Hegelian philosophy—maintains with the limit seems in the end to apply integrally and equally to Husserl.[6] If philosophy can think the limit, it is not in the sense in which it would put itself at risk *at* the limit, at the place of its dissolution or at least of its contamination by an Other that is radically Other, but always in the sense in which it makes the limit the very object of its thought. To maintain a connection with the limit means, for philosophy—how could it be otherwise?—to *think* the limit, which it simultaneously recuperates as *its* limit, emptying it of its power of destabilization and returning it, ironically, to being the internal engine of its own deployment. Thus, Derrida sees the limitation that is negativity for Hegel as resembling Husserlian *Limes*. The limit appears as a domesticated alterity, an internal usage localized at the point where knowledge and the absolute reciprocate.

What does this mean? It cannot simply be a matter of *crossing* the limit, if it is to be maintained within philosophy. It must be located at the *internal border* of the philosophical,[7] but in escaping the temptation of a negating gesture, of conjuration and recuperation, that we see after Derrida. How? Faced with this aporia, we must remember Heidegger's principles of interpretation: "it will be a matter of unveiling its positive possibilities, meaning its limits," says Heidegger regarding the ontological tradition.[8] This means that the limit, far from indicating the prevention or imperfection of a philosophy, is, on the contrary, its own possibility, since its possibility is its unthought. If it is thus necessary not to conjure up the limit but to unveil it, this is because it is properly the richness of a thought, an indication of its unexpectedness; that is, its unforeseeable inhabiting that will "invent" us as much as we invent it. This is the authentic positivity of the philosophical limit, not as the perfecting of a determination of closure but as an *opening* onto the indetermination of the possible.

I am attempting to challenge the "authors" we are addressing here in order to unveil the limit of the phenomenological method, since all three *start* to do so, in a more or less explicit manner and claimed as such in each case.

This limit is thus, again, properly an *opening*, not in the sense that it opens the determined by translating it into an absolute knowledge, but in making it an *initial incision* (*Riss*): not as the substance of a trait that designates a closure, but as the gash made by the incising trait, thus opening to the effect of the Other.[9]

Clearly we must not allow ourselves to be guided too strictly by these words, but it is significant that with regard to Husserl, who seems to deny the limit to the same degree to which he puts it to the test, Eugen Fink writes—I cite it once again—that "Husserl wants to return to the informal base from which formations emerge; he wants to grasp the *apeiron*, the *boundless*, not by being mystically destroyed in the night within which, according to Hegel's ironic formula, 'all cows are black'; he wants to seize it in its originary leap (*Ursprung*), like an *incision* (*Riss*) [emphasis added] cutting into the very ground of life . . . that is, he wants to seize time in his process" (EF, 184).

Let us pause to assess.

How is it possible to unveil the limit of intentionality and, beyond that, of phenomenology itself, without traversing it? This is the aporia the texts we are reading here must confront,[10] at least hypothetically, whether in a reflective manner or not.

We have tried to demonstrate that the limit is implicated in the notion of non-givenness, if non-givenness is what threatens to produce the emergence of presence to itself that characterizes intentionality, and if non-givenness actually constitutes the risk of a transcendence that is, as it were, *too radical*, and that would cause "transcendence within immanence" to be exploded through an excess of presence—or, contrarily, through a default of presence.[11] The notion of non-givenness is intrinsically ambivalent: in making us aware of the limit, it also presents the risk of crossing it. At base, there are two figures of failure here and, taking everything into account, the one is as valuable as the other: one can fail from the start by not knowing how to rise above the risk of failing; one can fail by acceding to the temptation to go beyond the limit, which implies at least having arrived at the limit's edge.

Any methodical reflection on the use of non-givenness in phenomenology is thus an imposition. This reflection is something Husserl never managed, never having thematized the notion. But it is nonetheless at work in his texts. The *Stimmung* of nascent phenomenology was antispeculative. As Eugen Fink clearly shows, at issue for phenomenology then was "to show things themselves without prejudice or systematizing construction, what they are and how they are, purely and simply and in a non-falsified manner." Further, "it wants to give 'to concrete things themselves' the first and last word. It wants to preserve them from being veiled by those who reconceal them with hasty 'interpretations' (*Deutungen*)" (EF, 113). And Fink continues with a substantial explanation of how this process renders possible an encounter with things themselves, liberating the experiencer "from what he proudly calls his system when he is a philosopher." But as Fink says, "The phenomenality of the phenomenon is not itself a phenomenal given" (EF, 120); "the appearance of the being is not something that appears in itself" (EF, 120). Thus, phenomenology is held in a tension, even a contradiction, forced to push its glance beyond the "presentable" given, "the thing itself," through its very care for the "presentable" given. To which one might object that, on the contrary, Husserl, and the majority of phenomenologists after him, elucidating the "medium" of all appearance (intentionality, for Husserl at least), discovers it as an appearance more radical, more perfect, than everything that appears, everything that is given, in and by it. It thus remains necessary that the perceived, sensible thing ceases to be the methodological model of donation. And out of this a certain suspicion might form: if the phenomenological glimpse is taken back prior to the thing that is given and "presentable," who can guarantee that it will regain the originary power to make appear, in that it itself is pure appearance, and in that it cannot be applied to the speculative constructions where, precisely, the thing that is given, "presentable," and thus describable, is not? The desire to grasp the root of all givenness opens up the risk of exceeding all giving, and thus of all control via intentional analysis; that is, at the very least, via rigorous description of the manner by which the given is given. Fink remarks that "it is significant that intentional analysis becomes, in the course of its methodical deployment, a sort of philosophy of life" (EF, 124), since it must flow back, in its requisite radicality, toward intentional life itself. And Fink's remark is extended and clarified by Derrida, who identifies in Husserl a "metaphysics" one of whose privileged expressions is "the metaphysics of life" (*OG*). Husserl's later texts addressed here, and in which the desire to elucidate the most originary—the auto-temporalization of consciousness—place the notion of the absolute at their center, can only consolidate the legitimacy of such a suspicion.

The urgent task imposed here, then, is to interrogate non-givenness, inasmuch as it opens up the risk of exceeding the constraints of intentional analysis, exceeds the need to hold to any description of the appearance of what appears.

This is what Eugen Fink does in the *Sixth Cartesian Meditation*.[12] Before offering our own critique, let us pause to take counsel from him. To do so, we need only briefly recount the problem Fink confronts in his § 7, requiring him to theorize non-givenness (*Nicht-Gegebenheit*). The influence of what could be called the phenomenologizing ego on the transcendental ego is disrupted, and this disruption is *time* itself. Faced with this problem, Fink must explicitly thematize the notion of non-givenness: he gives it his phenomenological stamp of nobility. In fact, he explicitly insists on the necessity of giving a phenomenological status to the limits of givenness, just where it seems that Husserl endlessly tested these limits without ever renouncing the need for an absolute givenness, and without thematically envisaging the unenvisagable: that there was a radical non-givenness that shakes the sovereignty of transcendental subjectivity. And in order to think at the very place of the non-gift, it is necessary that a descriptive phenomenology already taken over by a regressive phenomenology be radicalized—radicalized or exceeded?, that is the problem— into a constructive phenomenology.[13] What cannot be described must be constructed. And for a moment at least, far from "transcendences" and Hegelian reconciliations he implements forcefully in the *Sixth Cartesian Meditation*, Fink puts a certain tension to the test, a tension between the need to think phenomenology in its constructive moment and the "relative inconceivability of the idea of a constructive phenomenology." This "relative inconceivability" is maintained throughout the text's concerns in simple indication, even though any possible construction must consist of an implementation of a dialectic of the absolute—which will then quickly be employed to calm any concern!

The fruitfulness of Fink's reflections on non-givenness and construction is obvious in the context of contemporary French phenomenology: we must choose between a phenomenology, fascinated by the originary, that breaks with a necessary rigor in order to go beyond the field of description and consequently—on the one hand, quite often in some theological heaven, and on the other, a phenomenology that under the pretext of rigor stays firmly with the thing given, the "presentable"—that by refusing to return prior to the "presentable" toward the *how* of its givenness as a result of the radicality—which becomes rigidity—of its refusal, it finishes by contradicting its very essence in order to fold itself back onto a positivist project.

Fink teaches us that the best weapon against speculative constructions never confessing themselves as such consists of addressing the problem of construction head-on, even while assuming the necessity of construction and its irreducibly aporetic nature, from the viewpoint of phenomenological exigency. Confronted by fabricators of illusions, what could be better than clarity in recognizing and meditating on the limits of givenness? Or rather, faced with "uncontrolled" phenomenological constructions,[14] attempting to think the modalities of this control is preferable to a negating of aporias in originary givenness and to a repressing of a non-givenness manifested through its exclusion from the phenomenological field. Fink points to the essential modality of this control: constructive phenomenology must not produce an economy of constitutive phenomenology, must not circumvent it but, on the contrary, traverse it.[15] If it is situated at the limit of phenomenology, it is situated at its own internal border, at the very edge of phenomenology.

The risk—and what is at stake—is the *usage* of the limit in phenomenology. In other words, the stakes are situated such that phenomenology "manages," or more elegantly, "governs," its connection—or its non-connection—to excess.

PART II

THE FRONTIER OF TIME

It is now time to put our working hypotheses to the test:

1. The opposition between givenness and non-givenness should be operative in order for us to be able to configure the contemporary French phenomenological landscape, or at least this "family" characterized by an *excessive* practice of the phenomenological method laid out here.

2. Various ways of applying the limit should be in play. Our attention here will focus in particular on three of these applications: refusing to approach, transgressing, and bearing with the limit.

Why the turn toward time?

1. Because it is the very "place" where the *highest risk to the originary* is clearly developed, following an aporetic laid out by Husserl. Time, according to *On the Phenomenology of the Consciousness of Internal Time*, reveals itself as constituting the most profound place, the place of *Urkonstitution*, for a phenomenology remaining on this side of the form of the ego as viewed noetically, finally to be carried toward the birth of the flux of consciousness that only a hyletic, and thus genetic, phenomenology can confront.[1] This origin, for Husserl, could not be a simple origin (*Anfang*) or a simple grounding, if grounding is only ever a question of Cartesian repetition in the

theoretical order of the fashionable notion of origin. This means that the phase in which phenomenology is identified and theorized, that of the "second" Husserl—of the transcendental turn, the path of Cartesian reduction, of reconduction in the direction of the *Ur-region* of absolute consciousness; toward certitude and a sense of the density of pure immanence—is not as simple as it might seem. Origin—this is always already the case—has no simple self-presence. Despite the evidence of the Cartesian claims for consciousness, origin is complicated, just as it is always complicated for Husserlian claims, even if initially only implicitly and even through certain texts desiring not to recognize it.[2] This topic rapidly and decisively testifies to the *genesis* of the ego that ruins the temptation of a simple origin or foundation by installing the phenomenological glance, from the very outset, within the slippery terrain of temporalized/ temporalizing flux.[3] However, the Husserlian glance's enduring of a more radical temporalization seems to bring about a movement that emerges from Cartesian simplicity only to approach a Fichtean absolute. And in this movement, despite everything, there is an ever-greater chance of a non-foundational origin (Heidegger will think this through carefully) relieved of the axiomatic *archē* and telos in order to be redirected toward its first sense, that of "thrownness."[4]

The temporality of consciousness or, more radically, consciousness as temporal flux, is the focus of the most originary constitution as *Urkonstitution*: thus, phenomenological reduction becomes more than ever a movement against nature; a stream that suddenly wants to reverse its course in order to return to seize its emergence as and at its point of origin. In order to be worthy of this unprecedented task, the phenomenological method must go to the very limits of its resources, since it is never solely the mirror that consciousness attempts to associate with itself—the mirror that, wanting to be too faithful and thus transparent in the end no longer reflects anything; clearly, *Urregion* consciousness for Husserl oscillates between the status of phenomenon par excellence and non-phenomenon. In fact, it is the medium of all phenomenology, and thus, in its coincidence— which is always transparence—it is in fact phenomenon par excellence; this is to say again that without distance from itself, a distance from which a glance can be deployed, it cannot see itself and is thus what is "without phenomenon." And if an irreducible distance is assumed and acknowledged, precisely as a temporal gap, then the mirror becomes irremediably opaque; in this reversed direction as well consciousness is non-phenomenon.[5] This conundrum is marked in the following manner at least: the language required by *Logical Investigation I* at the level of simple, transparent, and straightforward expression is filled out, given flesh, and consequently "worked" in such a manner that the work's materiality must emerge through the gesture it resists—in such a way that traced within it is what both exceeds and precedes it. Phenomenology finds itself increasingly accepted as "negative phenomenology,"[6] whose grounding principle is that when in the context of the gift one moves toward what precedes all gifts and is thus not given—as this is a question of what gives, or of the very operation of givenness, an operation that does not perhaps presuppose an authentic donor—what then brings to appearance and names what has always already preceded?

How is it possible to speak of what has preceded all givenness, everything in the context of which I give myself the gift, and finally the operative concepts through which the meditating ego can describe givenness? It would be necessary to think and to make formulations outside the great commonalities of Western philosophy engaged by Husserlian phenomenology, especially the link between form and matter. But then, clearly, "words are lacking," and phenomenology becomes apophatic, sharing the aporia of all the philosophies turning toward origin, in particular all idealisms,[7] and one must ask how one might know whether the process is better effectuated from ectype to archetype, from copy to model, from the least presence to the source that irrigates it—as we have asked philosophy to do since its Platonic origin. Or is it that, on the contrary, I do not project, in some retrospective illusion, any model or source other than the very place where I was born and where I am already inscribed (in Heidegger's words, "being" apart from "*the* being"; the "transcendental" apart from the "worldly" in Husserl's)? The "ontic model," in Gérard Granel's expression, is not the model for what is given as a model, or, more exactly, for what is given as a gift.

2. Because to turn to time is to turn to the monstrous requirement that consciousness always be aware of itself: this is the aporia insisting to Husserl that the transcendental ego is not born and does not die or that it dies, thus affirming its absoluteness, and that also makes him pay close attention to the process of its passive genesis.[8] To maintain these two contradictory constraints implies that consciousness is *self-contained*. This double bind is nowhere more decisive than in Husserl, given that he directs consciousness toward passivity and "frees it of the selfhood" provided by birth, through the same movement by which he accentuates the activity of its masterful ability to conjure up the very thing being sought and that risks contaminating this power itself. This is self-constitution's wager: the astonishing need to seize upon the *Ur* in and through the *Selbst*. This is manifestly the *hybris* of the phenomenology of time: if consciousness is lived uniquely as finite, then there can be no *hybris*, no more than if it were lived absolutely as absolute; *hybris* results from the fact that it wants, as absolute, absolutely to grasp the finitude that it is. And this can be reversed: it wants to suspend itself in its very finitude, as absolute. *Hybris* consists of attempting to be perceived as infinitely finite.

   This self-containment that is self-constitution must be a privileged aporia for us, if we attempt to install ourselves at the limit of intentionality by suspending ourselves on its internal border.

3. Because the question engendered by this aporia initiated by Husserl and inherited by the thinkers on whom we are focusing is the following: if what escapes me does so radically, do I lose all connection to "that"? But to radicalize affection destroys it: it flows beyond all my powers to the point of no longer being connected to me, no longer affecting me: my passivity, being "too" absolute, disconnects me and is no longer passivity.[9] If I must be connected to what affects *me*, how can I then not "return" the connection, if it is true that I risk dissolving affection in the minimal activity of accommodating it? How can I enter into a connection with what affects me without circumventing it?

This is non-givenness as such: precisely what is at risk. Non-givenness is only "absence-producing" absently. Non-givenness is not absence of affection but is rather the humiliation of a power,[10] or at least its obfuscation.

In non-givenness I do not live in the lightness—a form of freedom—of one who is without heritage, of one to whom nothing has been given, but in a sense as always already despoiled. And this flight, this gift, must be maintained in view, in the temporal gap.

We must attempt to characterize the various ways of enduring—or refusing to endure—non-givenness as the very limit of givenness, in the exemplary matrix of originary temporality.[11]

Toward a reconfiguration of the landscape of contemporary French phenomenology

This part of our inquiry must engage with a reconfiguration of a field at which we must look in order to categorize differing practices of the limits of givenness. We will work toward the point at which givenness and temporality originarily cross, supported by ways in which these two threads—that of givenness and that of temporality—develop most explicitly in the works we are reading, and to draw one thread toward the other, since they are intricately interwoven.

We will consider two issues: one focuses on the perspective both Michel Henry and Emmanuel Levinas give to *On the Phenomenology of the Consciousness of Internal Time*; the other, on the way in which Jacques Derrida and Jean-Luc Marion, each in his own way, make the gift and/or givenness originary.

The comparative framework will allow us to lay out a landscape and thus to avoid being closed into any single thought process. It will permit us above all to see a proximity behind any apparent opposition, and inversely.

Hypotheses for our work will be:

1. Levinasian and Henrian thought seem to be opposed as the radical need for transcendence and for immanence, leading toward destruction of the Husserlian matrix of "transcendence within immanence"; nonetheless, they share the intimate proximity of obverse and reverse. If this can indeed be shown, we will ask, what does this unexpected and ambiguous relationship teach us about each thinker's position?

2. Even beyond the explicit intersection between the problematics of the gift (Derrida) and of givenness (Marion), Marion never ceases to claim a relationship with the Derridean aporia of the gift as impossibility, inasmuch as this aporia in some way would initiate it: it thus lays claim to a filiation. But to what extent does this claim, about which we might wonder if it is not significant that it must be *shown*, is not destined to obliterate a perhaps irreducible gap between one and the other of these problematics, a gap so important that it signifies less difference than opposition? Why would this gap be carefully "reversed" by Marion? What does that mean?

This will not be a matter of proceeding to an exercise in comparison having no other end than itself. The comparison can be valuable only if it is connected to the underlying structural hypothesis here: that the discriminating factor lies in the various manners of managing the limit of intentionality (i.e., of givenness). To juxtapose Henry and Levinas is to bring Michel Henry, in some respect against himself, onto the side of accounting for this limit, while his philosophy, as a philosophy of the plenitude of presence, ignores all limits. It will also mean indicating a gap between Henry and Marion, even though there is an explicit affinity between Henrian presence and what I am calling Marion's "super-presence" that, as such, presents itself explicitly as a transgression of all limits. And to manifest a gap between Derrida and Marion means marking—explicitly—a gap between Levinas and Marion, despite the affinities between the problematics of seeing and the icon,[12] if what separates Derrida from Marion is what connects him to Levinas.

Behind all the affinities and even the amphibologies, the landscape is disturbed whenever there is a relationship—without naïveté regarding the sharpness of this split—between what survives the work of the limit and what only ceases to keep it at bay.

1

At the Limits of Intentionality

MICHEL HENRY AND EMMANUEL LEVINAS AS
READERS OF *ON THE PHENOMENOLOGY*
OF THE CONSCIOUSNESS OF INTERNAL TIME

For anyone wishing to map out the field of contemporary French phenomenology, intentionality—the central theme of phenomenology in general—and its crudest testing out, which begins when Husserl orients it toward time, confronts it through time, constituting a privileged or strategic "place of passage": a place that cannot be avoided even if it is but rarely traversed.[1]

1. I propose here to follow two trajectories, Michel Henry's and Emmanuel Levinas's, and to show that they install themselves in precisely the same "places" within the Husserlian problematic of time, though they can never meet there; it is as if they take the same route but in opposite directions.[2] In order to carry all this out, we must first describe Henry's reading of *On the Phenomenology of the Consciousness of Internal Time* through his "Hyletic Phenomenology and Material Phenomenology" (*HIC*, 7–42), and then we must attempt to demonstrate the mirror inversion of Levinas's analysis of the same Husserlian text in *Otherwise Than Being: or, Beyond Essence.*[3] In this process of "reflection" (which is clearly non-thematized by our central figures), there is clearly on the one side, intuition, and on the

other, its image. This is a matter, I would rather boldly suggest, of
the same thought seeming to work against itself.

2. But this internal risk is relayed through another regarding the fruitfulness and the limits of the phenomenological method.

Two initial courses of inquiry:

a. Why, when interrogating the limits of intentionality, is one led toward time?

   Clearly this is because "time-objects" are, as such, resistant to intentionality: since Augustine we have known that caught between
   being and non-being, time will not permit itself to be stabilized in
   a *logos*. But what gives the Husserlian problematic of time its originality is that Husserlian time is a "strange" object for consciousness
   since it is revealed as the originary being of consciousness itself—an
   originary describable neither as "beginning" nor as "foundation"
   in the logical sense of these terms. Time is basically the "place"
   in which intentionality, as the power of producing all things, as
   the pure act of being thrown into the world while remaining itself,
   seeks to be given to itself. *On the Phenomenology of the Consciousness of Internal Time* attempts to conjure up origin as aporia, since
   origin threatens to conceal itself in the same gesture that attempts
   to seize hold of it (a gesture of which it is the origin). In searching
   for its origin, the Husserlian intentional glance sees itself as an "object" in the form of a *more originary intentionality*. Faced with this
   task, Husserlian phenomenological method must create the ideas
   of passive synthesis, double intentionality "ratified" in longitudinal
   intentionality, transversal intentionality, and operant intentionality; these are all ideas about which we might wonder if they do not
   remain "haunted" and thus made opaque by the very aporia they
   seek to absorb. The need for originarity implies that the sought-
   for intentionality be required and presaged as "non-objectivizing"
   (since it is more originary than any objectivizing glance) and "passive" (since it precedes all constituting activity, and thus the opposition between activity and passivity). This is a kind of intentional
   chiasmus, bringing forth aporias comparable to those of the corpo-
   real/carnal chiasmus: intentionality—despite all of its "goodwill,"

so to speak—remains "objectivizing,"[4] and thus "contaminates" that with which it is connected—its "object," precisely—giving it its own materiality, which seems inevitable since it is itself what it seeks to understand, and above all since, being unknown—or more widely constituted—it consists precisely of being held in the pure glance it is. Yet, as one might suspect, it thus also loses itself, caught up in the vertigo of wanting to be known as other (non-objective and passive) and of needing to be known as identical to itself, to know itself.

Thus, the attempt to encounter itself in time is its proper limit, insofar as it is the power to know, and more generally to constitute, that intentionality encounters.

b. That said, why turn to Henrian and Levinasian readings? Proposing to radicalize Husserlian reduction judged as insufficient, they then "extend" intentionality to the point of breaking the matrix (of "transcendence in immanence"). The matter at hand has thus to do with a pressure inflicted on intentionality—and the degree to which intentionality can withstand the radicality of that pressure—or even the violence of a rupture.

If perhaps it would be necessary to conclude with intentionality's destruction [*défaite*] in the sense in which intentionality would be "un-made" [*défaite*], it would still also be necessary to note that in the texts on time[5]— and this is the reason for making this choice—Henry and Levinas work toward the same immanence of consciousness, time being precisely that: the place in which conscious intentionality confronts its own destruction, with no other resource than itself to "leave itself there"; time is the place in which intentional consciousness confronts its limit *in itself.* This suggests that phenomenological discourse has no access to other resources than its own for achieving its own release: the operative power of intentionality, and it alone.[6] From this point of view, as we will try to show, Henry's and Levinas's steps are exemplary.[7] To remain at the limit means that one gives it the ability neither to remain on the inside, nor to go beyond it.[8]

The time has come to begin our reading.

If we wish to start out originally, Henry and Levinas are interested from the outset and nearly exclusively in "impression," as *Urimpression* ("givenness"), but retentionally modified ("given" in and through intentionality). Temporality, sensibility, and/or affectivity of impression, and intentionality, are originarily tied together. This originary unity (impression/retention) forms what Desanti calls a knot. Can this knot, which "makes" the time of un-making, the defeat or *dé-faite*—if time is in a sense nothing other than the very thing that defeats all substance, its own first of all—be untied without slicing it to pieces?

Let us take Michel Henry's course first.

For him, this is a matter of thinking the most radical immanence possible—only immanence is in fact radical—since *The Essence of Manifestation* shows that all manifestation, since it presupposes the gesture of opening a horizon, would not know how to support itself. (What "is thrown outside" would not know how to be grounded or how to receive.)

Thus, Husserl offers Henry the radicality of a method, a phenomenology (which Henry, however, judges to be insufficiently radical),[9] but also a field: immanence. But it is a half-hidden field, lost by Husserl himself. In fact, Husserl's phenomenological trajectory is consecrated to seeing that intentionality is thoroughly Ek-static, and not only that: under the pure glance of intentionality, the "ontological collapse" comprises the loss of immanence.

And this is because transcendence of seeing is from the start *form*, horizon on which a content is then built, but it is never itself content; principle or law of connectivity and of deployment but never itself what is connected or deployed. Henrian phenomenology thinks itself as integrally material,[10] reversing the traditional preeminence of form over matter, extracting itself even from the very duality form/matter (true, § 86 of *Ideas I* presents hyletic phenomenology as an autonomous discipline, but by rendering the discipline impossible within a Husserlian framework). In other words, since theoretical thought makes us "see," it must always turn toward what does not always allow itself to be brought beneath the eye of intentionality in the same objectivizing way—despite Husserl's respect for differing life experiences; toward sensation or, more precisely, toward *affectivity* (since sensation opens the transcendence of the sensed): such is Henry's understanding of Husserlian impression.

If intentionality—as Ek-static transcendence—cannot itself be given, it must still be sought, more "profoundly" hidden, behind intentionality, as an other giving, giving itself and giving intentionality. Auto-donation of self to self through self: this is the definition of sentiment, of affect, for Henry. All phenomenological analysis leads toward it.

Thus *On the Phenomenology* appears to Michel Henry as the strategic text in which Husserl has, as it were, "lost sight of" *Urimpression* (precisely by excessively holding it in view). But at the same time, this text is also where impression's remarkable power of "arche-" and "auto-" giving allows itself to be perceived: if only the text can lose sight of it, then Husserlian analysis can use all of its forces to seize upon impression as "newness" (thus betraying it, if radical novelty is precisely what surprises and overflows all constitutive data). And—which is worse in Husserl's eyes—it is because *Urimpression*—betrayed—allows its strange power to be seen, despite everything, that intentionality is thoroughly radicalized though its forces (such as the problematic of double intentionality).[11] In brief, this text in which intentionality triumphs over impression—in a Pyrrhic victory since it loses what it has sought at the very moment in which it pretends to give it, and thus loses itself since the quest was entirely one for its origin—is also the text in which *Urimpression* ephemerally succeeds in showing itself, but it can only *be* ephemerally (through the idea of the living present, for example). That is, if time is Transcendence par excellence, the place where intentionality is more than ever Ek-static, this is only because solely in it is the immanence of impression made so threatening. "The entirety of *On the Phenomenology* is directed simultaneously at disguising and conjuring" (*HIC*, 38).

We must lay out the main steps of the taming, the domestication of *Urimpression* by intentionality, according to Michel Henry. First, and throughout, impression does not give itself to itself but is given "as being there *now*" by an intentionality. This is the ambiguous layer of "originary consciousness" that, in pretending to show its origin, gives itself to itself (*HIC*, 35). The process is thus inescapable: when there is a "now," this is a "just past," then a "past"; in brief, time. *Urimpression* is *non-realized*—condemned to time. "What then is time?" For Michel Henry it is only the non-reality of the "not yet" (of protentional intentionality), and more exemplarily, of the "already more" of retention. From this point of view, the privilege accorded to retention in *On the Phenomenology* signifies the derealizing power of this non-reality, time. As for the present, it is thus according to Husserl only an ideal limit, a non-realization of the hyletic gift for Michel Henry. Intentionality, at base, does not submit to a crude test by time as a "stubborn" object; on the contrary, it blossoms out as time, as non-real and non-realizing process: Michel Henry uses expressions such as "failure," "destruction," ontological "collapse." It might be said that in *On the Phenomenology* intentionality is perturbed by time but emerges stronger still from this test since it then recognizes time as forming its own proper field. And all other outcomes will have been unenvisagable through the constraints of intentionality.

Longitudinal intentionality is the culmination of the non-reality of intentionality in time. If there is time, it is the fault of intentionality that "kills" what it holds in view, emptying it of all matter, of all hyletic flesh: the non-reality of *transcendence* is the non-reality of *form*: formal transcendence is time. From one perspective, intentionality mutilates itself, producing itself as intentionality in its auto-mutilation. Henry pursues this process of non-realization in *On the Phenomenology*, the salient moments of which are:

1. That flux itself is prioritized, even if it is always flux of hyletic matter, of form as such.

2. This implies a privileging of *retention* or, more precisely, of the articulation of impression and retention in *modification* (impression only being given to—and in—retentional modification).

3. Thus, *Urimpression* wisely makes itself the content of the "form" of now since it is no longer given except through its coming into flux at the point of now, and not through itself. This is for Henry the most "profound" falsification. Not only is impression distorted in being so constituted, but the structure of ecstatic temporality is injected into it in such a way that it ends by defining essence: impression will then be thought as perception turned toward spatial, but above all temporal, exteriority: a "now" is nothing other than a glance toward a new now. For Michel Henry, the "murder" of impression in and by time is this completed.

4. The notion of *passive synthesis* attempts to revive its rights to impression's passivity, but this passivity is not radical since it is not a "dormant" activity: it is what remains of a production already having

taken place, but a production nonetheless. This is really and despite everything a question of synthesis.[12]

In this way Husserl, not realizing what he pretends to give himself, is caught in a balancing act: the more he conjures the disquieting strangeness of impression for intentionality, the more (increasingly timidly) he conjures up the "void," non-reality at which he thus arrives and that he did not wish for, in affirming the specificity of impression's originarity "that is not itself produced,"[13] as living-present. But he is immediately returned from this second pole toward the first, in the impossibility, from where he now finds himself, of thinking radically.

Where will Michel Henry's trajectory take us?

One must be struck by the fact that Husserl's question, which was already Augustine's, "But what is time?," is not at all Michel Henry's when he reads *On the Phenomenology*. Time, thought as transcendence par excellence, is the very contrary—or the contradictory—of the reality of immanence. It is the "reverse" of what alone interests Henry: all of his philosophy can be seen as the need to unburden oneself of time. In fairness, one must nuance this analysis: insofar as it is "affection of self," immanence is inhabited by an internal "movement"; this is what gives itself, is given, is received, and is before all else this very "process." It is the venue in the self of the Self, of Life, and not of the dead immobility of the/a thing. And in his later texts,[14] Henry wants to see "authentic time." Without betraying his first instinct to denounce Ek-static time but, on the contrary, to reinforce it, he thus gives himself the means at the very core of his categories to "think" time and not simply to exclude it. There would be a great deal to say on this "inversion" (what is a non-Ek-static time?; what is the status of a phenomenological language that pretends to account for it?), but that would lead us too far from our subject.

At all events, our working hypotheses are clear:

1. If philosophy seems to lean toward the exclusion of time, Michel Henry sides with phenomenologists who confront time and who therefore work on the immanence of consciousness, and never with anything other than the resources of phenomenology (its operative concepts). If it is necessary to "transcend" the constituting

consciousness, it would not be by leaving it for a "higher mark" of some theological kind but by digging deeper into what is hidden. Life is, so to speak, "under" the consciousness traversing it, but in no case is it elsewhere, that is, "beyond."

2. Therefore, if Michel Henry exhibits the limits of intentionality to the point of excluding it from his phenomenology as the cause of all evils (all transcendences), he nonetheless does so *apart from* the practice of phenomenology, "from the interior." Once the "defeat" of intentionality is accomplished, then the problem of knowing whether the contents of Henrian phenomenology are thoroughly phenomenological remains open. The fact remains that Henry does not place himself beyond intentionality but arrives at its limit in and through phenomenology. He arrives at the point at which intentionality—according to his interpretation—burns with all its fires (Husserl) or throws off its last fires (Henry). He arrives at the limit where if intentionality wins, it loses; it loses impression as *such*, as pure surging forth into appearance.

Let us be clear: in the negative sense in which limits signify impotence, Michel Henry displays the limits of Husserlian intentionality, incapable of revealing—let alone masking—Immanence, Life, Matter, *Urimpression* (in the Husserlian lexicon), that are just so many "names" for pure presence. Given that his philosophy's task is the revealing of what manifestation, "making-see," hides, Henry expels intentionality. He is one of those who is seen as a "revealer of the absolute," as it were (more specifically, this could only be Life revealed in him and in his texts), and not as a thinker of the finitude of limits. Nonetheless, from a point of view exterior to Henry's position, the attempt to stay on this side of intentionality and to "exceed"—or to pierce through—the transcendence of language could appear as eminently aporetic. From this viewpoint Henry clearly directs phenomenology and his central theme, intentionality, toward their limits. One question rises up: is it necessary, at the risk of becoming lost, to test the most authentic radicality, or does it exceed the limits in the Kantian sense of the term, the revelation of immanence proving, in a moment of equilibrium, a construction beyond the field of phenomenologically lived experience?[15]

Briefly, then, let us test the hypothesis according to which Levinas and Henry follow the same route but in opposite directions. In a sense, in reading *On the Phenomenology* the former begins where the latter finishes, and vice versa.

While Henry denounces an Ek-static temporalization of the immanence of affectivity that *is*, even though it excludes, time, Levinas regrets, on the contrary, an incapacity to think time radically as *diachrony* (the Levinasian name for authentic temporality). Where Henry wants to think what *is not* Ek-static time, Levinas wants to think what is *more* than Ek-static time.

For Levinas, being (the Same) is nothing other than the act of gathering all alterity to itself. It is thus in a sense thoroughly contradictory and, since nothing escapes him, self-destructive. It is necessary as a result to think that it is always opened by the Other, who thus gives it to himself. This "process" "is"—in its "Otherwise than being"—temporality par excellence, *diachrony*.

Traditionally, time is thought as a mixture of being and non-being, the alterations of being. As a process of alteration, time is the Other.[16] In a sense, Levinas could only be "installed" in the problematic of temporality. And, at base, all of his philosophy can be interpreted as an effort at the inversion of signification that philosophy since the Greeks gives to time: that it not be "lost" but what gives; that it be fruitfulness and birth.

Because *On the Phenomenology* confronts intentionality with the "unconstituted" in it, with what in it escapes him, reading it is decisive for Levinas's construction of a philosophy of diachrony.

In *Otherwise Than Being; or, Beyond Essence* we find the same *type* of reproach to Husserl, and the same *type* of exploration of debt, as one we might read in Michel Henry.[17] If Henrian debts and reproaches, on one side, and Levinasian ones, on the other, are both rooted in the contents of the differing—and opposing—senses, they nonetheless have the same structure. But at a more radical level, the sense-contents of these two philosophers are not symmetrically perfectly—or even proportionately—opposed, insofar as their structures arise from the identical.[18]

Husserl would present the diachrony from the same gesture he was incapable of thinking radically, as a response to Henry's reproach that he had not been able to think immanence, and to Levinas's of not having been able to think transcendence.

These seemingly contradictory protestations in fact constitute the same claim, but the different moments or terms of the process have exchanged names: Levinas's *fustige* frames recuperant intentionality as not allowing *Urimpression* to exist or, more precisely, as "Otherwise than being" for itself, but he inverts interpretations of the ideas in play—we might in fact say that it is Michel Henry who inverts Levinas's interpretation. Henry calls recuperant intentionality "immanence," since *Urimpression* has the connotation of alterity. The confrontation between these two readings of *On the Phenomenology*, however, rests on a *commonality* beyond the opposition of their motives, since from Henry to Levinas, if intentionality and *Urimpression* exchange their qualities of transcendence and immanence, transcendence and immanence for their part reverse their respective connotations of inauthenticity and authenticity.

While Henry thinks *Urimpression* as an "arche-" and "auto-"giving that is purely immanent to *affectivity*, Levinas interprets it as *sensibility*, as the primordial gap between sensing and sensed, meaning that there *is* a sensing and a sensed. *Urimpression* is the first gap of/in the self, and thus a self can exist without succumbing to its own weight of immanence. Impression suffocates under itself and "emerges" from itself, says Levinas.[19] He speaks of a primary retreat with regard to the self, from which the subject emerges: from a first departure that "produces"—and this is in no case a matter of a constitutive act—all engagements with being.

This *Urimpression*, pure immanence for Henry, is transcendence for Levinas, since he thinks it as what un-makes [*dé-faite*], alters, opens intentionality out, and thus gives it Being, rather than as what excludes it. If for Henry the suffering of immanence stifled under its own weight returns to itself in *jouissance*, for Levinas it must already be liberated from itself. This power to astonish intentionality is not solely what disturbs it, not what it attempts to conjure up; it is also what allows it to be, rendering it "lighter." (The "obviously ontological" denounced by Henry has a positive function in Levinas.) Clearly, it is important to confront this paradox: *Urimpression* "makes possible" its own possibility: intentionality (whose fabric constitutes the field of the possible). This is the very definition of the present: "the real preceding and surprising the possible."

But intentionality brings *Urimpression* back into order, assigning it a place in the flux of time. Levinas and Henry describe the same process: intentionality domesticates *Urimpression*. The living-present as non-objectivizing and non-objectifiable consciousness and even, if it is possible, as unintentional consciousness, can last only for an instant.

As Levinas explains, the "gap in the self," the originary dephasing that "is" *Urimpression*, is accessible to consciousness only if the gap separating the two poles is already doubled by what brings about its reabsorption: intentional lived experience maintaining the distance between the poles and *in doing so*, spanning it. Throughout and always, precisely for "being," *Urimpression* is inhabited by the intentional consciousness that *still* awaits it, or *already* recuperates it. The disrupting novelty of *Urimpression* must be the origin of time, as spontaneity in which "activity and passivity are absolutely confused"; that is, as "creation." Yet in fact time is always injected into its origin, which it thus conceals and domesticates, the only way for it to approach a being, a substance, stabilizing it by its glance.

The two readings of *On the Phenomenology* by Levinas and Henry are convergent: intentionality is opened out and completed as temporal and longitudinal, and *Urimpression*, for Husserl, is dedicated to time (Husserlian time being able only to be an intentional merging). To find time is to "lose" impression, precisely in holding on to it.

But Levinas, as opposed to Henry, does not think that one can or must thus exclude intentionality and language, which envelops it and makes it possible (since it is a primordial "already-said"—of passive syntheses). In fact, Levinas assumes that diachronic impression, originary gap, can resonate only in intentionality. If Henry requires not only that intentionality not have the *last word*, as it does in Levinas, but also be excluded from the phenomenological field, Levinas for his part tries to *open* intentionality onto its Other, implying that this opening, as such, is inscribed *within* what opens. Thus overflowing, intentionality subsists, since it is given to being through what overflows it. This is the Same of intentionality, as the *Pharmakon* of diachrony: what threatens to kill it, and yet the sole place in which it can show itself. It cannot be overemphasized that if diachrony gives to being—and in this sense the *Pharmakon* exists only thanks to its "patient"—it is the Same of intentionality that locates the immanence of existence where diachrony can deposit its trace. (This is where an ineluctable balancing act that is ceaselessly returning from the "otherwise than ontological" originary of diachronic transcendence toward the immanence of the existent and the *logos* guarantees its framework, which is itself primary as the very basis of all manifestation and of all "speech": this very movement is itself originary.) Levinas is confronted with the task of inscribing the necessary *articulation* of time as the unknown of diachrony onto time as intentional weaving. In the strictest sense this describes the *limit* of intentionality.

And this is where the limit is perceived as emerging from a viewpoint *interior* to intentionality itself, not "elsewhere." It is from this point that the philosopher and the phenomenologist speak, out of the immanence of intentionality itself, out of phenomenology's powers of elucidation. Alteration is at the very heart of immanence and nowhere else, and exemplarily so in the texts on time. Transcendence in time is above all "retroscendence," "a transcendence *backward*, out of the immanence of the conscious state" (*DE*, 103).

Let us take stock. We might say that Husserl, in *On the Phenomenology*, reinforces intentionality's powers of recuperation in order to permit himself to come face-to-face with the strangeness of time, in that regard showing fidelity to the principle of the *absence of limits* of objective reason as put forth in the *Logical Investigations*.[20] Reading this text, Michel Henry requires, on the contrary, the *expulsion* of intentionality, and especially of triumphant intentionality in the form of time, which masks authenticity. From a resolutely interpretive viewpoint, we might hypothesize a text needing to maintain itself well within the threshold of intentionality and to give access to the absolute that has thus been rendered, paradoxically and radically, the test of the limits of intentionality's powers. Levinas claims to assist in their *fragilization*, in explicitly assuming the limit. Moreover, it is significant that language and its powers of elucidation have only very recently been elevated to the status of "problem" by a Michel Henry who sees in Ek-static time not a threat to the powers of manifestation of the *logos*, but an inauthenticity of the same fabric, to be expelled—for him as well—from the field of phenomenologically lived experience, while for Levinas the question of diachrony is simultaneously that of the limit of the Said—and not just the gesture expelling it.

To conclude, and leaving aside the connections of "reflection"—reversing and deforming—that seem to unite the Henrian and Levinasian readings of *On the Phenomenology*, let me clarify how they are fruitful in my probings as they attempt to orient us in the French phenomenological field.

In working through the question of time, Levinas and Henry agree about nothing other than what the dedicated resources of the phenomenological method offer them. They implement, exemplarily, the concepts of *intentionality* and *Urimpression* as *operatory* concepts in Eugen Fink's sense. An "operatory" concept is precisely that which remains in the shadows such that it illuminates the concept being thematized, one that is not being made clear because it is the very medium of the research: the very act of carrying the flame thus remaining in the shadows. *Urimpression* and intentionality offer us a dance of shadows and light, the one being in the shadows even as it illuminates the other, reciprocally operating each other and thus simultaneously unconstitutable and non-elucidatable. *Urimpression* remains within a shadow that escapes an intentionality that *in a sense* it always precedes, and intentionality also remains in the shadows—which are however, in the framework of Husserlian phenomenology, the power of producing all elucidating and constituting light; it tracks its own secret in *Urimpression*, the key to its own enigma, and that wants to be the key to all enigma. Is this not the phenomenological operativity that Levinas and Henry radically test out? In proposing this, we are saying what neither Levinas nor Henry has said. And above all, Michel Henry, who needs to touch the obscure clarity of immanence, behind the inauthentic light of Ek-static representation. But for us, what we read in these two thinkers is less a content of thought than a manner of working intentionality to the limit. "Limit" here is close to understanding, in the sense used by mathematicians: what is never attained and known in itself, but out of which understanding is possible, and what is never itself known other than as this function. In this sense, would intentionality and *Urimpression* not "limit" themselves reciprocally?[21]

2

Anticipating Phenomenology

JACQUES DERRIDA AND JEAN-LUC MARION,
THE IMPOSSIBLE AND POSSIBILITY

1. The Time of Ordinary Phenomena and Phantoms (Jean-Toussaint Desanti; Jacques Derrida)

Our focus here is to put in perspective the various ways in which Jacques Derrida and Jean-Luc Marion determine and inhabit the originary problematic in which the issues of temporality and giving cross and provoke each other. We will only tangentially refer to Marion's texts, starting out with a reading of *Réflexions sur le temps* by Jean-Toussaint Desanti. This will merit some prejudicial explications.

Without any doubt Desanti's work more than justifies our attention, all the more because we do not know precisely how to use it here; we will do so only in a skewed fashion, within the perspective of our limited problematic. In locating the affinities between Desanti's *Réflexions sur le temps* and Derrida's *Given Time*,[1] it is necessary to mark a direction that is hardly discernible, yet as we will try to show, decisive for the field of French phenomenology, in the end reconfiguring the entire explicit design of its topography.

Laying out this road sign, and thus tracing the route linking Desanti and Derrida, is a way of demonstrating the gap that separates Derridean thought of the gift as loss of presence and impossibility, from Marionian thought of givenness as profusion of possibility and presence. The many signs Marion erects as guides on his route in the Derridean direction, as though toward an origin, invite us to ask if other routes are not cleared through Derrida, and which of these routes would be lost and perhaps even carefully reconcealed in Marion's texts. The fact that this route-clearing is fruitful is the condition that, a posteriori, legitimizes our suspicion regarding Marion's strategy regarding Derrida.

First, it is important to separate the Derrida of "Derrida for domestic consumption" in Marion's *Reduction and Givenness* and that of "Esquisse d'un concept phénoménologique du don."[2] And how better to mark the contrast than to specify what brings Derrida closer to Desanti in their phenomenological analysis of temporality? It is not *explicitly* what might be called Desanti's structuralism that is in play here but rather what it *implies*: the need to spotlight the intentional constraints *within* intentionality, in refusing to dream, *beyond* their "circuit"—an ontological pole capable of grounding them (a transcendental subjectivity, or even a theological pole), and another, at the most dangerous moment: when intentionality is confronted by its most intimate other, temporality.

Certainly, Desanti's *Réflexions sur le temps* can be read as a book in which the author, as he says, plies his trade of more than fifty years, that of philosophy professor: in that case one would be reading a beautiful pedagogical meditation on the texts of Plato, Augustine, and Husserl concerning time.

Of course—and Desanti even recalls it here—the moments of reflection on philosophic texts are for Desanti always synchronized with his activities; the historian of philosophy is actually what he must be only insofar as he rethinks, for and through himself, what there is to be thought in the texts he is reading. And in *this* reading exercise I am indeed all alone, the author being precisely the absent other leaving me unaccompanied and in some respect disabled in the face of the need to inhabit the fabric of indicative marks he has delegated to me. To read texts is already to interpret them; and to interpret them is already to be a philosopher, to be called to produce one's own proper thought. There is no pause—but, on the contrary, a perfect reversibility—between the need to inhabit another's thought and the need to produce one's own thought; to be a historian of philosophy is to be a philosopher, and inversely.

Thus, Desanti's *Réflexions sur le temps* is the work of a philosopher rooted in the philosophical tradition insofar as it sets the requirement, and runs the necessary risk, of bringing texts alive here and now, meaning always rediscovering them, but doing so *otherwise*; that is, in truth. And it is clear why these are the conversations given to reading: a written text is like the *mise en abyme* of a philosophy that must first be lived in the living present of an "I" put in question by an interlocutor. Dominique-Antoine Grisoni, who assumes the role of "co-producer" of thought, nonetheless insists that "it is a matter of a true book," *written*, and not of the raw exposition of a recorded interview. Lying behind this formal notice is one of the great lessons of Desanti's philosophy: all philosophy is the continuation of a lifestyle that lays itself out in a present and roots itself in an actual body, given that life always declares the style of problems I must think in order to live.

Since philosophical problems are always there, even in the most ordinary life—this bus in the Rue du Bac, this agenda, and so on—the historian of philosophy and of the philosopher "naturally" speaks a language, as it were, that tends toward minute descriptions of the conditions of appearance of everything that appears even in ordinary life: this is the language of phenomenology.

Let us come to the "object" of these variations: time.

Time is not simply the "object" of these conversations. In *Réflexions* Desanti has "business with time," all the more so in that he speaks of it only because it offers the spectacle of an ego meditating on events through a temporality by which it perceives that it is less the object of its discourse than its worrying inhabitant, and even more radically the secret inhabitant of all subjectivity.

And if Heidegger has been able to say that no philosopher worthy of the name can avoid the problem of time, Desanti qualifies this in that, in a sense, one can *begin* only by clashing with time (even if this originary gesture of philosophy remains somehow concealed).

This first philosophical variation must be with time if it is true—as Desanti claims—that all discourse, and not simply philosophical discourse, is born in and through the inaugural difficulty that there is speech. In fact, the discourse is entirely the need to gather together again—to re-collect—precisely what has been dispersed, and the quintessential experience of this "dispersal" is the experience of time. Even before I decide to speak about time, the need to "speak of time" has been originarily manifested. Time makes me speak since it is the very opening of the dimension of the—its—enigma. Desanti writes that "discourses on time are always strange. At one moment, they seem to fail themselves in some fashion, and thus to need to be restarted, but in the other direction, as if it were necessary to rediscover a route on the high seas" (JTD, 52), and to install oneself in this need of recommencing such as that carried out by Plato and precisely of the problem of the origin of time, toward the formulation of this enigma as the lived opacity of subjectivity to itself in Augustine.

But this track, which constitutes the first part of this book, after having unveiled the originary disquiet of time—"what is closest is unveiled to thought as the most distant" (JTD, 80)—brings us face-to-face with the requirement to (re)depart from time as intimately lived, as "temporal behaviors."

It is important to confront this originary existential situation of the discourse emanating from the requirement to have to speak (about) time, that time "is" only insofar as it is spoken (about). The thread of time and the thread of discourse are tied together in such a way that the knot linking them in fact precedes them—constitutes them. And a third protagonist must be added to this scene: what can be said of the circumstance by which one might think that these two threads could be conjoined?—might we call it "subjectivity"? And does it not coincide at this point with the knot, less its producer than its result? In other words, is not this third thread the "weaving" of the first two, from which their "fabrication" results? "Subjectivity" is born of the very gesture by which time is given; it thus confronts the very thing that splits it: it is "un-made," "de-feated"—and at the same time "made," *fait.* This is the very problem Husserl situates in the *Urkonstitution* and that Desanti takes up again.

The second part of the text that follows consists of a close reading of *On the Phenomenology of the Consciousness of Internal Time* (of 1905), oriented by the need, through description, to "untie" the knot of time and of discourse, which clearly implies not *cutting* it.

After having worked through the overall Husserlian analyses—and particularly the famous diagram of time, focusing on the status of the "reduced model," with its "simple" operational virtues that it "dynamizes," we will enter the heart of the enigma: how to account for a characteristic of the past—and of time in general: "being" pure presence and pure nothing. Our glance will thus stop on the originary cell (*aa'*), the initial unity of impression/retention: the pure emergence of what surges forth in its irreducible novelty, with all spontaneity (impression), is always recuperated in a retention. The need for phenomenological analysis is measured by its capacity to describe a paradox where it had been feared there was a contradiction.

Like Husserl's, Desanti's strategy is very precise. It is a matter of "reinterpreting," which consists neither of "going beyond" nor, certainly, of simply reproducing. To use a spatial metaphor, this is rather a matter of "taking a step inside," in a gesture both close to and distinct from the Heideggerian *Schritt zurück*, since it is Husserl who in a sense goes too far in agreeing to the straightforwardness of a transcendental "coupling." Desanti maintains that Husserl wishes in some way to conjure up, rather than to explore, the troubling neglect of itself that temporal self-constitution signifies for "subjectivity." And it is the position of a transcendental, as originary power and absolute self-givenness of all things, that is in question:[3] the notion of "transcendental subjectivity," even a still-implicit one, that Desanti suspects to be "hovering" over the lessons of 1905.

This suspicion can be formulated thus: is transcendental subjectivity not a theoretical and textual substructure that betrays the very thingness of the Time-phenomenon? Is it a "cape thrown" over the immanent "overflowing" that is Time, translated through an "effect of transcendence"? To work *truthfully* in phenomenology implies that one works "without a net," without the redemptive and recuperative shadow of some transcendental authority.

But how then to re-start Husserlian analyses of temporal behaviors, to remake the economy of the transcendental? This is Desanti's question.

Transcendental subjectivity is the result of a reduction of rigor in Husserlian analysis, betraying a central theme of phenomenology: "intentionality." This is why, according to Desanti, constructing the economy of the transcendental is the only way to be truly faithful to Husserl.

But we must track the overall lines of this interpretive analysis. The phenomenologist's glance is cast upon the originary cell (*aa'*), impression/

retention. The question, then, has to do with the type of gap that allows me to be connected with the "having-duration" that transports me from *a'* toward *a*. The naïve response that comes immediately to mind (and that must be put aside), is "memory." One remembers oneself only at a *past moment*: memory implies that there was already a past, already time; it comes "after" time and thus does not constitute it essentially.

It is this gap, Desanti says, that Husserl calls intentionality.

So we must ask, "What is the specific intentionality that must be opened in constituting time?" Yet, in the face of time, intentionality seems to be sidetracked, precisely because time is less what faces it than its secret inhabitant, or perhaps, more radically, what it itself inhabits. Intentionality—pure, lived experience, pure "being connected with"—is confronted by what "overflows" it. "Intentionality is thus disturbed by something like an inferior limit, a sub-jacent flux," according to Desanti.

And thus the problem is how to cancel this limit's effect? It certainly does not return to erase uneasiness through time, thanks to the "beyond-ness" of intentionality in a transcendental subjectivity that is, by definition, "non-disturbable." As we have seen, for Desanti such a transcendence conserves nothing, neither disquiet (time) nor disquieting (intentionality).

To refuse to resort to the "authority of transcendental retraction," to be disillusioned by this phantasm, and to reject phenomenology for a sphere in which it would be necessary to endure remaining in the pure immanence of consciousness without recourse to any "transcendent" aid, where if there were transcendence, it would be the overflowing of time that would be in play: a break in the insideness of an opened consciousness, a "retroscendence"; these are Desanti's problems. From the perspective of method, that would imply holding fast to intentionality and being held to its own operatory resources. The road we have taken into the trap must allow for our getting out of it, as Desanti explains (JTD, 150).

Through describing intentionality, one can elucidate its secret disruption, the form of flux (of time) whose substructure it forms. According to Desanti, it is through the notion of intentionality that Husserl designates—and masks—the very thing that must escape as a "magma," "invisible" yet organized. Intentionality is thus not Desanti's last word: his analysis situates him relative to an "inside" that forms the basis for intentionality, an intentionality that thus simultaneously demonstrates and conceals its own ground. The form of substructural flux is accessible only *through* intentionality; that is, through piercing it, but never otherwise than through its mediation.

Desantian analysis is absolutely coherent. It interprets Husserlian intentionality, in the end bringing to light the—ineluctably paradoxi-cal—relation that unites it with the substructural flux of time. There is thus an *elsewhere* of intentionality, but this elsewhere is not a *beyond*, not a mysterious transcendence that it would be tempted to phantasmize in order to be relieved of disturbance and of the need to have to endure time. This elsewhere is inside intentionality: it is its very "here" since, in fact, the heart is graspable only through its mediation.

From a methodological perspective it is necessary to hold fast to in-tentional constraints, signifying not giving in to the temptation to ground intentionality in an element that would be a stranger to it and would have the ontological weight of a cause, an ultimate reason. What Desanti has in view is the temptation only to give weight, ontologically, to the pure, *empty* lived experience that intentionality "is" by definition. Intentionality is a pure arc that throws itself toward: thus, in order to avoid the fact that this arc seems as though "suspended," not grounded, one might be tempted to add to its weight either by one end or the other; in its origin—and one is here touching on a transcendent egology—or at its opposite pole—and here one must deal with a theology (in fact, "subjectivity" is thus given to being through transcendence). Adhering to intentionality's own resources thus means for Desanti that what is being held to is the pure *form* of lived experience. And in fact, Desantian analysis is thoroughly "formal," managing to hold on to its form without ever appealing to any content. Describing the intentional arc, Desanti utilizes letters that are like empty marks and thus resist, he says, the temptation of naming and dreaming of inhabitants, ontological contents for these empty marks. Yet he remem-bers that all Western philosophy perhaps consists of these dreams.

And where is respect for these constraints leading us? To the imple-mentation of what Desanti calls the "circle of opening," perhaps?

If we want arc $\overset{\frown}{OT}$ (the Origin of Transcendence being inhabited only by an X and an X') not to seem to support itself anywhere, without grounding itself in one of the two poles, we will have to think of it as "an arc of recall": $\overset{\frown}{OT}$ implementation of the arc of recall, of the dual, is a requirement of the intentional arc. Indeed, lived experience as such is empty but needs to be replenished; it is the connection between these two characteristics—being "empty" but needing replenishment—that makes it "be" insofar as it "is," that pushes or precipitates it toward X'. Were there only emptiness, there would be no lived experience; were there only the "full," there would no longer be lived experience. Thus, the pole designated X' must give itself and refuse itself simultaneously; it must give itself *in* refusing itself—if it is in fact necessary to propose an arc of recall that always reanimates the intentional arc out of the empty pole X' precisely, recall to itself, an intentional arousal. The intentional arc and its double constitute a "circle of opening" in which the poles X and X' are constructed through the circuit itself without any help or exterior ontological "leverage" for its structure. Desanti does not say this, but we can go so far as to say that X and X', origin of lived experience and its goal, are constituted through insertion in the total systematic structure forming the circle of opening; of them we might say that their separation is their greatest link; and of the "circle" we might say that "what opens, closes."

The following remarks are salient here:

1. The constraints of holding tightly to intentionality and being held tightly in its own operatory resources must be respected: the "circle of opening" is "supported" in its own paradoxical circularity.
2. The inhabitant of pole X is strictly contemporary with the circuit, and even in a sense, "results" from it. At least, he is not its instigator: this is the end of transcendental egology.

Desanti, it must be emphasized, is oriented toward one of the recurrent themes of contemporary French phenomenology: that of the ego passive and deprived of itself (the Ego opens through the Idea of the Infinite for Levinas; the interlocutor-I for Marion, the blessed Cogito for Ricoeur). But this "outcome," seen at the end of a train of thought, is itself situated at the antipodes of the philosophies addressed here; as we have seen, it seems that it would be at the intersection of the two horizons of thought at work in Desanti, a certain "Marxist structuralism" (present in *Réflexions*, though implicitly) and phenomenology, in the transcendence of the traditional opposition between "Subject" and "Structure," that Desanti produces this inhabitant, the "circle of opening," that is not recollected in its own identity and that despite the fact that it is disseminated in this "opening-closing" structure with which it coincides.

Desanti goes so far as to call the inhabitant of the circle of opening *Dasein*, aligning himself more and more explicitly with Heidegger. And indeed it is the coincidence of *Dasein* and temporality that will be described.

If we were to propose a reading of the "circle of opening" in which our angle of attack was the problem of time, what might we discover?

We would discover that consciousness is not the pure compactness of a presence to itself but is rather nothing other than the very thing that must conform to the "circle of opening." The present in X, at the origin of lived experience, is thus only the *form* of a void, the form of its attachment to itself, separate from the pole X'. "The present, moreover, occurs only out of itself," says Desanti. Paradoxically, the X pole has the *first* experience of a *return* to its own identity; this return can thus not reveal it as massive, total presence: "X is recalled to its identity as self outside of self." And if it is recall that comes first, then pole X' in some way precedes pole X, the origin of lived experience. This dissymmetry signifies a character that is fundamentally the first of future form, as in Heidegger (who breaks cleanly with the implicit privilege of retention in Husserlian analyses).

Dasein is thus the pure form of a void whose content is only its own cancellation from the future.

But how is this unforeseen mode of being—"being" the very form of its cancellation—possible? How can it be, in being nothing but the form of its nothing? Desanti responds: precisely, in being its *form*, its *formulation*. It is as discursivity that subjectivity returns from its nothingness. The inhabitant of pole X, *Dasein*, is confronted by the need to "mark," to "designate," or at least to "evade," the absence of pole X'; in brief, to produce the *symbolic* (the form that is entirely a reference to the absent one). "Intimate consciousness is inhabited by the space of marks," since "what constitutes the mark is the function of return it exercises toward the absent one."

In its sinuosity, Desantian analysis leads to the promised place, the site "more originary" than the present where time and discourse are tied together such that the knot precedes and constitutes each of the two

threads in its pure form, a "subjectivity" made fragile by being only outside itself, a *Dasein*.

Comparing Desanti's *Réflexions sur le temps* and Derrida's *Given
Time* might seem risky and artificial:[4] no doubt their object is the same,
but the practice of phenomenological description, just as much as the textual practice itself, differs radically from one to the other.

However, Desanti and Derrida maintain one thing in common—in
very different ways: a *problematic* connection to Husserlian phenomenology; in fact, a connection so problematic that neither one claims it without
reservation, but that nonetheless both of them practice and question, and
not by accident.

One might say that Desanti conceives of the phenomenological description as a *moment* that is both necessary and necessarily transcended
in its course, in that he must denounce the foundational dream within
the transcendental ego—after having allowed it to show itself at the core
of a patient and minute description. As for Derrida, one might say that
he has a *peripheral* connection—which does not mean accidental—to
phenomenology: he is located at its border, its limit; can see things only
through texts, indeed texts themselves envisaged as the very signifiers of
the (problematic) access to things themselves; these for Derrida are the
problematics of the phenomenological project.

My fundamental idea here, my hypothesis, is that in speaking less
about phenomenology than *about* other contemporary strategies, and in
claiming it less explicitly, Desanti and Derrida *practice* it even more radically. They test out—in their quite different styles, I suggest—the idea
that the impossibility of following the phenomenological method to its
conclusion *is* to be truly faithful to it. And this test is most exemplarily
accomplished in the confrontation with time.

Derrida's *Given Time* marks out a very different site from the one
toward which Desanti leads us, and by another route. For Derrida it is not,
as it is in *On the Phenomenology*, a matter of manifesting the intuition, in
the Bergsonian sense, of the great founding texts on Time, but rather of
deconstructing (i.e., taking by surprise, in order to be taken by surprise by
them) texts that would qualify as marginal and to assess them principally
but not solely in terms of the history of philosophy, texts from Baudelaire

and from Mauss.[5] This is not a matter of describing ordinary phenomena but—and it *seems* to be the very opposite of describing ordinary phenomena—of describing a phenomenon refusing its status as phenomenon: the gift, a spectral phenomenon that in its undecidability thwarts any ordinary categorical oppositions or foundational divergences of philosophy, indeed of rationality in general: matter and form, sensible and intelligible, given and non-given. But (and this is where Derrida's proximity to Desanti seems most real and decisive) for Derrida it is a matter of describing the revealed phenomenon in all its phenomenality—understanding that this characterization of the gift could just as well be applied to *time* (we must and will return to this) by refusing to set aside the aspect of the analysis beyond what is in play, however restive it might be. These are both the aporia and the requirement that must be opposed to him.

In a sense, the question of the gift, posited as the question of givenness, is phenomenology's grounding question. Only rarely does Derrida refer to this question, but the way in which he does so seems decisive: he demonstrates simultaneously the limitations of the phenomenological approach and the impossibility of absolutely escaping from it. This is why we might say of *Given Time* that he practices the aporias of phenomenology as though taking dictation, the question of the gift redirecting givenness just as much as the impossibility of escaping it: if it is necessary to maintain that the gift does not rise to the level of an authentic and originary gift, it is only from the interior of a gesture of fundamentally phenomenological style that this impossibility can be manifested, by being put to the test.

Derrida shows that the gift is unknowable as a thing itself—it both appears and does not appear—because it grounds all exchange by originarily breaking it. Even more radically, he breaks and thus grounds all logic, all *logos*, as the armature of all possible visible worlds. Indeed, and here Derrida is closest to Levinas, if all acts of the Same, all exchanges, aim at reestablishing the order of the Same, then any such act is suicidal, since it purports to aim at reabsorbing the "play" making it possible, the gap in which it is deployed. One must attempt to remain at the point of the originary event that gives being in "disjoining" it, in hiding something of itself from it: as the gift. And what this disjuncture, giving the visible by breaking it, risks must be understood as a "phenomenological impossibility" (*GT*, 156).

If the gift gives all things, does it give itself? (To answer in the affirmative would be to take a Henrian path.) Is the gift given by some authority that could thus qualify as an "over-giver"? To be able to say of the gift that it gives itself to itself, that is, to situate it entirely within the gesture of self-mastery, would be blatantly to betray it, if it is nothing other than pure surprise: it can be the force of surprise only insofar as it is originarily surprised itself. If purity is the mastery of the self in the departure from the stranger, then there is no pure gift.

If the gift does not give *itself* of itself and by itself, can or could we identify the place of its givenness *elsewhere*?

Derrida shows that the gift, being incalculable, could not be determined, could only be *as gift*. The gift, if it is one, is concealed by the concept "gift," as well as in its very phenomenality: what is given to me can be only for me, at the same time, concealed, not-given. Given in being concealed, concealed because given—this is what characterizes the counterfeit money that for Derrida thus *symbolizes* (which is itself one way of giving)—but the word "symbolize" is being misused if it implies a regulated exchange between two orders—and this is true for any gift (any gift that could be called "authentic," at least; this is the critical threat at play in all authenticity).

Thus, and for the same reasons, we can hardly imagine the gift *giving itself*; it is nearly impossible to imagine that a giving authority could be located, simply having receded (and not in radically different form) *beyond* the gift, to the place of its fullest accessibility. More precisely, it would be unavailable only in being too full, like the "too much" of all availability, an over-presence, a too-full of presence saturating the field of givenness. This could only be a refusal to determine the gift, even within the immanence of the gift to itself, in order better to locate it *elsewhere*, in the figure of an "indeterminable" that is no more than a word, a place given or assigned to it. This is why it is necessary to hold firmly to the force of the rupturing of all *logos* and all phenomenality proper to the gift, and thus in a certain sense to the rupture of the regime of immanence itself, which, however, would not open out onto any *beyond* of the gift: "there is no beyond of the gift," as Derrida declares. He further says that the gift must "suspend its relation to the border," signifying that breaking the immanence by which *logos* weaves phenomenality does not necessarily mean acquiescing to the temptation to install it *beyond*—in *belief.*

If the gift *is* in fact the gift, its concealment is endless, its deferral originary; it could not be redirected toward, "reduced to" any originary gift-giving authority, nor to anything that could be identified as such—and the magic trick called theology, which consists of identifying just such an authority as the unidentifiable itself, could thus simply not be plausible. To designate an originary givenness that would give only itself, being an overabundance of presence, would be to misunderstand that "true" generosity gives nothing, gives the nothing: "a gift must not be generous," according to Derrida. In addition, this would be to reinstall a fiduciary logic, despite all claims to the contrary, that would convert the absence of the gift into its even-here and to-itself, the gift as counterfeit money, as a letter of credit promising the glittering gold of a super-presence (in the) beyond.

From this perspective, the note Derrida addresses to Marion's *Reduction and Givenness* (*RG*, 72) is decisive. Recalling a close relationship with Marion's work, the note marks out a radical distancing at the very heart of this proximity. Along radically different routes and despite the proximity of their practical aporias, unlike Derrida's text Marion's thus claims *success*, a return to an *ultimate* givenness. There is in Marion an ultimate reduction that moves toward an ultimate givenness that gives the gift itself; an ultimate givenness that, since it is no longer concealed, is determined; it claims to be the undeterminable, for me, of what overflows my lived experience, all the more in that it is a question of what is absolutely present to itself apart from itself—an indeterminable with regard to intuition, given that it is a question of what absolutely determines *itself* in its presence to itself: as a phenomenon that is saturated, pure—as good as gold, so to speak. Authenticity and authority from the very thing that gives me sight when I avert my eyes, that my glance undermines, and that I therefore *believe*—since I must believe in what shows itself absolutely apart from itself. This is what Derrida calls *the name of the father,* and what Marion returns to (and thus *in a sense* speaks).

In this way the constraints "proper" to the paradoxical and phantomic phenomenality of the gift are not respected; the impurity of counterfeit money, as concealment, is denied.

But which of these two gestures is more phenomenological?—the one explicitly following Husserl's wishes, giving the originarity of all givenness by situating it beyond phenomena, even beyond the gift (that is, paradoxically but consequently, even beyond all phenomenology, according to Marion); or the one denouncing the impossibility of all ultimate reduction, while manifesting this impossibility from the very interior of the place of the gift—which is perhaps *still* the place of the *logos*?—of the immanence of phenomenality; that is, *despite everything*, from the very interior of phenomenology (as for Derrida)?

Through his need to respect this paradoxical phenomenality of the gift, Derrida is directed by the conundrum of describing an originary, irreducible differing—what gives even as it steals, if not *time* itself? In its paradoxical phenomenality, the gift "is" time itself. The question is therefore what can be said about time? What of the gift? And the question declares itself to be badly formulated, in that the link between the "saying" of time and of the gift cannot consist of a simple exterior connection: all operations of "saying" are intercalated between us and the thing itself, deferring it; but it thus gives, since givenness occurs only in concealing. The text, which Husserl calls a spiritual object, is spirit in the sense of the phantomic, is fundamentally a phantomic object, a mixture of presence and non-presence, given in the very refusal of givenness.[6] The text itself, an unreimbursable debt constituted by the infinite delay of what it speaks about, as a result lacks generosity, transferring the debt to the receiver— and this is therefore what it gives: debt. In a sense, if we can speak of total presence while still recognizing that it is not total presence; if we can speak of ghosts—that is, to let them speak, or to let them speak in us—this is in order to retain a little of what is lost to and in them if they are nothing but their escape, their flight, and thus to recognize them as such. Is not allowing to escape that which *remains*, fully itself *in* its escape, to be given it, as such? What remains is a *trace*.

And if these *accounts*, these *narratives*, among the multiplicity of discourses, are so important, it is not only because the double constraints of the gift's absence and presence in *this* life, *this* time, culminate in them: if the gift is entirely *this* event, tearing the fabric it has woven (the fabric of being), and if what is at play there can be named otherwise than with the name "time," then the account is not merely one among the *logoi*, but all *logos*, as seen through and in the narrative account. This comes back to saying that all life "is" *trace*, to be found nowhere but in a trace of itself.[7]

Anyone wishing to be oriented in the field of French phenomenology can learn much from the originality of the Desantian approach. It constitutes, perhaps, an essential point of focus that can help us avoid many possible pitfalls in contemporary phenomenological discourses.

Desanti's reflections take place serenely precisely in the gap, the opening in the recent debate over the "theological turn in French phenomenology," as Dominique Janicaud calls it. Our next step must be to confront his reading of *On the Phenomenology* with that in Marion's principal works,[8] while still understanding the risk of "theological intoxication" by reading Husserl's text through an unambiguously atheistic phenomenology, immanentist and strictly operational in its formalism, though nonetheless capable of thinking a *passive* subjectivity that thus breaks through any transcendental naïveté.

We will thus discover a very strong link between Desanti's phenomenological requirements and Derrida's, even if this communality manifests itself very differently in the two (a formalism holding all ontology at distance in Desanti, an ontology perpetually thrown into crisis as hauntology in Derrida), in the common space of the temptation to reabsorb and suture over the loss of any fruitful presence of *time*, as and in a *beyond*. Facing off against the thinker of the saturated phenomenon diverting his gaze away from time in order to embed it in the superabundance of *presence* (Marion) stand the thinkers of ordinary phenomena (Desanti) and of spectral phenomena (Derrida); that is, of *time* as such. And it must be understood that even beyond terminological differences, the stakes are the same: to describe the collapse of presence *just as* of the immanence of this presence, and to describe it as not being simply and flatly a dead loss but the generous gift of this life itself, insofar as it is what it is only in its loss of generosity. In this sense, phantoms contain nothing *extra*ordinary, or rather all ordinary phenomena are spectres, since spectres are *here*. They oppose a force of inertia, the paradoxical inertia of time passing, to any passage into the *beyond*. They are *sur*-vivors, in the sense that it is only thus that one is truly living, in this fragility, this precariousness.

And if it is necessary to implement a "phenomenology of the un-apparent," it is not simply in the slightly flat sense of having to move toward manifesting the still-unexplored horizon of the visible, a potential visibility remaining unexploited. It is more that it must make appear what cannot be seen, what is never given, givenness itself. This would lead us to leave behind all ordinary phenomena, the "common law" as Marion calls it when he hierarchizes phenomena, locating and orienting the glance as if from low to high on a graduated scale for measuring presence, moving toward a phenomenon that is invisible in the sense that it refuses to allow me to see it even though it can see itself, toward a phenomenon beyond. The invisible is such all the more when it surprises the visible—at the very core of the visible. The gift of the world, breaking through logic in order to bring it about, is recuperable neither here nor elsewhere; or rather, there is no elsewhere but here. That is the paradoxical constraint that must be respected if ordinary phenomena, the infraordinary, are to maintain their high value, a task all the more formidable, perhaps, given that no one, concentrating the gaze on a pure presence beyond, really wants to believe it: to describe infraordinary spectrality without yielding to its double bind; its undecidability not at all being an unspecified and weakened mixture of presence and non-presence, but rather the contradictory necessity of being at once presence *and* non-presence, of *being* only as being absent; of being given only by withholding itself.

This is because they lack the presence of which spectres, ghosts, are the only true apparitions.

At base, ordinary phenomena are unapparent, since we do not notice them.[9] And although we focus our gaze on them, they divert it, not toward the elsewhere of full presence but onto a confrontation with their own absence.

Must we not, then, prefer the meticulous work—done without fanfare, without any declaration of phenomenologicality—and for good reason—of those who, like Desanti and Derrida, orient themselves (however indeterminately) toward the diverting of phenomenology, which maintains as a central tenet the elevation of the spectrality of the originary phenomenon whose presence appears in order to collapse? Must we not prefer that to a phenomenology forcefully asserting the quintessentially Husserlian requirement of returning to the full presence of an originary, in an ultimate reduction that would culminate in the Husserlian reduction to the transcendental ego and the Heideggerian reduction to ontological difference, thereby discovering them to be simple preparatory stages of its own gesture? Clearly—and the texts focused on here offer a greater test of this than they claim: the former place us in a double impossibility, that of phenomenology itself, but also of absolutely abandoning it. Only from "within" presence is what presents it, in eating away at it, present; only from "within" discourse is presence *affixed*—and "phenomenology" named—and only "there" can the impossibility of this discourse itself be manifested. In order to engage with and in phenomenology today, must we not—patiently—endure this double bind, in order to give birth to it, indefinitely, at the core of its diversion, just as all phenomenology *gives* itself at the very center of its disaster, which is only to "give time" to time, and to a time that gives us everything?

2. The Impossibility of the Gift: *Within* the Extreme Possibility of Givenness (Jacques Derrida; Jean-Luc Marion)

We must return to, and deepen, our analysis of what is at stake in phenomenology, and of the very thing it envisages in the abyss that has seemed to hover behind the apparent proximity between Derrida's and Marion's phenomenological practice.

This time we must work through Jean-Luc Marion's *Reduction and Givenness*,[10] attempting to determine the extent to which Derrida resonates in it; this is doubly legitimate in that Marion both claims a close affinity to Derrida and aims at determining the pure form of the call.

Marion takes up the Derridean critique of the primacy of presence as determined through the figure of objectness, uninterrogated by Husserl, even if he then pushes it beyond itself, reverses it, and finally turns it against itself. This reversal—meant in the sense of "reversing" a glove—is clearly the engine of Marion's research,[11] or at least what activates it,[12] and is perhaps even its very heart.

This reversal brings Marion and Derrida into proximity, but—this is at least the hypothesis we will follow here—it is pushed so far that it produces a tear, a gap: Marion's phenomenology, far from being in solidarity with the Derridean text as though they were recto and verso, completely estranges itself from the force of its call and does not allow itself to be affected by it.

Marion's text, aiming toward the pure form of a claim or call, though it claims a frequently cited and discussed proximity with Derrida, is nonetheless deaf to the Derridean call, through the very fact of the *other* call, which it designates as the more originary claimant.

One cannot help being powerfully struck by Marion's disqualification of time as temporal gap, in favor of the thematic of presence through which *Reduction and Givenness* operates.

Even more prejudicially, but in keeping with this question of temporality, a reader of Marion, occupied with phenomenological necessity, could not fail to be astonished in the face of a text that presents itself less as the provisional description of phenomena ceaselessly glimpsed on the horizon than as the impeccable *construction* of an "order of reasons."[13]

Looked at more closely, this "order of reasons" has less the form of a nexus than of a nerve pathway along which, from a departure point firmly established from the outset, each stage prepares for the one that follows, will transcend it, and will redeem it. This order is not initially presented as what *is*, a logical order, but as a progression in the elucidating of phenomenality that takes an axiological form and thus one of hierarchy, at least in terms of phenomenological values.

Finally, and this is decisive, *Reduction and Givenness* claims a particular outcome; indeed, more radically, it claims the ultimate outcome, in the form of a "third reduction" beyond both the Husserlian and Heideggerian—a "last reduction."[14]

This carefully constructed, linear, and monological work, "conclusive," as it were, is located at the opposite pole from the Husserlian text: zigzagging sinuosity, the need for analytic description—ceaselessly diverted, ceaselessly maintained—which means perpetual rebeginning as well.

My claim is that Marion's text can succeed—and can thus set out—only because it has in a sense *always already arrived*. The Husserlian text can only succeed—and can only accumulate false departures—because it always carries within it the inscription of the impossibility of setting foot on the promised land.

In the strictest sense, we can only engage in a discourse *without surprise*. This is the paradox that must be kept in view, that is foundational: discourse pretending to move toward the place of the most radical surprise, the place of interlocution, would be, for that very reason, the *least* surprised and, perhaps, the least surprising. At this point we should remember our very first remark about the content of this discourse: it speaks not of a temporal gap but of presence. The connection of form to foundation would thus be less a connection of the production of signification than a pragmatic and minimalist one.[15] The discourse *of* presence—and here it is necessary to understand the genitive as just as subjective as it is objective—canceling all temporality: its own as much as the one it speaks about, or rather doesn't speak about.

But is it not *time* that ceaselessly surprises us and, even more radically, captures us?[16]

Reduction and Givenness is a conversation that, since it does not run the risk of inventing anything new—of being affected—would lead nowhere other than where it already was, *in the name of* a more radical affection, and in the form of a dominant progression. As such, since it sees itself as the ultimate, affection inverts its power and is betrayed.

What authorizes this diagnostic that, term for term, contradicts what Marion brings to his own text? He says that "indeed, the two preceding works [*God Without Being* and *On Descartes' Metaphysical Prism*] *unlike the third* [*Reduction and Givenness*; emphasis added], could assume the acquisition and demonstration of their conclusions."[17]

But the effort here will be to show that the manner in which this last text *functions* is absolutely significant. First, though Marion cannot be reproached for using phenomenology to analyze other texts,[18] and even less to invoke it against this or that argument, we might still be surprised at the kind of connection he maintains with the texts he cites, in close attention. One could say that he in fact *instrumentalizes* them.

In this regard, we must examine Marion's reading of Derrida's reading of Husserl's *Logical Investigations* in *Speech and Phenomena*, in "The Breakthrough and the Broadening," the first chapter of *Reduction and Givenness*. (We will then propose, and then confirm, that the same scenario at work in Heidegger occurs in the last chapter of *Reduction and Givenness*.)

For Marion, unlike for Derrida, this is a matter of showing that signification is autonomous relative to Husserlian intuition. In fact, if this is the case, and since signification could not know in *any* case how to *give* anything—let alone how to signify anything—then givenness is not limited to the determination of presence in the interdependent figures of intuition and objectivity.

As part of his demonstration, Marion will in some fashion, *temporarily*, become more Derridean than Derrida, recognizing the originary Derridean gap in the very place in which Derrida marked it as averted in order to oppose it to the Derridean reading of *Logical Investigation I*: as non-presence marked radically at the level of signification and its expression, not simply circumscribed and reverting to simple indication. This then permits a cleverly orchestrated reversal: against the Derridean philosophy of the gap, Marion here restores presence, not against Husserl but—in a very Derridean way—by carefully scrutinizing Husserl's unthought. Marion detects a thematic of presence irreducible to intuition.

And finally, in support of these claims we should quickly follow the argument in § 4 and § 5 of this chapter, which constitutes the heart of Marion's counterreading of the *Logical Investigations*, in which he reverses the Derridean interpretation against itself.

This is then a matter of opposing the Derridean interpretation that would terminally undermine the metaphysics of presence in Husserl's *Logical Investigations*, recalling that Heidegger, on the contrary, foresaw "being" as exceeding "beings" and thus metaphysics. But these two interpretations would be in opposition if we succeed in demonstrating that in a sense Derrida is correct—situating him within the order of presence—and that Heidegger is also and even more correct—the order of beings and thus of metaphysics as ontotheology is exceeded. From this it would be necessary to conclude that Derrida is not correct in confining Husserl within metaphysics since he is even more fundamentally incorrect in connecting "metaphysics" and "presence," metaphysics as the reign of beings never only being a derivative mode of presence, and never presence as source (recognized in the Husserlian word for givenness, *Gegebenheit*). This is what Marion wishes to demonstrate. How does he do so?

He reveals a *decision* in Derrida's reading. This decision is a vital one, supporting *Speech and Phenomena* and the entire interpretation given in it, but it is nowhere legitimated (*RG*, 35–37); the decision is "intuition pervasively governs the 'metaphysics of presence' . . . intuition alone achieves presence" (*RG*, 36). This decision determines the validity—because it first of all determines the coherence—of Derrida's reading. Indeed, Derrida can then demonstrate that, on the one hand, all of Husserl's explicit efforts attempt to think the autonomy of the intention of signification through its connection to intention, while, on the other hand, as though despite himself, Husserl would bring intention back toward intuitive fullness and, in the end, subordinate intention to it, intention never being merely the awaiting or the desire for intention. But why could Husserl only connect intention to intuition? Because intention left to itself can only collapse, if it gives nothing and gives itself as nothing, if it is incapable of furnishing any presence autonomously: a void such as this is inconceivable—simply "is" not—only by association with a fullness it puts in quotation marks. All other possibilities are unenvisagable, at least within the frame of a *logos* that gathers presence—Western philosophy since its Greek origins. Following Marion, we can see just how much the Derridean decision to make intuition and presence reciprocal is decisive here, since it is the pivot point of argumentation allowing Derrida—according to Marion—to show that Husserl contradicts himself.[19]

Consequently, Marion, citing a number of passages from *Logical Investigations I* and *VI*, can show that intuition is not the last word of intention, that the intention of signification is indeed autonomous. As an example Marion cites the case of mathematical ideality in geometry:

No mathematical ideality can be found in the space that is indeed lived that is adequately full; inadequation, and thus the overflowing of intuition by intention, and its surplus through signification, far from constituting an exception, enunciates an absolute rule: signification of the *straight line*, or of the *curve of the equation ax + b*, or even of the *triangle*, never to be encountered as adequately full in the lived experiences of intuition properly actualized by a consciousness. (*RG*, 40)

This decisive asset permits Marion to show that Husserl, far from delivering intention to intuition—and as a consequence of its self-contradiction—on the contrary, critiques the error of having done so (*RG*, 43). Derrida has misunderstood (*RG*, 44). It is a fruitful misunderstanding, in that it puts its finger on what makes the Husserlian aporia even more radical, and thus even indicates the way to its transcendence inasmuch as it is true that it is in being brought to the highest danger that one finds "the means to exit from it": to Derrida the aporia; to Marion the release from the path on whose threshold Derrida rests. In fact, if intention is not promised to intuition, and if despite signifying nothing, intention cannot *not* give something (by way of presence), then there is a mode of presence that is not reduced to intuition, and thus that intuition—presence that "makes" metaphysics—is but a mode of presence, of givenness.

Yet what legitimates Marion's reading, aside from the detailed discussion of Husserl's texts?

1. Considering it self-evident that a reading that saves an author (here, Husserl) from contradiction precedes a reading that leaves the author in contradiction, in that it will more fully satisfy the need for rationality.[20]

2. Designating the Derridean decision according to which intuition deems the entirety of the "metaphysics of presence" as non-legitimate.

To which it might be objected:

1. Derrida seems not to say, not in *Speech and Phenomena* or elsewhere, that Husserl simply contradicts himself. Rather, Derrida shows him to be caught in a double constraint, a double bind, an aporia in the strongest sense of the word. And Marion clearly knows this: "Derrida's interpretation largely avoids the oversimplification ascribed to him. Husserl's *Investigations* return, in his view, to metaphysics only in that they reach the outer edge of the field of presence; they arrive there only because they fail to transgress it" (*RG*, 34). And it is not certain, even if the complacency within the aporia can be turned into a rhetorical "trick," that the decision according to which philosophical texts can be saved from aporia is not philosophically suspect.

2. Clearly, the Derridean reading precedes a decision—what reading does not? But this decision seems to reside less in the determination of presence as intuition than, more generally and fundamentally, in "deconstruction" itself—that is, at minimum, in the suspicion thrown onto all given presence. And this decision repeats itself by displacing itself, in the initiatory rupture of the very act of philosophy that for Plato and Aristotle is called "astonishment."

Marion's counterreading also proceeds from a decision, which can be easily demonstrated.

Marion moves toward presence as though this were as simple as changing its name—it is no longer intuition but givenness—in order to extract it from metaphysics, and as if what Derrida demonstrates is not already worth as much to givenness as to intuition (and of what importance are these names?). Marion desires presence. It is only out of this desire that he can produce a contradictory reading, in reversing it and using it as a springboard for deploying his own proposal. Presence in givenness (that is, freed from metaphysics) is only to be glimpsed in *Logical Investigation VI* insofar as Marion's reading of it has *previously* taken root there; this is the decision of presence.

It is possible to say two things regarding this decision: (1) it does not recognize itself as a decision, averts and masks, beneath the cloak of demonstration, the aspect of contingency lurking secretly in all decisions as such, and (2) it attempts to circumvent an unease characteristic of the doing of philosophy, a need to "account for," then experiences its own vulnerability, its own precariousness, in the irreducible enigma of the glance's conversion, in which it is born.[21]

A perusal of the first chapter of *Reduction and Givenness* reveals its strategy—that is, at the very least, that it is oriented toward an already-chosen goal without ever having taken account of this choice in the course of the process itself.

Beyond the fact that Marion himself lays claim to this strategy, as we will see, we must determine the ways in which his trajectory is strategic and specify what in all strategy is in opposition to phenomenological research.[22]

A strategy is always decided, and thus closed in on itself, as opposed to a *research*, and even more to a phenomenological research that must be allowed to open through the phenomenon.[23] Thus, the question posed here is confirmed and legitimated: has the Derridean call been heard and understood by Marion's text, which speaks so positively of it? Is the first chapter of *Reduction and Givenness* actually affected by *Speech and Phenomena*?

What would be required in order for that to happen would first be to accept the idea that the hegemony of presence *can* be suspended, or at least threatened. In order to be able to play the game of presence and nothing-ness in Husserl's text otherwise than parodically, we must already have brought presence itself into question. But how *not* to see that the empire of presence is precisely what renders one blind here as elsewhere in *Reduction and Givenness*, presence as that which is never put into question, given that it is precisely the inception of all questions?

How *not* to see, then, that the erudite debate over the interpretation of *Logical Investigations I* and *VI* is finally secondary relative to the deci-sion of reading that is its precondition?

Is it possible to analyze the marginalization of the index in favor of the expression of a signification that is always oriented and, as it were, magnetized by intuition, like the symptom of the primary uninterrogated of presence (Derrida), or can one go so far as to accord the autonomy of signification to intuition as in *Logical Investigation I*, in order better to discover presence elsewhere, exceeding intuition, as in *Logical Investigation VI* (Marion)?

These questions can be decisive only if we accept the disruption *in advance* of the very thing we ourselves carry, in being carried toward a text, what we carry in our glance and what makes it possible to see, this glance itself: we must accept the disruption of the actual field of the glance.

Marion invites this risk in *Reduction and Givenness*. He engages in a dialogue with Derrida's reading in—and never beyond—the intact, undisturbed field that precedes it. According to our analysis here, then, we must conclude that *Reduction and Givenness* is, despite—and in?—its multiplicity of discussions and tributes, rendered deaf to the Derridean call.[24]

But Marion's proposal increasingly has the appearance of a dia-logue that is careful to permit the other to speak—Derrida's analysis is restored—in that in fact it consists of a faultless and unhesitating augmen-tation that is all the more impeccable in that the prior certitude in which it is written has been left intact.

We must note, with the other objective of *Reduction and Givenness*, the same effect of deafness—though toward Heidegger this time—pre-cisely toward what Derrida persistently demands from Heidegger, and what Marion persists in returning to—and at the same time not to hear it; what Marion never ceases to assert, in order to circumvent it.

Marion's strategy is the same: to radicalize Heidegger against Heidegger's own text, turning him against himself. More specifically, Marion radicalizes the thought of the Nothing as "nothing of nothing," freeing up the terrain for the greatest plenitude. In fact, the Nothing in Heidegger, giving being, is thus for him in some way subordinated: the Heideggerian nothing is still deduced *from* being, as Levinas loves to say in *God, Death, and Time.* The nothing, presented as the reflux of all beings—as, in the strictest sense, not being—comes to coincide with a sense of being that is the nothing of beings, since—and this is decisive—being is the promise of all beings: being without beings, since it is the very matrix of all beings.

Thus, the thought of the gap between being and beings-as-nothing does not lead radically toward a "nothing of nothing," a nothing that promises only nothing: for Heidegger, this is the limit of all phenomenology, and thus of all philosophy, if it is true that he understands the originary and matricial question as, from the start and immediately, the question of being. Just as for Descartes, doubt is from the outset, and in a sense always already, methodological, for Heidegger the nothing is reciprocal with being, given that it is from the start and always seen through being.

It is perfectly legitimate to attempt to unlock the Heideggerian unthought from its connections between Nothing, Being, and beings, and further, to push beyond this unthought: this is apparently what Marion does, pushing the Heideggerian text in the direction of the "nothing of nothing" before which Heidegger in some respects retreats. But this operation can conclude in a textual mechanics that does not fail precisely because it produces a discourse in which we can ask if it truly allows itself to be radically affected by the nothing. Marion can reproach Heidegger for not having gone to the very limit of the nothing, of not having left himself the last word—which would have been to confess that he did not have the last word—although he *plays* with the nothing, plays the nothing against being, *in view* of presence: he manipulates it. And this demonstration never fails to betray an absence of affection, betrays the fact that nothing has occurred since the nothing is not past, because we did without the nothing.[25] This discourse emerges from presence, in view of presence, and thus has always made of the nothing the means of its achievement.

And is it not necessary—contrary to what Marion constantly repeats in a gesture that can seem to reveal denial just as much as self-con-
viction—to say that *Reduction and Givenness* is from the outset installed
in the very place requiring us never to leave it once we have penetrated it:
faith?[26] It is only from this place that the nothing, which can hardly any
longer be but a simulacrum of itself, can be countered and overturned
through its radicalization.

The nerve center of our suspicions about the phenomenological
nature of Marion's enterprise is clear: while it pretends to pierce further
than what remains unquestioned in Husserl (presence determined in the
solid figures of intuition and objectness), and in Heidegger (presence determined as phenomenon of being), it remains, according to our analysis,
inside, within, unquestioned itself: faith;[27] that is, within the indetermination of presence, within presence as determination.[28] (And it is true
that what is here neither determined nor determinable is from a certain
point of view unquestionable.) Therefore, on the contrary, in figures that
are certainly as such limited to the presence they inhabit, the Husserlian
and Heideggerian texts produce just *the experience of this limit*, since it is
necessary to conjure it up.

Jean-Luc Marion addresses this question of faith as a necessary presupposition, directly, since for him it is posed through the editorial process
of the *Revue de métaphysique et de morale*. And he clearly distinguishes *On
Descartes' Metaphysical Prism* and *God Without Being* from his third transgression beyond being, *Reduction and Givenness*. Indeed, whereas the first
two rest explicitly on a *positum*, a prior given that takes a proper position
(the history of philosophy/faith), *Reduction and Givenness* firmly neces-
sitates presupposing nothing, not giving, from the outset, any content. As
a result the arrival point, no longer being already-given before departure,
will be seen as "void" or "empty" (see "*Réponses à quelques questions*," in the
Revue de métaphysique et demorale, 1991, no. 1, 67). This is a way of saying
that nothing of what it is is acquired at the beginning—and, it thus seems,
at the end. We find in Marion a confirmation of the hypothesis that success never comes to one who misses the first step, who proceeds only in
and through lack.

Does this mean that we coarsen the procedure of *Reduction and Givenness* in reproaching it for what it explicitly guards itself against?

Note that the "emptiness" in question corresponds in *Reduction and Givenness* to the fullest presence; that Marion's text installs itself at the very place of the void, requiring its philosophical and phenomenological operativity, and that it claims pure presence as such—what will then saturate saturated phenomena.[29] This is disconcerting but understandable.

Indeed, when Marion evokes this "void" or "emptiness" required by the absence of presupposition, he implicitly thinks it as a "nothing determined," a not-"this", not-"that" (thus replaying the Heideggerian schema of Being that has nothing to do with a being, against Heideggerian Being itself: what would not even be Being—in a trumping of the originary). But thinking of this kind leads to the very opposite of a nothing of nothing: it leads to the very indeterminacy of presence, the *purest* presence not limited to any determined figure (a being, objectness, or even Heideggerian Being, which would—still—be a determination) and thus a presence more complete than any of the particular figures in which it reveals its source and measure.

The undetermined, as the undeterminable, is in the end not the void: on the contrary, it involves the purest plenitude. It is, properly speaking, in our marrying of the gesture of higher phenomenological risk that we might say that Marion does not go to the conclusion of his gesture:[30] pushing the nothing of Heideggerian beings toward the nothing of Being is always rendered "unaffectable" by the spectre of the nothing of nothing.[31]

Thus, everything is suspended. If the "empty square" shows itself as being full or, more precisely, as the revelation of what is never *a* fullness, all the more in that it brings plenitude itself into question, then the discourse of invention applies to all stakes. It confesses—and is even legitimated in claiming—that in fact it permits itself to claim, by what precedes it. Marion explicitly addresses this in "the nothing and its demand."[32] Despite Marion's denials, it is precisely faith that is at stake.

Marion shows that since the transition between the Nothing and being fails if one separates it from the Nothing, Heidegger is, according to Marion, led to conclude that

it is necessary to undertake it [the transition] out of the intimate end—being itself; the gap between the Nothing and being can only be traversed through its extreme end . . . ; this ultimate begins with the end—the call of the distant, being—
and with the beginning—the near Nothing, where we are. (see *RG*, 278)

This trajectory, designated as Heidegger's in the instauration of the motif
of the call of being (*Anspruch des Seins*),[33] Marion, faithful to his methodological principle, adopts and radicalizes it, making it a matter of "transcending" the call of being in "the pure form of the call." We can see where
this subreption is played out: to conclude that X both exceeds and precedes
me, that it thus *must emerge* from X—and from the outset, though it seems
to proceed from the self in Marion's discourse, that it *can* emerge. To give
oneself the means of evading the "where we are," and what is more, to go
elsewhere, that is, to *give* oneself this elsewhere, this ultimate, and as given,
makes it a beginning: this is precisely what seems non-phenomenological
and, more generally, non-philosophical, if philosophy always begins in the
near-at-hand, and if phenomenology—even that of the unapparent—must
maintain itself on "this side"—*where we are*, and only to foresee of its other
side what of it disturbs the phenomenality that is the here-itself. Certainly,
it is necessary to show, along with Marion, that the I is exceeded. But what
a remarkable yet ambiguous manner this excess assumes in order to produce
it (even if "as such"). And is this not what must be called "faith," this manner of giving what exceeds, thus fixing it as an ultimate, indeed as a ground
from which to depart (at least in the unfolding of discourse) even while it
is a matter with regard to the thing itself of an irreducible "base"? It is as
if I could directly relay the words of this "base," since in its largesse it already speaks and overflows presence. The act of faith is situated, first and
most profoundly, there, in that decision—which as such is always already
made—this is the presence that addresses itself to me and has need of me.

This decision, of which the "nothing of nothing" could not know
how to constitute the first and last word, is precisely—faith.

Marion's discourse can thus claim an absence of (determined) presupposition only for this quite paradoxical but thoroughly coherent reason: he is rooted in presupposition itself; presupposition as indetermination that can be reversed—the pure form of presupposition.[34] This results,
finally, in the tension we cannot fail to note between, on the one hand, the
need for indetermination—for a negative phenomenology[35] that permits

retention within the limited figures of boredom and unsettledness of the very thing that is inexhaustible, thus preserving the reserve of presence; and, on the other hand, the temptation—since this is a question of plenitude itself, and above all of the nothing—to taste of this plenitude and to identify it. Final paradox: it must be identified as the unidentifiable itself, and we must name it, if not with the name of the "unnamable," then with the name of the unnamable, that of the Father: "'Hear, Israël, Yahweh our God, Yahweh alone' (Deuteronomy 6:4). This is confirmation that another call—the call of the other—can dismiss or submerge the first call that launches the claim of being" (*RG*, 295).

This is the process through which the universality of faith ineluctably particularizes itself. Such dogma subtly claiming faith as such for itself is thus revealed as never being anything but *a* dogma.

It is another way of locating this tension, this paradoxical and denied process through which the pure form of the call and/or the indetermination of presence come to be particularized: the question of the saturated phenomenon.[36]

The saturated phenomenon accommodates the presence that thus saturates it, which claims privilege over what is known as ordinary phenomena, saturating it for the lived experience envisaging it. Marion is careful to show that the saturated phenomenon is a "phenomenological type," integrally describable through phenomenological analysis since it is more radically required and legitimated through it. Consequently, the historical event, the work of art, and Christ can all be described as being saturated phenomena *on the same basis*, and finally that what receives a phenomenological analysis should not be confused with an apologetics. Yet, since saturated phenomena are not pure presence themselves but still-determined figures, despite everything—which permits them to foresee what cannot be glanced directly; saturated phenomena will thus be susceptible to hierarchization according to the "rendered" presence they authorize. In this way, one phenomenon might claim to be slightly more saturated than others: Christ, for example. How would it be possible to misunderstand that this does not emerge from a phenomenological description, nor even a phenomenological description of faith, but from faith itself, and one particularized as Christian;[37] and further, that such a hierarchy is possible, like it or not, declared or not?

Therefore, and to conclude this analysis at the same point at which we entered it (the viewpoint of posture and manner), we must recall that Marion does in fact claim a strategy but, he says, a different strategy, in *Reduction and Givenness*. It might be called a torqued strategy, since it consists of not giving itself as a strategy. The inhibition of thought is not installation in faith but the effort needed to mask it under the guise of phenomenology. At least the masterful strategic gesture is not inhabited by a denial.

The effort here has been first of all to explore the way in which Derrida's *Given Time* is separated from Marion's *Reduction and Givenness* (see Chapter 2, Section 1), and then to show how *Reduction and Givenness* does not recognize in the Derridean call the merits of having opened this breach in order to circumvent it (Chapter 2, Section 2).

Although these analyses considering how *Given Time* "works"—and is worked by—*Reduction and Givenness* were already quite advanced, Marion published "Esquisse d'un concept phénoménologique du don," a reading of Derrida's *Given Time*. Thus, Marion reveals explicitly what he had first indicated in "Réponses à quelques questions": that his work on the givenness of presence originated in the problems he found in Derrida's text.

On the brink of accepting that our analysis has been overwhelmed and thus disrupted by this new piece of contrary evidence, we actually find there, it seems, a step-by-step, term-for-term confirmation of the gap that exists between the two bodies of thought.

The opposition between temporal gap and full presence is *interdependent* with thoughts tending toward it, thoughts to which it has always in some sense given their orientation. And if the interweaving, if not the originary ambiguity, of both position and thematics renders undecidable the problem of knowing which decides the other, if we keep to our method, we still enter Marion's text via his position.

Marion begins by ascribing to *Given Time* the phenomenological value of having identified this positionality as such. But whereas Derrida designates it as structured by a double bind, forced to juxtapose the gift's existence precisely in the place of its impossibility, in a paradox refusing to let itself retreat into a simple contradiction, Marion attempts to

demonstrate that the impossibility laid out by Derrida is at once the mark
and the condition of possibility of a "higher possibility": that of the pure
presence of a present as "givenness" itself (we will come back to this). Only
under these conditions, for Marion, can the impossible possibility of the
gift be saved from contradiction.

1. Thus for Marion *from the outset* Derrida's proposition is understood
   only as a means or tool of presence, as an intermediary proposition,
   a launching pad for the liberation of Marionian presence.

2. We see further that Marion's thought here claims the force of demonstration: any obstacle presenting itself will be immediately transformed into a means for going further, as a problem rather than an
   aporia,[38] and this is the case as a result of the very force of Marion's
   decision. If the gift as Derrida speaks about it is impossible, then its
   truth must be liberated elsewhere, "higher up" on the scale of this
   kind of ascendant dialectic: this becomes impossible for Marion *not*
   to think; it has always already been decided. We might remark in
   passing that Marion's discourse transforms paradox into the promise
   of a greater clarity, claiming for it the force of the order of reason and
   leaving Derridean thought "behind" it—thus paralyzing itself in its
   own impasse, in its active passivity, in this enduring lack of progress,
   poised on a unsettling and shifting—if not irrational, at least non-
   rational—frontier. This has the secondary consequence of allowing
   Marion to give (i.e., to produce) his discourse as *having nothing to do*
   with the irrational, and in particular with the irrationality concealing the act of faith.[39]

   The fact that impossibility *must* be the sign of a higher possibility
is the exemplary mark in the distinction Marion makes here, the
difference he lays out in *Reduction and Givenness* between presence
and present.[40] While Derrida conceives presence as always affected
by absence, indeed by the radical absence of the nothing (the impossible possibility of presence), Marion (still suspended within the
ontotheology of presence) is forced to show the "essential" difference
between the overabundance of presence as he defines it and a simple
metaphysical understanding of presence. This is why he says that we
must subscribe to the Derridean critique of presence, since it forbids
remaining "in presence, understood as the permanent subsistence

of beingness within the self."[41] But Marion reproaches Derrida for not going far enough on the path toward the impossibility of the metaphysical gift, Marion's own text claiming to float above the objections levied at Derrida. But Marion is the one who goes "too far," transgressing the limit of impossibility and being deluded by the question of a test of whatever limit there may be, his murky course inscribing the test precisely—and by that very fact—on the selfsame path of the metaphysics of presence. Fundamentally, and despite what Marion says regarding his own "transcendence" of metaphysics as being supported by the Derridean springboard, it is Marion's proposition more than Derrida's that exposes itself to the danger of extending the ontotheology of presence: for Marion, simply distinguishing "the present" from "presence" is enough to escape *to* ontotheology, by making his "deconstruction" the launching pad for his transcendence toward a higher, finally liberated, possibility.

3. Finally, Marion and Derrida can be opposed to each other in terms of their claims regarding the possibility of any test of the impossible; of the profusion of presence[42] to the ungenerous deficiency of spectral presence in what is always absented; and finally to the will to purity of the meditation on originary contamination. This reading requires our close attention to the inflating of the semantic register of purity in the texts on which Marion focuses here (*Reduction and Givenness* and "Esquisse d'un concept phénoménologique du don"). For example, among others: "thus to extract the gift from the economy and to manifest it according to pure givenness" (ECP, 84). And it is always the same opposition we can see emerging from differing viewpoints through an originary positionality, a particular manner of being connected to the limit.

Marion's gesture, initially and throughout, claims that it transgresses limits, and we can only be struck by his numerous explicit determinations of *thought as transgression* in the texts we are considering here.[43] And we might finally wonder if a *systematically* transgressive gesture is truly subversive: crossing a frontier means never remaining there, never putting it to the test—one that is always that of the impossible.[44] In a sense, such a test has always already canceled the impossible, and, in this context, the border is always conceived as the closure of other territory; it *is* only in light of this other territory (in this case, pure, full presence). The purity of its project purifies the fields determined by it. This purity also, in its clarity, allows us to cross it. It separates two "homes," so transgressing it, one leaves behind the comfort of being at home (however devalued it may be as mundane, "living being," "common," as Marion says) only to be ensconced in the comfort of another. Here or there, for Marion transgression always in the end finds its place, neutralizing all passage, all processes of radical alteration; transgression as the means for something other than itself, canceled at the very place at which it succeeds.

Thus, transgression, to exaggerate slightly, would cancel and reverse the very thing it explicitly requires: a departure from ontotheology in the radical passage (without any possibility of return) of an *I* taken by surprise and decentered by what irreducibly exceeds it in exceeding all presence in the form of the living being, decentered by what in its excess never allows for determination or stabilization as any "home."

Derridean thought—as thought that tests limits—on the contrary, thinks limits only insofar as it does not cross them. Located on the border as a result of a necessarily precarious, unstable, and finally impossible installation, Derridean thought awaits what will never arrive—which thus arrives. Caught in an interminable detention, disappointed in its waiting since the gift exists only in its absence of generosity, and thus disappointing (that is, giving), it marches in place in the very place in which it cannot take place: the frontier.[45] This enduring of the limit, in which alterity presents itself in order to be refused, as we have seen, is temporality itself.

And what is being investigated here is the double bind of the gift presenting itself perhaps less *as* a Derridean *thematic* than, more radically, in the *manner* or style of this thought.[46]

At the conclusion of this part of our inquiry, a concern appears: to what extent have we not simply replicated Marion's analyses in *Reduction and Givenness*, even while we critiqued them through their connection to Derrida? To what extent is our reading not rendered deaf to their appeal—to what calls them (opens them), calls *in* them, and thus permits them to call (to open a philosophizing subjectivity and to give it to itself)? To what extent are we not always closed to Marion's work, in deciding from the start on an attitude of general suspicion in our approach to these texts?—a "deconstruction," in the worst sense of the term, as suspicion that simply says "no" rather than as exposition saying "yes" to what takes us by surprise?

And we will have done all of this in the most decisive manner, though it is precisely this that is in question: the capacity to allow ourselves to be affected by what arrives at the limit without in one way or another canceling the element of risk in all surprises.

Certainly, Marion's proposals occupy a unique place in this chapter's economy.

In fact, we have tried to show:

1. That the thinkers on whom we have focused practice a phenomenology at the limit by allowing themselves to confront non-givenness, within the context of temporality.

2. That Derrida is the one who takes this practice to the limit and thinks it as such: as what decenters phenomenology at its border while holding it at its inner edge—that is, still as phenomenology— at the very moment in which phenomenology is divested of the certitude of its closure and of its purity.

3. That Levinas and Michel Henry, each in his own way, test out this limit in a (deforming) mirror image, and in conflict with temporality, Levinas explicitly, Henry all the more so in that his practical methodology contains precisely what his thematics ignore.

4. That this practice of putting the limit to the test of non-verification is not separable from the *risk* of the limit's verification: this is why we must suspend all conclusions pretending to validate the *totality* of a corpus. Nothing, at this point in our process, allows us decide one way or the other, to decide who holds to the limit and who does not. On the contrary, if the analysis of time seems to be the exemplary place at which to confront the limit, have we not already indicated the paradox wanting the test of the limit to imply precisely the risk of transgression, and thus perhaps already transgressions of the work, just as much as indications that the risk has been taken? At minimum, at this point it is important to cease believing in the homogeneity of the corpus, and even to prepare to envisage failure—in this case the verification of limits—as accompanying and in a sense *making possible* the test of phenomenology.

Marion is isolated in this problematic: he is the counterexample, the one who does not, according to our critique, in fact put the limit to the test. Significantly, his "object" is presence (or the present), and the temporal gap. Marion is the one who, differentiating himself from Levinas and Henry, exposes himself to Janicaud's reproach regarding the theologization of phenomenology,[47] a theologization amounting to a loss of being poised "this side" of the frontier; his is a gesture that dreams beyond in order to implement the encounter what it needs: the figure of presence in the ontotheological sense since, after Derrida, as we have seen here, *all* pure presence is ontotheological, not simply presence in the mode of (a) living being. This would be a matter of an absolutely unsurprising construction since it remains ontotheological and phenomenologically uncontrollable, given that it radically exceeds phenomenology.

Marion's gesture of theologization cannot escape positivism any more than any other such gesture, though his reconcealing and disguising culminate in *pure* phenomenology. It is a virtue of faith as decision, that of unveiling the Greek affinity for the *logos* and the phenomenon (for phenomenology, perhaps), for its self-sufficiency, which reminds philosophy that it also results from decision and thus, as such, from ungrounded contingency. Thus, philosophy defines itself when its other reveals it as a vulnerability that must be exposed. The call of the Infinite (in its religious sense) does not function for Marion as it does for Levinas—as what destabilizes, blurs, and finally upsets the supposed purity of the field of immanence of the *logos* and the phenomenon. On the contrary, its entire effort is aimed at attempting to domesticate this theme, within the constraints of a phenomenology thought as being pure in its "as such": this works against the writer's will, as the dissolution of those constraints, the dissolution—in its domestication—of what it is questioning, or as both.

Clearly, the reading we are giving these texts lacks generosity. At least the radicality of Marion's project—which is in a sense its other—reminds us that it (it especially) can proceed only from a decision that conceals something irreducibly arbitrary within itself. At least, if Derrida is correct, we can hope that this lack of generosity will lead to something else. Finally, for lack of anything else, and only if it can come to pass, we might hope that this "enemy," even "ungrateful," reading will have been of use in sketching a phenomenology of the concept of the gift, as gift.[48]

PART III

THE TEST OF SUBJECTIVITY

If a fruitful way of positioning ourselves in the field we have been exploring has so far consisted of engaging in a confrontation with non-givenness, and if temporality is the exemplary terrain for the aporia of non-givenness, we must now advance our analysis by looking at the (necessarily paradoxical) order of non-givenness.

And it seems that this must be the complete *test* of the limit—certainly not its transgression, its traversal, or (and this would come to the same thing) refusal to face it.

But what is subjectivity if not precisely that, a *test*?

In modern metaphysics, in Descartes for example, subjectivity is the point of immanence situated at the intersection of the gnoseological and the ontological axes, from which the glance is torn and to which one must turn in order to carefully review all the evidence, to put it to the test.

More important still, the most traditional idea of the subject as foundational is from the start described as what essentially *lies beneath* or *supports* its accidents.

Even supposing that it could be possible to disunite subjectivity from the axiomatic of modern metaphysics, would this not still remain a pure test of the self? It is in this test—and perhaps even *as* test—that subjectivity becomes ipseity, becomes true subjectivity in this pressing against the self that already has a bond with the self.

Is this not in a way what is in play when Husserl, in *On the Phenomenology of the Consciousness of Internal Time*, isolates *Urimpression* as this surging forth of pure immanence, as nothing other than the context for acts of consciousness, that for which they occur? This point-source, always already supporting what takes place outside itself by defeating, "unmaking," demolishing it, Husserl calls "absolute subjectivity" (*CIT*, 99).

One powerful characteristic of the writers we are reading here is to have placed the question of subjectivity at the center of their work,[1] and to have thought to put it to the test. The expression "the test of subjectivity," as in Michel Henry,[2] and that resonates with Levinas's formulations as well,[3] signals not that Henry would return to subjectivity in order to "have" one or more tests, but that subjectivity is entirely a test and "is" nothing other than that.

1

Subjectivity in Contemporary
French Phenomenology

What of subjectivity resists—and perhaps even returns—in contemporary French phenomenology?

This is the question that must be asked in acknowledging that Levinas and Henry are philosophers of subjectivity; when we note, in a manner more ambiguous but in a way perhaps therefore all the more destabilizing, that Derrida's final texts deconstruct subjectivity only to let it remain haunted by "something" "irreducible" about it, in a gesture in which Derrida distances himself from Heidegger and comes closer to Levinas.

Thus, it seems, Heideggerian "destruction" (and certain of its avatars sometimes fertilized by "structuralism") had in a sense eradicated what could appear as the most massive Husserlian "transcendental naïveté": pure Ego.

Thus, Merleau-Ponty also oriented the phenomenological glance toward the world as being proto-ontic and, at the same time, pre-individual and pre-subjective, in a sense *anonymous*. This glance has such acuity that a family of contemporary French phenomenologists, chiefly Marc Richir and Jacques Garelli, can attempt with real phenomenological legitimacy to describe the originary in the form of the pre-individual and, even more radically, of the pre-subjective itself.

Emerging from this fracture in the current phenomenological field: the originary—all the more originary in that the idea of an imaginary is not deeply disrupted—understood as being in the same place as subjectivity, *or even better*, specifically not being subjectivity.

This, then, is the question: with regard to subjectivity, are we concerned with a return to a naïvely metaphysical motif or, on the contrary, with the recovery of a fertile disquiet with which we can never be finished?

The problematic of the subject

Engaging in philosophy means finding it both easy and frequently necessary to make use of the notion of the "subject," precisely to the degree to which it is difficult to speak about it, to make it the "object" of any discourse seen as philosophical.

This is well understood, but we must quickly remember why this is so, why the notion of the subject presents itself in the end as an "operational" rather than a "thematic" concept, to use Eugen Fink's terminology.

Paradoxically the subject, as the basis for all being, insofar as it is self-based (or at least as what represents everything insofar as it is represented), seems unascribable. This is a disconcerting claim—it stops one for a moment, and the subject appears as a constellation or a nebula of connected notions that can be partially recovered but that cannot coincide, that can be called this or that through their proximity but that are sometimes opposed to each other.

Yves Thierry says this very clearly:

The subject is, then, so to speak, not the situated person or consciousness to which the world appears or even the ego instituted within an irreducible separation from this constitution of the world; it is like a to-and-fro-ing among these three instances of which none is an isolated entity, and in which each one is the pole of one kind of relationality for which the other two cannot be substituted.[1]

The subject is a "to-and-fro-ing"—the hide-and-seek of modern philosophy!—capable of multiplying instances in which it can take refuge, and thus it no longer *is*: Me, I, consciousness, personhood, man, woman, subjectivity, self, individual, ipseity . . .

This is an astonishing diffraction of what, at least in its exemplary (Cartesian) form, is given as basal and thus as interiority, since in order to be such, it must establish itself—that is, at the very least to separate itself from the world. As a result, as the simplicity of the absolute (of what has no other cause than itself), I give myself to myself in the transparency of certitude, even if it is not an obvious one.

But clearly such obviousness, unquestionable in itself, will be able to appear as unquestioned given that we move from an attitude of credence to one of suspicion. The subject appears as a blind spot all vision prepares for yet that cannot be seen. Such are the surprises of all originarity and thus of a subject presenting itself as fundamental substance. In this sense it is obvious and unquestionable, since the evidence for it is imposed on sight. This is true for the same reason, according to this framework, that it can be perpetually hidden from sight at the very point at which one might suspect it to be an illusion. And these two phases, the obverse and reverse of the same problem in their radicality, lead to another: the subject is then even more exalted, even more humiliated, as Ricoeur says in the preface to *Oneself as Another*.[2] When one digs deeper, the serenity of a self-certain absolute crumbles in the face of these polar reversals.

And looking even closer, one might say that these phases of opposing excesses serve not only to stress the history of modern and contemporary philosophy but to disclose the tensions already inscribed in the notion of the subject, tensions that are the very object of concealment. Here we must remember that in Descartes' third *Metaphysical Meditation*,[3] the absoluteness of the cogito is relativized, since it finds inscribed at its heart the idea of the infinite confronting it in its own finitude, confronting it in its paradoxical situation as a "second-order absolute."

If this tension between finitude and infinity, between passivity and activity, singularity and universality did not exist, would the subject *be* the subject? Would not the best way to destroy the subject be to defuse this tension? One aspect of philosophy's history insistently suggests just this: it is initially in its exaltation that the subject can die, in being too full of itself. Thus, for Spinoza, for whom the discourse of infinite substance has unique and absolute value, and for whom the first-person formulation of the cogito no longer takes place, it must be said that "humans think" and that therefore the forming of the first person in Descartes signifies this tension between universality and singularity: if the universal in the Cartesian text says "I," then all "we" is required through it—though in the sense of "each one," not of just "anyone."

But to connect these internal tensions back to the notion of the subject basically manifesting it as both aporia and concern for its reconcealment would be a gesture trapped in ancient history, since the subject seems to have succumbed to these tensions, these specific wounds.

Finally, it is "structuralism" that must be charged with dealing it its last blows.

We must place "structuralism" in quotation marks because of the fact that there are many structuralism*s*. Nonetheless, among the common traits we could group into the same family is an effort to elevate the subject's mysterious prestige, an effort aimed not at any suppression but at laying out the conditions of its production, giving subjectivity the "surface effect" of structured systems, systems in which there always remains an "empty square," of "play" or of "difference," in order to allow them to be productive and to be transformed. The subject must be placed within the localized structure. Structure as such is anonymous: it does not have to be *self*-affecting nor to live *itself* as meaning in order to produce being and signification. The subject, as Deleuze says in "How Do We Recognize Structuralism?,"[4] is precisely the authority that *follows from* difference, from the empty place. This space must not be filled up: its emptiness authorizes circulation, and thus production, within the structure. And this is precisely the subject of modern metaphysics: the solid and "congealing" filling up that arrests the fertile difference within structure, internal difference that arises to extend beyond itself and to "fill" in, finally to claim that it is itself origin when in fact it is "surface effect."

In "structuralism," then, the subject is less suppressed than fragmented, atomized: always nomadic, moving from place to place; individuation, but pre-personal, according to Deleuze (GDH, 190), which might be translated as "singularized event"—but one that cannot as such be tested as a Self, an ego.

The subject is not suppressed in the sense in which it would be caricatural to say that structuralism does take the subject into account, in order to expel it. The subject is, however, suppressed *as such*, since it no longer has any claim to be foundational, and since it is simultaneously "objectivity" laid out for the glance, to be captured in the "play" of structures (even if it should be seen as the uncapturable nomad).

This is, in broad strokes, a sketch of the problematic horizon of the notion of subject.

The subject in phenomenology

Phenomenology has participated and continues to participate in this "work" on the subject, on exaltation, humiliation, deadliness, and—why not?—resurrection. This participation—this at least is the hypothesis being explored here—can teach us a great deal, as much about the nature of phenomenology as about that of subjectivity. Phenomenology is one of the protagonists of this debate on the subject, all the more so in that it "redoubles" the subject within itself, inscribes it within itself. We can identify certain symptoms of this.

As Deleuze declares in the opening pages of *Nietzsche and Philosophy*, Husserlian phenomenology can seem to be a refuge that in the strictest sense is "reactionary" for the connected figures of the subject and consciousness. And more than the thematics of pure Ego and pure consciousness, this is the reductive gesture of a return to the origin that gives rise to these themes and directs them. (Deleuze, however, is able to say much more complicated things about phenomenology!) Inversely, Michel Henry denounces the structuralist model of many recent decades, at the beginning of his *Material Phenomenology*, debates that critique phenomenology as "a matter of allowing for recognition of the very essence of philosophy," as the most profound research (i.e., research leading it toward life as subjectivity). Jean-Toussaint Desanti, on the other hand, tries to bring structuralism and phenomenological methodology together.

Phenomenology is thus attacked as a refuge for the traditional metaphysical subject, contrary to its claim to being the place in which subjectivity might clearly be revealed to itself (as in Henry), or even as a place for engaging in the "destruction" of the subject. Phenomenology does not allow the subject to remain intact, and the subject does not allow phenomenology to remain indifferent, with regard to itself most of all.

Since Husserl, phenomenology has seen its fundamental existence—and these things must be said very allusively in this introductory form, describing what appears *as* it appears—as dedicated to the central task of destroying the subject, in the sense of traditional metaphysics (that of

Descartes). Indeed, the subject as solid, static substance is seen in it as what most powerfully occludes the field of appearance. If the constituted object obliterates the "how" of its appearance, the substance-subject constructs it even more fundamentally, as ignorance of the constitutive movement of appearance with regard to itself: the constructed world, through a process of projection, occludes not only the given as given but also the very process of its givenness, its constitutive movement. Intentionality—since that is what is in play here—is the breaking up of the static substance of the Cartesian subject, denounced as a mere retroactive and retrospective "projection" of the worldly real onto its source. Yet if the "first Husserl," of the *Logical Investigations*, refuses to connect the flux of consciousness with an ego that is precisely denounced as a derivative, worldly agency, the Husserlian text still sees emerging there, at its core, this "marvel of marvels," the pure Ego: Husserl sees in it a dynamic tension (to which we will return); for the moment we must read it as a dynamic tension rather than defuse it, dissolving it in chronology and thus in the evolution of Husserlian thought.[5]

That said, the dynamic movement of desubstantialization, as is now widely accepted, is accentuated by Heidegger: *Dasein*, as being, can be "itself" only outside of itself, as pure projection. Consequently, as Gérard Granel says in "Lacan and Heidegger," "*Dasein* thus does not indicate *what* we are but *that* we are, and without '*quid*': that we are not *nothing*, and consequently that there is nothing more to know."[6] *Dasein* "is" the very destruction of the subject as ground and as presence-to-itself. If it thus no longer contains anything in its paradoxical, ecstatic mode of being—if it is henceforth to be seen as perspectival aporia—*Dasein* can only be understood within the context, the "circuit" or circulation, of Being, which is itself never living being.

Whatever may be the case with its differing modalities, the fundamental task of phenomenology—to liberate appearance as such—is necessarily linked to the destruction of the subject. How, then, can this effort be tied to structuralism? This is Desanti's goal, for example, when he reinterprets doubled (Husserlian) intentionality in terms of a circuit of opening (which is not without its evocation of Heidegger's association of *Dasein* with Being): this is a gesture that appears as a requirement of the formalizing of these motifs as bequeathed by Husserl and Heidegger. This formalization underpins the phenomenological need for the "destruction" of the substantialist metaphysic and thus of its most articulate expression, the subject—that is, subject as then called to the place of its production within the structure.

Yet the Ego "reemerges" in "Husserl," and even triumphs there.

Does this mean that Husserl does not go far enough, or even that at a particular moment (that of the idealist turn) he betrays and misleads himself, as certain of his disciples have claimed? Or is it to say that he only pretends to dismiss the *in*authentic figure of the subject in order to reveal the authentic one? And if the latter is the case, why still name the "it" thus revealed the "subject"?

The response to these questions depends on the response to another one: is our choice only between lamentation over the Husserlian "repercussions" in and for traditional metaphysics, on the one hand, and, on the other (and inversely), applause at the resurrection of the metaphysical Ego, in itself, "unchanged" and even more resplendent than ever? Or is a subjectivity without the resurrecting of the Ego another possibility on which one might focus? This is a possibility that in certain respects reflects Husserl's increasing need for egological subjectivity, though it would still be entirely open to reproach as the reinstauration of a transcendental Ego.

At this point, in order to better understand the question of subjectivity in our central figures, we might focus on the state of this question in Husserl, since all three, to varying degrees, take positions relative to this heritage.[7]

Husserl's *Logical Investigations* does not test out the need to refer the conscious, lived experience of an Ego that has been denounced as strictly worldly. Why is this so?

The notion of intentionality itself, since it is in a sense pure "emergence from self," seems to imply a liberation from all prior mastery.

However, even if it is an "exploding out," Husserlian intentionality cannot be without links back to itself, lest it run the risk of being dissolved in the pure multiplicity of what cannot be "assembled," what collapses and thus cannot be said.

Moreover, the intentionality that appears gives form in the sense that it forms itself: there is—there must be—a *sequence* of conscious lived experiences, a *form* of the flux of consciousness.

But then what *Logical Investigations* requires, to take up the formula Deleuze borrows from Bergson,[8] consists of thinking "the multiple without the one." Husserl follows this course in *Philosophy of Arithmetic*, and then in the first of the *Logical Investigations*, principally in the definition of multiplicity as "a domain uniquely determined by the fact that it is subjected to a theory of form [*donnée*]" (*LI1*, 274). Dastur cites this passage, making the following comment on it: a multiplicity is "a domain of objects defined uniquely by their established relations within a formal system, a domain to which we have access only through the formal system in question."[9] A common example of this is figural unities: we talk about a *column of soldiers*, sensing here something like a "structuralist accent" before the term existed.

In a sense, Husserl "applies" this conception of "multiplicity" to consciousness.

What is important to understand here is that multiplicity, insofar as it is multiplicity, is always a unity: there is no need to conjoin it, to frame it, or to constitute it as a figure of the One; it is always already united and thus has no need of being united (see DL, 74). The significance of this is that there is no need to inscribe it as a subject, to enclose it in a subject, to connect it to the form of a subject nor to a subject as center. Unity is here immanent to a consciousness that is itself constructed from this same consciousness: there is no need to associate it with a mysterious weaver who would be its origin, the instauration of mastery and, finally, its end. No need to return it to a mysterious home that, paradoxically, would make it simultaneously center and closure by keeping it outside of itself because prior to itself; that is, despite and through that very strategy, more profound, deeper than itself.

There is no subject—no Ego—because there is no agency of rising above, of extending beyond conscious lived experience that would connect them one to another. The lived experiences of consciousness are not my own to be reconnected to a "third" that preexists them as an immutable center: I am in each instance ego, Me, in each of those experiences; my ego is only that: the faculty of being connected to conscious lived experiences at any given moment (which is ceaselessly changing).

And yet Husserl introduces an Ego that is, so to speak, triumphant, in *Ideas I*. What is happening here?

What is taking place is a way of dissociating from the judgment long dominant in phenomenology through which Husserl is misled: after *Logical Investigations* he asks himself if there is not a shadow of the Ego, despite everything already in intentional consciousness—if the Ego is not already "there."

This hypothesis—paradoxical but significant and coherent—was formulated not by phenomenologists who were already in thrall to the Ego but, on the contrary, by a Jan Patočka[10] and a Jean-Toussaint Desanti.[11] Both of them, attempting to think an asubjective—or, at the very least, a non-egological—phenomenology (which does not mean *without* a subject, but where the subject is assigned to a locality and is always constituted), do not avoid the difficulty. They set out to measure the implantation of the theme of the Ego in Husserlianism, to measure the solidity of the link between egological subjectivity and Ek-static intentionality. But from the outset they cannot avoid the difficulty in diagnosing a return to traditional metaphysics: if Husserl comes back to the Ego, is he not then constrained by that very choice?

Let us spend a moment with Patočka's comments. He locates "Le subjectivisme de la phénoménologie husserlienne à l'état naissant [The Subjectivism of Husserlian Phenomenology in Its Nascent State]" in the *Logical Investigations V* and *VI*, writing that "the non-intuitive, the mode of the 'improper,' 'deficient,' givenness, figure here as indications of the subjective" (*QP*, 203). What does Patočka have in mind?

In order for what is given in a non-intuitive manner—for example, "the thing" when I experience it as a name naming it, or "worse," as graphic sign—to thus be given (despite everything) even with its deficit of presence, this deficiency must be compensated for *elsewhere*: notwithstanding the lack of presence in the "object," the signifying object is given to me because *I* give it to myself; this presupposes that primordially, originarily, I give myself to myself. The non-originary nature of the given is captured and maintained by the certainty the gift—or the "what gives"—has in itself: like a pure sphere of immanence with no gaps relative to itself—that is, a pure presence to self, a pure certainty of self. "*I*" is the name imposed when naming the necessary here: all givenness implies *the pure immanence* of a presence (to self) that underlies and endures it. And this immanence is subjectivity, since it asserts that a presence is truly and plainly that only in order to be presence *to* self in a self-mastery through which it gives itself to itself in apodictic clarity. The Ego is thus born through the very movement of giving, to use a Cartesian figure, as substance—or at the very least, presence—that is truly substance only in order to be certainty of self.

In other words, there must be a *reserve of presence*—that is, truly presence only as subjectivity—to endure intentional Ek-stasy, the gathering of presence to itself where all things are given. "Transcendence in immanence": the famous Husserlian schema articulates itself exemplarily and fundamentally as transcendence of appearance in the immanence of subjectivity.

What is thus revealed as intolerable is the idea of a plane of immanence weaving itself with nothing that could serve as a center, a closure, or an instance of transcendence; and further—it can never be overstated—it is givenness, the confrontation with the "how" of the appearing of all things, revealing the necessity of an Ego. This view is confirmed by Rudolf Bernet when he explains in *The Life of the Subject*[12] that the manuscripts of Group C consecrated to temporality in fact speak much more to subjectivity than to time, since the Ego appears essentially as having the function of conjuring up the gap as fundamental and temporal, and that burrows the lived experience of consciousness into the memory or imagination such that what escapes me is *not* what is properly given to me as such (neither the "imagined" nor the "remembered")—it is myself: I have the experience of a "depreciation" (of self). The Ego's *function* of reestablishing the continuity of myself with myself is put in danger by these specific givens of memory and imagination.[13] It is within this contact, this connection of self with itself, that the *I* arises, as a Me in the strong sense, an Ego.

The enigma of givenness thus in some respect constitutes the Ego as the point of immanence that must always endure it, close it off, in order to allow it to be.[14]

This, then, denotes the ambiguity in the Husserlian Ego that is widely exploited by the phenomenologists we are focusing on here: a necessary originary, it appears in the end to be less a grounding and a sovereign power than one already betraying its own weakness: it is what ceaselessly *re*tains and *re*centers. And is not making this claim the same thing as suggesting that what is *prior* is the very gap itself that must be reduced? If so, is there not already in the Husserlian Ego something like the passivity of endurance?

Let us review briefly.

There is thus an alternative for the post-Husserlian phenomenology whose source is the evolution of Husserl's position regarding the Ego; that is, primarily in the difficulty of holding together the two Husserlian requirements through which we have begun to work ("to free the intentionality" of the Ego, on the one hand, and on the other, to posit givenness and to assure its durability precisely where it seems to be in danger, thanks to the Ego).

In the deepening of this alternative—of which each side is a figure of retreat before what is essential to the other—in its "digging down," what is played out is, it seems, more than "the destiny of subjectivity for phenomenology," the destiny—or at least something important to this destiny—as much of phenomenology as of subjectivity, in an encounter that is as decisive for the one as for the other.

Let us explore briefly the two directions taken by this bifurcation.

On one side, the effort is increasingly to expropriate—"ex-appropriate"—the subject from itself; this involves possibly radicalizing, so to speak, the Heideggerian *Dasein*, a task that thus implies, if this nothing of beings (and even this nothing of being) is still "expressible," pulling it back to a horizon that is "older" than itself (this is Being for Heidegger, The World for Merleau-Ponty), and even to "melt" it into this horizon, redirecting it as if toward its authenticity. In fact, from this perspective, it is being a self (individuated, reflective, or simply "ipseized") that is inauthentic:[15] ipseity perpetually *solidified* risks obliterating that older movement (of Being, of World), even when it is nonetheless produced by it. Ipseity for Merleau-Ponty, for example, is a parasite on being that must never be retained but return there. Anonymity is the truth of the Ego.

The I is nothing if it is a pure event (and as such always expropriated from itself) in Being (or The World). "I, truly, that is no one, that is the anonymous," writes Merleau-Ponty in a work note from April 1960.[16] And further: "Is it what thinks, reasons, speaks, debates, suffers, plays, etc.? Obviously not, since it is *nothing*" (*VI*, 299). Clearly, this Heideggerian/Merleau-Pontian line has managed to tie itself to certain representations in "structuralism" (even if others, like Garelli, have always opposed the need for a "moving" originary, within a structuralism always suspected of being positivist, installed within the given and consequently horribly "mechanical").

Yet in contemporary French phenomenology there is an entirely different family—the one we are analyzing here—redirecting us toward subjectivity as originary.

This family includes Michel Henry and Emmanuel Levinas, though Jean-Luc Marion could also be added, at least from this point of view. Rather surprisingly, from the perspective of the subjectivity question we can also invite Jacques Derrida in. Or rather, we might see Derrida as "family-less" in contemporary French philosophy, in the sense that Derrida is never "at home"—and never where he is expected. In his later texts he seems to distance himself from clear links to structuralism (without, what is more, even having properly "spoken structuralist"), on the one hand, and from what could link him to Heidegger (again without his ever having properly spoken Heideggerian), on the other. It is not just that he stopped laying out Western philosophy's dream of pure presence and the dreamer of this dream, the subject, as the figure fullest of pure presence and thus as the most complete phantasm, but that in a movement that seems to veer away from Heidegger toward Levinas, Derrida wants to work at the very *limit* such that in this limit-work (of the philosophical and of presence) it is "always with self that one meets" (DA, 116–17).

That said, just what is it that characterizes this family (Henry, Levinas, Marion) and its guest (a somewhat *différant* Derrida)?

Would Henry, Levinas, and Marion restore the Cartesian subject? Certainly not! Would they, like Husserl according to Heidegger, reintroduce elsewhere and in another form what they would destroy at a certain level (the cogito)? Certainly not!

At least as much as the members of the Heideggerian/Merleau-Pontian family, they deconstruct transcendental egology, finding support in Husserl, from the elements destabilizing this transcendental egology.

We must remember that both the motivation and the principle of the critique of subjectivity are identical and require the same radicality in the Heideggerian/Merleau-Pontian family and that on which we have focused. However, in the latter family there is perhaps not simply a *return* of subjectivity, if we mean by "return" the simple repetition of an unchanged metaphysical motif, but rather a *new birth* of subjectivity: a new subjectivity invented not in that these thinkers invent something that *was not*, but in that they make us see what we have not previously seen, what was perhaps obliterated by the modern subject although (despite everything) surviving within it.

This subjectivity no longer contains anything of the conscious *Ur-region*'s absoluteness, nor of the constitutive powers of the transcendental Ego. As much as Merleau-Pontians and Heideggerians they destroy the transcendental subject, but from a "resistive" subjectivity that is nothing other than a fragment of itself, a subjectivity that is not a constitutive power, an originary that is no longer supported by a base (which, if we examine it a bit more closely, was not, moreover, already the case for Husserl, since for him the origin is "complicated" by an ego that is without beginning and perpetually generating itself), a subjectivity that is no longer only a pure *test*, not even an *experience* since experience still implies an activity of the *I* through which what affects me begins and is reconstructed. Consequently, since it is not even "my own" experience, this test is all the more not "my test" but "me as a test." This me, this ego, that in its passivity is no longer really a me but merely a self, is designated as "self riveted to itself," an expression one finds as extensively in Levinas as in Henry.[17] Irreducible, hardly Husserlian, since it is its pure passivity—in a sense its poverty—that makes it less a profuse source (as are, each in its own way, Husserlian living-present and Heideggerian Being) than the ground that must be maintained, and that can be maintained only through being assigned to its specific place: a specific starting point must be assigned to it.[18]

And what if subjectivity were only that, a powerless destitution that thus can do more than all previous powers, and that thus can only— ceaselessly, through its disasters—be reborn?[19]

If we do invite Derrida—if he invites himself—into this problematic, it would be through the question of the gift,[20] through which he has moved increasingly toward Levinas: the Other "faces" me. The problematic takes up this "face-to-face"—paradoxical both since it is the very distancing of *all* confrontation, and since it is dissymmetrical—as primary. It can be addressed, in this context, only from the viewpoint of an anonymity or an intersubjectivity preceding and enveloping the Other *and* the

Ego, thus allowing philosophical discourse to be deployed as an extension *beyond*, from an ipseic point of view. The self—no longer independent, but a Self—is given to itself, assembled and caused, by the other. It knows only one case: the vocative. It is caught in an irreducible retardation onto the Other that as a result, paradoxically but as a consequence, makes it *absolutely primary in its solitude*, trapped and driven back into the solitude of existence:[21] an originary ipseity. Derrida certainly does not here simply repeat Levinas: specifically, he insists that the Other "as such" is impossible, that the gift "as such" is impossible. This impossibility ceaselessly *returns* as its own phantom.

In a manner close to Levinas's but already different (more different even than from Marion and, in a sense, opposed to Henry[22]), Derrida also, like the others, thinks a subjectivity with which one can never be finished: as a pure weakness deriving its force from its poverty.

If *this* conception of subjectivity is born in *this* phenomenology, it is not by chance. The test of subjectivity occurs through the common phenomenological style in which this family first appears to us: as practice of phenomenological method carrying it to its limits, and that, wanting to go to the very end of its radicality, risks (again paradoxically) the destruction of its proper constraints. In short, it is an *excessive* practice of the method we recognize by its specificity—in contrast to the Merleau-Pontian method that also scans the limits but as so many zones of encroachment of the visible onto the invisible, focusing not on the violence of a rupture or cut but on the lability of an unknowable profundity.

And this violent and excessive methodological practice is like an attempt to go against the grain by imitating the movement of a phenomenological givenness that is itself violent and excessive—traumatizing, as Levinas would say. And yet, does this traumatism not claim that only a subjectivity as pure originary passivity can put it to the test? If there is traumatism, does that not imply, in the same gesture, an entity susceptible to being affected by it, an entity as such born, "ipseized," by testing it?

Excess brings about the self that endures it. Excess, first in its manner, gives being the test that proves it; the test that as such is always first of all a test of itself. In very different guises, a movement of tense rigidity going to the very limit of rupture is "deployed" in Levinas, Henry, Marion, and Derrida.

In addition, one way of understanding what is at stake here would be to mark the contrast with Merleau-Ponty. Through the flexibility of the winding together of the visible and invisible, the Merleau-Pontian self can be dissolved in(to) the World in order to reemerge from it (significantly, it *emerged* from it), always, though hardly at all *and* already more. The self "steals into" the World. Thus, World is originary and not the self.

Thus, I have juxtaposed Levinas, Henry, Marion, and, in his own way, Derrida, in order to deepen the study of this underlying ascription of self's necessity. And if my claim regarding these thinkers is correct, it implies simultaneously moving to the very place of traumatism in which the Self is born.[23]

2

The Birth of Subjectivity in Levinas

Why is subjectivity originary in Levinas?

Many aspects of Levinas's philosophy would seem to render this subjective originarity improbable if not impossible. First, because the very notion of originarity to be found there is reworked and put into crisis, all beginning and all grounding origin crumbling into anarchy. Yet paradoxically, concern for originarity is not only redirected but radicalized through a gesture that explodes all foundation: hyperbole does not cancel reduction as re*ducere* but, on the contrary, exaggerates it, and for this very reason deprives it of any evidentiary basis, any grounding in which it can come to rest. And then because if it is in fact necessary to find an originary in Levinasian philosophy, is it not the Other that must come to occupy this place? Is it not the Other that gives me to being?

Finally, because anyone wanting to argue the conciliatory hypothesis of the co-originarity of other and self would be forced to recall that between other and self a temporal gap is in play. Through such a co-originarity it would thus be necessary to understand all *other* things as a simultaneity and/or a symmetry.

And yet in quite different ways, from *On Escape* to *Otherwise Than Being* via *Existence and Existents* and *Totality and Infinity*, subjectivity never stops being a central theme for Levinas: a decisive role is reserved for it, and in an originary place where the connections of being to what being is *not* come together.

How to understand what it is that requires the originarity of subjectivity, if not by following the steps of its invention in Levinas?

This means that to follow Levinas's steps is to discover a *mise en abyme*: the path by which Levinasian philosophy invents the notion of subjectivity consists precisely of describing the very movement of the birth of subjectivity. At the very place of originarity, legitimacy cannot be a redirection toward some antecedent entity: it maintains itself entirely in its *birth*.

One way to understand what is at play at the point of birth for Levinas is to mark its contrast with Heidegger's position on the birth question.

In a sense, Levinas *inverts* Heidegger, first in that as Claude Romano shows,[1] Heidegger entirely omits the analytic of birth in *Being and Time*. The fact that he omits what Levinas insists on is significant: if *Dasein* is "being-for-death," Levinasian subjectivity would then be—though Levinas never states the formulation explicitly—"being-for-birth." And this difference of understanding regarding the birth phenomenon is interdependent with the inversion of status of the notion of *death* at play between Heidegger and Levinas: death is "the possibility of my impossibility" for Heidegger,[2] while it is "smothering in the impossibility of the possible" for Levinas (*TI*, 27). If, as Levinas says, the meaning and the ipseity of an existent are decisive in its birth and not in its "for-death," then birth is stronger than death, and then "it [life between birth and death] unfolds in its own dimension, where it has a meaning and where a triumph over death can have meaning."[3]

We should take a moment to gauge the contrast between Heidegger and Levinas on this birth question.

As is well known, in the anguish of death *Dasein* recoils before the nothing, a nothing that thus reveals Being to it. As being-for-death, *Dasein* grasps itself as existence proceeding toward death: its being as pure possibility is revealed to it as such, precisely and paradoxically, in proceeding toward the end of all possibility. In fact, death thus shows that it *is not* in any of its ontic realizations, taken one by one; fear of death revealing being to it as nothing, and simultaneously as its authentic being as Ek-static; it *ipseizes Dasein* in the paradoxical mode of "outside-of-self."

For Levinas, on the contrary, if the meaning and ipseity of subjectivity seem to be decided through birth, then for him dying is a difficult thing.

A formulation such as this requires some explication. It does not mean that Levinas along with many others repeats that death is merely difficult, nor that it is a reminder of the tendency to flee from the authenticity of dying. Certainly he does not deny death in favor of an absolutized life. Levinas describes the difficulty of *truly* dying. He is, in fact, a thinker of finitude, if it exists, situating finitude elsewhere than in mortality.

Why such suspicion regarding this paradoxical experience—that is nonetheless absolutely obvious—of death?

Because in a sense there is something even worse than death, something that obliterates death *and* birth—since truly to die one must be born, and inversely. *Worse* than death is the impossibility of death that is also the incapability of death. Incapable of death because incapable of birth: this is the *spectre* Levinas profiles. This modality of existence, which Levinas explicitly opposes to the anguish of nothingness and/or of death in Heidegger, he calls "the horror of being" and/or "the horror of the being": this marks out the incapacity to escape from being, and first of all from the event of being. His philosophical emblem is the spectre, the living-dead, frequently evoked in his reading of Shakespeare or, as here, of Poe:

The horror of being interred alive, the persistent suspicion that dead is not dead enough, that in death one *is*, appears as the fundamental emotion of Edgar Allan Poe. . . . The character finds himself enclosed in a tomb, destroyed; but in this destruction, trapped in existence, a situation the character transposes in death itself, as if to die was still *to be* at the heart of nothingness.[4]

What is at stake in this opposition between Heideggerian anguish regarding nothingness and Levinasian horror of being? For Heidegger, it is this nothing watching over us, and its test that distresses us, that as a result reveals the authenticity and the ipseity of *Dasein*. The horror of Levinasian being, just as much a test—in the strictest sense of the word—does not have the positive virtue of authenticity and ipseization; on the contrary, it means risking dissolution in "the impersonal anonymity of being." This inversion from Heidegger to Levinas is perfect: being responds to nothingness, less inauthenticity responding to authenticity (of a nothingness that produces being) than the dissolution of what is *truly not* (that is, of what is not ipseized) *being too much held* within the brute fact of existing, and finally, the risk of anonymity responds to ipseity.

And what does this Levinasian inversion allow him to think?

It allows him to direct his attention toward being, to turn away from nothingness. But does his analysis of the horror of being make Levinas, as opposed to Heidegger, a thinker of nothingness? On the contrary, the horror of being, as we have already seen, is horror at being, in that it actually signifies the difficulty of escaping being, for example, in showing that the nothing promising us death (Heidegger's nothingness) is not radical, is released *once again* from being: death is not dead enough. Levinas does not envisage a being without an effective nothingness (like Bergson, for example), on the contrary, showing that Heideggerian nothingness released once again from being is a task orienting it toward an understanding that wants to be a more radical nothing: a nothing freed from being itself, not "deduced from" being or "in view of" it.[5] That is, a nothingness not ensconced in being, not toward or as a counterpart of being, but a nothingness *beyond* being[6] with no intrinsic connection to it, in the sense that it is neither simply the mere nothing of being nor even a nothing of being per se, but an Otherwise than being: this radical nothingness not explicitly named by Levinas in his early texts, those concerned with analyzing the horror of being and thus negatively discerning its various contours, will subsequently be named the Other, Transcendence, or Infinity, and the trauma it inflicts will be on the side of birth, not death.

Chronologically, Levinas undertakes the analysis of the horror of being in those first texts, though they do not yet evoke the semantic network of the Other; this network will subsequently tend to move increasingly into the foreground—without canceling those first analyses but being supported by them—and to culminate in the Otherwise than being.

We can account for this trajectory by stating that it follows the very movement deployed at the limit of being, a movement in which connections between existence (the raw fact of existing), existing (ipseity), and Otherwise than being.

In order accurately to describe the connection between us and the Otherwise than being, it is necessary preliminarily to have completed an initial task: we must describe the escape—the birth—of subjectivity out of being.[7]

In fact, if there is such a thing as "the horror of being," it is because Levinas describes being as an anonymous, impersonal event, a pure veil of undetermined existence: in order truly to be, one must necessarily be torn out of being, evading it. This is a matter, in being born, of being determined, of being "carved out" as an individuated being: I emerge to personalize myself on the preliminary horizon of being that Levinas names the *il y a*, the "there is." The *il y a* is a "bad" being, or rather a "bad" nothingness, since it is neither radical being nor radical nothingness: it is the night of spectres, of the living-dead. To be, truly, is to be Self, as individuated being, and more precisely as a *self*-individuating being—ipseized being. And this ipseization takes place in birth as emergence to the *il y a*.

So, truly to be is to be a Self: to have a beginning and thus an end. Spectres do not know how to, and cannot, die since in a sense they are not born but rather are dedicated to the indetermination of raw existence in the *il y a*. They haunt us, because they are implacably "from" being, all the more implacably in that they are without contour, without determination, and thus ungraspable. They are incapable of escaping from being and thus ceaselessly return: they must have had a beginning in order to have an end. In other words, in order truly to be is to be a Self, and to be a Self is to be an *interiority*, to be separate from the world. Levinas describes this, borrowing an expression from Jules Romain, as the ability to "make tracks for the interior" (*EE*, 116). To be an interiority is to be born and thus to die: beyond the truism according to which only what has chronologically begun can finish, it is necessary to grasp the significance of separation and thus of absolute immanence, both as events of birth and death. Birth has a dignity superior to that of death for Levinas because if death can attest that I am (that I was) an interiority, this does not decide anything: what is decisive is to be born. Birth is in this sense the condition of possibility for death, insofar as it is truly death and not a simple return to the indetermination of being, not that half-death that produces spectres. Thus, *my* death, as radical event, will testify that my life will have been *my* life: the fact that I will die one day protects me, "waiting," from death as dissolution—and what is more, it attests that in the meantime I was an absolute interiority as such, an interiority on which, as interiority, no worldly event took place; an interiority that as such does not allow itself to be integrated into the world. My death (as an event that puts an end to my interiority and thus completes it as such) retrospectively *witnesses* that in the meantime I have triumphed over death (as dissolution in the *il y a*).

We should note in passing that in presenting itself as a phenomenology of birth, Levinasian phenomenology does not propose any less of an elucidation of the limit phenomenon of death, rendering itself capable of giving an account of the rigorous methodology of its frameworks (never distinguishing, it is true, as explicitly as I have done here, between death as dissolution in the *il y a*—spectral half-death—and death as paradoxical certification of the absoluteness of interiority), even if it is in relieving it of the ontological dignity Heidegger ascribes to it.

Let us press this further.

It is easy to see why birth has such decisive importance for Levinas. To be born is to escape the *il y a*. Why is it necessary to escape the event of being as anonymous? Because for Levinas true being is ipseized being, is being itself: the plenitude of being and ipseity are originarily "reciprocal."

That said, two problems (at least!) remain.

1. Could it not be said, against the case being made here, that the non-foundational originary Levinas envisions is not in fact subjectivity but the anonymous *il y a*, next to which subjectivity would be secondary since it emerges by escaping from it?

2. What is the Transcendence, the Other, the Infinite, whatever its name might be here, in the process by which the existent contracts the existence—is born—that I am describing? Must not that "originary" title, however, return to it in the end—and was it not anarchic? Is it enough to say that it is *first* necessary to contract existence in order *then* to encounter the Other, in an order that, if it is not reduced to mundane chronology or to an equally mundane mechanical causality, does not any the less imitate their simplicity, and that would agree with the chronological order of Levinas's works?[8]

Let us begin by confronting the first of this difficulties; an examination of the second will naturally unfold from a treatment of the first.

If the *il y a* was the originary, then the mechanism by which subjectivity is connected to being would hardly be different from what, for example, Merleau-Ponty describes in his late works: individualities that start out in the world (or being) emerge from it and never cease to communicate with this anonymous ground, as no more than its parasites. Only the coefficient of ontological axiology affecting various different terms of the mechanism would be inverted: if for Levinas ipseity is given a positive connotation and anonymity a negative one, for Merleau-Ponty—though we cannot say that he is the exact opposite, since individuality is no more depreciated for him than is anonymity for Levinas—it remains that individuality finds its authenticity only in being able to rejoin the anonymity of the world until it melts into it, and all the more in that it was never radically cut off from it, never escaped from this anonymity that will always, through that connection, have the surplus dignity of a source, an origin.

But precisely if ipseity wins out over the *il y a*, then the *il y a* is not its origin, in the sense of a matrix: it provides nothing (and above all not *the* nothing). The Levinasian *il y a* is not Heideggerian nothingness that produces being and, thereby, beings; is not the Husserlian living-present that brings forth all being and all sense of being; is not the Merleau-Pontian world that in the depths of its interlacings produces all ipseity: it is sterility itself. And yet it is true that without the *il y a* there would be nothing. Subjectivity, like interiority, must be conquered *against* the *il y a*, this *il y a* that does not possess the fruitfulness of an original source but rather is significantly described by Levinas as a threatening night (threatening to dissolve all identity): I am not born from the *il y a*, as for Merleau-Ponty; I am born in a chiasm of the world, *against* the *il y a*. In this sense, one gives birth to oneself: it is always the self that must be brought forth—that only *I* can bring forth. If dissolution in being is ceaselessly threatening, is in some sense antecedent, it is only meaningful for a self, only emergent from a self: subjectivity as nothing other than an assignation to self is irreducibly originary. This originarity, paradoxically, is nonetheless all the more constraining: Self is riveted to itself, existing only in the movement riveting it to itself.

The paradox of this originarity is all the more original in that it is irreducibly preceded by and caught in an originary delay that Jean-Luc Marion describes thus: "Without any doubt, another possibility remains: that the *I* sees itself as non-originary and derivative, in such fashion, however, that the status 'derivative' itself becomes as though absolutely originary" (*RG*, 1).

This other possibility that Marion places in opposition to the metaphysics of the triumphant subject, and to the sterile aporias in which it cannot help sinking, but that does not consist—in the face of the declaration of the bankruptcy of the metaphysical subject—of a dismissal of the totality of all subjectivity, on the contrary, is the very one that since his first work, *On Escape*, Levinas never stopped exploring.

Levinasian subjectivity is reverberations, an echo chamber—nothing but an echo—of that to which it concedes an originary delay, one that assigns it all the more to the originarity of its *position* as to a point of view that is, as such, finite: it is intrinsically a being of birth. And that is not without forcing the content of this subjectivity into a complex "process" whose principal moments are the following:

1. I am born in order to escape from the *il y a*.

2. I am not a pure, transcendent movement, a pure escape from self, a pure consciousness in the Sartrean sense, but on the contrary, I am driven back to myself. We cannot radically escape the *il y a*. Moreover, it might be possible that to do so would not be desirable: in fact, the *il y a* lends me being. And if I rescue it in terms of its spectrality, I would be nothing without it: in some respect it is the primal matter of subjectivity that tears away even while carrying with it, or more exactly as being nothing other than it, a scrap of the *il y a* that will be, so to speak, concentrated in subjectivity. I am a true self in breaking away from the *il y a*; that is, also in determining it and thus making it denser: in this movement, I am born as a point of pure immanence—the early Levinas would say a hypostasis, a "self riveted to itself."

The notion of the *double bind* in its Derridean sense seems once again to describe in the most rigorous way possible the process by which the pure exigency of departing from being and the impossibility of so doing are held together. This is a matter of departing from being as *il y a* and, in the same movement, entering into the self as "truly being." This departure is thus in a sense a false one, since it must have made a contract with existence: to have signed a contract with it, as Levinas says in

Existence and Existents. And at base, beyond the juridical sense of this expression, we should understand it to mean that it is necessary "to be reached" by existence, and further that it must be subjected to a movement of "contraction."

Subjectivity is nothing but a hyperbolic, endlessly restarting process in which the escapee's transcendence is already reversed in the immanence of hypostasis, and inversely, and so on, "reversals" and ambiguity that are not the symptom of deterioration and lability but of the reversal of "for and against" provoked by the violence of the hyperbole that pushes a moment of subjectivity to the point at which, strictly speaking, it is no longer tenable, carrying subjectivity to the limit of a schizophrenic effect precisely, however, where it connects with itself. This is the process that the early Levinas calls the "dialectic of the instant." This idea of dialectic must be understood to contain the will to identify a movement at the very core of the givenness of hypostasis, even though the proper word for it is (still) lacking. But as we must understand, this movement is not dialectical in the Hegelian sense: if movement exists, it is not the deployment of logic in its execution; if negativity exists, it is not domesticated as the engine of the deployment of the rational.[9]

We can see an exemplary presentation of this hyperbolized reversal in Levinas's study of limit-phenomena, as related to that of birth and interlaced with it via dream sequence, insomnia, and awakening.

And in a surprising way it is initially the dream, or more precisely the very possibility of sleeping, that Levinas connotes positively as a symptom, even as a condition of ipseity.

Indeed, to be a self, to be born as Self, is to possess the possibility of escaping to the insomniac's obsession, since insomnia is a way of being threatened by the *il y a* if it consists of this hyperlucidity in which the silhouette of individuated beings is stamped onto the obsession of a pure presence.[10] Consequently, the ego/self surges up, so to speak, in the very possibility of "making tracks for the interior"—of sleeping. To sleep is to be a Self, an interiority, within the possibility of withdrawing into the self. And to be a self *already* presupposes a separation of self from self, to be withdrawn. Ek-stasis returns to itself in the immanence of interiority, and the immanence of hypostasis is already carved out of the gap in the self, in order to *be* self.

But this sequence of cascading reversals is itself always already completely inverted.

Interiority is already no longer dream but immanence as mastery of self, as wakefulness—what modern metaphysics calls a consciousness. (In a complex movement, the dream is not in a simple opposition to wakefulness, to the vigilance of consciousness, but rather makes it possible.) As a result, insomnia as connection to the *il y a* sees its signification reversed: in the later Levinas it takes on the positive function of awakening the consciousness that is drunk on itself, drunk with its powers.[11] It is what sobers up the Ego from its consciousness—on this point one must concede being sufficiently of the other or the nothing to play this role!—even when consciousness deprived the Self of its fascination with the night of the *il y a* in which it risked being lost in anonymity.

Within the vertiginous play of these reversals, in order to recognize oneself, there it is tempting to remark for early Levinas insomnia is negatively defined as a threat to the *il y a*, and for later Levinas it takes on the sense of a true alteration of the consciousness it then praises. An ontological order is thus revealed, even if it is only gnoseological; but in any case—and this is essential—it is an order of which the chronological history of Levinas's writings is the manifestation.

From the viewpoint of subjectivity, this separation into periods would be something like the following:

- From *On Escape* to *Existence and Existents*, by way of the *il y a*, Levinas analyzes the existent (subjectivity) born in existence (the event of being), insofar as it deals with the originary event whose analysis forms the precondition for all others.
- In *Totality and Infinity*, the interiority of the Ego is specifically described as escaping from being and placing itself apart from the world, of being originarily fractured by the Infinite.
- In *Otherwise Than Being: or, Beyond Essence*, the departure from being is finally not so much found as named, as an escape more radical than the existent's escape from an existence that is never anything but a departure from being but still held within the horizon of being, a radical nothingness that is not the counterpart of being and in view of which it becomes necessary to critique the bad nothingness of spectres; this is the anarchic originarity of Otherwise than being.

It thus appears that subjectivity is not the immanence of an interiority already in default through alterity, that is, out of phase with itself and prevented from taking root in a base self.

It seems that the motifs foregrounded in Levinas's works, pausing to read it in this way—as following an order—are numerous and powerful, the least powerful not being his claim of a method proceeding by a hyperbolic exasperation that is the very opposite of a deduction in that it conceals all ground, all foundation, at each stage of thought, rather than ensures it.

It is also reductive to read Levinas's development as organized as, first, analysis describing the emergence of the existent on the horizon of existence, then, second, association with the fracture of the existent through alterity—this could only be second since subjectivity must be born *first* in order *then* to be fractured by alterity. As for the "refinement" manifesting the order of the analysis as the inversion of the order of things that would be taken in the wrong way (the alterity of Otherwise than being would be "the most originary" originary of the process), it belongs fundamentally to the order of logic that Levinas proposes to put in crisis.

Clearly, it is not certain that one might escape radically to the logical deduction in philosophy—nor would it be desirable—and moreover the torture Levinas inflicts on the *logos* does not have the naïveté to believe in finishing with it, escaping it.

It therefore becomes necessary to read Levinas otherwise.

We might begin with a hypothesis that even if it is not named in the early works, it is somehow foreshadowed in the altering force of the Otherwise than being, since it is already at work. Indeed, if it aligns itself both *against* the *il y a* and *in* it, has not the birth of subjectivity *always already* put itself under the aegis of the Other—the Other as the mark of the primordial split with itself we have been noting? (A gap that in its ambivalence can be read positively or negatively—and is this not the Other at the heart of the Ego announcing itself in the ontological signification of the vomiting Levinas analyzes in *On Escape*? This would also be a premonition of the Infinite!) The analyses of describing birth less in the connection with the *il y a* than as the trauma of alterity are not only *not* opposed to the early Levinas's analyses but make them even more explicit.

One might be tempted here to evoke a reciprocal enveloping of connections between subjectivity and the *il y a*, on the one hand, and connections between subjectivity and the Other, on the other hand, each one presupposing the other in the originary short-circuiting of all priority among them, whether chronological, logical, or ontological. The *il y a* creates the milieu for the birth of subjectivity without being its origin, without being what *gives* it; the Otherwise than being creates the origin—paradoxically anarchic—of subjectivity, an origin that thus presupposes even more paradoxically that a point of immanence, *a* subjectivity, stabilizes itself—is *born*—on the unstable ground of the *il y a*.

The conceptual image of this "reciprocal enveloping" clearly says something about the "process" at play, but it risks making it too logical and more particularly too stable. (How might one describe it differently?)

In order to proceed as we have been means returning to an analysis of the retardation of an unprecedented, absolutely unstable movement: that of the temporality of diachrony, or more exactly of temporality *as* diachrony, which is how the later Levinas characterizes radical alterity: as temporality itself, no matter what temporality, temporality revealed as the violence of interruption that is (paradoxically) the fertile renewer (but otherwise) of the connection it has broken, in the very gesture by which it breaks it. Subjectivity provides an exemplary application point for diachrony—it is thoroughly diachronic: immanence in interruption and simultaneously interruption in immanence, that is, temporality itself, and a temporality in which the accent is on separation and rupture to the detriment of continuity—but certainly not in the pure and simple annihilation of the latter.

This, then, is my hypothesis: diachrony is always already there, though not named, in this "dialectic of the instant" in which the existent relates to the *il y a* as its secret engine. And I am proposing substituting the atemporality of a central intuition whose sole expression is gradually transformed in becoming increasingly specific as the conception of a Levinasian oeuvre in which chronological linearity guides the existent in an orderly way from its birth in the *il y a* toward the trauma of alterity. Or better, this intuition is precisely that of diachrony, which is to say that it can exist rigorously as itself only as thoroughly diachronic.

This is in no sense a denial of the intrinsically temporal nature of Levinas's oeuvre; it is, on the contrary, a manifestation of the fact that true temporality is not a linear accumulation moving from a beginning to an end across an irreversible order of intermediary stages. True temporality has never begun (in the sense of a point of commencement) and will never finish, if it is always the flickering of interruptions already reversed as *re*beginnings: birth(s), continuity as perpetual *re*birth(s).

This diachronic oeuvre never *only* addresses diachrony itself; its movement is always a *mise en abyme*.

We must, therefore, begin with the birth of subjectivity, since I can only ever discover one thing: precisely that I can only begin at the beginning; that is, at the point at which I am assigned to myself. And this discovery is not canceled but reinforced by a second discovery: the beginning is not what one first believed it to be, does not have the simplicity of a nostalgia, but is *perpetual* rebeginning, always inhabited by an internal phase shift.

Didier Franck is correct that Levinas, in scrutinizing the way the existent born from existence in *Of Existence to Existents*, proposes something more radical than does Heidegger, who does not interrogate the emergence of the being on the horizon of being and who leaves ontological difference unfounded by inscribing, from the outset, this interrogation within the horizon of being. But to be precise, we must remember that the emergence of this specific being, the existent, is played out *at once* entirely within the solitude of being torn from the *il y a* and entirely within a connection with Otherwise than being,[12] the Otherwise than being that is the finally radical nothing "surprising" subjectivity at the core of the *il y a* and pushing subjectivity out of "it." Only the notion of diachrony can save this paradox from contradiction and allow it to be glimpsed—but never more than that.

One can only begin through subjectivity, in fact through the birth of subjectivity, because subjectivity is never anything other than that, a beginning, as such devoted to an essential and originary solitude,[13] an originary solitude that is never canceled but rather made possible by the radicalism of its derivation: the Otherwise than being precedes me so absolutely that I am all the more as-signed to myself *and thus* to the only place from which I can depart, originarily—even though I must also renounce the pretense of self-grounding and of all mastery in presence to self.

This is the vertiginous, diachronic flickering that makes Levinas's subjectivity originary—that is, simply subjectivity, since what is a subjectivity that is *integrally* deducible, derivable, other than that?—at the very point of the dismissal of all the powers it has invested in modern metaphysics, and in particular the power of a self-grounded self from which all others flow out. And indeed, this power flows out such that it is more the immanence of a radical beginning the more it is radically *delayed* through the Otherwise than being sustaining it.

3

Born to Life, Born to Oneself

THE BIRTH OF SUBJECTIVITY IN
MICHEL HENRY

The notion of birth is a decisive one for Michel Henry's philosophy and, inversely, what Michel Henry says about it gives contestable but fruitful clarity to the limit-phenomenon of birth such that birth is more decisively revealed in the direction of subjectivity.[1]

We must first recall that Michel Henry did not thematize birth until late on in his writing. His first works, from around 1990,[2] do not, to my knowledge, thematize the notion of birth. I am thus characterizing Michel Henry's philosophy as one of the refusal of birth.[3]

And this statement is not invalidated, it seems, by recent texts, even if it must now be understood in a more restrained and complex way.

Let us recall briefly the central idea in Henry's thought.

Key for Henry is "denouncing" the forgetting that has taken place[4]—and has place—as much in ordinary conduct as in the Western philosophy that can only make complete the error of common sense, of what is sometimes called Immanence, sometimes Life, sometimes Affectivity, sometimes Revelation, sometimes Subjectivity; these different names, corresponding to different characteristics of the very thing that is here in question, pure immanence, without a gap in itself, crushed against itself. Immanence has two fundamentally connected characteristics: absence of distance from self and, thus, not to show itself in any outside.

It is easy to see why I have been able to attempt to characterize Henry's philosophy as a "philosophy of the refusal of birth": to be a self, indeed, authentically—(even if it is in a non-explicit manner, the opposition of inauthenticity and authenticity is clearly "functioning" in Michel Henry)—is *not to come to the world* and as a result not to be separated from the origin. Yet birth—as it is commonly understood—is precisely that: a separation. It is an "arrival" only insofar as it is a separation. To be a self, for Henry, is equally to refuse separation and visibility, the first being the opening for the second.

Birth is thus an exemplary limit-phenomenon, the place of a species of crucial experience and not "a phenomenon among others" for Henrian intuition. Birth is determined in a sense entirely as exclusive, since birth— to be separated and to come into the world—is already to die: birth, as coming into the world, and death, are equivalent.

But this is a characteristic of phenomenology by which Henry attempts to integrate all phenomena (though beyond the range of his thought, it can seem to be less "integrative" of phenomena: in refusing to be delayed in coming to the world, does it not simultaneously refuse the diversity of what is to be seen there?). Thus, the phenomena seeming to consist in their entirety and bit by bit of the stuff of the exterior world—or even that make exteriority—are not purely excluded by Henrian phenomenology as we might have expected: essentially, language (which makes visible the absent thing, and which even, so to speak, "absentizes" it, unrealizes it), time, the alterity of the other. The phenomenology of pure immanence is not without time, language, others. On the contrary, it is in immanence that we discover "true" time, "true" language, and "authentic" alterity. These "phenomena" are thus like the results of a positive coefficient that will reverse nature and its powers: they can then be addressed as "living beings," "transcendentals," or even "phenomenologists." The challenge is allocating to language, time, and the alterity of the other a coefficient powerful enough to save them from transcendence and to inscribe them at the heart of immanence.

Henrian reduction, the inverse of Merleau-Ponty's unachievable reduction, arises from an all-or-nothing logic: it is radical and has no residue.[5] This is why, if one "resists" the intuition of Henrian philosophy, it will seem to be a phenomenology "without phenomena" since it has no "outside." On the contrary, if one looks through Henrian eyes, then everything reappears in its authenticity, in the obscure clarity of immanence.

(A remark in passing: Henry, who frequently critiques Hegel as a thinker of the deployment of manifestation as logic, is himself constrained to a posture of reception akin to Hegel's—a posture of reception with which it is very difficult to avoid: either to be inscribed from the outset in his philosophy thus to be required to adhere step by step and integrally to the tissue of statements it lays out, or to be kept on the outside and be required to "reject it as a whole.")

Before entering into the core of things here, into the epicenter of the question of the birth of subjectivity, let us consider one preliminary (and prejudicial) question: why is Michel Henry not content to exclude these phenomena that seem to consist only in the illusion of exteriority?

Because it is necessary for him to "recuperate," if this is the correct word, "something" initially perceived in the outside, and moreover *as* the outside, but in needing above all not to commit the error for which "all other" philosophers are reproached—to understand and to retrospectively project Transcendence into Immanence, and thus to corrupt the latter.

It must initially be demonstrated that these motifs, at first perceived far outside, in truth—in *their* truth, in their effectiveness—are "from" Immanence. But they are not *absorbed* into an absolutely compact Immanence, so dense that it contains no gaps. Rather, they permit the thought of what is truly Immanence, inhabited, Henry claims, by an *internal movement.*

But once Ek-static critique is in operation, this task cannot be completed. The critical phase—which for Henry is particularly negative—can only prepare the essential: it can only describe Immanence.

Immanence, as Henry never ceases to repeat, is Life, Affectivity, Revelation, Ipseity.

And it is important to him at the very highest point of this thought to posit, and to legitimate phenomenologically, the originarity of this equivalence. Indeed, it permits the short-circuiting at its very root of the first and most substantial objection one might make against his thought: that it is a kind of autism, an enclosing within the self that thus can say nothing (whom to address? and why?) and that in light of the Parmenidean aporia remembers that there is nothing to say (what can be said of the One, other than that it is?). Moreover, speaking would already be "peeled off" from the One, its "peeling off" and "articulating" of itself to itself like a predicate—that is, doing violence to itself.

1. Immanence is not a pure and simple identity to self—"empty" and thus solidified in something like a death—that would give forth nothing (even if what it gave forth was always giving itself and, more fundamentally, as being nothing other than itself). For Henry, this is precisely Life itself (a *phusis*, a blossoming, but a paradoxical blossoming in that it could emerge only to itself, in itself). It is "arrival in self"; we will have to account for this particular fruitfulness.

2. Immanence is defined as the pressure of the Self on itself (of Life on Life). This is why it is affectivity: Henrian affectivity is affection preceding all exteriority and thus all representation. This is a primordial difficulty we must revisit: we must account for this *gap* presupposing the "erasure" of "Self" *against* "self" even when one situates oneself "before" all exteriority.

3. Immanence reveals, shows—only itself; it must show only itself—but it shows. Here too there must be a connection of self *to* self at the very "place" that (of what) precedes all Ek-stasy. Life, as arrival in self, is immediately Revelation, since Revelation is nowhere but in this movement of exiting from self that takes itself with itself, and that thus coincides with an arrival in self (as movement in self of the Self of Revelation is distinguished from the manifestation that is thrown far outside).

4. Immanence is nowhere other than in the test, the pressure, in which it is erased against *itself*. A Self emerges from this test. Immanence is Ipseity, Subjectivity.

Briefly, as we have seen, immanence is what it is only insofar as it is inhabited by what could be called an *internal gap*, even though it could seem that all gaps could be dismissed as co-natural with exteriority.

It is absolutely necessary to withdraw language, and above all others and time, from Ek-static transcendence, by giving them the title "transcendental": to describe and ground, phenomenologically, this internal separation.

The phenomenology of Immanence, as phenomenology of Life, had to "think"—to describe—birth not as "arrival in the world" but as "arrival in self"; as the perpetual self-engendering that is Life.

What is more, it seems that the major aporias Henry's phenomenology proposes converge at the point of birth—and that his phenomenology never laid out:[6]

- How to think a temporality in and of Immanence, if all temporality *seems* to implicate an Ek-stasis, a temporal gap?
- How to think others as being in Immanence itself? That is, how to test the alterity of others if it must above all else not have a face?
- Corollary: Even if it is presented as a philosophy of ipseity, a possible objection to Henry's philosophy might be the question as to whether, if it is Life that comes to self, who is self, who is a "Self," how is it *my* "Self"? Is it its "Self" or is it mine? In vigorously denouncing the Freudian unconscious and other structuralisms as dissolving originary ipseity, as well as Merleau-Ponty for whom all ipseity emerges from a primordial anonymity at the crux of an interlacing of the World with itself, as an "anonymity of the outside," even though it denounces all that, Henry runs the risk of an "anonymity of the inside." To cite a Henrian image, Life plays the role of a subterranean shroud preceding all the individual Egos by which they are nourished.[7]

Describing birth is thus crucial, since this also describes the arrival of an ipseity to itself (which implies tying ipseity *and* the "arrival"—that is, temporality—together) *in* Life itself *and* as the coming of Life to itself, without the latter being required to cancel the former.

Additionally, if it is possible, phenomenologically, to take proper account of the fact that an absolutely singular ipseity whose singularity is affirmed relative to Life itself arrives *in* Life—even if it is in Life—then *more* ipseities are possible (each singular relative to others and to Life).

To think birth is thus to think the internal gap, the fundamentally dynamic gap, in Immanence, since it is *procreation* (internal circulation within Life that, however, produces the singular and the new in it, without the intervention of any outside), since it is Life itself at the place where all of its expressions converge: time—as fecundity and not as loss of being, of others, of ipseity.

After having brought to light what forces Henry to describe something as a transcendental birth, we can see what description, what content, he then gives this notion, and if what is thus proposed reveals the un-expected challenge thrown out by the very thing of Life: to think this internal, dynamic separation with no outside, but contrarily as the very heart of Immanence, as the "Immanence of Immanence."

This is the pathetic effort of Henry's thought to think the pathetic, originary effort of Life.

Let us recall quickly the negative significations of birth.

Birth must above all *not* signify "arrival in the world": it must thus absolutely not correspond to the results of the act of "creation." "To en-gender wants to say all, except to create, if creation designates the creation of the world, this phenomenological opening of a first 'outside' where we have revealed to us the entire reign of the visible" (*IAT*, 131), writes Henry (agreeing, by the way, with Levinas).

This is the process:

Life is Life only insofar as it is the test of itself: it thus *is* entirely in the movement of connecting with itself, of arriving in itself: Life is nowhere other than in the node of Life with itself.

To this we must immediately declare a first objection: the Self (Life) being *from the outset* connection to itself is thus primary exteriority (permit-ting Life to separate from itself). It must, as a precondition, "exit," in order to return, or even to come, to Self. Life is initially "two" in order to be "one."

This is the "classic" objection that Henry short-circuits from the start—from inside his intuition—saying that this objection comes from "outside," can be stated only by the one who has been "mislaid" "far out-side." (He cuts it off at the roots by denouncing it as a false problem.)

Inside Life—and so much the worse for the *logos*, for logic, which are both "the outside itself"—there is no Life separated from itself, "Life" and "beside" it "Life," then relinked by a connection that reattaches them to each other. No, what is first is the link itself that in itself preexists all the poles it connects and then causes them to connect. This dynamic link, which is pure "arrival," pure "internal circulation," constitutes the heart of immanence, "the immanence of Immanence."

That is, interiority, the intimateness of life, is nowhere other than in this "crashing against self." This looping back of life on itself "makes" a "Self" (its "Self"). A life that does not make a loop or a knot on itself is unthinkable—it would not be Life. This test is "co-essential" to Life.

And this is where things become complicated. This loop occurs in/ of Life (if we concede to Henry that a connection can be the economy of an outside where it is deployed, where it can be "inside," the "inside" it- self of Immanence; Immanence as interiority), and without this (internal) loop Life would not be Life: the enlacing, the loop, is a condition of Life in the sense of "that without which Life would not be Life." It produces a modus, an expression—a revelation, we might say, since nothing outside it is mobilized—of Life, in such a way that Life would be nothing outside its test, its revelation—yet, however, in a sense Life preexists it since it is Life that is enlaced. Life is nowhere other than in this enlacing. This means it is its very enlacing, and its before (since it is what is enlaced in its enlac- ing): this paradox trembles. But Henry escapes it—as always—by saying that it is untenable only for one situated in the light of the world, in the calculation of mundane time.

The "gap" from life to Self that it is—this Self that is this very gap entirely—"is" life itself as self-engendering (*IAT*, 133): what is at play here is immanence without the outside of the pure movement of self-engen- dering: Life is itself confined, from itself, as itself. In other words, it auto- affects; it is what gives, the gift, and the given: and this "process" "ties" itself into a Self. For Michel Henry the notion of engendering signifies *reciprocal interiority* (*IAT*, e.g., 101, 108, 116, 163) of the different moments of this "process."

To clarify the paradox in a fruitful way—in a way that saves us from the contradiction of the aporias we discussed earlier: if Life is nowhere but in its enlacings, and if, however, no one exhausts Life—since, on the contrary, Life always precedes it and is embraced in it—then *many* inter- lacings are possible. Intersubjectivity is thus possible, and even necessary, since it is a matter of considering that among the plurality of singularities there is each time an enrichment of Life that is enlaced anew.

It is understood that in the notion of engendering always understood as self-engendering, Henry wants to write, precisely, the originary move- ment of Life, movement in which it is entirely held—as this unexpected movement through which Life does not leave itself but comes to itself, is carried in itself (apart from itself).

But how is it with this ipseizing and ipseic engendering for the ip- seized Self that is born in it?

If the Self is not exhausted by Life—that is, held entirely within it, inversely, is Life not exhausted by Self?

Doubtless, from the outset Henry short-circuits the objection of saying that Life is a first, anonymous veil to which all ipseity must be redirected and in which it must eventually be dissolved in a return to its authenticity.

In fact, Life is its "ipseizations." This is not a matter of redirecting different ipseities to something other than themselves, since Life is nowhere but in them (in its ipseities). (Redirecting different ipseities to something other than themselves is precisely the error that Henry rejects—projects?—in Romanticism and/or the Freudian theory of the unconscious, thus exonerating himself from the charge he merely reactivates the Romantic thematic of life as Absolute.)

Nevertheless, the question reappears at a deeper level: in order to be a true one, an ipseity must be its ipseity *for itself*. But for Michel Henry the real question is one of knowing if it is really the self that the Self tests—or if it is Life that *in itself* tests the self; this is not the same thing, but Henry would say that indeed there is an equivalence between these two movements. This is the problem that must be underlined: is it my Self or the Life-Self that is in question?

Michel Henry's challenge, the aporia he is testing—the aporia in which his thought, so to speak, comes into itself and connects with itself—consists of this: wanting to think the perfect coincidence and the strict simultaneity of two movements: the one by which a Self comes to itself, *and* the one by which Life comes to self, such that the second movement does not cancel the first, respects its originary model, while the first takes place only in it, only at the heart of its absolute and irreducible originarity, an originarity that is always already old.

It is from the point of view of the Self that the unfolding of this process I have just described by implicitly borrowing the viewpoint of Life (since it is originary—"the most originary") must now be readdressed.

So, is it possible, from the viewpoint of the Self, to take on the delicate problem of this internal gap, this internal movement, while holding firmly to what might be called (in non-Henrian terms) the double bind of the thought of Life—a double bind that is only a contradiction for the light of the world!: to think a gap that is sufficiently intimate and interior that it can in no way be Ek-static, *and* that is marked as irreducible—the only way of making possible a movement that would be an affection (it would be "self-")—a gap not absorbed by a pure immanence without differentiation, by an absolute night in which all cows would be gray?

To be born, for a Self, must not signify nor be separated from Life, nor depart from it—and yet that implies its radical distinction, its not sinking into its undifferentiated night—and that life must not, cannot, ever be an undifferentiated night. To be born, for a Self, in a sense implies *needing nothing from Life, while life has given it everything.* As we have seen, Michel Henry explains that even more radically the Self needs nothing from Life *because* Life has given it everything.

In order to confront this aporia, Henry distinguishes two auto-affections or, rather, two senses of auto-affection, a strong one and a weak one (*IAT,* 135).

The strong sense of auto-affection is appropriate to Life and to it alone. It is a radical auto-affection in the sense that Life is absolutely in every moment of the process: it is Life that affects, it is Life that is affected, and the content of affection is nothing other than it. It is what gives; it gives, is the giver and the gift. It is "everywhere," but would not be itself if it did not deploy itself thus, in a deployment that is paradoxical since it is entirely interior.

And there is a weak sense of auto-affection that is important for the Ego. In the auto-affection of Life, the Ego is auto-affected, but in such a way that it is not itself but Life that casts into itself. The Ego is fundamentally passive: it is not posited; it is given to itself. (While Life, in its pure absoluteness, situates itself within the division between activity and passivity: it is absolute activity that as absolute has no outside in which to be deployed, and that is hardly any longer an activity; activity for it is carried to a point of absoluteness so radical that it is reversed into passivity—and adversely.)

The Ego is passive: it is received as a "burden"; it does not give itself to itself but in such a manner that—and this is decisive—it is nonetheless not a hetero-affection. This is the paradox that must be given the means of managing: the Ego's passivity does not presuppose a preexistent Ego affected from the outside by something it has not decided. This passivity is in a sense more radical since it signifies that the Ego does not preexist the affection in and from which it emerges.

It is affected inasmuch as it constitutes in its entirety all the content of affection, but it is not the power of affecting (giving). However, affection is so radical that it engenders the Ego such that this engendering link could not be exterior: it is the very interiority of the Ego. (Engendering could not occur from the Ego's exterior since it does not preexist it.) It is thus *because* affection (here, passivity) is absolutely radical that *as a result* it does not come from "outside."

This is what "happens" in birth: there is a linkage with reciprocal interiority that not only preserves but even "causes" the Self as absolutely singular, as, so to speak, an originary of the second level—that is nonetheless an originary.[8]

Life, in being self-engendering, creates the Self as self-engendering: this is the paradox that must be kept in sight.

Michel Henry says it thus: "If the Self is expressed spontaneously in the accusative, it is all the more because it leaves it to the explication that is its own, not of being affected itself but of being constantly self-affected" (*IAT,* 137).

"To be self-affected," not "I self-affect myself" or "I am affected (by)": in this expression that puts the "self," the "auto," in the passive voice, we read the paradox of passivity that returns in a form of autonomy, of being pushed to its end.

From the viewpoint of Henrian intuition, Life is the before *in which* I am—while remaining irreducibly "my before," and which is in me, in me such that it makes up my ego itself.

The Self emerges from Life in such a way that it no longer only interacts with it, at the very point of its emergence, and this emergence is radical. It is seized (by) itself, even if it is not the origin of the gesture that thus fastens on itself. It too is pure immanence, and in this sense is distinguished from the Immanence of Life: it is created as an "auto-": it is born.

What is gained in this process?

1. From the point of view of Henrian phenomenology and from its own proper movement:
   As we have seen, birth as "arrival in the world" is denounced. But as "arrival in self" of Life *and* of Self—of Self/Selves—it is at once essential—what must be described in such a way that the intuition of pure immanence is pushed to its end, and thus legitimized—*and*

what risks the most in resisting it—the place where the major aporias to which Henrian philosophy converge and that are hardly only
the different expressions of the same fundamental aporia.

2. From the point of view of the phenomenon of birth itself:
      While we may normally frequently—justly—insist on the di-
mension of separation inscribed in the phenomenon of birth, on the
trauma of birth, Henry insists, on the contrary, on the *reciprocal
interiority* of the procreator and the procreated, while not denying—
and indeed thinking precisely *there*—the dynamic gap that makes
birth birth.

      In this sense, he emphasizes the opposite pole from that insisted
on by Levinas. But that said, Henry does not deny what birth ex-
pects of that gap, and in fact does everything to describe it as the
essential element inside the frames of thought that would initially
seem already to have prevented it. And the problem is, thus, that this
thought wants, on the one hand, to be radical, not compromising
with "Transcendence," and, on the other hand, needing to find in
itself what is normally accorded to Ek-static transcendence—and
that I have referred to by the non-Henrian term "gap"—in carefully
distinguishing it from Ek-static transcendence.[9]

      Is any reading possible *other* than a work of the *accentuating* of
one of the poles to the detriment of the other?

      This proves that to *cut* absolutely between these two poles—
immanence/transcendence (even when revisited as non-Ek-static
gap)—would be less radical in its description of phenomena than
its mutilation.

3. Finally, from the point of view of subjectivity:
      Since it is never only a question of this in the very analyses that
sometimes produce this bias.

Understanding subjectivity through birth permits Henry, like Levinas, to
account for a paradoxical originarity in subjectivity: it is originary, but it
is "preceded by" *because* this radically so. An expression of Jean-Luc Marion nicely captures Henry's description of subjectivity: "The I is non-originary, is in some sense derived, even though its very derived status makes
it absolutely originary."[10]

We might here take a possible objection into account.

It might seem that the description given here of the movement through which Life *and* Self come into themselves, the one as much as the other, is in fact gently shifted with regard to that produced by Henry. And this shift, perhaps in order not to be immediately perceptible to an eye not trained in Henrian exigency, could appear to be an awkwardness, or even nonsensical—or, even more seriously, a betrayal, and a voluntary one. This shift seizes us, though we understand it and hope for it as a form of fidelity in the very center of infidelity.[11]

Where is the infidelity?

In our redefining of Henry's analysis regarding the birth of a living being, of an ipseity, in Life, we have avoided the supplementary protagonist that for Henry is indissociable from this event: the First Living Being who accompanies each birth, who is present in each authentic birth, since it will have "always already" rendered it possible. And this First Living Being is named Christ.

Without doubt, the paradoxical "logic" of the "movement" of birth is incomprehensible for Henry, if we remove the decisive element. Yet this is what we have attempted to do: we now tend to legitimize this path, our own path.

What is the status of the First Living Being? It is, precisely, "Archi": "Archi-son," "Archi-ipseity," "First Living Being." And yet while Henry does not say it exactly thus, it is the first time in which the still-undefined advent of the Living Beings who will follow are possible: in order for Living Beings that are—each time—ipseized, to ceaselessly come to Life, there must have been a *first* time.[12] The importance of this first time, this inauguration, is immeasurable: it accompanies each singular event, each birth.

Why is this *first* time *necessary*; why is it alone capable of acting in such a way that ipseity can be born?

It short-circuits the fundamental objection addressed here very near to the origin.

I have tried to show that one of the greatest difficulties the Henrian conception of birth encounters consists of holding together the originary absoluteness of Life *and* the radical ipseity of the Living Being in its singularity: indeed, while Life is a matricial Absolute, the Living Being endlessly risks being subordinated to it. How is it possible to avoid thinking this last as integrally derived from an Absolute that would be only one of its expressions, and consequently subordinating its singularity before the authority of the Absolute from which it comes?

This proves that the *function* of the First Living Being in Henry's analysis of birth, and beyond the analysis, in the very *thing* of birth, consists of transcending this tension.[13] In fact, the First Living Being is precisely the first not to *receive* the life of Life but to *give* it: it will give life to all the living because it will itself make a gift to Life, to Life that nonetheless gives all that is given. It will give ipseity to Life, its first ipseity; it will make Life escape to the indetermination of its absoluteness, to the indetermination of its profuse fertility.

Here I must make one remark.

This gift given to Life by the First Living Being—and that is truly in a sense the gift of life since life would hardly be life if no living ipseity appeared in it—thus this gift, the First Living Being will *always* have made the gift to Life, since it must itself be thought as "Archi," as inscribed under the heading *arch*. The installation, in the transcendental dimension, to Michel Henry is supposed to assure the possibility of escaping to what is unthinkable—if not absurd—in an irreversible, linear chronology being deployed in the World, namely, the *simultaneity* of the antecedence of Life over the First Living Being *and* of the antecedence of the First Living Being over Life itself. The first antecedence comes together easily: Life is the source of all life. Let us stop for a moment on the second: the First Living Being is a radical event, inaugurating itself in the very movement in which it inaugurates ipseity, and in which it "makes possible" something like ipseity. In fact, what is essential here is to understand that it *does not receive* its ipseity from Life.

In a sense—and only in a sense,[14] I can claim my ipseity only from myself. It would be more accurate to say that I always coincide, and always have coincided, absolutely with my ipseity, so much so that compressed against it I have no power over it. But nonetheless if I do not "give" my ipseity to myself, it still cannot come to me from elsewhere; it cannot be, so to speak, imported, from a "place" older than myself, at the heart of which it would have had to be conceived: if this were the case, it would always already have been a garment too large for my absolute singularity; already a generality, the idea or essence of my me, my ego.

Consequently, the First Living Being gives life to other Living Beings, in that it has given Life the capacity to engender ipseities, and this gives it its own.

From a certain point of view, it is the *form* of ipseity, the *archetype* of ipseity itself, since it is what provides ipseity to living beings. But this formulation must immediately be corrected, since the first ipseity that will produce all ipseities must above all not, as we will see, return to this form and to the general; it is not even the first singular "incarnation" of what would be the "principle of ipseity": the First Living Being, in the event of its appearing, underivable, unrepeatable, and irreplaceable, can transmit ipseity only to such a being. What Michel Henry wishes to grasp here is the possibility (and the effectivity) not only of that appearing but also of the *transmission* of ipseity—insofar as such a possibility does not betray itself to the sole condition of engaging in the shortcut of detouring through the general (as the idea of ipseity), detouring through an absolute fabricator (anonymous Life), a detour that would kill ipseity.

Such a configuration of the exigency of thought has certain implications.

First, the kind of temporality in which connections are made between different arrivals—those of Life, of the First Living Being, of Living Beings—must be understood as properly consisting of what Henry calls "transcendental time." This is a temporality heterogeneous to mundane, continuous, cumulative, and irreversible chronology that is, however, no less radical, now seen—and in complete coherence with what preceded it—under the sign of the discontinuity of the event.

What must be kept in view is the fact that the event, if it is truly singular, must be in some sense susceptible to the proper name, as the mark of its absolute singularity. This is its double bind: it seems to need to *identify* the event in order to perfect it as such—in the same gesture, it is true, that risks causing its own loss in concretizing it, in concealing the event-ness of the event in a "larval" form of substantiality: the proper name, the *identification*, of the event of the First Living Being is, for Michel Henry—Christ.

Christianity must be recognized, according to Henry, as a—as *the*—radical phenomenology.

We are thus led toward the problem Janicaud identifies as phenomenology's "theological turn," since though we cannot seriously reproach

Henry for having imported theology into phenomenology, we can formulate this problem of the "theological turn" through a trajectory that wants to be seen as internal to a vein of Henrian exigency and that has attempted to follow this exigency closely, to the point that the problem itself arises.

It is possible not to be greatly convinced by Henry's investment in Christianity—and seen properly, it is in large part an "investment": Henry uses Christianity as he does Descartes or Husserl, for example, recognizing what is most profound in them: *his own* intuition of Life's radical immanence. One might jokingly almost say in this context that what is authentic in Descartes, Husserl, Marx, or Christianity is what Henrian philosophy announces regarding Life. More seriously, it is Life that will have, to various degrees and in various ways (and all the more in that it will have been recovered), bored pervasively into these diverse works.

But clearly we cannot remain at this level of analysis.

We must be more specific regarding this suspicion of "theologization": first we must investigate not simply a *connection* between philosophy and faith—this would be entirely inappropriate—but rather a connection between philosophy and faith such that the first is *founded* on the second. Next, we must show that *faith* can, with difficulty, remain a vague mystery with an undetermined "object." In order to reassure itself, it is as though driven by a fundamental need to determine, to *identify*, the source to which it is connected—(this in order subtly to name it with an unpronounceable name, to identify it as the unidentifiable itself). This is why there are religions or, more specifically, positive and determined dogmas that are such only in that they are suspended in the worldliness of a history: faith is never reduced to them, however, though they are its necessary supports, as it were (even if it consists to a large extent in the negation of this support).

Thus it remains to determine the degree to which Henrian philosophy, in *I Am the Truth*, exposes itself to the charge of being *founded* on a Christianity understood as itself resting on a determined, *identified*, dogma.

A stance such as this makes as clear as day the analysis that we have done on the immanence of Henry's exigency of thought, according to which all birth of an ipseized Self presupposes a First Living Being as first ipseity that, as such, must be if not identified then at least caught in a *process* of *identification*.

There seems to be a necessary confusion between transcendental temporality and worldly temporality; as an embedding of the first in the second. The First Living Being must not be undetermined, must be *identified*; its very existence consists of nothing other than this gesture. Thus, it is *singularized* as event at the very core of transcendental temporality, this singularization being required to ring out, to announce itself at the heart of mundane and Ek-static temporality in order to make possible a "second birth" for those who have forgotten that Life is in them: Christic incarnation, in this Henrian context, is this event of transcendental "stuff" that will resonate in the Ek-static World without being contaminated by it.

Thus, Henrian thought is—though without pretending to do an instant summary of it[15]—a "weak" reading making poor usage of the ambiguity of concealment between worldly temporality and transcendental temporality: like all dogmatically religious readings, Henry's claims for itself alone the appearance of a transcendental event cutting through the worldly, declaring itself to be best at recognizing the ability to present— albeit confusedly—transcendental immanence, or at least not to betray it too much. This would provide, for example, the measure of all other historical religion, Judaism in particular, relative to Christianity: quite allusive in *I Am the Truth*—though this is happily not this book's project— this kind of positioning is nonetheless not absent; and it is not without its reminders of Hegel in "The Spirit of Christianity and Its Fate," even if that in no case manifests the unhelpful nature of Henry's book regarding religion-as-law (and of the lack of love, if not hate).

To explain more fully: I am in no sense castigating a philosophy relying on the specific experience in which faith seems to be a privileged agent and that possesses at least two connected traits: moving toward that which does not "give onto" the World and without which nothing of the World could be given; and testing an ipseity that in a radical passivity cannot be lived as being its own proper origin.

I am not even suggesting that philosophy's task is the integral acclimatization (or at least the most integral possible) of such an experience within the exigencies of a discourse of "returning reason" to the "how" of the appearance of phenomena. *To identify* what is at play in such an experience, whether it is *in* philosophy or *in* religion, is the best means of losing it.

The practice of philosophy is the constant testing of this experience as its alterity, holding it at its limit.

So we will have to be satisfied with asking this question: if we can think that Christianity is the field in which Michel Henry tests the limits of philosophy, the treatment of the question as he presents it in *I Am the Truth*, the position he takes there, risks ceding to one of the two branches of the double bind we have already addressed: given that this stance exposes itself to a test that is older than philosophical discourse but *identifies* it (in Christianity),[16] does it not risk canceling it as such?

Would it not need to expose itself to the double bind of being required *simultaneously* to "identify" and "disidentify" this test and this event to maintain their event-power?

And that can be accomplished only in an unstable discourse that must ceaselessly be retracted, "restated" (i.e., identified anew), and thus this discourse, for which no *final* identification could be possible, could only remain irreducibly aporetic.

Henrian ambiguity, according to which the figure of Christ seems *at once* what the phenomenological step accomplishes *and* what already grounds it, as perhaps irreducible, opens out the temptation of a philosophical *beyond* in which one might proceed to an identification of the provenance of living ipseity (thanks here to the determination of Life in its connection with First Living Being).

Our attempt to reimplement the Henrian description of "transcendental birth" through the economy of the First Living Being is thus condemned to emphasize the aporetic aspect of ipseic subjectivity to Life, since it returns to us deprived at the point of suture regarding the one and the other in their first contradictory exigencies. But this gesture *also* refers back to a preference for moments of the philosophy of Life in which this last is affirmed, in the disquiet of a perpetual repetition of the shock to the self (which thus implies passing through a desensitization) to those for whom its arrival in them has the tendency to identify (and thus to fix) them.

Such a torsion as this, inflicted on Henrian thought, returns for us to accentuate a dimension of itself that it risks hiding somehow—in a very explicit manner when it relates to Christianity—and that nonetheless constructs the question from which it wishes not to turn away: that of the attempt to think radical immanence such that it contains an originary gap within itself as the sole manner of being properly itself. From a certain point of view, the question of the articulation of Life for each Self born into it is a reformulation of this exigency.

In emphasizing the aporetic in such an exigency, in that it is a double bind, we have attempted to be true to a hidden thread of Henrian thought that could only appear at the cost of being untrue to a part of itself.

It is, perhaps, not insignificant to implement this gesture precisely with regard to the question of the birth of a Self.

4

Spectral Subjectivity According to Jacques Derrida

With only very rare exceptions—when, for example, he is in some way "obliged" to do so, as in an interview[1]—Jacques Derrida never takes the question of subjectivity as the central theme of his work.

However, even if it is never in the spotlight, the question of the subject is an insistent one in Derridean texts, and not only in the form of an exemplary reminder of the metaphysics he has set out to eradicate with a gesture that is simple and without nuance: the subject is not the scapegoat of deconstruction.

Let us recall briefly some of the stakes of this insistence, this "resistance" to subjectivity at the very margins of a work that will in turn be carried to the margins of modern metaphysics. In a surprising reversal, is it not the central motif of the metaphysics of presence, disrupting "deconstruction" at *its* margins?

- Since *Speech and Phenomena*, the impossible possibility of the words of Poe's M. Valdemar, "*I* am dead," comes to haunt and deconstruct the pure presence to self of the Husserlian consciousness that ceaselessly reassures itself in its interior monologue.

- During the period in which the thought of différance was being elaborated as a *grammatology*, the question of the *signature* signals at once the deconstruction of subjectivity—this time less as presence to self of fundamental substance than as presence of the singular event of Self—*and* the insistence of a subjectivity that, like signature, precisely, persists in its very effacement.

- In recent texts (since 1985) the motif of subjectivity is constantly at work, in a lateral manner—as if only this approach was capable of being appropriate to it—but more and more obsessively, it seems.

  And here are some indices: "Ulysses Gramophone,"[2] for example, adheres to an "auto-position of self in the *yes*" (UG, 131) that brings about a "reference of self to self." This certainly is not a matter of a reinstallation of the metaphysics of presence—this *yes* is "preonto-logical" and therefore "older than knowledge" (UG, 121)—but the decisive motif for Derrida, the distance and/or the originary delay is now complicated, perhaps even concurrently, even if it is in no case a contradiction or a correction, through the movement—we must return to this—of an "affirmative" "force" that is older than the origin, older than all origin, even if older, strictly speaking, than all affirmation, a "force" in which Self is always already promised.

  Beside the texts devoted to this archi-originary *yes*—and not in contradiction with them, rather on the contrary[3]—of others, more or less explicitly in dialogue with Levinas (if not consecrated to Levinas)—Derrida "invests" a domain that could be called religious,[4] if it is true that from a certain viewpoint subjectivity—not as ground but as interiority—was invented by monotheism: what is thus principally in play is the "I am here" of Abraham that gives itself integrally to God to be given to him by God in a paradoxical relation that is a separation.[5]

- There is something like a "revenance" of subjectivity in the "last" Derrida; and his most recent texts remain haunted by an ego whose spectral character is affirmed and demonstrated, in a paradoxical manner whose spectrality is "affirmed" and "demonstrated." This spectral ego, finally, will lodge in this test of the limit, this aporia. In fact, as we have already seen, in the practice of the aporia, in the very test for the thought of the impossibility of being closed once again on *self*, "it is always to oneself that one returns."

For reasons we have already explored, we are not reading Levinas, Henry, and Derrida as "authors" in what is conventionally called their "evolution," a practice that at the very least tends toward decryption of a hidden teleology. Here, it is not a question of reading Derrida as working through a structuralist demolition of subjectivity toward a return to subjectivity in such a form that one must wonder if it repeats the metaphysics of presence or if it is truly new; in a form that might make one ask if it is absolutely naïve, since it is a question of subjectivity, of pretending to completely destroy the metaphysics of presence.

A reading of this kind misses the true aporetic nexus. That is, the motif of subjectivity is always at work in Derrida's texts, insofar as it is at work. And that is never simple—that is, oriented toward a solution that if it is not decisive is at least decidable. And the question of subjectivity constitutes a point of suffering—and also doubtless of *jouissance*—in the Derridean text, one to which it never ceases to return and on which it ceaselessly insists, literally, on "pressing," as one aggravates a scar in order to replay endlessly the experience of the cut precisely where it is covered over. In other terms, the question of subjectivity is the point of auto-affection for Derridean thought, on which—at once most incidentally and most necessarily, in what Derrida calls a *destinerrance*—it continuously folds back.

Let us return briefly to the highest stakes posed in light of this hypothetical reading.

If the Derridean gesture has some association with structuralism(s), it has never suggested the idea that it would be necessary to demolish the subject (a project that, moreover, is not even imputable to any structuralism that is part of this caricature). Its reticence regarding structuralism comes from the fact that if it is justifiable that it (structuralism) redirects the subject toward conditions of production, this would mean simultaneously substituting another figure of presence for the subject, one that would remain beyond question: the reality of structure, as a given.[6]

This reticence is the double of another connected formulated in *Positions*:[7] structure ignores the entire force *animating* it. This old text of Derrida's certainly does not say this, but reading a text like "Ulysses Gramophone," with its insistence on an archi-originary *yes*[8]—an archi-originary *yes* that is sometimes (and quite accurately) described as *intakes of breath* that precede all propositions,[9] and even all questions—this reading, then, allows us to think that Derrida has from the outset been sensitive to what might obscurely be given the name of "soul," and thus to subject and/or subjectivity, in the very gesture by which he has complemented the structuralist disassembling of the triumphant subject-substance.

The Derridean gesture toward Austinian pragmatism is, from this perspective, analogous to the one aimed at structuralism (though more critical). We must recall that Derrida recognizes in pragmatism the merit of having defeated the imperialism of the constative and the descriptive, and thus (and above all) of the supposedly fundamental metaphysics underlying it, namely, substantiality as such: in fact, only that which has nothing to do with substance can describe it. Manifesting the fundamental and original role of the performative in language is thus an operation that defeats the hegemony of the substantialist model of understanding being. But immediately Derrida uncovers in the pragmatic another strategy for the redirection of the metaphysics of presence, as belief in the pure presence to self of living speech, presence to self that culminates in the *speech act*.

But this "deconstruction" of the pragmatic, since "deconstruction" can never be reduced to a skeptical demolition, nor does it ever leave, in terms of its central concerns, emerges unscathed from its encounter with the pragmatic.

It is in this perspective that we must insist on the importance, in Derrida's texts of the 1970s and the beginning of the 1980s,[10] of analyses dedicated to the proper name and the signature.

And remember its stakes: the proper name is in a sense exemplary of the illusion of the present-living-being: it is its spokesperson. It is charged with signifying the singularity of a pure presence to self. But clearly it manifests—and implements—rather, the impossibility of presence to singular self of a concrete individual: indeed, a concrete individual can truly be itself only at the instant at which, for example, it grasps itself, or in the instant of an act of enunciation. The pure presence of the "I, here, now," as pure instantaneity, is by its very nature fugitive, already gone. It is thus necessary to guarantee presence beyond its own transience: this is why my proper name is the only thing to survive me, the only thing to allow me to transcend and to conjure my mortality, my finitude, a finitude that always accompanies me, always preceding the event of my death in the instantaneity of my presence to myself (an instantaneity signified, for example, by the Cartesian cogito).

Consequently, the proper name can assume its function only through already being detached from the singular present-living-being it names: my proper name is my proper name only in being capable of being *repeated* by *others*, elsewhere, and, above all, when I am dead. It is the possibility of a repetition that will always have betrayed and rendered impossible the pure event-ness of my existence; it is, already, ideality—that is, the iterability made possible by writing, by the scriptural trace—that detaches itself from my life. As the personal pronoun "I," the proper name is what it is only by being already of the order of the general, only in already detaching itself from my concrete individuality. It is more than clear that thus the proper name betrays and saves in the same motion, a motion whose ambivalence is absolutely indivisible.

It is my death itself, insofar as it is at base an indefinitely iterable trace, deserted by living speech. But it is the tomb of writing, death itself in this sense, only in order better to save me from the strict instantaneity of my live presence that is always in the process of self-cancellation, and that, without it, would always already be dead. In other words, we see here that pure presence to self is in fact contradictory, even impossible, that it is indeed possible only in having been pervaded by its very impossibility, since the proper name both says and constitutes the originary impropriety permitting me to escape the self-cancellation of the instant.

Thus, there is no "proper" name, and not simply because my name is never my "proper" nor even my property, but more radically because it disappropriates myself, and thus only allows for an attempt to be myself, to appropriate myself, at the price of this originary disappropriation.[11]

A decisive remark regarding the question of subjectivity must be inserted here.

Originary disappropriation must not be presented as the *truth* of the pure event-ness of presence to self—this last thus being denounced as an *illusion*. Originary "exappropriation" does not cancel the event of a singular presence to self but, paradoxically, uniquely makes it possible: it will have been truly itself only in the impossibility of its completion. And it is legitimate to indicate that the proper name, as originary impropriety, far from effacing it, *is* only *in view of* the singular event of a presence to self that it thus "expropriates": "the absolute appropriation is the absolute expropriation" (*Glas*, 188). Even though there is no "proper," expropriation is always reappropriation. Therefore, the Derridean text—since deconstruction does not efface, does not cancel the event of presence but returns it to itself in liberating it from the illusion of its stabilization in a grounding substance, without being contradicted—will have made a place for the presence of the event: an event that is ceaselessly reappropriated.

The problematic of the signature continues and deploys the problematic of the proper name. Indeed, it appears as the attempt to inscribe within the text the singularity of a present-living-being who marks the fact that this text belongs to me and, above all, that in it I assure myself of my ownership. Thus it is returned immediately and naturally, against the signature's desire. In that it is a textual trace, it is already detached from "I-here-now," delivering the text to others. What is "proper" to a signature is to be revealed, however much it may resist, as counterfeit. This is why the signature event wishing to be an event of appropriation already calls the countersignature reappropriation. Any countersignature can only ever promise *its* countersignature, and so forth endlessly: appropriation to and of self can never be completed; the improper is originary.

However, we can see here once again the fundamental idea that the deconstruction of the "proper" in the signature, far from canceling the proper in favor of the originarity of the im-proper, reveals a non-substantial presence that cannot stabilize itself through any determination, which is its weakness but also its strength: what is not a base subject does not, as a result, lend itself to "deconstruction," surviving but escaping it. This is a matter of the fragile presence of the unforeseeable event demolishing all substance rather than bringing it forth—of a signature, for example—that is not simply a disappropriation of self but always also (and in the same gesture) the appropriation of self. This event, exiled from the self, is then identified as an address or a message.

Far from pretending to exhaust the richness of Derrida's treatment of the proper name and the signature,[12] I want here simply to demonstrate that the deconstruction of the substantial subject, of the immanence of presence to self, does not cancel everything signified within the notion of subjectivity but rather unveils the event of presence—presence as event—and the need for the appropriation of self.

Now we must address Derrida's later texts, in which we can see in *the most insistent way*, I think, what always resists deconstruction: an archi-Originary Self.

These texts, from the end of the 1980s and the beginning of the 1990s, are inscribed within the horizon opened out just as much by the problematics of the question of the gift and of temporality as by Derrida's increasingly explicit approach to Levinas's issues. In particular, Derrida increasingly shares Levinas's concern for a Self thought out of the Abrahamic "I am here." The general problematic controlling our inquiry will require us to examine these texts closely.

Clearly, our reading will be governed by a very simple hypothesis, hardly more than a statement of the obvious, which hopefully at least has the merit of destroying a bias, just as Descartes teaches us to do; that is, we readily recognize it, while twisting Derridean thought far in the opposite direction from one tending toward a majoritarian, or even caricatural, reading.

Suffice it to say that if Derrida teaches us that presence is always already haunted by an originary delay, that all "living speech" works through the textual gap that has already destroyed its supposed purity; if Derrida tells us that in a general way "death has always already seized life," he is also, at the very heart of this gesture, the thinker of the living word "as such," of life "as such." The quotation marks around "as such," denying it its naïveté, do not cancel it since the deconstruction that has trumped the Husserlian reduction is no less faithful to him in the friendly gesture of what it given. Derrida is not the one who says that there is no living voice, that fundamentally there is only text; that there is no life, only death. He is the one who says "simply" that the voice is always complicated, that life is always complicated, and above all that they are nothing but illusions.

Let us be clear about this: to refuse this caricatural Derrideanism is not to accede to a radical deconstruction, not to dull its edge by maintaining, despite everything, a bit of presence mixed into the originary delay. On the contrary, it is to emphasize that deconstruction's radicality is not simple but caught in a double bind, which means, paradoxically, that to unveil the affection haunting presence is finally to reveal it "in and as itself."

And the test of this double bind is played out exemplarily in the place of subjectivity as archi-Originary Self, this breath that says "yes."

And this is in fact a question of—what?—of whom?

This "yes" or "I am here" is certainly archi-originary in the sense that if it did *not answer "present,"* no relationality could be established. Before all description, all affirmation; even before all questions and issues; even further, before the *speech act* "yes" reduced to its phatic function, to its function of facilitator of dialogue, it is the silent punctuation that will already have acquiesced—or, at least, received the speech addressed to it, and will thus have given birth to it.[13] This is a source older than all modes of speech, older than all language in general: in this sense the "yes" is not even a word. However, paradoxically but consequently, its archi-originarity does not contradict and even presupposes that it is—by the same stroke—absolutely secondary, and if not derived, at least brought up: it is only a matter of *responding*, of correctly answering "yes"; that is, always answering, in a certain sense, "I am here." A somewhat awkward image for describing what is at stake here: it is as though the archi-originary "yes" was the vibration of a pure potentiality that, as it were, "coagulated," and thus appeared, heeding a call older than it but that, without it, would already have collapsed. And we must add that the potentiality in question is not the simple separation by quotation marks of what must be acted out, and that its "coagulation" is not properly an acting out as substantialization.

This "yes" constitutes a Self in that it self-affects as a Self at the very center of its integral exposition. This is what Derrida's commentary on the Abrahamic "I am here" means, echoing Levinas's commentary: because nothing of what I am comes from me, I am myself because the divine light illuminates and even "sees" what remains to me completely sealed shut, *secret*—that I am an *interiority*. In a paradox that has reversed the evidence of the Cartesian subject to himself is to be completely naked to myself—I am an *I*, or more precisely a Self, brought about by the gesture that originarily held him hostage to himself.[14]

If we examine this archi-Originary Self more closely,[15] this affirmation that is not yet affirmation *of* self but that, however, within the passivity of its radical exposition, emerges, says "yes." In other texts, in order to speak this passivity that without betraying itself as passivity, nonetheless draws, so to speak, from itself, Derrida proposes the interjection "come!," as the mark, older than language, of the "will"—how paradoxical!—of an integral exposition.

I have retained here certain traits of this archi-Originary Self, of this "yes" older than language. It is promise, it is of the order of the voice, and more precisely, it is of the order of what within the voice presents itself as breath and rhythm.

It is promise.[16] This means it is nothing substantial, as a promise is not effectuated action. But at the same time it is entirely there, exposed, as I am there, entirely, in my oath. As a mode of appearing or of paradoxical presence, not only in that it is not that of a substance but that of a performative—but in that this performative itself is quite strange since it is traversed by—and even holds itself entirely within—its own withdrawal or its own effacement: and am I not in a sense entirely there in my promise when, for example, I say to you, "I would come!" (which means, certainly, that I have not come and that perhaps I would never come)? It remains nonetheless that this is a question of manner, doubtless infinitely fragile, precarious—to promise: this is already and simultaneously to risk failure of the promise—to be present, to be *there*.

And yet is it not thus, uniquely, that one is "truly" present?

While it retreats from appearing, from the visibility of substance, the Self is not, as one might be tempted to conclude too quickly, *beyond* all presence, and thus beyond itself—if being a self is all the *less* to answer "present." (This prompts us to say that deconstruction does not cancel, does not eradicate all subjectivity.) The Self is present otherwise, outside visibility, outside substantiality. One would be tempted, in emphasizing a trait that, it is true, is less clearly marked by Derrida, to say that the deconstruction of the metaphysics of presence while stumbling onto subjectivity as that archi-originary "yes," discovers that it is not, as it believed it was, the integral destruction of all presence. Destroying the primacy of presence as substantiality, and still that of presence as appearance, begins to butt up, like its defendant's body, against another kind of presence, strictly invisible and non-substantial. (Should we still speak of presence? Let us leave this question suspended for a moment. It is never a case of absence, on the other hand.)

We must also remember the analyses Derrida consecrates to the voice as such.[17] The voice is the invisible, in essence and not by accident (to cite the traditional distinction). The voice has an absolutely radical invisibility, different from the hidden, that is basically still a mode of visibility, or at least a way of being inscribed in it. The voice is not defined as the negation of the visible, nor as any possible declension of visibility: and yet in my voice I am there, and even perhaps I am in no way truly there, other than in my voice.

Here we can establish a connection between Michel Henry and Jacques Derrida.

In a configuration of thought completely different from Henry's, Derrida lays out a manner of being present that defines itself by its very invisibility; that is, as refusing itself visibility, and, more radically still, being elsewhere than in visibility. We can recognize here the fundamental characteristics of Life according to Michel Henry, in that for him Life is entirely affectivity. In other words—and the parallels can be extended—Life's invisibility for Henry also means that it does not concern itself with substance—if substantiality always means a form capable of being seen.

To say of Derrida that despite everything he is a thinker of presence, that to deconstruct substantiality he "drills down" toward another presence[18] that presents itself as the Self has, it is true, something of the overly simplistic provocateur about it! To show an affinity between the Derridean gesture addressing delay as originary and the dead as always having seized the living, and Henry's gesture affirming life as pure originary immanence, might seem to evoke the same immoderate taste for gratuitous paradox: do these two gestures not stand in opposition to each other, term for term?

Such a connection will correctly allow us to clarify what has been said—and what has not yet been said—of Derrida so far.

What has *not* been said here, in fact—above all—is that Derrida can discover, beyond the figure of presence as substantiality, another figure—the only authentic one—of presence. What has already been said is that the deconstruction of presence is not the promotion of an absence, of a nothing or a nothingness that is, so to speak, autonomous. And since this means that there is always (a) presence to which delay, in order to be originary, is attached, one is always *attached* to presence, which then means at the same time that presence, always complicated by a gap in the originary self, never as pure as it thinks itself to be, is thus no less—and

184 THE TEST OF SUBJECTIVITY

is thus only—presence. The constraint requiring the Derridean gesture of the deconstruction of presence, because it is a double constraint, a double bind, also requires it (always increasingly invisibly) to *affirm* presence even within its originary complication: "the truth is necessary," Derrida writes. In fact, Derrida never advocates for a radically autonomous, pure nothingness that is basic to presence, and that would, moreover, never have been anything more than a reversed imitation of the purity of substance: an uncomfortable, reversed double of the metaphysics of presence.[19] The originary gap is not at the foundation of a presence that, as such, is derivative and inauthentic. The logic of deconstruction is more complex than any simple linear order of ontological derivation, because "the thing itself" is. And if pure presence is a chimera to deconstruct, so is the pure originary gap (of all presence).

Consequently, this double bind requires me to say that I am never myself, lord of my presence to myself, and simultaneously that thus and only thus I am "truly" myself. There is no "as such," no subject, no subject-as-such, and yet "it" is at the very center of the extreme fragilization that makes it undergo deconstruction, that reveals the subject "as such,"[20] since it is truly only itself by surviving its being made most precarious: strictly speaking, it is always a shadow of itself—thus, and only thus, is it truly itself.

The Self, complete in the fragility of the breath of its voice, is only itself at the edge of its destruction or its defection.[21]

In other words, and to return to the theme on which Derrida increasingly insists—that of spectrality—there is a Self only as spectral. *I* am only a spectre—the *I* is only a spectre—Derrida teaches us, but at the same time he shows us that only phantoms are truly living.

And the connection we have here established between Derrida's spectral subjectivity and Life as Henrian subjectivity permits us to "contrast" it—albeit by slightly "forcing" the contrast—with Derridean thought,[22] to make the affirmative life of the spectre appear in it precisely by demonstrating that the spectre and the (its) archi-originary yes to life are always and consequently tied together. We must separate the Derridean philosophical emblematic of the spectre—for a time, at least, since nothing can easily or permanently escape its caricature—from its simplifying caricature: the spectre is not the cadaver. It is essential not to acquiesce to a certain tone of morbid fascination.

There remains one characteristic of this archi-Originary Self that has been underlined but that has still not been explored, and that must be clarified in all its consequences: certainly, the archi-Originary Self is nowhere other than in its voice, or more precisely, it is entirely in the breathing, the tone, or the rhythm of the voice.[23] We will not look more deeply into this here, but this semantic network indicates precisely that only at the point where presence is destroyed is it truly presence: [24] if the voice is really irreducible to the visible in which all substance is profiled, breathing (at least metaphorically) speaks what at the very center of the living voice, that is, the gift, never gives itself. The rhythm and tone of the voice, though unformalizable and incalculable, are also what break the interior voice, and thus (only thus)—paradoxically—"subjectivity." It is important to emphasize that it is these traces—rhythm and tone are but traces that are always concealed in plain sight—that, breaking or at least originarily disordering my presence to myself, give me my *intimacy*. And they give it to me as *living* intimacy, as my living intimacy "'as such.'" The rhythm and tone of my voice, irreducibly ungraspable, "slipping between my fingers," as pause or silence at the heart of my voice, are a "yes," an originary acquiescence that animates it and in so doing, gives *me* to myself as a *living Self*.[25]

This is a problem that has been left suspended, on hold until now to be used as regulative evidence in our analysis: this originary complication of presence, this trace at the heart of all life, giving it itself *as life*, plays out in exemplary fashion and in a sense fundamentally as the originary node of a Self, of a radical subjectivity.

In fact, to say that a Self *is* a Self only insofar as it instantiates a rapport with itself, that it is a presence to itself, is simultaneously to say inversely that presence is presence only when connected to itself, and even always "reassured," in a present, to itself. Moreover, it is a constant of traditional philosophies of subjectivity to think this as the pinnacle of presence: subjectivity is thus the reserve of presence, sovereignty as the looping of presence onto itself.

This can help us understand a decisive aspect of Derrida's interrogation of subjectivity. First, putting aside all unnuanced simplification, it is necessary to hammer home the fact that the Derridean gesture does not cancel subjectivity as such (but rather discovers it as completely other than what it thought itself to be and, in the strictest sense, non-self-reflecting). Now we must add that Derridean thought *does not dissolve* the traditional figure of the subject as subject-substance and/or base (or reduced to its transcendental version): this is not simply a matter of Derrida's exhibiting archi-originary ipseity in emptying the subject of traditional metaphysics, but rather of saying that this subject of traditional metaphysics, as such, is if not legitimate at least ineluctable, and in one sense, necessary.

To say that all subjectivity is already spectral subjectivity is not only to say that its presence to itself will always already have been destroyed but also that, conversely, this presence to self, finding its force in its very precariousness, resists, acts as an ineluctable return: as the resultant spectre, it haunts. To reveal the subject as spectral is to perceive that in no case is it possible to defeat it: presence is impossible to escape.

As a result, it is necessary to coordinate with this spectre: the subject is necessary just as eating is necessary.[26] Any "one must" or "it is necessary" here connotes neither logical necessity nor moral obligation; it is rather a "one must" that says nothing other than the necessity of contingency, the necessity of "making do," of calculating and negotiating.

And must one not negotiate with the subject, in that the subject is itself precisely entirely calculation and negotiation?

If all that is given is given only in the very movement in which it is refused while making a gap—and this is where Derridean différance holds mastery over any gift—the gap is what it is only in not being without connection with that from which it deviates. Too radical a gap, one that would radically break with what it breaks—that is, with presence, the presence that is solely susceptible to being broken—would cancel itself, since it could draw out the little being that is itself only through *still* being "connected to" presence. This is why différance is nothing other than its mark or trace—a trace that can be left only through the immanence of presence: presence is what it is only by always being disrupted, separated from itself—even though it consists entirely of the effort of conjuring up difference—but it is necessary *also* to say that the gap—variation—is what it is only by attaching itself to presence. In addition, the task of showing that presence never has the purity it claims must add to it the task of showing that there is no pure variation (one common to all presence): this is the double bind. And the subject is entirely this obligated presence, which is nothing other than a preoccupation with giving presence confidence in itself. It is a calculation that connects to itself, for itself. The Self emerges from the very gesture of calculation, of preoccupation (with self), of appropriation: strictly speaking, it even merges with this gesture and is thus always in some sense preceded.

The subject negotiates with what is endlessly torn off from itself; it is precisely this negotiation with what one cannot negotiate and with the one who does not negotiate: with the absolutely radical movement of transcendence that perpetually decenters it.[27] This is the harsh spotlight that we might, for example, throw onto the Husserlian ego (to which one can never make too many references), indicating that it is in fact less "center" than movement of centering ceaselessly relaunched, less "identity" than the effort and the exigency of identification of self within the constituting of what—of what *it*—is given.

The subject is nothing other than the (egoistic) movement of adhering to self. And while Derrida formulates the essence of the subject as a "one must eat well," this statement is in a sense neither allegorical nor metaphorical; on the contrary, the subject declares itself directly and entirely within itself, if all of its activities—even the most theoretical, the most apparently detached from biological "eating"—consist of eating, that is, of "making the body," "making presence."

From this point of view, the subject is the opposite or the contradiction of the gift, if the gift, paradoxically but consequently, always conceals. But to say this is to say that it is thus not unconnected to the gift, if it is the focal point of immanence and of presence—or at least the point that has this ideal for itself—alone capable of putting the gift to the test. Consequently, the subject is what could never exist if the gift could not fracture it, but also what would be nothing without the gift, since the gift is where the test takes place—the gift being nothing but the test's taking place: the subject gives the gift/test.

As a result, by identifying itself at the place of its presence to itself, the subject "is" also the gift being concealed from itself: what is always in play, as has become clear, is the breath, the rhythm of the archi-originary yes we began by describing. The subject "circulates" from one to the other of these poles, never allowing it to pause at either of them. And to speak of "circulation" between "poles" is already to rigidify and "mechanize" what is precisely, as we have already seen, the ungraspable breath of "spectralization."

The frontier between the inside and outside of the subject, then, is *blurred*—though this blurring *is* the frontier. And to blur the frontier does not mean to efface it but rather to give it the pretense of originary purity.

The overdetermination of the frontier—that is, what modern metaphysics has ceaselessly engaged in; lured by a pure presence to self that unfolds in the gesture of separating from (the extended thing, for example, to return to the paradigmatic case of the Cartesian cogito). But conversely, to absolutely efface the frontier is to risk caricaturing originary undecidability in the confusion of the mixture: and this is why the subject is ineluctable and even in a sense legitimate, a "one must be the subject well" in order to reguarantee the frontier in perpetuity.

There is in this a double bind with which the subject entirely coincides; indeed, the subject is nothing other than this double bind; that is, it endlessly circles from one to the other of two contradictory constraints—in such a way, however paradoxically, as to localize itself as more specifically at the calculating pole, since that is what marks *its* frontier. It must be said immediately that the other pole, that of alteration, is in its own way more originary and more intimate. But let us stop there. We must break with the vertiginous spinning of this double bind: this is the only method of escaping it.

One last detail: the nature of the connection linking subjectivity as originary yes to subject as egoic (if not egoist) recentering clarifies the ineluctable nature of the latter.

If Michel Henry can designate an auto-affection, a connection from self to itself, more originary than all reflection from self, and even than all substantiality supported by one form, for Derrida, an absolutely pure self-affection, in its need precisely for purity, does nothing but imitate the most fundamental trait of the metaphysics of presence.[28] Thus, the archi-originary yes cannot be apprehended and conserved in its purity; it will already have translated into the subject, within the metaphysics of presence just as, inversely, the ego-substance and/or base will never have had the empire it thought it had. The connection between the one and the other is a connection of *contamination*.[29] The subject's spectrality is only that:[30] the derangement of presence to itself through a separation from self (and conversely). The subject-substance and/or base already contaminates auto-affection in the archi-originary yes, in a contamination that at once betrays and saves: and the gesture consisting of expelling the traditional figure of the subject under the pretext of bringing to light a more originary subjectivity disfigures spectral subjectivity as much as that which consists of being entrusted integrally and without remainder to the subject.

Thus, the different characteristic traits of subjectivity are woven together, according to Derrida. And if in his texts a specific assemblage does not occur, this is because the "clarification" we have wished—in a naïve and awkward gesture—to be in operation can only result in an already-excessive rigidification that betrays the surprise produced through all subjectivity, and where all subjectivity is produced. It is in dissemination that subjectivity is best "given."

But it is also true that there "must be" pauses, even and above all in the most unrestrained rhythms. There "must be subject" regarding the Derridean discourse on the subject itself.

PART IV

PHENOMENOLOGICAL DISCOURSE
AND SUBJECTIFICATION

We will now bring the threads of Parts 1 and 2 together—temporality as limit and subjectivity as test—in order now to see them in the context of their redoubling in philosophical discourse.

And perhaps this will be surprising: phenomenology is, in fact, the patient description of phenomena in the face of which it must in a sense efface itself, ignoring all expressive "depth." Why, then, spend time on its discourse as such, let alone on the texts it provides us?

As I cannot overemphasize, in the final chapters of *Otherwise Than Being: or, Beyond Essence*, Emmanuel Levinas shifts the question of the test of subjectivity step by step from the domain of experience—the phenomenological discourse on which we are focusing here—toward discourse per se, discourse characterized by *diachrony*: this diachrony, like subjectivity, is exemplarily, if not originarily, of the order of philosophical *Saying* and of *Said*.

We must remember that the analyses of subjectivity undertaken here all converge on a subjectivity framed by either accusative or vocative grammatical categories *called* subjectivity. The sources of this call, this appeal—all the more so given that the notion of "source" is itself in crisis—are Being (Heidegger), Life (Henry), the pure form of the call (Marion), the Other (Levinas/Derrida).

And we must read there the placing in crisis of the metaphysical axiomatic laid out in the notions of cause, of base, of "reason." Substituting for the link between the reality of the cause and what it grounds is another linkage, whose model is provided to us through language's performative dimension: subjectivity, as such, is called or convened, entirely caused by the act addressed to it and that in no case precedes it. The connection between subjectivity and what causes or precedes it, on the one hand, and the effect of its cause, on the other, is incommensurable. In fact, this latter connection presupposes the opening of the horizon of substantiality.

Consequently, the call in question here no longer arises from the language of the project of truth, and even less as the vessel of meaning—if sense, as distinguished from reference, is still constituted from the gravitational pull of the latter. Language is thus not what describes, states, or poses a content of meaning but rather what makes being from beings, and first of all from the *I*; the *I to which it gives birth*.

Philosophic discourse appears as the *echo* and even the *amplification* of precisely what is at play on the scene of beings, or more precisely on that limit where the scene of being is itself (immanence, as Levinas would say) given to itself as nothing other than the painful solitude of its initial inhabitant.

Let us briefly lay out the implications of this other gift, of this other configuration of connections between subjectivity and language.[1]

First, primordial language demonstrates the immediacy of the event: this is why Levinas understands it through the "category" of *Saying*; *Saying* as the radicality of the Word-event that above all else signifies the intentional constituting of meaning, before all noemes and, in general, before all the thematics gathered together in a *Said*. And if we might say of *Saying* that it *signifies*, then signification emerges in the paradoxical pragmatics of an act that is itself situated entirely in the radical passivity of its *exposition* (to the Other).[2]

Consequently, the Word-event of ipseized, finite subjectivity combines the radicality of its passivity and the radicality of its performative force in the figure of *witnessing* and/or of *attestation*.[3]

Finally, the immediacy and the event-nature of language implied by such a configuration mean that it is the register of the *voice* (as of *inspiration* and *breath* for Levinas and Derrida), more than that of *text*, that is foregrounded in such a problematic.[4] Make no mistake: it is certainly not the empirical fabric of sound that is in question but the immediacy of the voice to itself, as a corporeal and even carnal intimacy.

But for all the thinkers addressed here, the voice's immediacy to itself finds itself, in one way or another, affecting an intimate separation from itself, a constitutive gap in its very immediacy.

This has to do with a configuration accentuating the "thesis" of the originarily constitutive gap in a unique way, since it insists on the idea that these are the intimacy and immediacy that are thus themselves manifested in this variation from itself.[5] To cite an exemplary indicator from Levinas: because the gap is not denied, this does not at all mean that the notion of the *trace* is effaced; because it is important not to caricature the originarity of the gap as *hegemony*, one must avoid the exclusivity of the textual register and of writing in order to maintain and retain a *voice* and/or a *speech act*.[6] Quite significantly, the notions of *echo* and of *resonance* often substitute for that of *trace* in *Otherwise Than Being*.[7]

In the final analysis, my hypothesis is that the works we are reading here speak less of the way in which subjectivity is brought about in an originary test—a "trauma," as Levinas says—and that they do not cause, do not *give birth to*, the subjectivity of the receiver, the reader. How do they do it? In the trauma consisting precisely of a "staging" of originary trauma of the Self in a discourse that itself "mimes" this trauma only insofar as it is situated nowhere other than in the temporality of the syncopated movement of the birth of a meditating subjectivity.[8]

In "Awakening and Birth. Some Remarks on Emmanuel Levinas and Michel Henry,"[9] I laid out the global nature of the problematic to be explored in what follows. My question there was: In what way do Henry's and Levinas's texts traumatize their reception? Seeking the answer to this question implies an attempt to discern these texts' general style: a traumatizing style because it is itself traumatized by excess. The remark through which these texts dealt explicitly and significantly with birth and awakening provided a thematic point of departure, and the subsequent analysis led to the conclusion that excess of immanence (Henry) and excess of transcendence (Levinas)—from a particular viewpoint, and only from that viewpoint, these two bodies of thought that seemed absolutely opposed are intimately close, like the two sides of a single intuition—join together in the fact that the untenable aspects of these philosophies are most fertile in the risk they perpetually run—the risk of sterility and destruction. As I wrote then:

Why and how are we to read Michel Henry and Emmanuel Levinas? Are there not, without doubt, in their work phases of "excess" and, consequently, of "slipping" out of phenomenology, but is there not a phenomenology that is not exposed to this "outside"? And if these phases of excess are not in themselves confrontation outside—they signal, on the contrary, that the limit was reached, that the test of the limit had been considered to be too radicalized—do they not at least testify, as if negatively, to having run the risk of exposure? In a sense, Henry and Levinas are "bad" masters. But to make a good master, do we not need a bad master, a master who makes it possible for one to be absolved of the relation that unites us with it, as Levinas said? (215)

Our task here, then, has been to examine the way to test out the limit of the phenomenological within that necessary risk of excess—excess that is necessarily already the "excess of excess" that is marked as the refallen. If our reading hypotheses are proven correct, then the movement of these philosophical discourses that the practice of excess takes to the threshold of rupture will have the performative function of causing the traumatized birth of the meditating ego-addressee, in the "staging" of the birth of meditating subjectivity that shows itself in them.

In fact, as I have tried to show, this problematic is now moving us toward a study of rhythm; that is, toward a study as much of what these writers we are studying have said *about* rhythm as of the rhythm of their phrasing.

Before entering into the heart of the matter, let me make a preliminary remark about the economy of our route: in the following pages, the commentary will be centered electively on the works of Levinas and Henry, and this will not be the elaborate study of rhythm according to Derrida, nor the rhythm of Derrida's phrasing. This sidestepping—only one of the expressions of a difficulty I mentioned at the beginning of this book: that of knowing Derrida to be more difficult than any other, perhaps, to integrate into a family—calls for a brief explanation.

First, it is essential to remember that Derrida speaks about rhythm often, and in terms that manifestly inform our analysis here; thus his definition of style as *éperon*, spur, destroying presence, identifying it, in *Spurs*, as *Nietzsche's styles*. Thus his insistence on what, rebelling against the syntax and the grammar constraining language, finds its accommodation in the fragility of tone or accent, and even more in what forms the heart of a tone or an accent: a certain unique rhythm. In fact, it is basically always a rhythm that makes an event, in the sense that it is incalculable, unforeseeable, and thus irreducibly singular. It is also always a rhythm that provides what a voice provides, however much it shies away, "in essence," from all integral givenness. An example, among many other texts:

Everything is summoned from an intonation. And even earlier still, in what gives its tone to the tone, a rhythm. I think that all in all, it is upon rhythm that I stake everything. It therefore begins before the beginning. That is the incalculable origin of a rhythm. (*MO*, 48)

Derrida teaches us that the notion of *tone* comes from *tonos*, the Greek term signifying "the extended ligament," and that consequently *tone* is what connects beings under tension, *tendu*; that is, brought to the brink of rupture (Tone, 25).

Deconstruction, thus, emerges, as we have seen, from a cut, a rupture freeing the unthought of a text by allowing it to be disrupted, one might say to be "wounded." And this rhythm for Derrida—in an affinity with a certain Levinasian rhythm—can and must be described, but it would be too mutilated to be isolated from the *other* Derridean rhythm; this is precisely the problem we face here: if it allows itself to be apprehended as a certain violence of rupture and of excess, according to the angle of our attack, the Derridean rhythm cannot be defined by this aspect alone. It is at this point that we might become embarrassed by our approach here. It must be said that the Derridean gesture is on the side of nuance rather than of contrast, in that it stops at the ambiguity of the undecidable, which brings it close to Merleau-Ponty. Derrida's ideas of "originary dissemination," of "originary undecidability," imply a style that, so to speak, undetermines itself. Derridean deconstruction, far from the violence of Levinasian hyperbole or the "tautologies" of the Henrian text in which Life expresses itself, insists on being more nuanced, less trenchant, through its infinite patience with the details of texts.

To hold this ambiguity in mind requires formulating the hypothesis that the Derridean text is entire, as it were; it is the regulating of a double bind whose two terms are constituted by, on the one hand, concern with undecidability and originary dissemination and, on the other, by the motifs of trait, of cut, of wound, of the trauma of the invention of the other. From this perspective, what Nicole Loraux explains regarding Plato—which, she says, she reads along with Derrida—seemingly has value for Derrida himself: "I would say gladly that in Plato everything plays out between *Khora* and *khoris*. Between *Khora*, neither sensible nor intelligible and thus the principle of indecision, and *khoris*, which separates and isolates."[10]

Our particular angle of attack allows us to privilege the Derridean motifs of the trait, the cut or wound, the double bind, and the aporia, all on the threshold of the impossible, of the gift as impossible or the lack of generosity, to the detriment as much of the patient sinuosity of the deconstructive gesture as of the "stirring" of style edging toward originary undecidability. This is, perhaps, a matter of interpretive manipulation, of our way of attempting to wound the Derridean text. And perhaps we might also see here an evolution of Derridean thought that, without ever ceasing to hold firmly to both requirements of the double bind, seems to move increasingly toward a testing of the impossible and of the cut—and thus toward Levinas.

Whatever the case may be, Derridean rhythm seems to be dedicated to complexity. And with the intent of emphasizing the significance of the general problematic of the book without proceeding to outrageous simplifications, we will attempt to avoid in the coming pages the complexity of the Derridean corpus, and we will focus our investigation on works in which the rhythm of the discontinuity of excess and of the trauma of rupture are clearest and, as it were, simplest: the works of Henry and Levinas.

With this focus in mind, let me lay out the reasons for an interest in rhythm as such.

1. Rhythm is one of the essential components of an author's style. And if style is this uniquely singularizing difference inscribing the subjectivity of the writer as affectivity within a text, and that thus makes the writer an author, a "writer" and not merely an inscriber, then we must study it, since the texts we will read come to us in the mode of excess—the excess that is always a gap with regard to a normative limit—and as the producer of performative subjectivity (as much that of the addressee as of the addresser).

2. The concept of the notion of rhythm since Plato—and doubtless much further back than that—is pervaded by a tension. Latterly,

rhythm is thought of as a formal principle and at the same time a principle of order, of organization: it is regularity in repetition—*measure*. But even more recently, on the contrary, rhythm has been seen as what menaces form, apart from form itself: unformulatable—and even *informe*, fluid and unformed—within all formulation, the incalculable within all calculation.[11] One can clearly see here the separation, the difference infusing all repetition. In fact, it would be more accurate to speak of an ambivalence in the notion of rhythm seeing it simultaneously as signifying the measure of cadence and the excess of rupture, the one in the other and the one through the other, given that repetition presupposes difference: in rhythm, form and the rupture of all form, continuity and discontinuity, are linked one to the other: rhythm is exemplarily aporetic.[12]

3. Our focus on rhythm is not a return to the stakes of writing or even of language itself but an originary given of phenomenology as such: if the hypothesis that all of this work has aimed at, the claim that givenness is possible only on the basis of non-givenness, is in fact legitimate, then all of phenomenology is related to rhythm—if rhythm is precisely what threatens (and thus gives birth to) form, that is, if rhythm is the discontinuity that breaks it.[13]

Also sharing in Benveniste's analyses, Jacques Garelli remarks that if rhythm is thought of as a form, and even as a schema, it is only as the form of a fluid element, and consequently—and this is the supplementary step explored by Garelli in association with Benveniste—he will say that rhythm *is not in fact a form*, even if it is at least partially linked with form. Rhythm lies beneath form, is more originary than form that is already a kind of objectivity. Rhythm arises, then, strictly in terms of the pre-predicative (and consequently can only be approached indirectly, through "reflecting judgments," as Garelli says, echoing Kant). All approaches to rhythm in terms of an objective time that could be counted and measured are invalid: the mechanical process of counting syllables is never tantamount to making a poet; the mechanical aspect of metronomic cadence is never solely responsible for making an interpretive musician. But it is not enough to say that rhythm lies beneath objectivity; rather, that it is still deeper than that, since it lies beneath phenomenality itself. And more precisely, it might be said that rhythm lies beneath phenomenality as its given, and thus as its own intimacy. In fact, rhythm, older than all substantiality—than all identity and all alterity, as Garelli says—is not nothing. It is—and Garelli expresses this in terms borrowed from contemporary physics, through which he implicitly tests out rhythm—"energetic potential." It is the oldest force in all substances, even older than all phenomena that open out into phenomenology itself. Phenomenology can exist only insofar as each rhythm is a "way" (I would not dare to say "a way of being") of the movement of temporalization proffering each phenomenon to us in its singularity, each in its own rhythm. A phenomenon is truly a phenomenon, radically appearing, only on condition of being, strictly speaking, an apparition, taking a horizon of expectation by surprise, interrupting: in Garelli's words, rhythm is a power of *dephasing* that prevents the phenomenologization process from "refalling," falling asleep, congealing into phenomena—and thus into "substantialities" in their respective, singular identities. Rhythm ceaselessly awakens phenomenality, recalling it to its primordial metastability: that is why it is nothing that can be foreseen and calculated (Garelli shows this effectively in his analysis of poems, for example, Mallarmé's and Rimbaud's, both of whom he shows to be powers of dephasings, emergences, and bendings, meaning that nothing of them is foreseeable to the reader in the unfolding of any reading).

I subscribe to *nearly* all of Garelli's analysis of rhythm, some aspects of which I will describe below. We differ, however, on one decisive point: for Garelli, rhythm situates itself at the hinge between substantial individualities and the primordial pre-individual base from which they come and to which they must return as if toward their true anonymity. Thus, in its metastability, rhythm is like the breath of this anonymous base, calling it back to itself; it is the already-dissolving lability that it makes appear.

But our writers address ipseic subjectivity, as we have seen, as originary in its own way, implying that the rhythm of phenomenalization will in no case ride on the emergence from and the immersion in all individualities within the anonymous base of what Merleau-Ponty calls The World. I cannot, according to our three writers, adopt—or even propose as a transcendental, which would be carnal—a point of view older than my singular subjectivity, which would permit me, if not to assist at least to hold as primordial, the shading of the feature designating each singularity in the originary metastable base.[14] Consequently, for our central figures rhythm loses fluidity, is no longer a dissolving flux, and gains in the power of rupture. Since it can be apprehended only from the perspective of an ipseic, singularized subjectivity, it is always lived as the test of an interruption, the interruption of the *jouissance* of self and of power over the self, interruption that paradoxically gives the self to itself.[15] It is the syncope interrupting all givenness in order to give it, originarily, to itself.

This discontinuous temporality, for essential reasons, resembles but differs from what applies to the lability of the flux, the phenomenological description toward its limit: what is there to see and what to say, not so much what *flows out*, but what *crumbles*; what in its crumbling will always already have preceded substantiality?

It does not allow itself to be integrally thematized in a discourse expressing, in an absolutely transparent way, an intentional constitution, as Husserl would wish but, on the contrary, only fleetingly indicating itself—all indication is by nature fleeting, incomplete, and this imperfect—in a language opposing the resistance and opacity of matter that is to be "opened" by subjectivity, by an author. This is indicated in rhythmic phrasing that—to state it too schematically—"mimes" and "performs" it when it is not able to say it (thematically).

A sentence's rhythm echoes that of phenomenality's discontinuous temporalization. This echo—since all echo is essentially distanced, an auditory trace—does not *say*, it *suggests* what the thematic *cannot* say, and it needs the thematic it contains to determine what it is, at least minimally, in order to escape radical indetermination. Inversely, the thematic needs rhythm to indicate what it cannot say. It is thus vital to scrutinize this interweaving of rhythm and theme in which each, handicapped, gives assistance to the other.[16]

1

The Rhythm of *Otherwise Than Being*
According to Levinas

1. Reading Levinas and Thinking
Entirely Otherwise

The name "Levinas" has, of course, already entered significantly into the history of philosophy and has become the name of a unique place in this strange landscape, a signpost for orientation in it. And if the history of philosophy, properly understood, cannot be reduced simply to a line of tombstones, it is because the names on them mark the important axes of theory and practice. "Levinas": the name of a way of thinking and living never before seen and whose like we will never see again, always available for questions about what is happening in the world, always available to respond to the ever-new questions perpetually addressed to him. Pure power of invention, it ("Levinas") eternally returns, all the more surprising though never completely identified, all the more lionized (that is, as the subject of idolatry)—or in a close, symmetrical gesture, broken, since in the end all idols are broken. Levinas's method of thought keeps coming back to us, quite simply, insofar as we have not *spoken* it, solidified it into a Said.

But this contribution to the "history of philosophy" is obvious when its name is Levinas, for at least two reasons. On the one hand (we will return to this), Levinas does not inscribe himself in philosophy's center nor outside it but at its limit. On the other hand—and these two are increasingly connected—since Levinas never ceased paying attention to the proper name and to its inscription in philosophy (to its inscription in philosophical text as signature), in that this is a matter of the echo of the paradoxical inscription of the face in phenomenology as what Jacques Rolland calls an "anti-phenomenon." Subjectivity as "unique identity" is at the center of Levinas's philosophy less as his theme than as what it produces—in the sense in which "to produce" is "to show," and "to show" is uniquely in manifestation. More precisely, philosophy as subjectivity produces *itself* as an "at this very moment" "here I am."[1] In addition, it tends to produce subjectivity otherwise, or rather the other as subjectivity: as interlocution, it is contained entirely in the act causing, giving birth to, others—the addressee par excellence. At base, Levinas's philosophical discourse *mimes* the very movement by which Otherwise than being makes being emerge. Philosophic subjectivity speaks about this scene in which phenomenology appears through what exceeds it rather than is produced by a miming of that excess—which, paradoxically, produces all phenomena by tearing them away from phenomenality. It emerges there and participates in its emergence: it redoubles, *en abyme*, the originary trembling of all phenomenality. And in confronting this strange spectacle, it initiates subjectivity: it "assigns" subjectivity to each person.

My subjectivity, then, is this "passivity older than all passivity," impossible for me to conceal, and is only that, since there *is* nothing else: my passivity, which is in a sense (and in one sense only) "nothing," is irreducible and originary, irreducible because originary. As a result (and through the same process), my subjectivity returns as the activation of responsibility: in the face of what is endlessly concealed, it is always already maintained, in its "needing to be" for . . . ; it is precisely this paradox: as the pure immanence of a hypostasy already signified and thus stable, it *is* only in the possibility of its own desertion, only in the possibility of breaking the chains linking it to itself, in the possibility of "going inside": this then means that it cannot hide from its "responsibility," its desertion loosening the grip of being that has taken it by the throat, thus giving it the relief necessary to be able to *respond*. Through this doubled movement, what breaks it makes it responsible, (re)installing it in the originary place that preceded the opposition between activity and passivity.

If we remember that "Levinas" is a proper name "produced" by a proper noun, this is still not to say that it turns toward the biographical in the psychological sense of the word, but that it exposes itself to these questions: If I install myself in Levinas's texts, what can I conceal from myself, and what must I perhaps then refuse myself? What is the *test* that, through philosophy, will "subjectivize" me, as a reader of Levinas?

In other words, if Levinas's text is in fact a powerful force of traumatism, then the question is: What is the best way to use this text? How should I expose myself to it, on the one hand, without allowing it to annihilate me but, on the other, still finding a way for this generative test to be my birth?[2]

This is the "irritant," and even the insupportable—and they are not the same—that one must anticipate in reading Levinas.

We see here first of all the caricatures of the Levinasian text. Such caricatures reside in the eye of the beholder (and the believer), and indeed in all readers whose desire is merely to *summarize*, but also—and this is the most troubling and the most interesting aspect of Levinas's texts themselves, or at least on their surface—first, that they *do not defend themselves* from being read as the simple *repetition* of a certain interpretation of Judaism and as its designation as that toward which all philosophic discourse migrates, finally to be erased in it—or at least where it finds its meaning. Or, second—and worse—it *allows itself to be read* as an elaborated version of the motto of contemporary humanitarianism.

Let us take a brief look at these two caricatures (which are only the most obvious): *it might seem* that in "Levinas" the philosophical did not stop at the limit at which it had to become uneasy with itself, though rather gaily crossed this limit in order to dissolve itself in the religious: "This relation with others, I call it religion." We must, however, quickly remember that in the first place Levinas never ceases claiming a distinction between his practice of interpreting the Talmud and his practice of philosophy (but is he convincing?). In the second place, the fact that in always claiming, neatly and cleanly, the overlap of his discourse with philosophy, he is careful in his philosophical texts themselves to avoid posing this problem in terms of a choice between philosophy and religion.[3] He seems to deny this approach all relevance: the inscription of the entirely other within the philosophical thematic, within its propheticism, does not for him "compromise" the philosophical status of his text—and even guarantees it: for Levinas, philosophy can occur only when it is already affected, contaminated—compromised—by its other.

In the end, Levinas only problematizes philosophy's relation with its other (religion) in order simultaneously to radically affect the sphere of religion as well: denouncing all substantiation, elevating transcendence beyond the phenomenon, and then beyond essence; forbidding its being named and revealing it as defection, he tells us that it *is not.* In this sense, "God" is only a word, a meaningful trace but nothing other than a word. No confession, no dogma can claim this experience of the infinite-as-meaning for themselves exclusively, and all of them are disguised as *a* truth (of being). We might then suspect Levinas—reversing himself—of dissolving religion in philosophy, given that the latter, as such, would be atheistic, fastened to the here-and-now through the endurance of nothing: "The authentic relationship with others I call religion." So is religion completely retraducible in Levinasian philosophy of the for-others?

Perpetually threatened by the two excesses about to be described is Levinas's very power not then to disturb both religion and philosophy, to expose them to each other? And thus to expose the fact that each of them is a *decision*—yet denied as such? The philosopher's decision faces him with the test of that *other* decision, faith, and vice versa.

The most appropriate model accounting for the connections between philosophy and religion *in* Levinas's philosophy is Derrida's interpretation of the *double bind*: philosophy as *always already* contaminated by its Other, Religion (since the latter is precisely the discourse *of* the Other—and the genitive is here as objective as it is subjective). It is the aporia of this aporia, the aporia at the heart of the double bind, the latter being at once the thought of contamination as originary (and thus the thought that in a sense neither philosophy nor religion exists in a *pure* state),[4] and that nonetheless, insofar as it has an effective real in the work of contamination, and insofar as it is not simply already mixed together so that nothing has an effect on anything else, that the *pure* is maintained "somehow," though already obscured by the blurring affecting it, and finally that we might be able even to think this blurring.

How must this double bind be managed? How does Levinas manage it? We can certainly not pretend to address these questions fully here. But in examining them, I want to find the reason for these irritating caricatures in terms of our present interests.

Levinas's texts put the double bind to work only through running the risk of transgressing limits, a transgression consisting of going beyond the philosophical and installing ourselves in this beyond, in the form of a false philosophy merely echoing religion (or is, rather, its excessive opposite, though Levinas is less subject to it in the form of a false philosophy reiterating "philosophy").

Not risking resuscitating the religious at the heart of the philosophical would imply saying not only that transcendence is nothing other than being—as Levinas continuously repeats—but also that it is the "nothing of nothing." But is Otherwise than being *still* recuperable along with being? Always in advance of the ego, it will have left its trace, but is it still connected to being since we must admit that it *will have been*, even if it is always already?[5] And how could it be otherwise since the nothing, as what does not even leave a trace, can be neither spoken nor thought; since, more profoundly, we can never be connected to the "nothing of nothing"? Additionally, even though the trace is necessary, it already contaminates; already within it, being contaminates. Levinas's discourse tests out this contamination all the more in not saying it: there must be a Said to embrace Saying, to allow itself to be disrupted by it and thus already to betray it, solidify it: this treason is neither specifically religious nor specifically philosophical; the flashing forth of saying is neither specifically religious nor specifically philosophical. Ambivalence strikes everywhere and redoubles.

Religious dogma flies into pieces beneath the blows of philosophical scrutiny,[6] all the more because the constituted philosophical *logos* must itself fly into pieces beneath the blow of the infinite extending beyond it. It is nonetheless true that even if Levinas actually ascribes to the second of these fundamental propositions, the first is to my knowledge completely absent from his texts. But this is precisely because he is a philosopher, because he endures the hardship of guiding this double bind toward the side of philosophy.

What is in play here is precisely the uncontrollable with which one can only negotiate, since it must ceaselessly renew *chance*—precisely in order to guide it. This uncontrollable, as I have indicated, since it must contaminate and since contamination exists only in order to maintain something of the purity beneath and in its very blurring, as the double bind implies a practice of the limit. It implies enduring the instability of a discourse that is like a high-wire act: perpetually uneasy on one of its two edges, and thus each edge made uneasy by the other. That is, an intrinsically risky discourse: risking falling to one side or the other. If excess is what upsets it (as, exemplarily in Levinas, the infinite in philosophy), excess is the risk of risking: an excessive practice of excess thus canceling it as such. This risk consists precisely of risking the cancellation of all risk. And it is what takes place when *traversing* the limit; the Levinasian discourse ceases enduring it in order to install it *beyond* (or on this side of it) in rediscovered comfort, that is, in a purity that is as though petrified and sure of itself, an effective purity: religion or philosophy, identified, determined, shielded from their closed frontiers. But this risk cannot be escaped because it is a question precisely of the risk of risk, of what returns the risk—philosophical discourse as endurance of the limit—that is risked.

And the mark that one has succumbed to this ineluctable risk consists of those moments in which the various phases of the constituted Said that are necessary for embracing the trace of Saying are "inverted" and "crusted over" in order to be protected from Saying, from what astonishes and upsets them. Avoiding all risk of invention, they set to work, in the mechanical sense of the word: the discourse assures and reassures itself through self-parody and self-caricature. And this caricature is neither "religion" nor "philosophy" but the one as the other when they betray what about them is surprised and surprising, disrupting and being disrupted, when they caricature *themselves.*[7] And thus they are strangely alike in that they both take on the immutability of the Same. They even encounter each other in caricature, which produces religion *repeated* in philosophy, in the cancellation of their respective powers of astonishing, which could lead, specifically, to the caricature of a clichéd agreement[8] to "take the bread out of one's mouth in order to give it to those who are hungry," as the humanitarian axiom—the laic version of the morality of charity current in democracies, itself currently caricatured as the democracy of the bourgeois individual. This is why Alain Badiou is not wrong when he says that to take Levinas's philosophy seriously requires disconnecting it from this caricature in order to restore its own force to it, its access to the opening onto (and through) the infinite; that is, to what defines the religious (see Alain Badiou, *Ethics. An Essay on the Understanding of Evil*). But Badiou draws the following conclusion: the power of Levinas's text resides entirely in its religious nature; it *cancels* philosophy, within itself, in favor of religion. And this is where he is wrong, since Levinas's philosophy critiques—or rather deconstructs—as though in advance, the axiomatic on which Badiou's very argument rests: the possibility of distinguishing and determining a pure philosophy and a pure religious sphere, and the necessity of protecting both. The infinite or the Entirely-Other is not the proper text for religion. The infinite or the Entirely-Other is not radically exterior to the philosophical; that is, not without a connection to it. This still does not mean that it can be accommodated *completely* in the philosophical. Here, in these "walks" or "borders" separating and contaminating the one by the other, religion and philosophy, the Infinite is the *improper* text itself. The one *is* only when always already affected by the other: the philosophical gives the Entirely-Other the support of its trace, while the Entirely-Other disrupts and thus animates the philosophical Said. They must both resist the temptation to cancel one *in* the other (a risk run by Levinas), and to refuse to maintain them as two exteriorities sealed together (which is what Badiou does, at least in his reading of Levinas).

We now understand why the Levinasian text can only expose itself to its own caricature.[9] And we understand that this caricature is inevitable, and even that it is caricatural in direct proportion to the risk it runs. This is how to account for the irritant in the reading of a certain Levinas.

But in engaging this reflection, we miss another: beyond the irritant, there is the *insupportable* in Levinas's texts. In the strictest sense, these texts produce a test that cannot be taken up. What do I mean?

This is not the least of the paradoxes in Levinasian philosophy allowing itself to develop as though at the surface of the superficial discourse we might call "slack" and that succumbs to the charitable, at the very moment when to *dig down*, if only a little, under this surface, would reveal the discourse of the for-others tainting itself with unexpected violence.[10] But we can pause only briefly in the peace of this originary opening to others, which endlessly reverts to its caricatural "love thy neighbor as thyself" toward its revelation as originary traumatism.

What we can see here is neither the violence of the analysis Levinas gives it (that is, as the act of the Same whose aim is to return to the Same "as an act in which I have not myself collaborated") nor the fact that he notes that the "real" is war—this latter, moreover, from the outset short-circuiting all pacifying caricatures and, all in all, idiotizing the for-others. No: what we see here is the violence of the other—violence to the genitive subjective—the other as violence. This violence is accented in the course of Levinas's work. And in *Otherwise Than Being*, it attains a paroxystic form that is semantic and, to an extent we will have to investigate further, "metaphorical": the body suffering torture: the "condition of the hostage," traumatism, returning primordially to the test—the ordeal—of "bleeding," of "stripping off of the skin to the point of death," of "enucleation" (eye gouging—blinding).[11] Subjectivity produces itself through the other's being blinded, broken, and bled out: there is something insupportable in these images, which might be found in similar forms in James Ellroy's patient descriptions of the serial killer at work (the difference between Levinas's style and Ellroy's is that Levinas's is less finished and consistent). Graphic violence "giving" the self to itself as co-equal with its pain; sadistic violence, if we adopt the viewpoint of the other—but it is precisely this point of view that I can never take.[12] Masochistic violence, then, the call of the other as violence. *I am*, being broken by the other.

Levinasian philosophy must be read as revelatory—and productive—neurotic machinery of neurosis, if not of psychosis. At work in it is obsession with the other; in fact, the primacy of the other-as-other—too bad if the expression seems contradictory—is *too absolute, absolute* to the point that it is no longer escapable, no longer "play" between ego and others. And my ipseity is nothing other than this "rivet" riveting me to the other and thus to myself, in and through pain.

Although in his first works Levinas defined subjectivity as the very capacity to *escape* to the omnipresence of *being* (see *EE*), by the time of *Otherwise Than Being* "being" is *chained* to the other. Alterity as liberation from the prison of the Same, as the very thing that opens, functioning as the strictest of chains, linking the being-in-debt, caught in a non-repayable debt, to the creditor. And that which also—and simultaneously—connects being to itself, returning it to itself in its being-accused. In the pointing of a finger I identify and accuse myself, for the *first time* turning my finger toward my own chest, saying "Me?" For the first time, in the interrogative fragility betraying my total exposure to the other, I become ego, become myself. Others give me to being, but I can never return it to others. Being nothing other than what others give me, I am nothing other than my pure *exposure*; the bare faces of others destroy my power because of its vulnerability and, already, persecute me, to the extent that I give them everything. But why is this originary affection, from *Totality and Infinity* to *Otherwise Than Being*, described less and less as paternity and teaching, as a caress and eroticism,[13] and increasingly as hostage guilt and traumatic pain? We will avoid psychoanalyzing the trajectory of the individual, noting only that without doubt, once again, ambivalence is pervasive and redoubling: what is most interesting is the rapport in Levinas that others always have with *jouissance* and suffering, which for Levinas are indistinguishable. If I am destroyed being, the trauma of alteration *already* comes back to me as *jouissance* of being; and the *jouissance* of being is already disrupted. And if it is the essence of being to persevere in its being, then alteration—change—can only be pain—and already the possibility of *jouissance*: in the strictest of terms, *I* sense myself only under the other's blows. And I am only that, this self that enjoys (from myself, since all *jouissance* is *jouissance*-of-oneself) having been subjected to the test of the other. I am born from the other in an irreducible pain that already returns as the other's *jouissance*. And this is clearly the test's conclusion, since it underlines the fact that alterity never produces experience, if "experience" is still my experience, recuperated affection, constituted and thus neutralized by the ego. A test as such is the unacceptable itself for the self born in it. Ambiguity, in the Levinasian sense of the word, reigns in this "process," connecting the self to others in an intricate originary of suffering and *jouissance*, not as liability and watchful indetermination—as in Merleau-Ponty, but as instability of a thread endlessly broken and repaired: thus the violence of alterity (as trauma or blinding, causing the ego to hemorrhage) will already have returned as eroticism or caress (at the point when losing one's grip infiltrates one's stability [*lorsque la déprise vient habiter la prise*]), when the other has revealed me to myself, placing me at the heart of my *jouissance*. As has been noted (see *MP* and Marty, "La hauteur et le sublime," 301–12), there is a Levinasian sublime: pleasure *in* displeasure, to which we must add that it is this specifically: as a blinking,[14] a quick alternation of phases of *jouissance* and of alteration that are themselves violent.

Why these insupportable, unacceptable "phases" of the Levinasian Said? And why are these insupportable moments surveilled by the risk of being too much? Why, pardon the expression, this "Gore" Levinas?

Certain phases of the Levinasian Said are strictly necessary, just as they are: marks of the infinite as unacceptable insofar as they can only provoke fear. The weft of the Levinasian Said has meaning only when disrupted, and when disrupting. As marks of the unacceptable, these phases must be untenable: they abandon us and we them. We cannot accompany Levinas there: we remain on the threshold—but we must go *almost there* with him in order to take the test of this limit in the best way possible. We must take it in the best way *possible*, while still remaining within the dimension of the possible, that is, the human. Rubbing up against the infinite, touching on the unknown, is the only way to truly take the test, never to the very end. Why? Because the "very end" of the test is hemorrhage. And what can quickly become far too easy. Everything returns to itself, and the risk is always going too far. The unacceptable, when caricatured, risks being far too tame.

We came to understand, in our study of the unacceptable in "Levinas," from that unacceptable heart, we will rediscover, as though backward, the very principle—the word itself is uncomfortable here—that makes its surface of irritating caricatures undulate: the risk of an excessive practice of excess. Those phases in which the infinite shines forth are the counterparts of phases of immanence, which they upset, and where *already* they lose themselves in caricature.

The serenity of this thought will thus have been nowhere: framed by its excess, it will always be diffracted in them.

The Levinasian text must above all not *retain* anything: this ambiguous text everywhere escapes; its "petrified" phases of the Said invite us explicitly only to go beyond them; its unexpected phases are merely untenable (or already reabsorbed). These texts are not reference texts on which we might depend, to which we might return as to an established Said: the infinite's excess is already exceeded in its caricatural violence on its upper border, or else risks fading away on its lower border by being solidified in its already-said. This is why those working with "Levinas" and attempting to remain at his heights are forbidden in a sense ever to say "Levinas *said*..." Levinas will have taught us nothing; he will have taught us to touch on the nothing, which can be done only in a discourse that is, strictly speaking, untenable, that always already no longer *supports* itself, and that for this very reason will never cease *returning*, never allowing ourselves to "be installed" anywhere, in no established Said. No thinker can possibly find the solidity of closure there, nor the comfort of any accommodation for thought—this text has rendered itself *uninhabitable*. And yet, all those who venture into "Levinas" to the extent of taking his test will be accompanied there by him as ineluctably as though by a shadow—or spectre, or revenant—as though by the affection of the other that will dislodge them each time they believe they can be stabilized.

Allowing the soft, sweet shell of excessive courtesy, of an "after you, sir," to melt away in order to taste the bitter seed of the trauma of the for-others, we must (always afresh) think entirely otherwise, within the trauma of endlessly renewed births.

2. Rhythm as the Question of Intentionality in Levinas

Levinas characterizes his own style of thought as one of emphasis or of hyperbole (see *OGW*). And in this sense, what we cannot say of any thought worthy of the name—to know whether it consists of an excess of style, style as ornament—can *above all* not be said of Levinas's thought. His philosophy is, from this point of view, exemplary: it appears as style; it is nowhere other than in its style. In fact, hyperbolic style is the rough draft of style itself, in that through excess it perpetually distances itself—to distance itself regarding distance itself, and thus as the infinite? Thus, it confronts the fabric of the Same, the apophantic *logos* that gathers, thus bringing to the light.

In fact, it seems that nothing must interrupt this hyperbolic gap, this continued (or rather indefinitely redoubled) distance with regard to itself, since it is what precedes the Saying of what is solidified in the Said (to return to Levinas's terminology).

Yet since the reversal of Saying requires the immanence of the Said to indicate it—without ever actually giving it—in the mode of the trace, immoderation must not be disconnected from moderation. Even if Levinas does not insist on it in designating the Said as what *simultaneously* betrays and embraces (in proximity with the Derridean problematic of writing as *pharmakon*), it is important to understand that there must also be moderation in immoderation. An excessive practice of excess cancels the latter, and thus cancels its subversive charge. More precisely, the very act of practicing immoderation must be moderate. We must also remember that hyperbole as such *figures* style: it moderates immoderation.

This points us to two connected dangers. If immanence does not give being to transcendence, if immanence does not offer itself as the place in which what cannot be presented announces itself in its very absence, then this "less than nothing" that is not without its effects, since it is disruption as the event of alterity, "is" no longer that disruptive nothing. At the same time, and symmetrically, since the Said ceases to permit itself to be disrupted, it sets itself to function mechanically, thus confirming its closure on itself.

This moderation within immoderation is like the internal limit to which the Levinasian gesture solidly affixes—but that it nonetheless threatens—the excess in which it situates itself *almost* completely.[15] This moderation-in-immoderation is something like a rhythm in Levinas's philosophy.

We should see what Levinas says about rhythm, which he thematizes in a very complex way in "Reality and Its Shadow," a text focusing on the work of art.[16] The work of art, from a perspective inspired by Plato, is defined as "part shadow." It is unreality—*internal*—Levinas insists, to all reality. It is desubstantialization itself, substance being on the side of plasticity of form. And rhythm is thus exemplarily—but not solely—localized[17] in music all the more in that sound is "the most detached quality of the object" (RS, 130), the least substantial, that Levinas links with music, and more specifically with sound. Thus, rhythm is negatively connoted because as the destroyer of substance, it signifies Ek-stasis, departure from self interpreted as "refusal to assume all responsibility. And so, Levinas says, it is necessary to *resist* rhythm. To listen to music, for example, is to *resist* dance, here conceived as loss of self.[18]

Let me quickly specify that Levinas's critique of rhythm is more complicated, in the strictest sense, than we might recall, because it is made up of different threads, more or less "thick" (apparent), woven together in such a complex way that they can seem contradictory.

And so this hesitation before rhythm as the power of ecstasy is deployed as reticence, expressed by Levinas in other texts on insomnia,[19] before rhythm as *refrain* installing the anonymity of the Same. The motif of critique appears to reverse itself, since rhythm is no longer condemned as the power of alteration but, on the contrary, as production of the immanence of being. More precisely, this is "bad" immanence at play, the immanence that congeals; therefore, this reversal is not the mark of an inconsistency, if we remember that the rough fabric of being or of existence is characterized for Levinas by its indetermination—that it is a threat to individuality, and more radically, to ipseity. There clearly is for Levinas a *bad* event of Alterity that,[20] in disindividualizing, far from being exposed to the other, dissolves in the Same, thus installing *bad* immanence (the one that is not ipseity but, on the contrary, the indetermination of a Same loosened and, so to speak, solidified). Rhythm is thus, as we have seen, *refrain*, and even more radically, it is dissolved and inverted in its repetition—which continues to the point of indistinction—as *humming* (see *OB*, 255). What does this mean, precisely? In rhythm the event of rupture tends to be effaced in favor of repetition, in which the loss of self is no longer violent enucleation that, paradoxically, delivers the self to itself through its test, but rather as a mundanity, repetition as loss of vigilance: sweet, slow dissolution.[21] There are two ways of losing oneself as ipseity: *I* can lose myself by exposing myself to an abduction that takes me out of myself in the violence of a rupture, but then all is reversed and the *I* appears from the test, now close to responsibility; *I* can also lose myself in allowing myself to be slowly corrupted by the seduction of the Same, through the stabbing sing-song of its endless repetition, a monotony that is all the more sure and effective in being entirely moderate, a moderate that as if being dissolved due to making the "self" a knowing consciousness, through acts that are precisely "measured," concluding by putting it to sleep through *too much* vigilance—concluding, paradoxically, by dissolving it in the quiet purring of its clarity.[22]

As always in Levinas, the same notion has its various characteristics, and eventually its powers, reversed, according to its insertion in thought, without its becoming contradictory. On the contrary, this is a matter of a recanting that must accompany all Saying in order to prevent it from congealing in a Said, thus betraying itself. At base, there must be in the movement of a "positive" recanting anticipation of the recanting that thought cannot fail to inflict on itself as it ensconces itself in the comfort of a definitive proposition, condemning it to the provisional, to the precarious. Thus for the sender, or at least for the receiver, the sole means of "understanding" consists in not hardening discourse through a will to put it in order, to control it, but rather to marry its own movement, to go with its flow. And the fact that no Said can go without recantation in Levinasian discourse does not deliver it to the bad liberty of being able to say everything and its opposite but, on the contrary, enjoins the reader to bend with the strong constraints of the singular movement of this thought in its necessity and its exigency: this is true no matter where, no matter when, no matter how the interruption and the reversal take place within it.

We can apply this declaration regarding the movement of Levinasian discourse when it takes rhythm as its theme to the status of many other notions in Levinas. But it is not a matter of indifference to propose now, with regard to rhythm, that in fact it is rhythm itself in the Levinasian sentence, in that its accents take place principally in the dimension of the discontinuity playing within it.

If we return to our reading of "Reality and Its Shadow"—this will even be the mark of its paradoxical but absolutely radical coherence, that is, characteristic of the blinking of Levinasian discourse—we will not be surprised to state that the distrust toward the power of the Ek-static in art, toward the force of transcendence desubstantializing rhythm, literally returns in a condemnation of art as reification, arrest, idolatry—in the movement giving phenomenology to itself.[23]

We must also not be astonished at being implicitly permitted (and even enjoined by Levinas's text) the task of *continuing* in a direction that the double bind at once forbids and orders.

Rhythm, at once absolutely present in the living and carnal intimacy of the speaking voice—and even more fundamentally than all phenomenality—and always already radically absent from itself in the incalculability of a rupture, an originary crack, is a power of destabiliza-tion. Can we not see in it the very force of *Otherwise Than Being*?[24] Even more radically, is this not exactly the way in which *Otherwise* presents itself in its withdrawal, the way in which it marks itself as being only its trace, in the disruption it leaves the landscape of immanence?

For essential reasons, I cannot explicitly claim such a direction; it is, however, increasingly suggested between the lines, especially in the revela-tions emerging from a certain reticence, but in the end more "positive," of the ontological status of art in the texts following the earlier "Reality and Its Shadow."[25]

Let us stop for a moment on these lines of Levinas: "Does he not understand [Atlan] unearthing by the brush—the simultaneity of con-tinuous forms, the primordial coexistence taking place on the canvas, the original spatiality of space that the brush itself affirms or consecrates—the diachrony of rhythm, or the beating of time, or the duration, or the life that denies this space of assemblage and the synthesis recovering and dis-simulating this life?" (JA, 509). These lines are decisive due to the radical reversal they imply in the Levinasian conception of art, and more spe-cifically of rhythm. And it is doubtless with no reticence that in the end Levinas recognizes in art in general, and in rhythm in particular, not the bad sameness of the *il y a*, but, on the contrary, the Otherwise than being that, as we have seen, is the paradoxical source of life in the very gesture of its interruptive force.

And here we must be very precise: even if we can identify an evolu-tion at work in Levinasian thought in this regard, this reversal has been "in preparation" since the beginning, at the very core of that fundamental modality of Levinas's thought as well as his phenomenality, according to and "in" Levinas: *ambiguity*. Levinasian *ambiguity* is not the concern of the "moved" or of indetermination, but about the radicality of a true reversal—at the very heart of a particular effect of simultaneity—because there is (*il y a*) ambiguity within it. Without this radicality and the sharp reversal within it being the least bit dulled, the two faces or moments of inversion are clearly there, united by their very tension, in each "stage" of Levinas's thought, the one working subliminally while the other works overtly. And this radicality of inversion maintains itself entirely within the nuance of its accentuation.

We will therefore not be surprised to see that even though the most obvious thread of Levinas's thought on art and rhythm is, in "Reality and Its Shadow," the denunciation of desubstantiation as dissolution in the anonymity of what he elsewhere directly refers to as the *il y a*, this thread is *already* woven into another, concealed and inchoate—a premonition only furtively indicated—according to which art has an "ambiguous value," meaning that it is *also* "in a world of initiative and responsibility, a dimension of escape" (RS, 145).

And certainly, at play in these radical inversions and perhaps already haunted by one another, is the rhythm of Levinas's thought (in this case, with regard to the theme of rhythm itself). Rhythm, as in Levinas's work on Atlan, is explicitly recognized as the very medium of *diachrony*, of the blinking or flashing of opposing phases that presuppose the unforeseen paradox of one thread rejoined beyond an interruption, however radical, and that engenders primordial palpitations animating all phenomenality and originarily disjoin it.[26]

In fact, if rhythm is like a trace, inscribing itself, writing itself, Otherwise than being—and it can inscribe itself only by leaving its trace, since it can know neither how to be "contemporary" with itself nor how to be plainly "given"—then must we not conclude that, as a consequence, it is in the rhythm of the blinking of Said and Recanted themselves, in the sentences of *Otherwise Than Being*—and here we would have to listen closely to the words of the title—that what can never be Said is "given," that is, thematized? It is, in a sense, between the lines of *Otherwise Than Being* that the Otherwise than being presents itself as nothing other than what disjoins them, prevents them from gathering into a theme, precisely at the point, nonetheless, of the same radical movement of meaning, of *vouloir-dire*, constrained by philosophical exigency;[27] the one in the other and the one through the other.

And this is why *Otherwise Than Being* is a work of art, and Levinas a writer. But no more than the Otherwise than being could thematize itself, the Levinasian text cannot reflect on itself, thematize itself, as a work. As work, it is *being done*, in the movement of its rhythm that must not be arrested even if only to reverse its own steps, on pain of congealing and thus betraying—reifying—itself: *Otherwise Than Being* is a work on the move—that is, a work existing in the rhythm of its steps.

218   PHENOMENOLOGICAL DISCOURSE

In other words, it is rhythm that *disputes* the work of intentionality without ever radically excluding it but by producing the signification of Saying at the heart of the trembling inflicted on it, moderating this trembling that would be lost were it to go *too* far, if it were, in the most simplistic sense, to destroy intentionality. If too much Said can kill Saying, ontologically, if too much immanence suffocates transcendence, then too much Saying also kills the Said: while the movement of Otherwise than being is entirely excess, excess also kills excess; the risk itself points to an excessive practice of excess.[28] This is why while Levinas's work cannot thematize itself as a work of art, it must immediately be added that it cannot thematize itself as a *work of art*. This means a shift of accent that it would lack as a work if its rhythm hardened through (self-)reflection, but that all the more—and contrarily—it cannot claim to be a work of art to the very end, if we understand by "a work of art" that which radically delivers itself to Ek-static rhythm, since then we would be dealing with an "excessive excess," finally reversing itself into its opposite.[29]

Such is the origin of the Levinasian reticence regarding rhythm and his remarkable analysis, of which this is part, and according to which in a sense to listen to music is to resist dance: to resist the *hybris* of a rhythm understood uniquely as rupture and absence of structure, and thus as the medium for the forgetting of self.

But what we now know is that we only truly dance within reticence, within dance's resistance. The fact that dance always contains moderation within immoderation,[30] which gathers the dancer to himself when he goes *too* far, is, moreover, what differentiates it from the pure violence of abduction. (It would be immediately necessary to construct the reciprocal of the proposition that we have begun to form, which is that dance is dance, never simply the repetition of a strict cadence, which within it ceaselessly regenerates excess within it.)

Between the contesting of the "Same" and reticence before the *too much* Other, Levinas's writing is dancing, and for whoever reads him, it is an invitation to dance.[31]

2

The Rhythm of Life According to Michel Henry

Even though he never speaks of his "tautologies" in the same way he speaks of "the tautologies of Christianity,"[1] it would not be a betrayal of Michel Henry to speak of his "tautological" style—so long as we place this in quotation marks, signifying that I do not hold them to be at the level of an impression of superficial reading that would judge Henry's text as being the flat, autistic repetition of Immanence (Immanence thus being too rapidly made equivalent to the category of the Same): it would, rather, be a question of a pure denial of reading. What we are confronted with is a massive aporia that constitutes a (musical) phrasing endlessly attached to itself, constraining itself in order to mark the very movement of Life, the authentic movement always coming into the self but never leaving it.

How to say what does not make itself other than "self," which does not even concede the relative alterity allowing for escape to Parmenidean silence in order to *articulate* propositions? What can we say about what does not *show* itself in any outside? How to "represent," for an addressee, what will never be more thoroughly betrayed than by this operation of representation? How to communicate, *to enter into a relation*, with Life? Even more judgmentally, why do it?

For reasons that are essential ones, the Henrian oeuvre does not pose these questions about itself.

In fact, since the Henrian text is always "reproducing" the movement of Life and being caught up in this movement, it is always in motion:

moments of "reflective" pause, inquiring metalanguage, marking the hesitation around the self and thus suspending the course of thought in action—these are hardly convenient to it and are reduced to an absolute minimum, to a strictly instrumental structure. To stop reflexively at the self in a sort of meditative paralysis sterilizing, or at least rarifying, affirmative discourse—that is what contradicts verbatim the movement and the immediacy of Life, insofar as it is thought within the register of force, of intensity, and of fertility.

If there are at the very least two general kinds of stylized philosophical thought that are symmetrically opposed—the one always seized by hesitations that keep it reflexively attached to itself, and the other, entirely immanent in its own proper movement, always engaged with itself without any exterior from which to examine itself (that is, also, without a *threshold* that would allow it to enter back in or to take itself fully out)—Henry's text is emblematic of the second kind.[2]

More globally and more radically, it must be said that doubt and, a fortiori, aporia, are not part of the diet of Michel Henry's discourse; on the contrary, his dominant, fundamental discursive register is affirmation.

Despite all this, I pose these questions in the very place of Henry's discourse as the ones his discourse will not ask, not from impotence but, on the contrary, out of respect for itself, since that is its "let it be." And what is such a gesture's legitimacy? Is it not both violent and derisory to pose questions to a text that has no natural place for them?

I will not open up this long, difficult debate but will be satisfied with one remark that, in the absence of a legitimation, carries with it at least a motivation since this gesture is made in *this* concrete, singular form, one that the Henrian text seems to forbid—certainly not in open, explicit violence but in the no-less-violent implicitness of a radical indifference to the reader *as other*. And this is not just another question—it is The Question itself, questioning as such, with regard to itself. Entirely self-contained, Henry's text at its core refuses all questions, in that it is alteration and paralysis, and a fortiori all questions addressed to it from an inauthentic outside and that, moreover, in a sense does not exist for it.

We can thus understand in passing that to interrogate this text's "tautological" style is at the same time—and even prejudicially—to interrogate oneself in place of the reader, to ask the unaskable question regarding the interior—unaskable *through* the "interior"—that of the *reception* of the work, which is clearly in a certain way the question of the very possibility of the question.

And to make the point more clearly, the question is absolutely legitimate for at least two reasons:

1. Because with regard to the philosophical work, we must ask ourselves what the situation is regarding the question, its critical stakes, the amazement in which certitudes collapse—this fundamental *Stimmung* of the philosopher.

2. Because *to read* Michel Henry requires, more than the reading of perhaps any other text, that one reflect on what he has already seized upon, and for this very reason, on a *threshold* through which to enter (and eventually to leave!): this is truly *vital* for anything desiring to be constituted as a philosophical subject through the reading of a work: here, of *this* work.³

So let us take as our motif the question of a "tautological" style.

One thing is clear immediately: in fact, Henrian "tautologies" do not precisely coincide, do not superimpose, and consequently they are not exactly tautologies; that is, the pure and simple foundation of an identity—and in the final analysis of the identity principle itself.

A first explanation suggested itself, one that perhaps must now be, if not discarded, at last recognized as insufficient: despite its explicit intention, Henry's text fails the test of declaring the affirmative plenitude of Life, the Life that by definition is irreducible to the apophantic *logos*—the apophantic *logos* from which, at least partially and from a certain point of view, the text emerges, even if only in order to solidly denounce its concealed nature. In close affinity to negative theology as its defending body, the Henrian text would be an apophantic. More precisely, since it does not proceed by a "negative path"—on the contrary, as I have emphasized, it finds an absolutely positive path—it should consist of a collection of *approximations* or *estimates* of the movement of Life. And this collection of approximations is endless since to circle in closer and closer to the constraint of Life by itself would by definition be no less dedicated to failure, having the apophantic *logos* for its medium.

This reading has the disadvantage of being absolutely exterior to Henry's problematic of the revelation of Life, not invalidating it but requiring one to listen to it in counterpoint and perhaps at first even to what Life says of its own self-revelation. No doubt, for Henry there is no "theory of the text" since, as we shall see, to "translate" the movement of Life is in no case to "reflect" it, and the text, since it appears through writing, is mediation par excellence (mediation that is originary for Derrida but is *certainly not* for Henry). Nevertheless, there is a place for the revelation of Life—a place that is even central and originary: it is only ever a question of the revelation of Life to itself in *The Essence of Manifestation*, since the revelation of Life to itself is the essence of manifestation.

In fact, Life is immediately and entirely revelation of itself, self-revelation: it is nowhere other than in the movement of connecting to itself, creating an *appearance*, since there is a movement by which Life is disjoined from itself (even though it is better to be conjoined with oneself). This appearance reveals itself to be absolutely heterogeneous in the mode of Ek-static appearance, in that according to the radical Henrian paradox—an unsustainable paradox for anyone thrown into the World but who acts as if he dared to speak of the very "evidence" of Life—in disjoining from itself, Life connects to itself, *gives itself* to itself. Life is thus entirely a "making-to-see," insofar as all authentic revelation is self-revelation.

We must not fail to notice here what I have designated as the central, originary aporia of Henry's philosophy: that the thought of immanence must be understood within the following double bind: the immediacy of immanence to itself—which makes it immanence—must be radical, but immanence is only what it is—Life—if it comes into itself, seeming to imply an *internal* gap making *connection as connection* possible, with itself. Consequently, the formulations taking this double bind furthest tend to think first of the immanence of the connection with itself.[4] Thus, the connection would in a sense precede the very "terms" it connects (it matters little whether these terms are Life and . . . Life, or Self and . . . Self). Clearly it is, strictly speaking, the embrace that comes first, in its immanence. Life is nowhere but in its coming, or in its embrace. We must leave undecided here the question as to whether such an embrace can be originarily immanent to itself, as Henry wants to say, or if in fact (and despite Henry) even an originary embrace cannot presuppose an outside separated from itself in order to be better rejoined with itself.

In any event, if we determine that Life is immediately self-revelation, because it is the immediacy of a connection with a self that came to itself—that is, is always coming in general—then a certain number of consequences unfold. One in particular is vitally important: the supposed aporia according to which we could not apophatically know how to represent the unrepresentable itself (Life) appears out of itself. Henry's philosophy is fully affirmative in the sense in which (according to itself) it does not confront the aporia, does not feel itself tested by it, since even more fundamentally it links to a sense of Life that is wholly self-affirmation of itself.[5] There is no aporia in "Saying of Life" since Life will always and immediately have been essentially its own Saying.[6] But understanding this involves destruction of the illusion by which we speak only through the apophantic *logos*, only through representation, through being open to this "evidence" that is older than all Seeing, and according to which authentic and originary Saying is not *representation* but *revelation*,[7] coinciding with the very movement of Life. It is only when one understands what *saying* truly is that one can understand that "the saying of Life" is, for Michel Henry, only the name of a false problem, a problem that is *not* one because it was badly constructed, badly posed; a problem that was, more radically, constructed from pieces of an answer already imposed.

This is the point from which a certain number of powerful characteristics follow, characteristics of Henry's position regarding phenomena that traditionally arise, in the broadest sense, from "language."

The most important of these is clearly what I have called the "tautology" that is merely the stylistic "form" of the movement of suppression in which Life is originarily held. Michel Henry identifies the self-revelation of Life as "words," indeed as being the Word itself. In fact, as words—or more precisely, as *only* words, since in all Henrian rigor there is, finally, no authentic Word other than "the Word of Life"—Life is nowhere other than in its actualization—its act—such that nothing can possibly precede it. It is pure force or intensity, which in this case means performativity (even if Henry does not use this term).[8] This is why the Word of Life arises from a practice and an ethic rather than a theory:[9] for each ipseity born into Life, speaking, this will be witness, attesting to the first surging forth of the self-revelation of Life in which it is held and that is held in it.

This attestation signifies that it is Life that is spoken in each self, always already, so that the question of the "transfer" of the Word of Life to the Word of each Self, from a Henrian point of view,[10] is never asked.

Once that is accomplished, the non-coincidence of the "tautologies" of which we are part finds a Henrian way of being included.

Life arrives in itself only in multiplicity, through the infinite, un-saturatable essence of the singular embraces that also come into Life as so many Selves. And this is exactly the way—without its being a question of an analogy here, since it is in fact the *same* movement that is in play, seen from a different point of view—in which the Word of Life is affirmed in a multiplicity of singular embraces that nothing can stop or saturate: as many embraces as words—and texts, and even, more simply, sentences—to transfer them. The Henrian text traverses the fields (ontology, aesthetics, politics, etc.) and the thought of writers with nothing being able to interrupt it, since it is only the witness of the movement of Life in its infinite rebirths, coming to attest to Life precisely where it was lost to "sight," was actually too much to be visible.

Thus, the text, having had a superficial and too-diligent reading, can seem "ceaselessly to say the same thing," to affirm the Same, to reveal itself as being infinitely reborn, though never exactly identically from one of its "proofs" to another, just as living individuals differ infinitely at the core of their communion in Life. And, in good Henrian logic—that is, according to the "logic" of the Life that is nonsense only for the light of the World, only for *the* logic—this is because it is Life itself and nothing but it, which thus endlessly comes into it with nothing that might intervene to make it a stranger; only its embraces, only its words are absolutely singular, incomparable among themselves.

We must thus reconsider our subjects of interrogation regarding the Henrian text.

If that text is not connected with aporia understood as paralysis, as prevention of access to truth, it is in fact connected to astonishment: each word being by its nature singular, it constitutes an event; it is at the very heart of the indefinite repetition of the coming-to-itself of Life, *surprising*. One might say that in reading Michel Henry, one discovers an astonishment without question, an affirmative astonishment entirely made up of "astonishing" affirmations. Perhaps in this context it would be appropriate to translate *traumazein* as "amazement": this would be a matter of saying yes to what is given, to what overflows, Life.

Radicalizing our reading of Henry, we might risk one further step: might we go so far as to say that despite everything the Henrian text is not without a connection to the aporia—a proximity from which in return the aporia could not depart without harm?

What do we see here? Always and ceaselessly this internal gap that we believed we could discern at the very heart of immanence. Life can be conjoined with itself only by cutting into itself, in the same movement, the gap that disjoins it and permits it—thus—connects it to itself: this gap cannot be sutured, since it is precisely the condition of the emergence of singular constraints in Life as being nothing but Life itself. This internal gap is, strictly speaking, the milieu of all birth, the matrix of Living Beings.

This consequently seems to indicate that in the same way, at the heart of affirmation—and indeed as its very condition, as what permits it to be reborn ceaselessly—there is a hole, a non-affirmation. This is certainly not negativity in the Hegelian sense of the term, destruction as the necessary engine of its own transcendence and thus of the realization of being. It is certainly not something lived painfully as a "lack," but it certainly is a hole that can never be filled: Life in its fertility and unsaturability; at the heart of the plenitude of its givenness the bottomless hole persists, the promise of Living Beings to come.

Despite the fact that the Henrian text is captured, deep down, by the aporia, we cannot deduce that negativity and doubt are triumphant within the Word of Life, but perhaps, on the contrary, that an affirmative image of aporia is possible, and even that in all aporias affirmation and life are present, which certain caricatural discourses perhaps forget.[11]

In Michel Henry we consistently face the fact that Life, to speak plainly, is not without constraints, and that the same is true for the discourse speaking it: he reminds us that *jouissance* is returned immediately in suffering (and inversely),[12] in the test of an embrace. And if this is a question of testing, it is because Life endlessly runs the risk of buckling under its own weight; it risks being *too heavy* for itself, giving *too much* of and to itself, thus putting itself in danger—which is translated into its Word by the paradoxical figure of an aporia—not through lack but through overabundance. What "overabounds" in each self-embrace is precisely the infinity of those to come that are all, and all *entirely, there*, in each one, given that it is Life that is there—and at the same time absolutely *not* there, since each reversal is entirely new, and since they would not know they preexisted in the ellipses of their possibles: clearly something like a radical non-duration exists at the heart of the "too-full" of Life's givenness.

Thus, at the heart of infidelity we believe we are showing absolute fidelity when we describe the Henrian text as being in the grip of aporia, though in an unanticipated form that is not without echoes in aporia itself.

This question of the aporia is one we encountered at the outset and have held in reserve until now, at least explicitly (we addressed it to the extent that it interlaces with that of "tautology" as aporia). This is the fundamental question of the text, of its usage and its reception, in Henrian philosophy. Let us review this.

We must do so carefully. If the Henrian text is never concerned with its reader, it is not because it mistakes her, denies her, or simply does without her; it is, on the contrary, because any relationship with "the reader" is sufficiently *immediate* that we would not know how to raise it as a problem for him: any particular problem is always already resolved. Henry's text does not unfold as enclosed, an autism within itself; on the contrary, as a singular embracing that speaks Life, it will always have been "communicated" with the reader, this other, singular embracing of Life by itself—without there ever having been the test of an encounter—because they will already have drawn the one and the other toward the same invisible source, Life. Thus, the relationship with the reader will always have been the very opposite of a problem, and a fortiori of an aporia: the "obviousness" of immediacy. We can see a particular stylistic trait here: in order to close in on themselves, "tautologies" are formulated in the mode of an *address* absolutely directly to the reader, with the *frankness* of a certitude.

For Michel Henry, it is thus bad to raise the problem of how to exit from the self in order to address another: once again, this is a false problem constructed from a misunderstanding of what Life is.[13] The painful test of the aporia of being placed in relation to others, of communication, will always be dissipated in the "experience"[14] of *communion* of Selves in Life. It is in the end not so much the Henrian text that makes us understand what Life is as our originary community of pairs of living beings that allow us to understand it most fundamentally.

We are one and all the children of Life, linked into a "reciprocal interiority" with that "Word-Ipseity" whose absolute singularity signifies "Michel Henry";[15] in it *I* recognize myself in my singularity because in the same movement I recognize Life there.

And yet, the Henrian text does not consist entirely of a speech act. It is, precisely, a *text*. That is,

1. As a *philosophic* text it is deployed in the element of the Ek-static *logos*; it weaves itself into the argumentative rigor of an apophantic *logos*.
2. As simply a *text*, it does not exhaust itself in the proffering of speech, but traces itself, inscribes itself in a material support.

Why must the Speech Act of Life, in its self-revelation, agree to compromise with its exterior, with the Outside itself (in two different versions: the empirical and the logical—but from this point of view the difference is unimportant)?

In order to respond to this question, since for reasons of essence there is in Henry no place for a theory of the text, it is necessary to turn toward certain indicators that are as such indirect.

But before asking *how* to inscribe Life in text, we must simply ask *why* to do it. The various elements of a response to this question may seem inchoate and scattered throughout Henry's work, no more than indications: its reader is essentially required to deduce them by connecting Henry's textual practice with the thematic principles of his philosophy.

If it is fundamentally necessary that Life risk itself on the outside, in the midst of the enemy, it is because it is *forgotten*, and that the challenge is basically to reanimate, for the reader, not its memory (which is a mode of representation) but its test. Consequently, we must search for the reader where she is: we must search each one of us as though he is thrown *at once* into the inauthentic, into World. And thus the Word of Life recalls to Life those who have forgotten and thus consent to be exposed at the core of contradiction.

We should stop here to consider the complex status as much of World as of Ek-stasy and forgetting in Henry. These three notions are linked, since the World is one of the fundamental modes of Ek-stasy that as such draws its entirely negative essence from being the forgotten of Life.

Although it consists of the negation of Life, forgetting is not summarized in it.

We should note that a large part of Henry's philosophy is written *against* Ek-static transcendence, meaning that, at least in the interior of the operativity of Henrian discourse, the notion of forgetting has a decisive function: it makes this discourse possible as support for the negation of which it in part consists. Had there not been transcendence to denounce, and even to set aside, how would it be possible to say Life, and why do it? And, in fact, to a certain extent the affirmation of Life in the Henrian text takes the indirect and diverted form of a denunciation, even a negation of transcendence.

We should add immediately that Henry's writings are never reduced to this, and that they essentially search into the "positive" movement of Life: into what we have been making the center of our research, his "tautological" style. Nevertheless, it is the urgency of the denunciation of this massive universal prejudice, the World—this forgetting of Life—that motivates and engages Henrian discourse. Had there not been this scandal, we would have had to allow the Ek-static *logos* to remain concealed—no need to write philosophy—not, in Henry, for it to be absorbed in a radical silence but, on the contrary, to listen to and already to speak the only word "speaking," the Word of Life.

At base, Michel Henry tests, in his own terms, what since Plato has inaugurated the majority of philosophical discourses: the original scandal in which we discover ourselves, paradoxically, to be *first* inscribed, thrown, into the inauthentic and the derivative, the primary characteristic of this situation for us being that we forget the authentic and take the inauthentic for it (this is in effect a powerful characteristic of illusion and/or prejudice: taking a given for its opposite).

The question Henry never asks, at least explicitly and thematically, is the following: how does Transcendence, strictly speaking, *arrive* at Immanence? *Why* the forgetting of Life?

A quick parallel with Platonism will help clarify this point: one might say, a bit too schematically but suggestively, that Plato is essentially consecrated to an "ascendant dialectic" that rises from the sensible world toward the intelligible world, interesting itself only late on and marginally in a "descendent dialectic," content with stating the sensible world in order then to rise up to a more perfect source, but that then asks a more originary question: why then has the *more* perfect given birth to the *less* perfect (and to the dialectic that, now installed in the *more* perfect even beyond Ideas and thus in the place of the One, tends to redescend toward the Sensible that the Neoplatonists, in particular Plotinus, are attached)?

If I may be permitted this comparison, we might say that there is no longer a "descendent dialectic" for Henry, or at least that it is only initiated in Henry's final texts.[16] The problematic (and there are no notable variations on this point from *The Essence of Manifestation* to the very last works) is significantly evident *from the start* in the dichotomy between Transcendence and Immanence, between Life and its forgetting as Ekstasis. But if Transcendence is derivative, inauthentic, then it can contain no necessity and no legitimacy. And its "why" remains largely enigmatic in Henry's work. Without interrogating Henry on what he has not (even nearly) said, or, certainly, reproaching him for what he has not done, it is still possible to bring certain elements of comprehension to the quasi-silence: would not accounting for the event of Transcendence, explaining it, already and immediately have been a beginning of legitimation?—a legitimation whose major requirement toward denunciation of Transcendence would see, so to speak, with an evil eye? In the grip of this tension, the Henrian text would thus only allow itself to express a "why" of Transcendence "halfheartedly," so that its argument would succeed in short-circuiting one fundamental objective: any reproach for not being able to account, within his framework, for an ontological event with which he is essentially concerned.

In Henry we read:

1. That Life threatened with suffocation beneath its own weight—by nature excessive, since it is superabundance itself—would throw itself out of itself in order to find some relief from itself, to soothe the suffering that it had inflicted on itself in the very movement in

which it is what it is.[17] And thus it would inaugurate the Outside
itself.

2. That to be an entirely separate subjectivity, an *I* must forget that
he contains what he is of Life, that he draws his power from Life.
That is the only way to be invested in his power, to be able to say
"I can," to be an ego. In fact, the only way of being himself is, from
this point of view—and only from this point of view—to coincide
so radically with himself that we do not see him, that we do not represent him, since such a gesture always presupposes the introduction
of distance. Fundamentally, to be an *I* means having no memory of
self or of one's birth, of one's condition as the Son of Life:[18] memory
of self, of one's generation and birth, memory as such, is in a sense
only an obstacle and a burden. There would thus be a form of legitimacy, and even of the necessity of the forgetting of Life, if I am
truly myself only in forgetting Life. Must Life not consent to being
forgotten, and even instigate this forgetting, so that its Sons can
truly be themselves, can at least take possession of themselves? As
Henry does not insist, for reasons we know about already, this would
mean that it is *also* necessary to forget Life, to be for World, in order
to be oneself (even though the essential aspect of his commentary
consists of his saying that one must rediscover the proof of Life in
order to be oneself).

Finally, we read:

3. That Life defines itself as the *immemorial*; that is, in the Henrian
context, as what has already escaped the representative structure
of memory. This definition of Life as immemorial has a significant
consequence. While it is obvious in Henry's logic that, on the one
hand, Transcendence has no proper essence, since it is entirely derived from Immanence as its desubstantialization, and that, on the
other hand, Immanence is "defined" only through itself, a decisive
change results: is saying that Life is *essentially* immemorial not making of forgetting one of its essential characteristics? And is this not
thus to accord to forgetting, and to World as its place, the status of
essential and originary, since it would interpose itself into the very
interior of the "essence of Life"? It would be insufficient to say that
Life shies away from World; we would have to say that Life "defines"

itself as shying away from World, and we would thus be defining Life in a necessary link with World. The device employed in this articulation is quite complex. To define Life as immemorial, as what is always already forgotten, is to define it as what escapes memory, and thus Representation and World, Representation and World being precisely the forgetting of Life: to live is to forget forgetting. Nevertheless, if Life occurs in the movement of refusing World, then it is *necessarily* World for which Life must refuse it. If World is the forgetting of Life, Life is then Forgetting of World (and the capital "F" of this second kind of forgetting indicates that it is a Forgetting constitutive of the essence of Life, a "transcendental" Forgetting in the sense in which it "works for" the authenticity of Immanence).

A consequence such as this is nowhere drawn out *in all its radicality* by Michel Henry, for two reasons (that are, moreover, opposites) already evoked:

1. Caught in the urgency of the denunciation of transcendence, it is not *first and foremost* necessary for Henry to draw out the available threads in order to formulate its "why."

2. Significantly, Life is the very thing that one enjoys in its connection to itself, without needing any outside that would thus subordinate it, and above all not the Outside itself. This is the central thesis of Henry's philosophy; to go against it would be to undermine the very foundation of this philosophy and, certainly, to commit the worst nonsense regarding Life. And the formulations evoked here, which seem to define Life with regard to World,[19] that seem to define it as the forgetting of forgetting, the forgetting of that forgetting that *is* the world, can be only pedagogical concessions to the light of World, a way of searching for those who are lost in speaking the only language that, in their distraction, they understand. It is conceivable that these formulations have an even more essential status within the framework of Henry's thought.

Nevertheless, ambiguity surges up—even if Henry's discourse immediately circumscribes, domesticates, and defuses it—and thus World and Life are rendered opaque. And it is not insignificant that this ambiguity surges up when it is a matter of the Outside and, what is more, when it is finally—above all—a matter of Word and Life consenting to risk themselves in their outside, to risk themselves in writing to the misled, to those who *no longer* understand the direct address of the words of Life. The text is precisely, exemplarily, this agreed-upon outside, this incursion into the enemy that cannot be done without risk, that cannot be made without the risk, exemplified above, of rendering opaque, rendering ambiguous, the Speech Acts of Life. More radically still, the text is nothing other than this risk. Is the risk of the text, as Henry implicitly thinks it, as a provisional and controlled sacrifice for the Word of Life, not rather that it has already concealed its immediacy?

At play in the response to this question is the degree of radicality of the forgetting of Life against which the question and its response must arise. And what is always already decided for Michel Henry is that the forgetting of Life in the World is not radical, is that those who are lost in the World have not broken their connection with Life. Even if they are survivors, shadows of themselves, spectres, they are still living beings: if not, it would be neither possible nor necessary to address them. What good is it to speak to the dead? Life must (we cannot *not* think it)—as the originary decision of this philosophy that implicitly borrows its formal apagogic reasoning in *modus tollens*—though occluded and repressed, survive clandestinely, in order to give to the inauthentic the bit of life it still has. And it is vital that, in the same movement, for each *I*, a "second" birth be possible.

We can see here, quite specifically, what for Plato has the thematic status and function of reminiscence: the only way of understanding that knowledge is possible is to ask if it has not been radically effaced and that, consequently, to learn is not to make surge forth once again, but to reanimate, to exhume, something that is already there; in fact, were I completely separated from knowledge and as though enclosed in error, having no sense of knowledge, I could not seek it. Similarly, for Henry, Life is an always-already-there into which one is always already plunged, but into which one never truly radically enters, and from which one never truly radically emerges—except, certainly, to die (but Life as such does not die).

And this decision logically follows since it extends the originary decision by which Life is the authentic and the Absolute from which everything, even and above all what corrupts it, is derived: all of *The Essence of Manifestation* is consecrated to showing that Transcendence would not know how to ground itself, that it owes everything to Immanence, and that thus Immanence subordinates Transcendence, acting as its support—in every sense of the word. And even though Immanence is occluded by Transcendence, it would not know how to be—"by definition"—altered by it: in its clandestineness it preserves the integrated nature of its force.

Such a philosophy, positing an originary Absolute that makes everything possible—thus, it is possible that this Absolute can always be isolated in its purity, which finally demonstrates that we cannot *not* think it—this philosophy is inscribed, despite everything opposed to it—in particular the devaluation of the status of form, of essence—in the predominant line running from Plato to Kant and Husserl (Life has the same function as the Idea or the Transcendental even though it also opposes it as the materiality of the affect of the transcendence of form).[20] And for this philosophy, which only pays lip service to the need to pass through that outside that is the text, it is always unthinkable that the text, secondary and instrumentalized, contaminates the purity of the Word of Life.

From this specific relationship between Transcendence and Immanence, from Life to Ek-static World, we could draw one final consequence regarding the connection to the text Henry's philosophy infers. Confirming one of our preceding analyses, we learn that the aporia at the beginning is maintained Platonically in the idea that there is no *true* beginning of Life, in the sense that as Living Being I am always inscribed in it.[21] Correlatively, the Absolute has no threshold: insofar as I am a Living Being, it is unthinkable that the Word of Life be completely dead for me. The Word of Life makes possible the text that degrades it and makes it opaque. Only the strangled echo of the Word of Life in the text permits me to comprehend the latter. To say this is to say that the Word of Life has, with regard to text, exactly the same status and the same function as transcendental language relative to empirical languages, according to Eugen Fink: beyond inscription in a derivative, imperfect outside (language, text), what is inscribed there is always preserved in its purity and its sovereignty, not in the sense of a nucleus of silence but, on the contrary, as the only authentic "language," the only one that can truly speak.

This connection to Fink, as much in the way of managing the aporia of the beginning as in the status given to the Word of Life, demonstrates what in Henry, despite all its nuances, returns to a "transcendental"—one that is openly claimed—that thus exposes it to all the classical objections that could be made to such a gesture. Namely, what authorizes me to make myself the spokesperson for the Absolute (i.e., of Life)? And who authorizes what might be called "hypertranscendentalism" according to which the Absolute (Life) directly, as it were, speaks up?

The response to this question, from the interior of Immanent "logic," is immediate and important: insofar as I am a Son of Life, its Word will always be said in me. The problem here is that since there is no threshold,[22] one is either outside this thought and thus confronts it without being grasped by it, or inside it, and thus literally absorbed by its internal coherence, deprived of all power of radical questioning. My entire effort here—a little against Henry's thought itself, but in order to be true to what is *also* his need—has been an attempt, despite everything, to short-circuit this alternative.

Let us go over the main idea of our course to this point.

We now know *why* the Word of Life must consent to be made text in order to go out to encounter those who are lost to it. We have also understood that this occurs only to the extent that its absoluteness is not threatened, and insofar as the lost were never absolutely so.

It remains, then, to understand *how* the Word of Life can carry out this remarkable project.

As I have pointed out, in responding to this kind of question, for various reasons we can only retrieve certain indices from it, certain indirect indications.

One could, for example, do so via the text Henry consecrates to the work of von Briesen.[23] There is an analogy, and more profoundly, an essential relationship, between the project Henry brought to von Briesen, namely, the paradoxical and remarkable attempt to inscribe Life in this outside par excellence that is the space (here, pictorial) and Henry's own project, which consisted at base of inscribing Life in the outside constituted through the philosophic text.[24]

Without going into inordinate detail regarding the analyses Henry devotes to the work of von Briesen, the designer,[25] we must pay close attention to the indirect instruction concerning Henry's textual practice we can draw from it.

Von Briesen's powerful originality is that he paints Music. More precisely, according to Henry, what von Briesen paints while listening to Music is Life itself. This is not uniquely a matter of saying, à la Schopenhauer, that music, refusing itself to space as the medium of exteriorization, would thus be close to the immediacy of Life as force, and that as a result, to draw Music is somehow to play space against itself in order to save it from itself. This analysis must be displaced by another, deeper one that explains (1) that it is not in fact Music that von Briesen draws; (2) that as a result the drawing does not function as representation.

In effect, we must understand that on the *occasion* of hearing a musical work, the rhythm of Life singularly and exemplarily completes itself within the individual living being von Briesen, as if the rhythm of Music aroused the rhythm at the heart of a singular ipseity signing itself "von Briesen." And it does this in such a way that from one of its poles of intensity to the other (the musical work, the draftsman), it is from a certain point of view the same rhythm, Life's rhythm, since the rhythms of each singularity are shared only through their first communion in Life, to which they endlessly return. Thus, for reasons pertaining to the way Life is lived and that we have already examined, Music refreshes a rhythm that is already there at the heart of the individual living being.

This in turn means that von Briesen need not *reproduce* one element (Music) in another (a drawing), these two elements being originarily strangers to and separated from each other. The model for the transfer of one substantive element (as an information) emerging from one medium toward another one autonomous from the first—is absolutely *not* valid for describing what "happens" when von Briesen draws.

In "echoing" Music, under its impulsion, an absolutely singular rhythmic configuration is born, as nothing other than a pale copy of the music that has catalyzed it. And in fact it is not Music that von Briesen draws: it is the subjective intensities that burgeon forth in him when he listens to Music. And thus to draw is in no case to translate—in the sense of transferring—from the ear to the sheet of paper, nor from the individual living being to the sheet of paper. To draw is to flash forth, to fulgurate—and in this word we must hear an absolute gestural im-mediacy—the intensity of (a) rhythm that is thus the more intimately united with all other rhythms of Life that must then be understood as each one *in* the others, since in them Life resonates *as* rhythm, in that it is singular.

All problematics of mediation are thus invalidated, along with those of representation as the movement from one medium to another, at the expense of a problematics of fulguration-as-immediacy that pre-serves (and in fact solely allows to be thought) the absolute difference among rhythmic configurations, one connected to another in their sub-terranean conjunction.

Consequently, the problematic of a pictorial apophatic, whose cen-tral question is "how to represent the unrepresentable?," and in terms through which one can conveniently express oneself—Michel Henry sometimes does so—is in fact inadequate, asks the question badly. Ac-cording to a Henrian motif already addressed here, it even produces a "false problem" where there is in fact no problem; where the mark of von Briesen fulgurates, flashes out, Life flashes out, and this is not a question of betraying any essence, since Life is not being represented.

If von Briesen's marks do not "represent," "reproduce," or "trans-late" (etc.) Life—and I have not employed this semantic register except through convenience and provisionally—what *do* they do?

If von Briesen's work is not an apophatic using pictorial representa-tion to say what Life is not, and to say it indirectly, what then is it?

I have used Henry's term, "fulguration," in order to evoke the radi-cal immediacy of the connection between the musical work in its sin-gularity and the pictorial work in *its* singularity, "piercing" the singular, individual living being von Briesen. This "fulguration" also says some-thing else: that von Briesen's *mark* represents nothing because, more originarily, it is itself nothing extended in space but rather what *incises* space.[26] The mark, clearly conceding the minimal inscribing it on the sheet of paper, is at a more profound level a mark tearing the space of the sheet, a mark drawn by force itself, by Life.[27]

Far from conforming to the law of Ek-static Transcendence, von Briesen's mark is its disruption. Far from seeming to represent Life, even assuming that that could (however imperfectly) be done, the mark is a trace of Life disrupting not this or that fulguration but Space as such and, beyond Space, Ek-static Transcendence as such. If "what is given to sight gives itself to us as not giving itself," this must be understood in a radical sense: as not carried out by the artist in a classically apophatic gesture of denying a representation by indicating that what one would like to represent will always exceed all representation; it must rather be applied to the space of a gesture stripped of all will and all representativity[28]—blind, as it were. The only effect of its living immediacy would be to disrupt space, to do violence to it. And this refusal to form even the least part of representativity, of exteriority, in the encounter with space is indicated precisely in the further step von Briesen takes taken through Kandinsky,[29] according to Henry, in the art of making Life shine forth as pure Subjectivity and Interiority "on" the canvas or the sheet of paper.

We could briefly account for this "projection" by von Briesen as follows: if the objective elements the painter assembles interest Kandinsky only to the extent that they correlate with interior and subjective tonalities, Kandinsky holds that subjective tonalities also correlate among themselves, that they come together in *configurations*. Thus, the idea of composition is a decisive one for him; the composition of the tableau is the best possible translation of the internal configuration of subjective tonalities. In this sense, Kandinsky *still* submits his painterly gesture, and more fundamentally subjective life, to aspects of the laws of exteriority and representation. Von Briesen painted in the dark, "meaning that each mark inscribed on the paper is totally independent of the one beside it" (GS, 54): he breaks the final link by which Kandinsky remained attached to space and representativity as such. The mark made by von Briesen's pencil, in space, is absolutely pure, preserved from all contamination in grounding spatial structures, and thus abolishing space in him as much as the space in which he works, his operations having absolutely nothing representational about them. Von Briesen's indifference to space, essentially contradictory to Kandinsky's, "is" nowhere other than in pure disruption, the pure violence inflicted on the space of the sheet of paper and, by extension, on Space as such.

Nonetheless we can still see, and perhaps more than ever, within this context of the most radical indifference to Space as such, an implicit tension within Henry's analysis. If von Briesen's draftsmanship is "minimal," or "extenuated," to use Henry's terminology,[30] nevertheless—and these expressions indicate it as well—its inscription in space is, *despite everything*, necessary. At this depth, and only at this depth, we rediscover the problematic of the apophantic. This is a matter of understanding that in drawing, Life can speak itself only *indirectly*, as what disrupts space, and only in that disruption. Therefore, as the support of its own torment, space is necessary; Life cannot declare itself without it. In other words—not Henry's, but hopefully connected with the vocabulary of Life—if the mark *wounds* the Ek-static space such that Life is recalled to Space only in the wound, will it not always, in fact, be confused with a *scar*? Is it not a *trace*, despite its desire for immediacy?

Henry's response to this question, which is always implicit, has already been broached: one can consent to recognize that this is the case, insofar as one immediately affirms that there is nothing there putting Life in jeopardy; that, on the contrary, in von Briesen's graphic design, Life agrees to address the lost and misled in order to gather them close to it, on the basis of the unbroken *jouissance* of its relationship to itself, which is also the intact purity of its Word.

We must approach Henry's work by rigorously applying its description of von Briesen's graphic work. In addressing von Briesen's drawings as absolutely singular, Henry's text—paradoxically but in a manner congruent with his own—indirectly, and perhaps without recognizing it, *also* addresses itself.

We began by addressing Henry's "tautological" style, and we must approach it once again in order to finish finally, by hearing it for what it is.

We have been able to say that Henry's "tautologies," in their looping forms, "mime" the movement of Life. I meant by this—and I stand firm on it—that the relationship to Life in Henry's text is never simply, and not at first, a relationship with signification (in the classic sense). But my formulation was rather awkward, since at its deepest Henry's style is neither "form" nor "mime." He says Life is singular *rhythms*: rhythms that will have ventured not into the Outside as constituted by graphic space, as with von Briesen, but in the Outside constituted by the philosophical text.

If Henry employs the notion of rhythm, however, it constitutes neither one of his themes nor one of his fundamental operational notions. Rhythm seems nonetheless precisely to fit what Henry calls (in fact, more often) "intensity" or "fulguration." These "tautologies" in which Life is finally simultaneously subject, verb, and predicate; these "tautologies" describing nothing but fabricating the event of Life, each time a singularity—flash forth, fulgurate, are the means by which the Henrian mark incises the space of the Ek-static *logos*. And, as we have seen, the mark can be what it is only in conserving the mode of Ek-static Transcendence to which it applies itself as the necessary support. This is why the mark of Henry's writing must always, in the same movement, consist of the rigorous fabrication of an apophantic *logos*.[31]

Henrian "tautologies" are the rhythm of life in writing and text, if rhythm is what disrupts all form at the heart of all sustained form; if it is what disrupts form without ever being merely destroying it; if it is what affects it and moves it.

And the rhythm of Life, of Henrian "tautology," is exemplarily disruptive, since it is collision and discontinuity, since it is *at the limit* of the supportable for the Ek-static mode in which it is inscribed, for the apophantic *logos*. Looping back on themselves, Henry's sentences do not, however, *wind around* themselves: they *embrace*; they *crash* against themselves. Far from any lability, suppleness, Merleau-Pontian encircling, this is how the rhythm of Life fulgurates.

In a sense—and only in a sense—Levinas's philosophical writing is an invitation to dance; it might be said that for Michel Henry the writing of philosophy is drawing; drawing only as von Briesen draws.

Thus, Derrida's, Levinas's, and Henry's texts each tend toward their own proper rhythm in order to put the rhythm of the givenness of all phenomenality to the test. For each of them this is a matter of reconceiving rhythm and never simply thematizing it or "representing" it. In fact, rhythm is precisely what, in a fertile traumatism, destabilizes all form in sustained form. All three, for reasons we have attempted to expose, see the rhythm of coming to appearance as an exemplarily violent rhythm marked by discontinuity. Consequently, the manner in

which they tend to bear witness to this is itself inhabited by discontinuity and rupture.[32]

It is the attestation within reeffectuation, through a singular style,
that has come to the support of a failing thematization. Within this
same perspective, Levinas is interested in the paintings of Jean Atlan,
and Henry is interested in the drawings of August von Briesen. And it
is, in part, in constructing an analogy between the philosophical acts of
each of these writers and the artistic act in which it is interested that we
have attempted to approach their conception as much as their practice
of rhythm. Constructing an analogy between the philosophical act and
that of the artist certainly in no case pleads for a confusing of the two.

We must insist here on two important points:

1. This assertion is as such entirely a test, since in order to be able
   to re-create, as singularity, the violent rhythm of the givenness of
   appearance, it is always necessary to run the risk of being exposed
   to it. Thus, enduring this test cannot be dissociated from the test
   of the self, of the birth of the Self at the heart of the test in which
   it tests itself as itself. This is why I can claim that in this sense (and
   only in this sense) Emmanuel Levinas, Michel Henry, and Jacques
   Derrida are authors *and* writers, insofar as these two categories can
   be separated from phantasms of mastery and absolute origin.

2. The texts of Levinas, Henry, and Derrida radically respect the
   philosophical necessity of an apophantic *logos*: they must be the
   fabric of a rigorous argumentation since the witnessing of the
   rhythm of phenomenality retains only a trace of the disruption
   inflicted by the philosophical Said. But this disruption, this echo,
   in return prevents the philosophical Said from gathering around
   itself, from being stabilized and from closing in on the quietude of
   a final word, a "result" guaranteed in its finished demonstration.
   In this sense it is in aporia, each in its own way, that these texts
   pay witness to the best of what they might pay witness to. Aporia,
   then, is revealed as fertile, since it is aporia that tests the rhythm of
   coming to appearance of all that appears.

I have tried to show here that this is always a risk. As our task has
been to put excess—to put what breaks—to the test, it endlessly risks

not holding itself to its highest test. And this is inescapable, since it is confronted by the unassumable. This risk is essentially that of an excessive practice of excess, the risk of solidifying excess by forcing the mark. These philosophies seem essentially exposed to their own caricature, for which we would not really know how to blame them if these moments of caricature actually declared that they are tests of the untenable. These excessive sentences are integral parts of these philosophies' rhythm, given that they have the power of not being fixed or congealed.

Conclusion

Our work on the philosophies of Jacques Derrida, Michel Henry, and Emmanuel Levinas has led us to put to the test a certain disappointment in their phenomenological practice.

A disappointment in the phenomenological method taken up as such by Levinas, who must exceed phenomenological description in the exposition of an ethical injunction—in order to perpetuate it beyond itself so that it remains faithful to its own needs. A disappointment in phenomenological method for Derrida, who has ceased meditating on the impossibility of pure phenomenology. But also disappointment—in practice—in Henrian philosophy, which nonetheless presents itself explicitly as the very completion of phenomenology as the self-revelation of Life. In fact, we have interpreted the Henrian gesture as being inhabited by the denial of an aporia that is thus all the more present as such, and, in a sense, all the more productive.[1]

This declaration is, however, ambivalent: regarding the disappointment of the phenomenology under consideration here, there is no doubt. But we have also attempted to show—without taking any rhetorical pirouettes—that the disappointment of this field in fact actually makes it more fruitful. Far from inviting us to conclude the adventure of contemporary French phenomenology whose common family resemblance is constituted through the practice of excess, this disappointment means precisely that this adventure can only be concluded on an ultimate outcome: exemplarily, it is constantly recommencing. This failure to provide itself phenomenality as such is not simply that of a method that should have tested its own incapacity to elucidate what occurs in experience. This failure is much more originary; it is the test of the impossibility of reaching the pure givenness of a phenomenality without remainder.

In the texts we have read here, phenomenology is lived radically as if it were always undercover, and even as if it required the opposite: the impossible.

In the judgment of Eric Alliez, "the impossibility of phenomenology" evokes hardly any emotion in us.[2] Phenomenology will have been for us neither the ultimate form of philosophy—philosophy being itself conceived as ultimate knowledge of the real—nor a school or movement to which one might come to defend integrity and purity. On the contrary, we practice it simply as a philosophical language that has wished to provide the means for articulating the enigma of being, one of the rare languages that in the twentieth century has not renounced this task or designated it as illusory—but there are certainly others. We have nonetheless installed ourselves in it as if in a field of problems in which the philosophical requirement to unveil being is *exemplarily* energized and radicalized, but without there being some monopoly to claim or to defend, so that the genre of the "defense and illustration" of phenomenology, as much as that of the declaration of its death—if not that of its murder—seems to us to be derisory.

We are thus in accord with Eric Alliez's conclusion regarding phenomenology's impossibility, but we must understand by these words the exact opposite of what he means by them. For Alliez, this impossibility—whose "theological" temptation would be the symptom—is to be understood as a simple failure, a sanction that invalidates the method and invites a conception of phenomenology as a historical movement that exhausted its energy and is not effaced, to the advantage of the philosophy of the future. For us also, this impossibility marks the limit of the power of this method, but insofar as this limit, far from signifying a completion to be effectively sanctioned, so to speak, historically, must be the "place" of its own practice, the "place" of a fruitfulness of the aporia finally delivered to the positivity of a result.

Phenomenology, as we have tried to show here, is less a field of problems than a field of *aporias*—the aporia being neither error as non-truth nor the problem that is the promise of truth, but rather the *suspense*, the *paralysis*, provoked by a double impossibility: that of the truth *and* that of the impossibility of truth. And is it not in fact the wager of phenomenology that the aporia of the aporia, the very matrix of all aporia, resides in the test of the non-givenness of phenomenality at the very heart of the need for its givenness? Going further, might we not say that only at the heart of the need for the most radical givenness could the proof of non-givenness be tested?

In addition, no more than there is pure phenomenon that can offer itself up without remainder, there is no pure phenomenology: as we have frequently indicated in the course of our investigation, phenomenology is cross-germinated with diverse "outsides"—and diverse types—that constitute at once the poles of resistance and of fecundity (a formalist structuralism for Desanti; ethics for Levinas; theology and even monotheistic faith for Levinas, Henry, and Marion; these differences come together within a mélange that is here represented only by Derrida).

It must be said of phenomenology that "higher than its possibility is its impossibility." This axiom is not in contradiction with Heidegger's: "higher than its effectivity is situated its possibility," but rather to Marion's reading; his is a reading that all of our work here has tended to legitimate.

It is an undiscussed, if not non-discussable, rule of phenomenology: finally to be more radical than the natural attitude shared by ordinary human beings and the positive sciences, phenomenology must tear itself away from the naïveté of doxology, which signifies nonetheless that this is nothing less than a matter of being attentive to the absenting of measured presence at the furthest stretch of the ontic. But divergences come to light when it is a matter of deciding ontologically on the domain thus opened: are we in the process of allowing ourselves to be affected by a purer presence since we have nothing that is substantial and static (Marion's view and, to a certain extent, Henry's), or are we allowing ourselves to be affected by absence as such—that is, by the impossibility of the "as such" (as suggested in this investigation)?[3] Adhering to the task laid out in the latter, as the good usage of phenomenology, means that the possibility of phenomenology can open itself out, strictly speaking, only in the test of the impossibility of the self.

And this is why on this point we have subscribed to Dominique Janicaud's recommendation that we practice a "minimalist phenomenology,"[4] as

1. a phenomenology that does not allow itself to be fascinated by an originary (however it identifies itself). The originary, as the matrix of phenomenality, through an essential necessity, tends to pull phenomenology into or "beneath" phenomenality—that is, in fact, *below* it—and at the same time to be promoted as first philosophy, which must jealously stand watch over its image and over the exclusivity of its dignity.

2. a phenomenology that thus ceaselessly renews its need to describe the emergence of sense at the level of phenomena in their singularity, allowing its glance to be reopened and to be provoked by all kinds of given phenomena—instead of locking it into a pretended originary phenomenon that we believe has demonstrated it, it is merely a construction beyond all phenomenality.

That said, this concern with not sacrificing "the prey (immanently appearing to intentional experience) for the shadow (pure givenness, archi-origin, etc.)" (*CPI*, 53), must not then be reversed into a naïveté that would consist of holding that we can reach the prey *without* the shadow—a systematic default that is in the end identical to what is being opposed here. In fact, is it not correct that to believe that one can detach from the shadow (of non-givenness) is not to restore naïveté of purity, this time as purity of a given that risks being constituted in positivity? As we have tried to demonstrate, prey does not allow itself to share the shadow, *remains* through essential necessity *in* the shadow. Intentionality does not know how to mount up to a knowledge, and the prey; the phenomenon does not know how to become prey—to define itself in its being through its capability to be grasped.

We must immediately make clear our concurrence with the recommendation made by Janicaud of a "minimalist phenomenology": the injunction against allowing ourselves to be fascinated by originarity must absolutely not be understood as an injunction to abandon our concern with the originary; it is in this concern ceaselessly redirected from the originary that the phenomenological glance can give the test that the originary ceaselessly escapes. And it is only thus, in this test, that it will be torn into phenomena from which it would like to come to rest in the quietude of its grasp; it is only thus that it can be protected against the risk of solidifying the phenomenon into positivity. This position is a perilous one: it opens out precisely the risk of what Janicaud calls the fascination of the originary, a fascination culminating in the *identification* ("theological") of the originary. But this, on the other hand, is the risk that must be run in order to avoid *identifying* the phenomenon, assigning it to positivity. These two temptations of identification are basically very similar to each other, obverse and reverse; it is the fragile exigency surviving this risk that will be furthest from these temptations, which here simply means "the furthest possible," always within reach.

Such is the ambivalence of the originary or, more precisely—and in order not to begin to identify—of what exceeds the phenomenological glance: it is at once what assures the fecundity of the latter—and what runs the risk of killing it. However, this is a question of recommending a "minimalist phenomenology" in the sense of establishing it from the outset, immediately, and "on the level," at the level of the originary is the best means of acquiescing to phenomenological exigency. It is always "from this side" that we must set out, from ordinary phenomena. Thus, for Levinas, it is in *this face*, singular and concrete, that the Otherwise than being is announced. We must finally separate ourselves from phenomena in order never to harden it, but without ever being able to detach from it completely, always remaining in the *tension* of tearing. The phenomenological glance must have the fragility and discomfort of being perpetually in the course of departing.

This impossible phenomenology is thus one denied the purity of givenness; that is, purity as such, the purity of a givenness of givenness (in advance of given phenomena), the purity of the phenomenon (even intentional experience) that, while we forget that it never entirely departs from its reserve—that it is always already suspended at the horizon of non-givenness—is no longer only a positive given.

The landscape of aporia

The phenomenon recognized as inseparable from what simultaneously evades, conceals, and brings forth was thematized in various ways throughout the figures we have read here, but all three find themselves in the same fundamental exigency: confronting non-givenness. The Derridean phantomic, the Levinasian "anti-phenomenal," the Henrian self-revelation of life, Marionian saturated phenomena—these are diverse translations of that exigency organizing itself relative to the line of division separating the (sur)presence and absence we have already addressed. If the phenomenon never offers itself forth plainly and integrally, this is doubtless because there is no goal without *Mehrmeinung*, as Husserl definitively demonstrates. More radically, what is always at play are not the degrees of fulfillment but the confrontation with the nothingness of beings. And this confrontation is *without degrees or distinctions*, confrontation with a phenomenality that is itself not *more or less* phenomenal, but entirely constituted through a double bind: that which requires of it that it simultaneously is nothing (of being) and yet the very thing that is given. The line of division between non-givenness and givenness is the double bind that allows for the ordering, in a pertinent way, of the landscape of contemporary French phenomenology. Is there any other way *not* to evade the test than to inhabit it in a necessarily precarious equilibrium?

We must emphasize that this givenness-in-non-givenness implies a certain test of temporality; as pure discontinuity, as pure rupture of the continuity of givenness, this test is certainly the most explicit one in Levinas, under the name of diachrony. It is, as such, at the limit of the thinkable, at the limit of that assemblage that is the *logos*.

It is in fact *against* continuity that Levinas, Henry, and Derrida think time. This cannot be done without audacity and peril, and perhaps not without failure; and, as we have seen, in times when failure is accompanied by audacity, as its shadow, as what at once warns it off and makes it possible. This temporality of the break is approached head-on and taken up as primordial temporality throughout the three writers we have read here.[5] But as we have often said, this break does not kill; it is in fact fecundity itself.

This discontinuous temporality is the very temporality of enduring the limit or the threshold. In fact, the interruption of givenness signifies at once that even here the phenomenon is irreducibly concealed, *and* that it would not know how to proceed in a movement of compensation that would open a horizon of givenness *beyond* the phenomenal that is already given: it is necessary to remain "on this side," on this border or limit at which phenomenality "flashes forth." In other words, this blinking temporality is the very test of the origin of the phenomenon for an *I* that is from then on a stakeholder in the spectacle that subjectivizes it and that forces it to its irreducible solitude of hypostasis: from the *I* to the spectacle that gives it to itself as originary spectator, there is plainly the irreducible, originary delay that always engenders the interruption of givenness, making it flicker.

Thus we might summarize the fundamental test common to all three of our central figures here. But it is true that what hardly needs repeating, but that we have tried to demonstrate, is less a matter of continuity of meaning—though that is necessary—than the movement whose nature ceaselessly destroys and ceaselessly renews the pragmatic, the performative, texts in which the voices testifying to this test resonate and that we have attempted to produce here as a supplementary echo.

The sole means of responding to this test is, for the texts we have been reading, to remake them according to the "logic" of the aporia. The aporia is the manner in which the discourse integrates the double bind of the givenness of phenomenality in the fact that the latter is only ever givenness through non-givenness. It thus lives as paralysis at the threshold of access to the phenomenon constraining the double impossibility as much of truth as of the absence of truth.[6]

Derrida claims the aporia, and Levinas formulates the injunction of recanting all Said, but Henry seems from the beginning to be a stranger to the logic of the aporia. And if the regimes of Henrian discursivity, on the one hand, and the Levinasian and Derridean, on the other, seem to oppose each other, this is because more fundamentally they are opposed to an ontology of full presence and an ontology of the gap and of absence. From this point of view there is a significant opposition between the Derridean claim regarding the spectre as philosophical emblem, of value to a phenomenology trapped in the double bind of givenness and non-givenness, and, on the other hand, the Henrian critique of spectres as symptoms of derealization common to the contemporary world; a contemporary world that adds it onto the wrenching of Life to itself that is itself the World, for example, in the technological production of virtual realities.

As the pure, affirmative revelation of life, Henrian phenomenology does not *above all* think itself in terms of the aporia, in the Derridean sense, nor of the difficulty and even the impossibility of describing what would ceaselessly escape, what would ceaselessly make the gap.

And yet, our plunge into the Henrian text will have shown us that the immediacy of Life to itself presupposes what, in non-Henrian language, we have called an internal gap, which allows him, even if—and because— it is *in itself,* still to *come.* This internal gap is decisive, if it is thanks to it that Henrian phenomenology pretends at once to concede nothing to the radicality of the intuition of immanence and to claim itself as the only authentic "rendering" of others, but also of time and, at a deeper level, of birth. And nothing allows for a decision as to whether this originary tiny gap permitting life to connect with itself is in fact the shadow of Ek-stasy denounced by Henrian philosophy as inauthenticity itself (and that it will have been obliged to resurge ironically within it—though in a quite re-fined manner), or if in fact it is authenticity establishing the Ek-static and hidden by it that is approached. But this decision matters little.

Consequently, the Henrian text seems to work through the aporia, and not simply because it is confronted with the classic difficulty of the apophantic (namely, how to speak the fullest presence?). Life is nowhere but in the multiplicity of its "coming to itself"; the text in which it reveals itself—specifically the Henrian text—will never cease to come to itself, in interlacings that are all the more tightly closed as they are shifted relative to one another. Nothing can stop, satisfy, or saturate the revelation of life to itself, the indefinite redoubling of its self-embracing: in a sense, it is solutionless, which results in this strange impression on the reader in con-fronting Michel Henry: the impression that he both always says the same thing and that it is never the same thing, the "tautology" of Life always be-ing pluralized in the plurality of its births, its "tautologies"—"tautologies" that are thus never really tautologies, since they are never simple repeti-tions of the identical. Only in its tiny gaps does radical immanence truly speak out. Reading Henry, we thus learn that the aporia is not loss and negation, and that the deceptive system it implies is never summarized in the simple experience of loss but is always a promise. In other words, reading Henry, we understand that the aporia is not incompatible with the regime of the *jouissance* of affirmation, and is perhaps even linked to it.

In making the gap at the heart of Life resonate, and the aporia at the heart of Henrian affirmation, we would wish to produce this effect of a return: to emphasize the affirmation of life within the landscape of thought where non-givenness and aporia are formed. We would thus learn to disconnect the Derridean version of this landscape from its possible nihilistic caricature, from its possible fascination with death, by recalling that the phantom is always and first of all the revenant; that is, the *reborn*.

Thus, the structural opposition between, on the one hand, the excess of plenitude in givenness (Henry) and, on the other, the symmetrical excess constituted through the decrease of presence in non-givenness (Levinas, Derrida), by no means erased and even thus made decisive, will be made more complex in a "contact at the heart of a chiasm."

Reading contemporary French phenomenology

In the final analysis, the texts that we have read here are "foreign." Inhabited by a traumatism, they are traumatizing: the performative or paradigmatic dimension of these philosophies seems to be decisive. And this performative dimension immediately signifies the originarity of subjectivity.

In all our texts, an *I* is "performed," as a "me" in the sense of each one and not of "no matter who": in its philosophical universality, this *I* supports the singularity of each one.[7] As the inheritor of the Heideggerian need of attestation of the event of being, it is born to have to assume the flashing forth of appearance and of absence to which this test is immediately witness. Thus, in the same movement, it arouses the philosophizing *I* of the addressee and presides over the test of the addressee's birth in assigning to the spectacle of the test its own birth into philosophical subjectivity. Additionally, we would gladly propose understanding the bodies of texts in which this study is interested as being relevant to a protreptic of a new genre: these texts, being true to the phenomenological task as properly understood, and despite the appearance of paradox, are less descriptive than indicative, or even prescriptive: they indicate a task, and even—and this is their specificity in the phenomenological domain—a test, to which the reader must be exposed. More than ever, they will be practiced in theory, will be theory *as practiced*, as being nowhere but in the *act* of thought.

Let us insist on the reader's place, as designated by the texts themselves, as being empty. Thus, in fact, these texts amount to an aesthetic of reception: in a rigorous paradox that our work here has tried to exemplify more than to theorize—this was not the task at hand—Levinas's, Henry's, and Derrida's texts manifest the infidelity that alone allows them to remain faithful to themselves. This call to an infidelity of reading lies at the heart of the indicative marks of the experiences of thought that they are, in their totality. This is indicated but never clearly expressed, necessarily and essentially: in that they are excessive, these texts need not be simply repeated, for two contradictory reasons. On the one hand, excess calls out to excess, the escalation in reading that one gives it, and never its simple reeffectuation. On the other hand, at the same time, it contradictorily indicates the need to control it, to measure it. This indicates a double infidelity. On the one hand, we must remain on this side of it, in the *caution* governing the test it is. And on the other hand, this is a matter of being integrally exposed to its own beyond, since it is never anything other than the injunction of the beyond. These two gestures form a double bind: they are nested one inside the other—the one through the other—as endurance of the limit.

In brief, diachronic writing requires a reading, a reception, that is itself diachronic. It needs, without ever being able to say it explicitly, a *phronesis*, a caution, in the use of its traumatic power: prudence and concern for the self without which excess, as excessively practiced, would be defused and would return as its opposite. A prudence and a concern for self that could nonetheless never be held onto, and out of which it would be necessary to call the excess that will expel us from it. This is the oscillation that must be tested ceaselessly.

In other words, the texts we have read here, and across which we have identified a diachronic writing, simultaneously control and liberate, since they order liberation from themselves as being true to their very requirements for liberation. Like diachronic writing, diachronic reception must thus be exposed to an unavoidable internal contradiction that leads to its fragility and its precariousness: it must be ceaselessly relinquished by the self in order all the better to be reconnected to itself, in a movement that

is not simply a logical contradiction that, in the absence of all normative constraints, would leave the field free for "no matter what" interpretations proliferating in inconsistency. On the contrary, it constructs a powerful constraint that *forbids* the petrifying of texts in their already-said, that forbids their solidifying into idols, in such a way, however, that the movement of desubstantialization to operate is oriented, as if in quotation marks, by the indicative trace of a need coming straight from the excess with which it *must* break. It *must*: the aesthetic of reception is, at the same time, an ethic.
[8] And the demand of inconsistency, in the sense of the fragilization of all substantialization, is not inconsistency in the logical sense of the word.

These brief methodological remarks concerning the task of an aesthetics of diachronic reception clearly indicate that we are hovering at the brink of the debate over the opposition between phenomenology and hermeneutics, between phenomenology and its "hermeneutic drift," as is sometimes claimed.[9] The aim of this expression is to clarify the opposition between a philosophy inspired by Husserl from one inspired by Heidegger and Gadamer. In the former, language, as a transparent and unproductive outer layer, is nothing but an instrument to be watched, and the requirement of any phenomenological watchfulness must be precisely to disrobe the "thing itself" of the veil the words have thrown over it when they are badly watched, in order to bring to light the prelinguistic experience of the intentional constitution of its sense of being. The latter—philosophy of Heideggerian and Gadamerian inspiration—would (according to the reproach formulated out of Husserlian "orthodoxy") make interpretation of the text the philosopher's goal.[10]

That phenomenology must confront the mediation of texts that are works of writing as such, without immediate transparency, is not at all contradictory with its need to be held—and to hold itself—as the highest experiment. In fact, the production of the texts we have been reading here, placed *en abyme*, continues and signifies the originary trembling of all phenomenality, the part of non-givenness that surrounds all givenness. Thus, to take a paradigmatic example, the Otherwise than being gives itself, in Levinas, only as that which disrupts the landscape of immanence: in the same way non-givenness, which is hardly of signification (if signification proceeds from the logico-linguistic power), is nonetheless signified, in that it points to itself as that which disrupts the landscape of logico-linguistic signification. And this is why it is at the privileged level of a pragmatics of rhythm, always united with a pragmatics of the *I*, that opposes and completes—completes in opposition—the need for the apophantic *logos* that we have claimed here. That done, we have not wanted to respond to the internal stakes of writing, but on the contrary, we have given ourselves the task of gathering together the originary trace, or echo, of the trembling, the flashing forth, of all phenomenality.

Reception of the disaster

We have just specified what we understand by the expression "impossibility of the phenomenology *of* excess" (in the genitive as much as the subjective and objective). We have arrived at a formulation—that of "phenomenology of the *disaster*." We are using "disaster" in the sense in which Maurice Blanchot works through this notion in *The Writing of the Disaster*.[11] That is, in the sense of a phenomenology (here) that, essentially carrying within itself its own impossibility as what simultaneously prevents it and makes it possible, does not force a renunciation even while it forbids all successful completion in the sense of the production of a specific result. What does force a certain "phenomenology of the disaster" is an indefinitely prolonged delay, an indefinite imminence, as much for the writer as for the reader.

This pathos of thought, this "state of the soul," which is proper to this phenomenology, is certainly not without its link to Husserlian writing, which ceaselessly seizes on the inchoate nature of its projects, of its propaedeutic and its returns, whose incompletion, though never desperate, is, on the contrary, the will to endlessness, and until the final breath, "always beginning everything again." Its specificity resides, however, in that it has definitively abandoned the certainty of progress, a certainty that for Husserl was nourished by the hope that, even if it is in the name of the ideal regulator, the plenitude of givenness is accessible. This phenomenology of excess, without hope of progress, having lost what Husserl calls "transcendental naïveté,"[12] is nonetheless far from being "apathic," without affect: on the contrary, it invites the risk of being precisely *too* affected—in every sense of the word.

This phenomenology of excess thus determines for the works that bear witness to it a test of a powerfully singular temporality, disconnected from all teleology and even from the need for continuity. This is, however, not a matter of an absence of temporality, but of the diachronic temporality we have described, of the flashing forth that reconnects, at the very heart of the radicality of rupture. This state—which is hardly one at all, since it is the pure instability of a movement—*this* movement—which is also hardly one, since in a sense it is fixed in time—is *the endurance of the limit*.

This is a work of and at the threshold—the threshold of the self for works whose completion is impossible but that will not properly speaking have failed, because they will thus have permitted the flowering of what cannot be overtly given, the "less than nothing" that produces all phenomenality. Always in gestation and in the impossibility of giving birth to itself, it nonetheless does not manifest the sterility of still-born thought that would have to be abandoned but, on the contrary, the promise of new births, within the fragility of diachrony. The endurance of the limit consists of assuming this indefinite flashing forth between phases that, already audacious, will pass beyond the limit, thus betraying excess in the very movement by which they bear witness to it. Flux and reflux of flashing that, suspended in its position, enclosed in the text of its *I*, remains on the threshold of phenomenality's secret, in the preparations for an essential departure indefinitely delayed.[13]

Therefore, this phenomenological writing of the *disaster* invites us to continue in a *reception* of the *disaster* to the extent of welcoming these texts, is simply to make them exist in the same movement in which they make me give birth to myself, in which they relegate me to the hypostasis of my *I*, in such a way, paradoxically, that they teach themselves the hard discipline of infidelity to the excess that they are—as fidelity itself—to themselves as selves.

The attempt to sketch out the landscape of this phenomenology that we have alternately called impossible phenomenology, the phenomenology of excess, or the phenomenology of the disaster—to express in three different ways the same fundamental trait—has only been possible within the precariousness of a diachronic reading, at once inescapable and unfaithful, that has wanted to replay, in its own proper rhythm, the test of subjectification at work in the texts we have addressed.

Abbreviations

AEL	Derrida, *Adieu to Emmanuel Levinas*
AH	Benoist, *Autour de Husserl*
AM	Montavont, "Le phénomène de l'affection dans les *Analysen zur passiven synthesis*"
AM2	Montavont, *De la passivité dans la phénoménologie de Husserl*
Barb	Barbaras, *La perception*
BPP	Heidegger, *The Basic Problems of Phenomenology*
BT	Heidegger, *Being and Time*
CC	Chalier, "Pour une pensée inspirée"
CD	Franck, "Le corps de la différence"
CIT	Husserl, *On the Phenomenology of the Consciousness of Internal Time*
CM	Husserl, *Cartesian Meditations*
CPI	Janicaud, *Chronos, pour l'intelligence du partage temporelle*
Crisis	Husserl, *Phenomenology and the Crisis of Philosophy*
DA	Derrida, *Aporias*
DE	Levinas, *Discovering Existence with Husserl*
DL	Lapoujade, "Le flux intensif de la conscience chez W. James"
DS	Nancy, *The Discourse of the Syncope*
DSD	Souche-Dagues, *Le développement de l'intentionnalité dans la phénoménologie husserlienne*
DT	Dastur, *Donner le temps*
ECP	Marion, "Esquisse d'un concept phénoménologique du don"
EE	Levinas, *Existence and Existents*

EF	Fink, "La philosophie tardive de Husserl dans la période de Fribourg"
EP	Granel, *Écrits logiques et politiques*
EU	Derrida, "Punctuations: The Time of the Thesis"
Éveil	Sebbah, "Éveil et naissance. Quelques remarques à propos d'Emmanuel Levinas et Michel Henry"
FA	Armengaud, "Éthique et esthétique: De l'ombre à l'obliération"
FD	Dastur, "Husserl et la neutralité de l'art"
FP	Poirié, *Emmanuel Levinas (Qui êtes-vous?)*
GD	Derrida, *The Gift of Death*
GDH	Deleuze, "À quoi reconnaît-on le structuralisme?"
GDT	Levinas, *God, Death, and Time*
GG	Granel, *Études*
Glas	Derrida, *Glas*
Gram.	Derrida, *Of Grammatology*
GS	Henry, "Graphie de la subjectivité"
GT	Derrida, *Given Time 1*
HG	Greisch, *Herméneutique et grammatologie*
HIC	Dreyfus, *Husserl, Intentionality and Cognitive Science*
HJL	Lenger, *La différence comme non-différence, éthique et altérité chez E. Levinas*
IAT	Henry, *I Am the Truth*
II	Levinas, *L'intrigue de l'infini*
IP	Husserl, *The Idea of Philosophy*
JA	Levinas, "Jean Atlan et la tension de l'art"
JC	Colléony, "Levinas et l'art"
JLC	Chrétien, "La dette et l'éléction"
JR	Rogozinski, "*Il faut la vérité*: Notes sur la vérité de Derrida"
JT	Taminiaux, *Le regard et l'excédent*
JTD	Desanti, *Réflexions sur le temps*
LI1	Husserl, *Logical Investigations 1*
LI2	Husserl, *Logical Investigations 2*

LP	Desanti, "Libre propos sur les *Leçons sur la conscience intime du temps*: Du temps qui s'écoule au temps qui s'écroule"
Marg.	Derrida, *Margins of Philosophy*
MO	Derrida, *Monolingualism of the Other*
MP	Richir, *Les méditations phénoménologiques*
OB	Levinas, *Otherwise Than Being: or, Beyond Essence*
OE	Levinas, *On Escape*
OG	Derrida, *Husserl's Origin of Geometry: An Introduction*
OGW	Levinas, *Of God Who Comes to Mind*
PD	Derrida, "L'éthique du don"
PG	Derrida, *The Problem of Genesis in Husserl's Philosophy*
PM	Marion and Planty-Bonjour, *Phénoménologie et métaphysique*
PR	Henry, "Parole et religion: La Parole de Dieu"
Psyche	Derrida, *Psyche: Inventions of the Other*
PTT	Janicaud, *Phenomenology and the "Theological Turn": The French Debate*
QP	Patočka, *Qu'est-ce que la phénoménologie?*
RB	Bernet, *La vie du sujet*
RG	Marion, *Reduction and Givenness*
RPE	Maldiney, *Regard, parole, espace*
RS	Levinas, "Reality and Its Shadow"
SP	Derrida, *Speech and Phenomena*
ST	Heidegger, *Schelling's Treatise on the Essence of Human Freedom*
STP	Granel, *Le sens du temps et de la perception chez Husserl*
TI	Levinas, *Totality and Infinity*
Tone	Derrida, "On a Newly Arisen Apocalyptic Tone in Philosophy"
TT	Granel, *Traditionis traditio*
UG	Derrida, "Ulysses Gramophone: Hear Say Yes in Joyce"
UP	Henry, *L'univers philosophique*
VI	Merleau-Ponty, *The Visible and the Invisible*

Notes

INTRODUCTION

1. The Heideggerian term "apophantic" defines the nature of the statement or sentence that does not present itself as a question or as in any way conditional, but rather as "factual"; this means that such a statement conceals any further or fuller contextual meaning the statement may have; e.g., "the sky is blue" is apophantic in that it presents itself as straightforward evidence, but that not only does not address implications of its own facticity but occludes further investigation into it.—Trans.

2. Janicaud, *Phenomenology and the "Theological Turn* (henceforth *PTT*).

3. See Wittgenstein, *Recherches philosophiques*, § 67 ff.

4. See Maldiney, "Tal Coat, 1954," in *Regard, parole, espace*, 21–26 (henceforth *RPE*).

5. "The gesture that catalyzes things as they are to us operates only according to the style of their presence to us, which only reveals the whatness of the world through the howness of our common reality" (Maldiney, 25).

6. Maldiney, ibid. It must be understood (and there is no reason to insist further on it here) that I am separating myself from Maldiney's analysis in that installation in the countryside identified by the names "Derrida," "Henry," and "Levinas" must lead me to think that the action of losing oneself in the countryside does not mean the dissolution of subjectivity in an anonymous originary as the locus of its authenticity, but is, on the contrary, the very test of solitary subjectivity in its originarity.

7. This is the claim of Michel de Certeau in *L'écriture de l'histoire* in 1987.

8. In addition, attempting to describe a family synchronically, as it were, our perspective does not consist of establishing a genealogical lineage; thus, I have reduced to the barest necessity any consideration of the Husserlian and Heideggerian heritage.

9. Henceforth, this operational perspective will cancel the objection according to which it would not be desirable to study absolutely contemporary bodies of work for those already completed, on the pretext that the former lack the distance that dissipates the "fog" of fashion and allows for objectivity.

10. "Take everything the philosopher has written, bring these scattered ideas back toward the image from which they have descended, raise them up, now firmly enclosed in the image, all the way to the abstract formula that swells out by images and ideas, then attach ourselves to this formula and peruse it in its simplicity, simplifying itself further, all the simpler because we will push onto it a great number of things, raise ourselves up with it, rise toward the point at which everything that was in tension in the doctrine is made more intense: we will then see for ourselves how this center of forces, however inaccessible, gives off this impulsion that produces *élan*; that is, intuition itself" (Bergson, *The Creative Mind*, 142).

PART I, CHAPTER I

1. H.-L. Dreyfus and Folledall make Husserl a precursor of classical cognitivism: of the principal tendency of the cognitive sciences claiming that intelligence, including human intelligence, can be defined by a calculation carried out through symbolic representations, whose model—which is highly explanatory— would be the computer (see *Husserl, Intentionality and Cognitive Science*; henceforth *HIC*). It is overwhelmingly important for them to show that Husserl, in describing "lived consciousnesses" as they are manifest in the world, i.e., in separating the laws of formal hierarchization from what he calls the *no me*, thus produces at the most fundamental and universal level, that of mental states, a syntax that had never been produced, according to him, at a strictly linguistic level (through Frege).

2. In other words, is it not a question here of what Gérard Granel warned us against: the return of "the worst of Husserl . . . in the form of a twinned renewal of spiritualism and scientism"; see "The Unexpressed of Research," in *Écrits logiques et politiques*, 84 (henceforth *EP*).

3. In "Punctuations" (henceforth EU).

4. Even if, factually, at least for Husserl, theoretical texts seem much more numerous than those implementing a method. We will take note, on the other hand, of the significant disinterest shown by Levinas, Henry, and Derrida—but not Jean-Luc Marion, it is true—in the definition and the description of the "technical apparatus" of the phenomenological method's operations, even when they are explicitly interested in it (see, for example, Henry's chapter "The Phenomenological Method," in *Material Phenomenology*).

5. See *The Basic Problems of Phenomenology* (henceforth *BPP*).

6. In the wake of the Husserlian thematic of absolute consciousness as *Urregion* (see *Ideas I*, § 49). And that he immediately describes consciousness as pure exhaustion of the self, then as negation, does not, on the contrary, call into question that it is presence to self: "The other indication that metaphysics can draw

on ontology is that the for-itself is effectively a perpetual project of the self qua being, and a perpetual failure of this project," writes Sartre in *Being and Nothingness*. The notion of "consciousness" is clearly one of the fundamental categories of Sartrean thought, and the determination of consciousness as for-itself, even if it ruins its grounding claim, is no less installed at the heart of being.

7. Thus, Gérard Granel characterizes the Derridean gesture. We will also explore how since *On Escape* (henceforth *OE*), Levinas asserts "excendance" as that which is in question. It seems that Levinasian ex/cendance can be understood only as excess. See the commentary on this Levinasian idea that Didier Franck gives in "Le corps de la différence" (henceforth *CD*).

8. Significant from this point of view is the difference affecting the agreement between the notion of ambiguity in its Merleau-Pontian context and its Levinasian one. In the former, it connotes the lability of the chiaroscuro, the "blur." Levinas asserts not the ambiguity of what does not allow itself to stabilize in the perpetual and imperceptible breaking of the living continuity of his deterioration, but rather the indistinguishable ambiguity, the "undecidable," of the "blink." See, for example, Levinas's interview with Hans Joachim Lenger in *La différence comme non-différence*, and the study by J. Rolland in the same edition, "'Divine comédie': La question de Dieu chez E. Levinas," especially 120. See also—and above all—*Otherwise Than Being*, where ambiguity, amphibology, and the equivocal appear frequently in significant and decisive ways (henceforth *OB*).

9. The case of Levinas is exemplary: if the human is a contemporary of Sartre and Merleau-Ponty, his work(s) can be received and understood only much later. This tends to confirm my hypothesis: the true constitution of a generation is theoretical before it is chronological.

10. "Intentionality as the crowning theme of phenomenology," is the title of § 84 of *Ideas I*; we might recall several passages: "It is intentionality that characterizes consciousness in the strongest sense"; "We should understand by intentionality that property of living beings 'of being conscious *of* something.'"

In the *Cartesian Meditations* (henceforth *CM*), Husserl says that "the word intentionality signifies nothing less than this general and functional particularity of the consciousness of being conscious of something, carrying within itself, in its quality of *cogito*, its *cogitatum*" (*Second Meditation*, § 14).

11. More precisely, intentionality is, according to Husserl, the specific mode of being—misunderstood up to the present—of consciousness. In fact, "intentionality" names within itself the essential characteristic that gives the consciousness of being a pure aim, of being in its entirety an arrow aiming at what it is given. And the movement of this arrow is strongly paradoxical, since as the a priori of correlation, it never departs from itself in order to encounter an exteriority that is already there, confronting it "statically." It is a description of consciousness that

perceives an entire horizon of understanding and that, already, conceals its own aporias. To mention two already engaged in the phenomenological tradition:

1. How to short-circuit, thanks to the a priori notion of correlation, the static opposition between the subject, on the one hand, and, on the other, the object whose reality would be attested to through its autonomous existence, so to speak; how to do that without reinvigorating a radical idealism that would transform the activity of constituting consciousness into an activity of creation? In other words, if the transcendence of the correlate of lived experience must be a "transcendence in immanence," must belong precisely to "intentional immanence," is it not connected, despite Husserl's efforts, despite the very dynamism of lived experience, to a risk of enclosure within consciousness?

2. There is another difficulty initiated in the discovery of intentionality: it proposes freeing itself from a substantial understanding that is, consequently, static, of the Cartesian kind, of consciousness. And could the Cartesian reciprocity between *consciousness* and *ego*—and even in any sense— be overcome? If consciousness is a pure arrow, it is no longer necessary to think like a grounding substance in the sense of a support that, as "gathered" on itself, it would "support" its accidents: as pure "bursting toward" it must even be liberated from the Ego, if that last is, on the contrary, the very movement of "gathering to itself" (and first of "*being* gathered to itself"). And obviously, certain Husserlian texts, those of the "first" Husserl, describe consciousness as an economy of the Ego: this is the way in which consciousness is described in the *On the Phenomenology of the Consciousness of Internal Time* (henceforth *CIT*) as the originary flux of lived experience whose unity is temporal: that is, here Husserl sees the economy of all Ego as a "pole of centration" assuring the unity of consciousness. This has not always been the case; on the contrary. We will return to this at greater length in Part 3, Chapter 1.

12. See *Phenomenology and the Crisis of Philosophy* (henceforth *Crisis*).

13. In *Philosophie première*.

14. On this question, see the remarkable "Translator's Preface" to *Philosophie première*.

15. "I would like to conclude, and in order to avoid misunderstandings, to indicate that phenomenology, as I have developed it, only eliminates naïve metaphysics, operating with absurd things within it, but that does not exclude metaphysics in general" (*Cartesian Meditations*, 156). This gesture is not without its ambiguities, as Jean-Luc Marion enumerates them: "Husserl's subsequent evolution—as we now know quite clearly—will ceaselessly and increasingly accentuate the strange imitation of metaphysics by phenomenology that, as though

fascinated by its most intimately strange other, will only attempt to demolish itself in order to better assert its heritage" (*Phénoménologie et métaphysique*, 12; henceforth *PM*).

16. Indicating from the outset that this is suggestive and significant, Levinas wrote a text entitled "The Nonintentional Consciousness," reprinted in *Entre nous*. Michel Henry, according to him, had published a text entitled "Phénoménologie non intentionnelle: Une tâche de la phénoménologie à venir [Non-intentional Phenomenology: A Task of Phenomenology to Come]," in *Intentionalité en question*. In the same section—"Vers une phénoménologie non intentionnelle"— in the same volume, is Gérard Granel's "La phénoménologie décapitée": to aim for the head is to aim for aiming itself, intentionality. It is true that within this program of "disintentionalization," from one author to another, a great deal of nuance exists. Levinas maintains something of intentionality in his very style— his brilliance? For him it is a question not of expulsion but of *inversion* (to use the very word Levinas frequently employs to describe the treatment to which he submits intentionality). Marion is largely of Levinas's view (less so in his manner than in his objective). Michel Henry places himself in the *elsewhere* of intentionality, out of all contact with it since, according to him, "intentionality arises only at nightfall. To say just a word on what *is*—when it is at least a question of the ego's ipseity—it always comes too late" (*Material Phenomenology*). But he is supported in this only through the reinforcement of his very negation. As for Derrida, if we leave aside his commentary on Husserl in which he clearly shows that intentionality brings presence to its culmination in the space of its ecstasy, he is (as I will show here) aiming at a *spectralization* of intentionality, even though he is hardly interested at this point in the technical concept of intentionality, and orients himself on the side of the aporia of the gift (see Part 2). Even though it is not directly a part of my field of interest here, we must remember that the combative gesture in Granel's manner of presentation is located entirely within the boundaries applied to intentionality as to the Chief after whom phenomenology has been written up to now, the Chief of Reason—the expression is pleonastic.

17. In *Transcendence of the Ego*, which Sartre wrote early on (1936; 1988), he designates the ego as "an inhabitant of consciousness" he qualifies as "useless." In fact, the ego appears to him to be an illusion retrospectively imported into intentionality from the sphere of constituted ontic reality. The ego, as static and auto-centered substance, conceals the transcendence without reserve of intentionality. And it is clear that Sartre later on will describe consciousness as "escaping to self"—an "escape" with Hegelian accents, since it would consist entirely of "self-destruction." Whatever would be involved in this gesture, Sartre does not in any case designate a *limit* to consciousness, a beyond or a non-beyond that would escape its powers but, on the contrary, connects it with absoluteness, even if it is then understood as "a transcendental field without subject."

18. "Despite the rhetorical aspects of this theme [the pure ego], I persist in thinking that there is something there, at least contra-Heidegger: it is not true that one can so easily be divested of this fruitful phenomenological theme represented by 'subjectivity' and, if I increasingly refuse to absolutize, it seems to me nonetheless that one cannot make it the economy of a certain number of properties, transcendental or not, associated with it and that solidly resist the operations of 'destruction' that have been brought to bear on them" (Benoist, *Autour de Husserl*, 7; henceforth *AH*).

19. "Phenomenology has been too quickly condemned in the name of a notion of the subject that it has tended to exceed. If phenomenology does not remain secure in the face of the crisis of modern subjectivity, it nevertheless occupies itself in seeking answers instead of leaping into peremptory declarations on the death of the subject" (Bernet, *La vie du sujet*, 2; henceforth RB).

20. Since the most fundamental structure of consciousness is the gift, this is therefore a matter of being directed toward non-giving. In other words, since consciousness is the medium of presence, it is necessary to invoke absence and/ or the nothing, or even better, and inversely, to identify an Ur-presence [*sur-présence*], a presence in excess of consciousness, a consciousness that, as a result, would cease to exhaust the domain of any possible presence. I will return to this theme.

[*Sur* is here translated "ur" in order to distinguish *sur* from "over" in the sense of "overflow" or "over-full"; the meaning here is rather the metaphorical "above," which has no English equivalent.—Trans.]

21. *Phenomenology and the "Theological Turn."*

22. "To confront [*buter*]" not in the sense in which the reduction encounters a resistance that would remain intact in it—an irreducible—and prevent its deployment but, on the contrary, in the sense in which it successfully attains its goal [*but*] and thus accomplishes its task.

23. See *Of God Who Comes to Mind* (henceforth *OGW*). Richir is quite close to Levinas here; see, for example, in *Les méditations phénoménologiques* (henceforth *MP*), especially the *IIIe Méditation* entitled "Pour une épokhè phénoménologique hyperbolique / Méditation hypercartésienne."

24. In order for a *gift* of what gives consciousness to itself to be possible, would it not be necessary—even if it were done with great subtlety—*to identify* this source? And would this not be the very gesture that would risk exceeding the constraints and the limits of the phenomenological method? This is the question we will test out here, with regard to Marion's philosophy (see Part 2, Chapter 2) and Henry's (Part 3, Chapter 3).

25. We will be led to interrogate the pertinence of this distinction, suggested by Janicaud, which does not mean to sidestep the problems it clearly lays out, but rather to give them their full aporetic force. The denunciation to which Janicaud

subjects them makes it, from the outset, a distinctively determined adversary, to the degree to which it determines itself, circumventing the problem rather than posing it, in aid of an idea of phenomenology that is consequently much less uneasy with itself. Obfuscating this frontier in order to make it more decisive runs the risk of being a *refusal* of understanding in the better part of those who denounce the theological turn in the name of a pure phenomenology well enclosed within its walls rather than those who tend (without perceiving or understanding it?) to substitute for phenomenological unease (in the name of phenomenology itself) an entirely different kind of rapport with the event of the appearance of that which appears: faith. What is more, we would risk, through each "faction," being identified as part of the other "camp." Too bad: that is a "good risk to run."

26. See Part 2, especially the chapter devoted to a comparative study of the impossible phenomenology of the Derridean gift and Marion's phenomenology of giving.

27. See Levinas, *Totality and Infinity* (henceforth *TI*).

28. The notion of *double bind*—of "double constraint"—initially elaborated by Gregory Bateson in the framework of the "Palo Alto School" most recently indicates this last contradictory (essentially parental) injunction that he situates at the origin of the pathological behaviors of the schizophrenic type: the child is subjected to contradictory injunctions and to the interdiction of attempting to escape this situation, which risks weakening, if not destroying, its ego. In Bateson the idea is that ordinary life confronts us fundamentally with this contradiction, testing whether formal understanding can be accounted for; there is also the idea that it is to be made, as much as possible, the test of the double constraint that one has the chance to exceed.

29. Derrida notes that Levinas expresses this idea in *Otherwise Than Being: or, Beyond Essence*. These passages are cited and commented upon in *Adieu to Emmanuel Levinas* (henceforth *AEL*).

30. On the Levinasian notions of Saying, Said, echo, trace, and, above all, diachrony, see Part 4.

31. Some examples: "In the copula 'is' shines, or blinks, the ambiguity of *essence* and of nominalizing relations. The Said as word is *essence* or temporalization" (*OB*); "gaping of an abyss within the proximity, the infinite that blinks in refusing speculative audacities, distinguished from the nothing pure and simple through the commission of the next to my responsibility."

The idea of blinking thus for Levinas indicates the radicality of the interruption paradoxically renewed beyond itself in what "resonates"—it would not know how to signify thematically—what for Levinas is more than originary, namely, the Infinite that gives all being-in-itself as having always already fractured. And this is the impossibility of an integral thematization of what will interrupt *all* thematization designating the idea of *ambiguity* in its Levinasian sense.

32. See *MP*, for example, passim, regarding "'phenomena' that are not at all positive but an indeterminacy that blinks in its phenomenalization."

PART I, CHAPTER 2

This chapter in part readdresses, by altering and amplifying it, my essay "Intentionnalité et non-givenness," in *Analecta Husserliana*, 50:101–13.

1. Let me clarify from the outset that I am not attempting here to provide an "objective" reading of Husserl or even to measure the size of the displacements that have occurred in the French readings of Husserl. I am interested in another necessary task. I will be satisfied here by determining a profile of "Husserl for domestic use" in French phenomenology, out of which it is constructed and through which it achieves the greater part of its phantasm, far from any objective Husserl—were such a thing to exist. This is why, for example, we will not concentrate here on recent important works (such as those of François Dastur) that attempt to reestablish the effects of the distortion that a reception in France universalized by Cartesianism would have submitted to the richness of Husserlian analyses, concealing psychological pathways and lived experience, and the monadological model linked to the latter.

2. For example, see §§ 3 and 41 of *Ideas I*.

3. This can be found in the notes he devotes in his translation to § 3 of Husserl's *Ideas I*.

4. Presentification thus perhaps means less in that, from a noematic point of view, it gives what is absent to givenness in perception, and gives it as such; that in terms of what it inscribes, from a hyletic standpoint, a gap, a fracture at the very heart of lived consciousness. This cannot be developed further here; see the very lucid remarks of Rudolf Bernet in *La vie du sujet*.

5. The manner we have of envisaging the connections between the theory and practice of phenomenology in our reading of Husserl intersects with that of Tran-Duc-Thao in his preface to *Phenomenology and Dialectical Materialism*.

6. Dastur, "Husserl et la neutralité de l'art," 26 (henceforth FD).

7. If most of the time originarity and *Leibhaftigkeit* are reciprocal for Husserl, consideration of the past requires their being distinctive, as Rudolf Bernet reminds us in *La vie du sujet* (RB, 304).

8. This fact makes possible the interpretive force so powerful in a Levinas or a Derrida; it also operates in Michel Henry even if he draws radically opposed conclusions from it: it provides him with the occasion to denounce the inauthenticity of the Ek-static gap. Levinas and Derrida privilege this gap—absence—to the detriment of continuity—presence—which must provide the thematic link with Husserl. For these three, it is a matter of adhering to a pure presence that for Husserl would already be betrayed; a pure presence that would be radically

immanent to itself to the point that, strangely but consequently, it would not even be deployed according to the continuity of flux.

9. This issue will be raised by Heidegger, Levinas, and Derrida as they explore whether one can think this nothing of the phenomenon as not "being" even a differed presence.

10. Barbaras, *Le perception*, 41 (henceforth Barb).

11. Without doubt the exploration of passive syntheses, of the ante-predicative in general, tends to place Husserl outside this frame, but one could hardly say that he *completes* the step.

On this question it is important to return to Anne Montavont's analysis of the phenomenon of affection in Husserl, in her "Le phénomène de l'affection dans les *Analysen zur passiven synthesis*" (henceforth AM). She shows that for Husserl "affective hyletic unities result from a passive synthesis, that is, a synthesis not actively constituted by the ego but, on the contrary, produced by itself according to the law of association" (AM, 124). From the outset, for Husserl passivity clearly indicates an anonymity of the life of consciousness whose emergence has no need of an ego, but in no case is it associated with an unconstitutable radically overflowing all powers of synthesis, all consciousness. In addition, Montavont shows that if anonymous affection precedes and motivates the cogito, the enacting of the ego, which fundamentally only answers to Husserl within the frameworks of thought that are his own, finds itself faced with "the necessity of responding negatively" to this question: "But is a unity that would not be for any subject thinkable?" Consequently for Husserl, "If I do not produce meaning [*sens*] at the outset (and it is properly the work of passive syntheses to make sense without concept, without subject, without the activity of synthesis since they are, on the contrary, constitutive of this subject), there is thus no meaning that would be available as such without me. The anonymous is already within potential or tendentious consciousness" (AM, 128). Montavont further develops these analyses in *De la passivité dans la phénoménologie de Husserl* (henceforth AM2).

12. A non-originary givenness is a givenness only insofar as it draws its power of givenness from originary givenness.

13. Michel Henry's philosophy is one of subjectivity, since it is always for him a matter of combating any thought of Ek-stasis that tends to undermine the subject, but nonetheless a philosophy without transcendental ego to the extent that the transcendental ego can be suspected of being a projection of the Ek-static; that does not exist as an instance of recuperative, conclusive synthesis; and from whom an Ek-static revelation of immanence has originarily emerged; it is a transcendental ego that insofar as it contains the possibility of glancing at itself, already betrays the pure immanence of subjectivity. We can thus understand why, when the dominant gesture in post-Husserlian phenomenology was to liberate

the ego's intentionality, Henry, in exact opposition, desired to liberate the subjectivity of intentionality and even of the ego.

14. See chapter 9, "Remarques sur Heidegger et les *Recherches logiques* de Husserl," in *Le regard et l'excédent* (henceforth JT). There he lays out the successive steps of Husserlian interrogation in the sixth chapter of the *Logical Investigation VI* and cites a certain number of significant passages from it, such as "the intention of the word 'white' only partially coincides with the color-aspect of the apparent object; a surplus of meaning remains over, a form that finds nothing in the appearance itself to confirm it" (Husserl, *Logical Investigations 2*, 273; henceforth *LI2*). Husserl insists especially on the fact that if certain characteristics narrow the field of possible perceptions, "being is absolutely imperceptible" (*LI2*, 277). And yet, if in phenomenology there is only what is given, then there must be "an act that renders identical services to the categorial elements of meaning that merely sensuous perceptions render to the material elements" (*LI2*, 280).

15. I owe much in these remarks to Desanti's analysis in *Réflexions sur le temps* (henceforth JTD). Certainly, everything at play between this "nothing" and this "everything" has nothing to do with a "quantitative" proportion of the given.

16. See Husserl, *Ideas Pertaining to a Pure Phenomenology*.

17. Husserl is reticent regarding dialectical schema. See, for example, Husserl's annotations in the *Sixth Cartesian Meditation* (*CM*).

18. See the introduction to *Edmund Husserl's Origin of Geometry* (henceforth *OG*).

19. For this reason, in a general way, the Husserl connection is privileged here, even if certain analyses evoke the connection maintained by one or another of our central thinkers to Heidegger. Husserl is the focus because he *initiates* the aporia that contemporary French phenomenology inherits, and because in Husserl the aporia is all the more effectively at work in that it hardly identifies itself as such, whereas Heidegger begins by making it explicit while drawing out its consequences.

20. Several exemplars, however:

- Levinas, in various interviews. With François Poirié in *Emmanuel Levinas (Qui êtes-vous?)* (henceforth FP). Or Hans Joachim Lenger, reprinted in *La différence comme non-différence, éthique et alterité chez E. Levinas* (henceforth HJL). It should be noted that in "The Non-Intentional Consciousness," reprinted in *Entre nous*, Levinas writes that "without doubt Husserl is at the origin of my writings."
- Derrida's link to Husserl is unambiguous: Husserl, at least thematically, is the culmination of the metaphysics of presence. Derrida sometimes evokes the ambiguity of his connection to Heidegger, an ambiguity to which Gérard Granel devotes a number of pages in "Derrida et la rature de l'origine," in *Traditionis traditio* (henceforth *TT*), where Granel shows that Derrida's

suspicions with regard to Heidegger—that Heidegger still works at the horizon of metaphysics while at the same time declares its closure—marks the concern that must always accompany Heideggerian thought—and in fact Derridean thought itself with regard to itself. This disquiet concerns the originary ambivalence that means there can be no originary purity and thus no pure outside metaphysics; and that belief is its worst form.

• Michel Henry's relationship with his ancestors is unambiguous. He recognizes Husserl as having glimpsed pure immanence by liberating models that are real and/or worldly—but reproaches him for already having lost it in intentionality, which is for him only a construction copied onto transcendence, onto the world. This is as much as saying that he refuses to allow Husserl what has generally been seen as his fundamental discovery (intentionality) and that he sees it as a motif received as aporetic ("Impression"); see *HIC*. Moreover, it happens that Henry declares that if it is explained in the language of Husserlian phenomenology, its "problematic" imposes itself independently of Husserl. Henry's connection to Heideggerian philosophy is, according to him, unnuanced: Henry does not see the most radical avatar of the hegemony of transcendence in a Heidegger to whom Henry opposes the originarity of immanence.

• J.-L. Marion declares that he places his philosophy in a process of radicalization oriented in the line whose first two steps were Husserl and (then) Heidegger. See *Reduction and Givenness* (henceforth *RG*), to which we will return in greater detail in Part 2, Chapter 2.

21. We will return to this, which does not exclude—and even solely renders possible, according to Heidegger—the discovery of the essentially ipseic nature of *Dasein*.

22. See particularly *God, Death, and Time* (henceforth *GDT*), in which Levinas explicitly formulates this reproach to Heidegger .

23. Levinas is even a thinker of the "less than nothing": "We find ourselves before a new category: before what is behind the portals of being, before the less-than-nothing that Eros tears off of its negativity and that he profanes. This is a question of a nothingness distinct from the nothingness of anguish: of the nothingness of the future buried in the secret of the less-than-nothing" (*TI*, 244).

24. The fact is that givenness, intentionality, and finally phenomenology can only be in play through the way they manage the link between possible and impossible, a link appearing explicitly in the opposition between Derrida and Marion regarding the method of working with Heidegger's statement regarding phenomenology that effectivity is not valued as highly as possibility. See Part 2, Chapter 2.

25. See Husserl, *The Idea of Philosophy* (henceforth *IP*), where the term *Gegebenheit* insistently imposes itself on Husserl's pen.

26. If Adorno could reproach Heidegger (and not without reason) for using such "star-words," it is nonetheless Heidegger who in *BPP* writes "what does 'give' mean, *'givenness'*—this magic word of phenomenology and the "stumbling block" for all others?" We owe this citation and its translation to J.-L. Marion, who comments on it in emphasizing that Heidegger signifies thereby not the scandal of vulgar rationalism or the magic of a pretended mystical enchantment that does not offer an appropriate attitude to what would be given.

27. This inversion of the intentional arrow tends toward the Levinasian gesture that, as we have already noted, found its initial impetus—while never made explicit in his most radical prolongations—in Husserl, if it is true that all representation, for Husserl, must be *caused*. See, for example, "Such a construct is pre-given to the extent to which it exercises an affective excitation; it is a given to the extent to which the ego *has responded to the excitation* [emphasis added, FDS] and turned toward the constituted by grasping it" (AM, 123–24).

28. It is clear, however, that Marion qualifies it initially and exemplarily through saturation, and not through excess, if it is true that it is only through a connection with the finitude of my representation that it is excessive, while it is in itself and with regard to itself that it is saturated.

29. Cartesian infinity—a saturated phenomenon if ever there was one—does not allow itself to be constructed apart from the finite.

30. Note that thoughts of non-givenness, of absence at the origin, do not exclude presence but *anxiety*, while the gestures of Henry and Marion exclude or dissolve all *radical* understanding of non-givenness, as fracture or absence.

31. Levinas writes: "Intrigue . . . tied together as absolute diachrony, and that will be a first priority of understanding . . . in the analysis, from irreducible proximity to consciousness of . . . , and describing itself in some fashion as its inversion" ("Le Dit et le Dire," in *L'intrigue de l'infini*, 165–94; henceforth *II*).

32. We are skimming over a crucial question here: do thinkers such as Levinas—or Marion—in disconnecting intentionality from all power of constitution in the proper sense of the term actually explode intentionality in thinking beyond it? Or as they suggest explicitly, do they show, contrary to Husserl, that the representation is not essentially linked to the power of constitution? It is important to work carefully through these words: either in separating the notion of representation from that of intentionality, or in separating intentionality from power despite all "theoretics" of constitution.

33. The notion of the trace appears very early in Levinas's itinerary and never ceases to be decisive. See "The Trace of the Other," in *Discovering Existence with Husserl* (henceforth *DE*), and "The Trace," in *Humanism of the Other*. And finally and above all, *Otherwise Than Being* where, among much else of importance, Levinas writes: "The intrigue of Saying that is absorbed in the Said is not exhausted in this absorption. It imprints its trace on thematization itself" (79). Or again, "the

trace of a past in the face is not the absence of a still-not-revealed, but the anarchy of what was never present, of an infinite that commands within the face of the Other and that—like an excluded third party—cannot be represented" (155).

Derrida comments on this other segment of *Otherwise Than Being*: "the trace of a withdrawal that orders it to the face" (*AEL*, 114). We will explore more deeply into the Levinasian notion of the trace in Part 4.

34. *Speech and Phenomena and Other Essays on Husserl's Theory of Signs* (henceforth *SP*).

35. From a certain point of view, Derrida's reading of Husserl follows in the footsteps of Tran-Duc-Thao. Derrida himself freely acknowledges this inspiration. My own reading here follows in this same vein.

36. Though this phrase perhaps needs no explanation, it is worth remembering that Derrida's *abyme* echoes the heraldic sense: a miniature version of an image within the larger "framing" one, thus "ruining" (*abîmer*) metaphoricity by making all images/terms identical; *mettre en abyme* is thus itself a ruined metaphor engulfed in its own intransigence.—Trans.

37. Since 1965, in a text that would become the first part of *Of Grammatology* (henceforth *Gram.*), Derrida "restores" to Levinas the notion of the trace, in order to thematize it. In *Margins of Philosophy*, this idea is thematized as being decisive in the deconstruction of ontotheology, and thus of presence. We will explore the fact that it is thus laid out in the context of a Heideggerian usage of *Spur*. Most important, the Derridean analysis of the trace is throughout simultaneously linguistic and temporal. It is designated as "trace of the trace" in an endless regression, as a radical trace to the extent that it does not revert to any full presence. In other words, the radical trace is with its "proper," its "own"; specifically, it can be thus only by in itself being without itself: "the trace is the trace of the effacing of the trace." Finally, since this is important for our inquiry, the trace can be located as such only insofar as it is the trace of an excess. See Derrida's "*Ousia* and *Grammē*: Note on a Note from *Being and Time*," in *Margins of Philosophy* (henceforth *Marg.*). The problematic of the trace becomes increasingly insistent in Derrida's work, in an increasingly explicit proximity to Levinas. See *Given Time 1:* (henceforth *GT*).

On the notion of the trace as being just as much for Levinas as for Derrida, and on the fact that the Levinasian notion of the trace informed Derrida's work very early on, see Greisch's *Herméneutique et grammatologie* (henceforth *HG*), particularly 49, 59, 82.

38. "'I am going to tell you what Derrida wants: he wants the reduction,' as Levinas would say," according to Alain David in "Je ne résiste pas aux larmes," 267–82 (henceforth PD).

39. "Then I am distanced, if one can so say, from phenomenology, unjustly, without doubt and not without remorse" (*Points . . . : Interviews, 1974–1994*).

40. Excess would thus be hubris. In a different sense, François Dastur asks this question of hubris in phenomenology, if not *of* phenomenology itself. He evokes the phenomenologist's pride in pretending to tear himself from his finitude in order to rejoin the absoluteness of constituant life—to sweep the objection away quickly; the second evokes a "hubris of the phenomenology of time that pretends . . . to bring about the appearance the very condition of all appearance." See *Donner le temps*, 65 (henceforth *DT*).

41. A reminder: "All originary donatory intuition is a source of right for consciousness; everything offered to us in intuition in an originary fashion (in its corporeal reality, so to speak) must simply be received for what it gives, but *without any longer passing beyond the limits* within which they are given (*Ideas I*, § 24; emphasis added, FDS).

42. We might distinguish, as Janicaud does, between a theological family that would include Henry as much as Levinas. Or we could describe a family of "transcendence" (Levinas, Marion). Or we could gather together the thinkers whose practice of phenomenology has been significantly informed by structuralism: Derrida, Desanti, Granel.

PART I, CHAPTER 3

1. See *LI2*. Cited by Souche-Dagues in *Le développement de l'intentionnalité dans la phénoménologie husserlienne*, 21 (henceforth *DSD*). Significantly, this principle is the central object of the work's first chapter.

2. An example: "What does infinity signify? The absolute!; the temporalization of human systems of monads; archontic systems that, as such, they enter 'the stage later on.' . . . The absolute is nothing other than absolute temporalization and always already its explication, as an absolute I find directly before me as my onward-flowing originarity, is temporalization, absolute in terms of originary being" (from Husserl's manuscript C I, 1–5, in Depraz, "La vie m'est-elle donnée?").

3. See "La philosophie tardive de Husserl dans la période de Fribourg," 184 (henceforth *EF*).

4. In the same order of ideas, it is useful to recall Husserl's consistent usage of the Kantian notion of the Idea as regulative principle.

5. See manuscript C8 I, 2 *a*: "We will here discuss a significant problem, that of the ego's finitude. This is a matter of the origin and the end of the ego's mundane life, naturally within its primordial surrounding world whose constitution is a separate affair. Birth and death are 'views' of the interior as *limes*." See Morabia, "Monadologie et trans-individuel."

6. See *Marg.*, especially "Tympan."

7. According to Karl Jaspers, the true function of the limit is "to still be immanent and already to indicate transcendence"; see Colette, *L'existentialisme*, 68 (henceforth JC).

8. *Being and Time*, § 6 (henceforth *BT*).

9. It will already be clear that what we are seeing here as the phenomenological method is similar to what Heidegger designates as the "neighborliness" between philosophy and poetry: he speaks of the *Riss* or even the *Umriss* between them; the *Riss* Derrida translates as *entame*; see *On the Way to Language*. Derrida gives a close reading of the text in "The *Retrait* of Metaphor," in *Psyche* (henceforth *Psyche*).

10. For Derrida, it is only possible to remain within philosophy—here, within the constraints of the phenomenological method; i.e., essentially on the interior of intentional constraints—but craftily, obliquely. This is a matter of showing how different texts in which one is interested engage in sleight of hand, or refuse to do so.

11. It is important, within the framework of our inquiry, to note that a deficit of presence itself constitutes a figure of excess, at least because as much as "superpresence" it produces a gap relative to a norm constructed through the adequate fulfillment of representation and even more through the consciousness's pure immanence to itself. The non-giving implied through absence does not allow intentionality to remain exactly within the comfort of giving, but rather results in disturbance if not in fracture.

12. *Sixth Cartesian Meditation*.

13. Let us specify that the notion of "construction in philosophy" originates in Schelling. It is vital that this notion emerge within the framework of German Idealism: it is a matter of *constructing* the history of *l'Esprit*, as spirit and mind (one could say absolute Spirit); it must be constructed because insofar as it is what it is, it would not know how to reduce itself to historical *facts*. See Heidegger's analysis in *Schelling's Treatise on the Essence of Human Freedom* (henceforth *ST*).

14. The expression "theological turn" appears first in Heidegger: he speaks of Schelling's *theologische Wendung*, thus declaring the gesture by which Schelling accomplishes, in his manner, metaphysics as ontotheology; that is, tending to know conceptually the being's totality, and thus to pose "the question of the ground of being, which has the name of *theos*—God" (ST, 94).

We should note that the "theological turn" in the thinkers on whom we are focusing here—Levinas, Henry, Derrida—for its part does not consist of a speculative construction pretending to speak the gesture of the Absolute (no matter how one can attempt to read Henrian philosophy), but certainly the specifics engendering suspicion of "theologization" that seem to interpolate the consideration for this problematic mode of giving, one that is faith in a connection to revelation—in seeing it, or not, according to circumstances, as a source of aporias. Opposing all systematization of the Absolute, this is the proper way in which philosophers have tested out what exceeds giving. Moreover, it is faith, more than theology in the strict sense of the term, that is at play here.

15. By thematizing the notion of "phenomenological construction," Fink was doubtless thinking of the thematization Heidegger gives it in *The Basic Problems of Phenomenology*: this course was given in 1927, and Fink edited the *Sixth Cartesian Meditation* in 1931–32. For Heidegger, the phenomenological method comprises three basic elements: reduction, construction, and destruction. In a sense, construction is the second step of the phenomenological process. The first step is constituted through reduction, which, in Heideggerian terms, redirects the being toward being. But Heidegger thematizes precisely what Husserl put to the test without ever explicitly formulating it: a certain insufficiency in the reduction; in fact, the reduction as a negative gesture characterized by being diverted from the being is not enough; it must "be carried positively toward being." There must be a "duction in the direction of being." Being is never precisely "simply in front of one" and must thus "be carried to the glance in a free projection": this is the task of construction, which is thus in a sense the decisive step in what returns to it to give access to the most originary—for Heidegger, this is Being—and to understand it as such (that is, as time itself). Obviously, in a Heideggerian context what appears here is the phenomenological difficulty according to which construction opens up the risk of speculation, since it manages the glance in advance of what is first shown. Briefly, in order to be complete, the phenomenological method must include a final stage that Heidegger calls "destruction" or "deconstruction" (*Abbau*); this last stage is implicated through the facticity of the *Dasein*, which makes it such that this third step is always already inserted into the tradition; thus, it must "deconstruct" received concepts in order to unmask the phenomenal ground they conceal as much as reveal. This gesture is not a negation of the tradition but, on the contrary, a "positive appropriation." At all events, what is important here is that even when the method is deployed according, so to speak, to a step-by-step chronology as we are doing here, more essentially "the three basic elements of the phenomenological method: reduction, construction, destruction, are intrinsically dependent on one another and must be grounded in their correlation." This correlation is decisive, since it returns inter alia to say—and this is important to our exploration—that the sole means of preventing the construction of what is transformed in a speculation absolutely freed from a desire for what is given is ceaselessly to "complete" it through the two other elements. More radically, it is necessary to practice the phenomenological method in such a way that its different moments are intimately interlaced with each other—in a sense, one within the other. See *BPP*, 41.

PART 2, INTRODUCTION

1. Certainly, the question of a genetic phenomenology is not explicitly raised in *On the Phenomenology of the Consciousness of Internal Time*. But the theme of genesis has unquestionably been present since 1905.

2. See, for example, Derrida's assertion in *The Problem of Genesis in Husserl's Philosophy* (henceforth *PG*): "the idea of an absolute foundation . . . will never leave Husserl" (16–17); see also *Ideas I*, § 1, and Fink, who, solidly supported by Husserl, defines Husserl's question as that of the origin of the world.

3. For more on this tension, see Derrida's *PG*, particularly the introduction. For an increasingly insistent affirmation of the Husserlian itinerary of refusing to accord a phenomenological pertinence to the problem of consciousness's origin, see Depraz, "Naître à soi-même," 85; there, certain parts of Husserl's late unedited works have been translated. On the accentuation of this movement that for Husserl defeats the origin's simplicity in favor of the idea that "the absolute is nothing but absolute temporalization" (manuscript C), see Dastur, "Le temps et l'autre dans Husserl et Heidegger," 385, who, among others, cites and comments on this archive.

4. On this question, see Schürmann, *Le principe d'anarchie*.

5. See DT, 65, and prior to that, Gérard Granel, *Le sens du temps et de la perception chez Husserl* (henceforth STP).

6. This is the case Dastur makes in DT paralleling the Granellian reading of *On the Phenomenology of the Consciousness of Internal Time*.

7. The aporia of idealisms is masterfully described, alongside that of materialisms, by Desanti in "Matérialisme et épistémologie."

8. It is true that Husserl saw and lived a contradiction, an aporetic tension, there, since the immortality of the ego *is*, for him, its *infinite* genesis itself.

9. We can see here the traditional structure of the circle of ignorance from Plato's *Meno*.

10. In the scholastic vocabulary revisited by Descartes, it could be said that non-givenness is a deprivation, not a simple negation.

11. In this aspect of our project we must remember the high risk to originarity implied in the manner in which the thinkers we are reading "manage" the confrontation with temporality, but it is a characteristic associated with this excessive gesture: the radical nature of confrontation with non-givenness leads it toward "describing"—insofar as it is possible—a temporality of *discontinuity* and *interruption*. See Part 4 and the general Conclusion.

12. The icon, according to Marion, like seeing for Levinas, is not a linking of representation with that of which it is the icon, and does not let it be constituted through the lived experience envisioning it. On the contrary, it only announces itself phenomenologically in disturbing the latter and gives itself to intentional

experience through going beyond its powers. On this matter, see Marion's *The Idol and Distance*.

PART 2, CHAPTER 1

1. This chapter is a revision of an article that appeared under the same title in *Alter* no. 2, 1994.

2. That Levinasian transcendence and Henrian immanence are like the recto and verso of the same intuition is a course I have developed in "'Éveil et naissance."

3. See chapter 2, "Intentionality and Sensing," part 3, "Time and Discourse," (a) "Sensuous Lived Experience." If it is true that in *Otherwise Than Being* Levinas radicalizes his analysis of Husserl's temporality, it remains true to his first, foundational intention on the subject. This is why I will refer only in passing to this text and to another older one, "Phenomenological Technique," reprinted in "New Commentaries," in *DE*.

4. This evaluation should be explored in greater detail since, regarding longitudinal intentionality, it is important to understand Husserl's effort to describe the intentional glance as it is tested out, as it sees itself, as subject, rather than seeing itself as object.

5. We will set aside here the question of knowing if it is to other texts by these same thinkers that we should turn. That *certain* texts do this is already sufficient at least to silence all global accusations of the theologization of phenomenology. This is not a question of canceling the aporia this conceals beneath the "theologization of phenomenology" but to demonstrate that it must be asked differently in order to be given its greatest force.

6. We must remember from the outset that on this point the symmetry between Levinas and Henry is not exact: they work at the limit in different ways. It is only from a viewpoint resolutely exterior to his thought that Michel Henry, holding to the absoluteness of Life on this side of intentionality, can be seen as testing the limits of intentionality. Our first heterodoxical effort at interpretation will consist of reflecting on a text by a writer—Michel Henry—for whom texts are never the essential thing, since originarily it is not texts that give us access to Life, but Life that gives us access to texts. See Part 4.

7. We should quickly distinguish them from those of Jean-Luc Marion, who is interested in Giving as *Presence*, but little or not at all in time as such. For Marion, it is as though the aporias confronted by intentionality in time were "offset" in another direction: that of God. This hypothesis, like the one classifying Henry and Levinas in the same family as those maintaining the aporia of time rather than among those who (always already) divert intentionality toward the theological, remains to be given proper support.

8. This in addition to the fact that the practice of the limit *also* implies that one is exposed to the risk of transgressing the limit, to the ability to do so. See Part 4.

9. See chapter 2 of *Material Phenomenology*.

10. Ibid.

11. Husserl thus distinguishes the transversal intentionality that "retains" the object's past duration from the "longitudinal" intentionality that is the flux emanating from absolute consciousness (through itself, so to speak).

12. Even if Husserl is forced to think here a synthesis without unifying instance and thus without a production without an agent of production.

13. See supplement 1 of *On the Phenomenology of the Consciousness of Internal Time.*

14. "Parole et religion" (henceforth PR); "Phénoménologie de la naissance," *Alter*, no. 2, 1994; *I Am the Truth* (henceforth *IAT*). We will return to this question, for example in Part 3, Chapter 3, and Part 4, Chapter 3.

15. On this last question, see Part 4.

16. It would be necessary to nuance this too-schematic characterization by recalling that at least for Bergson the long duration of being of the order of alteration is carried entirely within itself. It would also be necessary to remember that inversely, temporal alterity can only be thought "traditionally" as a relative alterity, still subordinated to being. And the Levinasian description of time must be understood in one sense as the need to radicalize and absolutize temporal alterity.

17. See 55ff.

18. This would be a question, strictly speaking, of an analogy, as a connection of proportionality.

19. See Husserl, "La technique phénoménologique."

20. On this point, see DSD, especially the first chapter.

21. In order not to slip into error in our attention to operatory concept, it is not a question of being consumed by risks that are purely internal to language or to texts, to Levinas's and Henry's texts reading Husserl's texts. My thesis is oriented by the need for a phenomenological description of phenomenological lived experience. It is necessary to say, for example, that *Urimpression* is less a concept than the shadowy fabric of lived experience itself. In a sense, it signifies phenomenology as aporia. And perhaps it is necessary to go so far as to say, in a Derridean manner, that it is not simply access to the lived that is problematic, but that all lived experience is labored impropriety. What calls to us to avoid being deceived is the possibility—which Fink leaves uninterrogated—of distinguishing (pure) operatory from (pure) thematic. We will permit ourselves, however, with certain precautions, to make use of this distinction since it is naïve to believe that we can avoid doing so.

PART 2, CHAPTER 2

1. See JTD and *GT*.

2. "Esquisse d'un concept phénoménologique du don" (henceforth ECP).

3. In fact, the pure Husserlian Ego, transcendence in immanence, *is not* constituted or constructed (see *Ideas I*, § 37).

4. I will not pretend here to work through Derrida's text as I have attempted—too quickly—to do with Desanti's, but simply to glance at it from nearby, that is, differently. It is not at all certain that *Given Time*, like Derrida's texts in general, moreover, invites a prosthetic reading exploring it step by step and end to end.

To summarize: In the text Derrida explores "Counterfeit Money," the short text by Baudelaire telling the story of the gift of a counterfeit coin to a beggar. Derrida's analysis shows that this is the status of all narrative and of all literature: giving gives nothing; it is a refusal of the very gesture of giving. In order to become aware of the process of *mettre en abyme* Derrida enacts throughout his work, we must perceive that the content of *Given Time*, what it *seems* to give, may be less valuable than its *style*, its wanderings, its long notes, the encounters it organizes between the texts that hardly seem related to it explicitly. One suspects that some readers react strongly to Derrida: "impostor!" Concealed behind the violence of this suspicion is hardly only the discomfort his misunderstood position provokes. More radically, it results from the *ambivalence* the reading of Derrida provokes: the promised analyses are almost infinitely delayed in their introduction; programmatic "openings" proliferate, often in notes, leaving the reader still hungry. In short, it is a text whose effects result almost entirely from deception. If *Given Time* addresses counterfeit money, at a deeper level it shows itself to be counterfeit money. But in reading it, one is taken by surprise in wondering whether such a text does not give more than a perfectly constructed text that produces no surprises, that always knows where it wants to go, and that thus moves as if ineluctably toward the authenticity of the fullest presence—where we would find, if not a swindle, at least a false gift.

One last comment. We cannot *render* justice here to Derrida's richness of analysis in *Given Time*, and we might even be seeing it through the bias of an issue that is not central to it but that nonetheless seems to be ceaselessly haunting: the question of the possibility of phenomenology itself. But *Given Time* is not one of those texts to which one can "return [*rend*]."

5. Respectively, Baudelaire's "Counterfeit Money" and Mauss's *The Gift*.

6. Notions associated with the spectre, distinguished this time from those of phantom, of trace, of gift as event of a temporality *out of joint*, in Hamlet's expression, are reconsidered in *Specters of Marx*.

7. We must leave to one side here the complex and rigorous proposition that Derrida, once again coming very close to Levinas, devotes to the trace as the

"place" in which discourse and temporality are mixed together, not as collected assemblage, a thematized content, but as the performativity of a mark.

8. It would be unfair to critique Michel Henry, and even Levinas, as one could Marion, for the theologization of phenomenology.

9. *Unscheinbar* must be understood in the sense of *unbemerklich*, as Dastur has suggested in a seminar presentation at the Center for Phenomenological and Hermeneutic Research, the Paris Husserl Archives, in 1992.

10. See *RG*.

11. See "Réponses à quelques questions," 69, n. 1: "no one more firmly than Derrida anticipates the central question of *Reduction and Givenness*."

12. See chapter 1 of *RG*, which focuses on *Speech and Phenomena*.

13. See the comments of François Laruelle in "L'appel et le phénomène."

14. See the final chapter of *RG*, in particular 305.

15. Since this distinction must be utilized with care inasmuch as it is naïve and naïvely metaphysical. But it is just as true as it is naïve to pretend to be able to think purely and simply outside it.

16. On the link between temporality and affection, see the research laid out in "Temporalité et affection."

17. In "Réponses à quelques questions," 67.

18. This precisely marks the fact that the givenness of the thing itself is never immediate.

19. This is the information at the end of § 4, entitled "A Misunderstanding of Signification?," 38.

20. What Marion calls a "contradiction" seems to be the unenvisagable even with regard to a philosophy worthy of the name: "Except to claim that Husserl contradicts himself from beginning to end of some lines, we must remember that . . . " (*RG*, 43).

21. We will be led to suspect Marion's text of concealing its rootedness in faith, as its nocturnal aspect that precedes the light of rational evidence, and we might even ask whether this gesture of concealment is not radicalized at the point of tending to cover the core of opacity that all authentic philosophy must assume as its beginning.

22. For Marion himself, this strategic posture does not contradict the exercise of philosophical thought. On the contrary, "one does not transcend a true thought by refuting it but by repeating it, or even by his borrowing the means for thinking with it beyond it," Marion writes (*RG*, 10). We must measure the ambiguity of respect when it prepares to treat what it respects—because it respects it!—as a means. In a sense, Marion's thought is driven from the start by the *calculation* of means and ends, even though it tirelessly attempts to approach the gift.

23. Certainly, the distinction between research and strategy cannot be made completely distinct. There is always strategy, calculation, in research, in the

incalculable; to deny it would be the worst of naïveté—the naïveté of believing in a disinterested, pure research that would oppose itself to a purely calculating strategy. The trick is not to approach research through strategy.

24. The Derridean call that, since it is not defused through a mechanical usage that makes a "trick" (we might almost dare to say a *Gestell*) out of it, is held completely within its disruptive force. One is reminded of the disrupted fields invoked by Levinas in "Wholly Otherwise," the section of *Proper Names* dedicated to Derrida.

25. Heidegger's return to the *border* of the nothing could, on the contrary, well mean that he has not ceased to be made uneasy by it: he retreats only in order to be only lightly grazed.

26. I am thinking here of Heidegger's firm opposition between philosophy as radical need for an absence of presupposition and theology as always presupposing a given, the *positum* of faith, which posits at the base of this last a positive science. On this matter, see Dastur's "Heidegger et la théologie." The Heideggerian texts on the subject are cited and commented upon.

27. Making faith and the unquestioned equivalent is not obvious. We must recall that in Christianity, for example—and this is more than an example in Marion's phenomenology—faith contains *in itself* an irreducible aspect of disquiet, of doubt. It remains, nonetheless—and this is what we have seen here— that faith consists first of all of this mode of specific adhesion that accords with revealed truth; that is, with a truth that does not give itself to reason through argumentation and rational evidence, and that even refuses and obfuscates them.

28. This is the core of Marion's argument: pure presence must be liberated from determination and thus from the limitations of figures that give them to metaphysics (including Husserl and Heidegger). It will still need to be shown that the claims regarding pure undetermined presence rise up to faith. And certainly questions of negative theology must continue to be posited regarding this kind of thought: are these figures that obliterate as much as they manifest the pure undetermined presence they designate—as negative theology says—or rather is pure undetermined presence never but a phantasmic projection that these figures operate, since they are figures themselves, irreducibly primary?

29. Marion "returns again"—voluntarily?—at least nominally, to the structuralist concept of the *case vide*, the "empty square" (see what Gilles Deleuze says regarding Lacan and Foucault in "How Do We Recognize Structuralism?"). This is significant in terms of the need for integral, and integrally immanent, rationality, that Marion displays here. We must remember, however, that structuralism, according to Deleuze, guards against the temptation to fill up the empty square.

30. And we must try to be the least naïve possible with regard to this gesture without losing sight of the fact that to pretend completely to escape it is doubtless still a figure of naïveté; perhaps the most radical one.

31. The spectre of the "nothing of nothing" is nothing other than the "nothing of nothing" as raised spectre, in the sense of that which does not permit itself to be conceptualized without remainder. On this question, see Derrida's analyses and my previous chapter, as well as the general Conclusion. Marion's text presents itself as a need for maximal conceptualization claiming possibility in the face of Derrida's impossibilities, which are often double. But does this not mean that he refuses to allow himself to be affected?

32. This is the title of the sixth and final chapter of *Reduction and Givenness*.

33. I will not focus on Marion's reading of Heidegger here. We will return to it. Let me simply indicate that we find similar comments in Levinas. But for Levinas this is a matter of strongly critiquing the idea that to depart from the end is possible and even necessary.

34. It thus becomes necessary to discern "phenomenologically" the "pure form of the call"; see *RG*, 296.

35. This is Marion's expression.

36. The reduction of our work was complete when Jean-Luc Marion published *Being Given* originally in 1997. This book is thus not fully discussed here. We might, however, refer to the problematic of the saturated phenomenon that will be raised again in *Being Given* through the reading of "The Saturated Phenomenon" in *PTT*.

37. Christ can be a saturated phenomenon only for one who *believes* in him.

38. The difference between *problema* and aporia, between, on the one hand, that which acts as an obstacle but also protects like a shield, and even "projects" like a springboard, and, on the other, the aporia as impasse and paralysis, is decisive. Marion's philosophy is a philosophy of the problem, while Derrida's is one of the aporia: this is their difference, and it is a profound one. In what follows I will attempt to show that, paradoxically, the aporia possesses, as such, a specific form of productivity, of fruitfulness.

39. This seems to agree with the very interesting hypothesis according to which the "obscure clarity" of faith—a way of understanding that consists of a black night for the light of reason—is located at the very heart of reason that, on the contrary, does not bring into question the need not to erase the abyssal difference between faith and reason that defines their very intimacy. On this subject, see Cugno, *Au coeur de la raison*.

40. "If presence demolishes the present (the gift in givenness), then it is necessary, in order to access the present, to subordinate it to presence" (ECP, 79).

41. "Gifts that give the most never give anything—no thing, no object; they disappoint waiting, but this is because what they give never appears to reality or to objectivity" (ECP, 85). This proposition perfectly summarizes Marion's strategy regarding Derrida: the first part goes along with Derrida, then is reversed by the second part, which makes it into its contrary, if not its

contradiction (the nothing is the ground of a presence that is not confined to reality and objectivity).

42. The possibility of which Marion speaks is, moreover, nothing other than presence as reserve, in a conjoining of the possible that does not make of it an actualizing power, a power that is logically and/or ontologically constrained, since it is entirely determination but, on the contrary, a pure undetermined generosity.

43. For example, see ECP, 82: "As well as the two interpretations of the expression 'the truth of the gift equivalent to the non-gift or to the non-truth of the gift' [Derrida], that the two meanings of the gift (as a given or a condition) present a frontier the crossing of which would give access to an entirely other determination of the gift than that given to contradiction by Derrida himself." It clearly seems that for Marion this is a matter of transgressing the frontier that Derrida enjoins us precisely to endure without traversing it.

44. We are attempting to show that this test of the impossible has a specific kind of fruitfulness, and that as such it characterizes Derrida's works.

45. The frontier thus understood is outside of "places": suspended among them, it escapes their system.

46. On the question of the limit and/or the frontier, on its redoubling in thought as the practice of aporia, see Derrida's *Aporias* (henceforth DA). We will analyze this text carefully in the Conclusion.

47. I say this even though our problematics of limit-practice attempts to transcend the way in which Janicaud poses the question. And we could almost reproach Marion for being taken in by the clean split Janicaud proposes in which phenomenology, falling back on positivism, is opposed to theology.

48. Since Jean-Luc Marion explains that placing the receiver of the gift within quotation marks, as "enemy"—one who denies the gift—and more radically as "ingrate"—one who does not believe in the gift—allows us to reduce the gift to the purity of givenness, as pure gratuity without in turn being removed from all economy (see ECP, 90–91).

PART 3, INTRODUCTION

1. This statement would need to be nuanced with regard to Derrida, though it might be said that from the outset the deconstruction of subjectivity never signified its simple eradication.

2. For example, Henry writes that "doubtless we can only test the world on the basis in us of this first test of self that is absolute subjectivity" (*L'univers philosophique*; henceforth *UP*). He then writes that consequently it is necessary to avoid projecting "retrospectively structures of representation on *a pure test damaged in its subjectivity* [emphasis added] and in which there is still no world and no relations that might constitute it" (*HIC*, 171).

3. E.g., the ego compelled or "assigned to self"; the ego as "traumatism," "exposition," "patience," as "pursued in the self," as "recurrence of ipseity," etc., in *OB*, 162ff.

PART 3, CHAPTER I

1. See *Conscience et humanité selon Husserl*, 16.

2. *Oneself as Another*, 27.

3. *Meditations and Other Metaphysical Writings*.

4. Deleuze, À quoi reconnaît-on le structuralisme?," 331 (henceforth GDH).

5. This reading of Husserl was developed in Part 1.

6. In *Études*, 56 (henceforth GG).

7. For a more complete treatment of this question in recent works in French, see Bernet and Benoist.

8. This formula is cited by Lapoujade in "Le flux intensif de la conscience chez W. James," 55–76 (henceforth DL).

9. Dastur, *Husserl*, 26.

10. In "Le subjectivisme de la phénoménologie," 189–216 (henceforth *QP*).

11. For example, in JTD, or in "Libre propos sur les *Leçons sur la conscience intime du temps*," 417–33 (henceforth LP).

12. See particularly the conclusion, in which a passage is devoted to "the genesis of ecological subjectivism," 300–307.

13. Rudolf Bernet also explains that as opposed to Sartre, who finds the Ego dangerous, Husserl, in the *Logical Investigations*, finds it merely "useless": he too will "use" it when he becomes interested no longer simply in the perceptive gift but in presentifications (those of others, or certainly and above all those constituted by secondary memory—and the difficulty points toward retention), that is, where non-donation is more radical than that of the simple spatiotemporal outline.

14. Desanti provides a powerful analysis akin to that being constructed here, in the wake of Patočka and then of Bernet, manifesting the same ineluctable slippage toward recognition of an Ego emerging from the very origin, from *Logical Investigation VI*, remarking about it that the difficulty posed by the fulfillment of the intentions of categorical significations—for example, a logical connector—could only arise through recourse to "I can" "as the intrinsic power marking the presence at a distance of having consciousness of a sense of the experience of an object" even though there is no longer *I*, as pure Me/Ego, in the *Logical Investigations*. See LP, 417–33.

15. More precisely, the Heideggerian self is ipseized, authentically itself, when it attests to the event of being that projects it outside of itself.

16. *The Visible and the Invisible*, 299 (henceforth *VI*).

17. Among many sources, see Levinas, *Totality and Infinity*, and Marion, *Essence of Manifestation*. Thanks to J. Colette, "Levinas et la phénoménologie husserlienne," 29, for this remark and this reference.

18. This idea of a ground, a "soil [*sol*]" with neither prestige and the ontological density of a foundation (*Grund*) nor the "generosity" associated with a source, but that has at once the contingency and the necessity of a departure point from which one can only begin and that one has not chosen is also held by both Henry and Levinas.

Thus, for example, for Michel Henry, "Kafka thus says 'Chance tells us that the ground [*sol*] you are holding on to can never be larger than the two feet covering it.' The fact that this is a matter of 'chance,' or the unbearable burden of life pressing on one, life's radical interiority, an interiority that adjusts moment by moment with itself, constructs it from inside like a test that is what it is not in exterior identity of a thing about which we might say that it selfsame—but that is what it is in that this test adjusts moment by moment to itself, sensing itself and testing itself thus" (*HIC*, 162–63).

Or, for example, for Levinas: "The subject takes it on. Its immobility, its fixity holds not as an invariable reference to some coordinates of the ideal space but to its *stance*, to the event of its position, which refers only to itself, which is the origin of fixity in general—the very beginning of the notion of beginning.

"The place, before being a geometric space, before being the concrete ambience of the Heideggerian world, is a base. It is through this that the body is the advent of consciousness. . . . It does not position itself; it is position" (*Existence and Existents*, 122; henceforth *EE*).

19. The thematic of birth, explicit in both Levinas and Henry, seems to be very enlightening with regard to signification of subjectivity in their thought. See Part 3, Chapters 2 and 3.

20. See Part 2, Chapter 2.

21. In both Henry and Levinas there is a need to think the immanence of self to Self within the concepts of immanence and transcendence phenomenologically disencumbered of all spatial connotations, and without giving up an inch of the terrain of the absoluteness of the Self's singularity, which both call "solitude." To be a self is to be *alone with* self: this is the intuition shared by Henry and Levinas. If for Henry that is so, Levinas thinks the alterity of Others as originary only insofar as he *also* thinks the Self in its solitude as existing as originary in its own fashion. These two closely connected notions, of "self" and "connection," then move to the foreground: there is only self in a "connection to self." In Marion's words, the category of relationality precedes the category of substance, which is thus freed of the traditional understanding of the notion of substance. This anteriority of relation to the Self is neither chronological nor logical: it is diachronic (Levinas); it is Ek-static, outside of time (Henry). It is necessary to signal this

originarity of the Self—that is, signified as solitude; it is also necessary to emphasize that this absolute solitude means that ipseity is such only in being in a sense originary to itself. However, it must also be emphasized that this solitude implies a gap, the "condition of possibility" of a connection, as "connection to self" and, paradoxically, "immediate connection." Finally, and still more paradoxically, this connection is in a sense a non-connection, since it consists of a rupture. The very intimacy of the Self implies a dephasing, a rupture through which it can reconnect to itself, indicating very precisely the "self riveted to itself" we have already seen, or "self cornered by itself," in both Henry and Levinas: that the self and the Self can be riveted presupposes a gap that is in some sense originary and that "gaps," distinguishing the self from the Self; but also that this connection can always be seen as a sequential scale—the metaphorical network of sequencing like that of weights or of ladings, or even of a "cul-de-sac," are largely and significantly mobilized as much by Henry as by Levinas with regard to the connection of the Self with itself—signifying the spacing out and thus the impotence of the Self with regard to itself, in turn signifying that it is *drawn back* to itself, that the originary gap it inhabits is not *initially* a space of "play" that would permit it to escape to itself but, on the contrary, the minute shift that requires it to test itself.

22. As the spectre is opposed to Life. But this is certainly not a matter of simple opposition.

23. Our travels through the question of subjectivity in Derrida, Henry, and Levinas are constrained by the problematic angle of attack we have chosen to take here, and that is in no way exhaustive, above all concerning Henry and Levinas. For a more complete presentation of this question in Levinas, see Bailhache, *Le sujet chez E. Levinas.*

Two important points we have not explored here.

1. It is hardly a question here of the fact that subjectivity is described in the register of a call, an interlocution; that is, as naissant within the performative power of the word. We will address this in Part 4.
2. I am hardly insisting here on the fact that subjectivity is initiated at an archi-originary level older than all substantiality and, even in a sense, than all identity.

Many analyses by both Henry and Levinas go in this direction. Levinas's "Unicity sans identité du Soi," Henry's "Hic absolu" explore ipseity *before* all identity of Self located in space, in the element of logic, in being (as substance or source of substantiality) or world (as horizon of what is given). Objective space, *logos*, Being, and even time when it is folded into a chronology as a "principle of individuation," are stable and homogeneous: one can thus count and compare what is being shown in them. In fact, one can count and compare (i.e., separate in the same movement by which they are connected) only what is comparable, what is of similar nature: clearly, number is only what is divided insofar as it does not change its nature. One can call "one" only what can be seen as homogeneous. The unicity of Self investigated by Levinas and Henry are situated in advance of the unity of identity that is, however, primordial in the philosophy—up to their work—of the *ontos* and the *logos*, of Being in the light of *logos*. It must be added that it certainly wants to be older than what modern philosophy is able to propose as the formulation of subjectivity: it wants to be older than all "representation of self" denounced at once as a garment that is always already too large for the absolute singularity of the test of self and as the betrayal of the immediacy of the test in the act of "holding before"; it wants finally to be older than all transcendental subjectivity in that for Kant this last is a form and, at the very least, a *power of identification*.

PART 3, CHAPTER 2

1. In Romano, "Le possible et l'événement," 84. (Unless we consider that the phenomenon of birth is "included" in the existential phenomenon of being-for-the-end—this is a hypothesis envisaged by Romano—and thus that we can only reproach Heidegger for having omitted it.)

2. See *BT*, 306ff: We have conceived death existentially as the possibility—characterized at a higher level—of the impossibility of existence.

3. This idea is further developed in "L'athéisme ou la volonté" in *TI*.

4. See "Il y a," in *II*.

5. In *God, Death, and Time*, in a course he taught at the Sorbonne in 1975–76, Levinas reproached Heidegger for a nothing that must still be "deduced from" or "in view of" being.

6. It is important here not to misunderstand the meaning of this "beyond": if it is a matter of a radical emancipation through a rapport with being, nothing would betray it more than to substitute for it, surreptitiously, the conception of "a being beyond," from which this practice of the limit "on the razor's edge" that we never cease to attempt to elucidate and that is always threatened by its own caricature. Thus, Derrida is absolutely correct when he writes regarding Levinas's thought that "it is not a thought of the limit, at least of this limit that is too-easily figurable by the word 'beyond'" in "At This Very Moment in This Work Here I Am," trans. Ruben Berezdivin and Peggy Kamuf, in *Psyche*, 143–90.

7. We begin this analysis by thrusting ourselves into the chronological linearity of Levinas's work, but it will become clear that we must reconsider this approach.

8. As Jules Rolland and Didier Franck, respectively, suggest in the preface to *On Escape*, and in "Le corps de la différence." Levinas himself seems sometimes to propose such a reading of his work, for example, in *Ethics and Infinity*. I am

certainly not denying this evolution of Levinas's thought, this displacement of emphasis that took place little by little. I will try to illuminate another movement in this thought, one that does not cancel chronology and its proper value. Levinas seems hardly to have applied this other movement to his development, though he describes it in *Otherwise Than Being* as valuable for philosophical discourse in general when understood in its authenticity.

9. The idea of combining "dialectic" with the "instant" is actually Bachelardian rather than Hegelian; see *L'intuition de l'instant* (1932) and *The Dialectic of Duration* (2000). Bachelard wants to think the instant as event, i.e., as discontinuity and rupture, *against* the radical continuity of Bergsonian duration, as multiplicity of co-penetration. From this viewpoint, Levinas is completely legitimate in suggesting a relationship with Bachelard, since subjectivity as hypostasis is written into a temporality of the event and of rupture; of rupture, at the very least, with the monotony of the *il y a* in its indetermination. But the Bachelardian instant is opposed to Bergsonian duration only in order to serve it better: the discontinuity of the event is in fact thinkable for Bachelard only insofar as it is "domesticated" by duration conceived as nothing other than its internal engine; the moment of discontinuity is "transcended" in a Hegelian sense. Clearly, Levinas's understanding of the notion of "dialectics of the instant" is in opposition to the final characteristic of Bachelard's "dialectics of the instant"; it wants to be *radical* discontinuity that is in no case recuperated through any continuity. In this sense, we might wonder if it is not the prefiguration of what Levinas will later call "diachrony": we will return to this theme.

10. See, for example, *EE*, 109–15.

11. See, for example, "De l'utilité des insomnies," in *Les imprévus de l'histoire.* See also *OGW*, especially note 24 in which Levinas allusively refers to himself, both reversing and maintaining the initial meaning he gave to insomnia and to the *il y a.*

12. This rapport of the existent with Otherwise than being, moreover, does not leave it less *solitary*, and even constitutes this originary solitude, since it consists entirely of a *delay*.

13. This is why the emergence of the existent in the *il y a* precedes the world-as-horizon in which everything given is given, or as totality of beings, beings as determined (as already having departed from the *il y a*). Consequently, this is why for Levinas subjectivity—in its very birth—is originary, and in no case the world—world from which a subjectivity irreducibly and *integrally* secondary, according to the later Merleau-Ponty, would emerge.

This originary of the birth of subjectivity in the *il y a* is such that it also precedes the opposition of the finite to the Infinite (see *OE*, 73–74). This is what will be surprising for Levinas, but that in fact absolutely follows. This is not simply a matter of saying that a hypostasis must initially be posited in order that it then be fractured by the Infinite. It is more radical: remembering that even if the trauma of Otherwise than being always envelops the self-confinement of subjectivity in the *il y a*, the latter is no less radically a *self*-confinement, out of a flawless solitude in which subjectivity binds itself to itself. It is impossible to overstate the importance of this statement: it precisely marks the distinction of this problematic of subjectivity from the theological question of the creature, at the very center of what must be understood as a strange proximity—one that is doubtless not simply negligible—of the one to the other.

PART 3, CHAPTER 3

1. A first version of this chapter, presented at the Cergy Conference on Michel Henry in 1966, was published in *Michel Henry, l'épreuve de la vie*, ed. A. David and J. Greisch (Paris: Le Cerf, 2000).

2. The notion of birth thus moves to the foreground, in particular with Henry's "Parole et religion" and "Phénoménologie de la naissance," *Alter*, no. 2, Fontenay-aux-Roses (1994), a preparatory sketch for *I Am the Truth*.

3. See "Éveil et naissance," 213–39 (henceforth Éveil).

4. This forgetting, however, has ambivalent connotations, since if memory implies a temporal gap and/or its representation, then so must forgetting, and the way in which it can manifest itself as such—that is, as what refuses itself to the world—in the world.

5. And this remainderless retreat from the world is possible, here and now, in its concrete movement, for this or that phenomenologist's work, because it has fundamentally always already taken place (which implies, moreover, its cancellation as an operation and as movement to the place of its originary): the phenomenological texts focusing on Life can do so only because Life is already their "essence," even if unperceived as such.

6. This lack of a summary of its "proper" aporias is another reason for desire to integrate all the phenomena characterizing Henry's phenomenology already mentioned.

7. In *I Am the Truth*, Henry neutralizes this objection, which was formulated in a particularly probing way in a reading of the final chapter of *Material Philosophy*, reexamining the error in what he calls "romantic thought" (*IAT*, 153). We should recall that in "Michel Henry entre phénoménologie et métaphysique," Michel Haar notes the relationship of Henry's philosophy with Romanticism, going as far as to call it our contemporary romanticism. Although it is incorrect to see Henry's thought as purely and simply philosophical romanticism—this type of gesture is always too easy—Haar's remark should not be forgotten.

It is important for Henry to separate himself from this connection, to break this strange proximity. And we might wonder whether romanticism has not taken the place of the scapegoat.

8. I will not insist here on the strong analogy between the birth of the self, according to Henry, and the birth of the Self for Levinas; this will be the object of the next chapter—the essential proximity consisting of what is decisive for both the one and the other: that the Self is "being born." There is something like a mirror system in the description of an "originary second-level" Self, but the mirror is a deforming one, in that the description of birth for Henry attempts the unexpected risk of describing an *integrally immanent* separation from immanence, while, as we have seen, the Levinasian description of birth is associated precisely with the point of "articulation" of the transcendence to immanence.

9. In its remarkable work of laying out a description of originary immanence, based at least in some sense against transcendence, Henry's phenomenology emerges as the constituter of the very heart of immanence that *must be* at the furthest distance from transcendence, yet that for the undisciplined eye absolutely resembles it. It pretends to tear away from a clear gesture, without hesitation or contamination, this strange proximity, "as if from dog to wolf." As we have seen, this reading (which will have needed to accompany this gesture absolutely) will only have accompanied it as far as possible, since it implicitly puts into question the very possibility of a clean and simple sharing between the "bad" transcendence of the departure of the self and the "good" gap of arriving to self.

10. As for Levinas, Henry sees it as is important to remark that subjectivity thus described is close to the "created" in the theological sense of the term, and whose birth very closely resembles a creation. It would be incorrect either to cover over or to reduce his proximity to an identity. In any case we should note that exactly as for Levinas (and in a more violent and radical manner) Henry insists categorically on the auto-procreation of creation. What is more, the birth of sons into Life is the opposite of creation. There again, the central motif of this differentiation is common to Levinas and Henry: the problematic of creation lacks originarity. For Levinas, it is necessary that departure from the *il y a* has taken place, thus presupposing a world. For Henry, it *gives* to the world (or, in its more radical form, it gives world).

11. In fact, what is it to read a philosophical text if not to place oneself within the indicative marks that are the requirements of thought that must be revisited as self-tests? This gesture explores from the interior the movement of another text that forces it into fidelity. At the same time, however, taking charge (in the first person) of the movement of the text given to me, I reduce it the freedom it gives me to be myself, so that I respect it absolutely just as one respects that to which one owes being a self.

12. The status of "First Living Being" seems to result from the capacity of Henrian thought to find the means as much for ipseity as for "intersubjectivity."

13. The following analysis rests on various passages of *I Am the Truth*, in particular pp. 158 and forward, such as, "In what sense and how does Christ give Life? In that no living being would be able to acquire Life if it had not been transmitted as Life having already received into itself the form of Ipseity, marked with its indelible seal. It is only a Life of this sort, a Life originarily ipseized, which is capable of rendering living beings the living beings we are—living beings who are transcendental egos capable of growing into their own skin, of growing in each instant of their being, growing into this Self they have received at the same time as Life. Only the one that has passed beneath the triumphal Arch of Archi-ipseity can come and go and find ground for grazing, to be one of those sheep who feed in the enclosure" (*IAT*, 158).

14. It is useless to insist on this since it is in fact this chapter's central problem: in order for ipseity to be ipseity, it must simultaneously be from a certain point of view originary to itself *and* that in its radical passivity it can absolutely not be its own origin.

15. This would be a matter of its caricature. A philosophy can never be reduced to its caricature; and if we cannot charge him with absolute responsibility here, we are still required to question him on the fact that it is never already forbidden in advance. We must question him on what *within* it permits the possibility of caricature as *surface*.

16. In making *identification* one of the criteria for the theologization of phenomenology—indeed of philosophy in general—I am agreeing with Jean-Michel Salanskis, who separates Heidegger's conception of Being from theology thus: "It [the Heideggerian conception of Being] contains no identification with the mysterious, infinite actor—Being—it introduces; it thus differentiates itself, I think, from what is generally called a theology. Being, in this account, is something with which I am presented in a manner necessary to thought, but that has no face, no history, no message; that wants nothing of me, at least in the first analysis" (in *Heidegger*, 66).

PART 3, CHAPTER 4

1. See Derrida, "Eating Well."

2. See "Ulysses Gramophone: Hear Say Yes in Joyce" (henceforth UG).

3. There is in fact no reason to oppose or even to rigorously separate the affirmative *yes* that is "older than all affirmation" of the Abrahamic "I am here," as is shown in the attention Derrida pays in various texts to the *yes* of God as *Unwort*, according to Rosenzweig in *The Star of Redemption*.

4. Without opening, in this note, the debate regarding the connections between the philosophical, on the one hand, and the theological (and/or the religious), on the other, I want here to indicate merely that the question is one of a "reappropriation" within the philosophical of a motif given first of all in the religious, in the disquietude of knowledge if this motif does not share irreducibly in the religious, and if the philosophical can approach him without yielding on his exigencies. In other words, the disquiet is knowing if confusion will or will not be established. And yet this urgent disquiet is doubled by its opposite, precisely that which as Derrida writes, "calls us back to the originary *yes* in the texts whose status remains essentially undecided, like all that says (the) *yes*, between the theological, the philosophical (transcendental or ontological) and the praise or the hymn" (in "Nombre de oui"). It is the test of this double constraint that must be endured when this archi-originary *yes* is in question.

5. See "At This Very Moment in This Work Here I Am," in *Psyche*. See also *The Gift of Death* (henceforth *GD*).

6. See, for example, "Structure, Sign, and Play," 278–94.

7. *Positions*, in particular the interview with Julia Kristeva entitled "Semiology and Grammatology."

8. On this *yes*, on Derrida's notions of force, of rhythm, and of tone, which for him are interconnected—notions that here appear within the theme of subjectivity—see Michel Haar's linking them with the idea of "non-grounding base" in "Le jeu de Nietzsche dans Derrida," 207–27.

9. "But at the limit, given that *yes* is co-extensive with every statement, there is a great temptation, in French but first of all in English, to double up everything with a kind of continuous *yes*, even to double up the *yes*es that are articulated by simple works of rhythm, intakes of breath in the form of pauses or murmured interjections, as sometimes happens in *Ulysses*: *yes* comes from me to me, from me to the Other in me, from the Other to me, to confirm the primary telephonic 'hello': yes, that's right, that's what I'm saying . . . yes, yes" (UG, 61).

10. See particularly *Glas* (henceforth *Glas*) and *The Post Card*.

11. One might, without being contradicted, also claim the opposite: my proper name is my proper name only on condition of not being my property, and more radically, of always having "disappropriated" myself.

12. For a closer study of this, see Rogozinski, "*Il faut la vérité*" (henceforth JR).

13. See the passage from UG cited in Note 9.

14. See *GD*: "The interiorization of the photological source [God sees into me] marks the end of the secret but the origin of the paradox, and is also the origin of the irreducible secret as interiority. No more secrecy means more secrecy " (100).

15. A methodological comment: I am here systematically utilizing the term *Self* to designate the "pre-egological ipseity" (to use another expression Derrida employs) at play. Derridean texts do not have this systematicity and this univocity: archi-originarity and the incalculable nature of what is in question here tell adequately why it is thus.

16. "The signature is always a 'yes, yes,' the synthetic performative of a promise and of a memory that conditions all engagement" (UG, 94).

17. See *GD*: "The absolute sense of invisibility resides rather in the idea of that which has no structure of visibility, for example, the voice, what is said or meant, and sound. Music is not invisible in the same way as a veiled sculpture. The voice is not invisible in the same way as skin under clothing. The nudity of a timbre or whisper doesn't have the same quality as the nudity of a man's or woman's breast; it signifies neither the same nudity nor the same modesty" (89).

18. We might thus designate Derrida as the willing partaker of Jean-Luc Marion's reading strategy, according to which the Derridean gesture of the deconstruction of presence opens onto something like a "super-presence." I have attempted to lay out this Marionian strategy and to show that Derrida's work is always opposed to it. See Part 2, Chapter 2.

19. We must completely agree with Rudolf Bernet when he writes: "The thought of 'différance' confronts the philosophy of presence not in the name of absence but of an indissoluble 'entanglement' of presence and absence, in essence and in fact, time and space, spirit and flesh, sense and sign, perception and imagination, speech and writing. The precise analysis of each of these multiple figures of 'différance' confirms that it should not be left to return to the form of a relation of dual opposition that in turn would lend itself to an operation of a 'reduction' deriving one of the terms from the other" (RB, 270).

20. One is tempted here to double the quotation marks ("'as such'") in order to signal that the "as such" lives on within its fragilization, and even that it lives on *only* thus.

21. It is very difficult to say what is at work here, since one is moving toward the originary, and even the archi-originary, and one can approach this expression only approximately and, so to speak, indefinitely, because each proposition requires deconstruction through the constraint, the bind, that doubles the one already affirmed. Therefore, if I maintain a certain "as such" of subjectivity beyond its deconstruction, this "as such" in turn requires deconstruction ad infinitum.

22. This is not this chapter's theme, but this connection no longer leaves Henrian Life unscathed, and indeed allows for the exemplary manifestation of the gap—to what point is it originary?—that always erodes and animates (see Part 3, Chapter 2). The connection might perhaps even demonstrate that despite

appearances, Henrian thought is not without its rapport with aporia (see Part 4, Chapter 3).

One could, consequently, suggest a reading hypothesis: to what extent is it possible, despite the rarity of allusions to Henry in Derrida and the total absence, to my knowledge, to Derrida in Henry, to read these two texts as forming a chiasm built around the tension, the double bind, of life and gap: two texts assuming the same tension though accenting them differently, each manifesting one pole of a tension that the other allows to act clandestinely?

23. See, for example, the passage in UG cited in Note 9. The subject is described as a *recovery* of breath, in the same way as in "'it is necessary to eat' or the calculation of the subject," it is designated as a *pause* in the rhythm. This means that the subject is "localizable" as that which breaks rhythm, rhythm itself thought of as the inverse of cadence, as what ceaselessly differs. Understood thus, the interlacing of rhythm and the pause inhabiting it is absolutely originary, since the rhythm is broken by the pause that, inasmuch as it is what breaks all stoppages such that the one is never without the other, that the one is always the secret heart of the other. We will return to this.

24. We do not know which Derridean text is principally and thematically dedicated to this semantic network, but insistence on dissemination in his remarks from the earliest texts, e.g., "difference is tonal" in "On a Newly Arisen Apocalyptic Tone in Philosophy" (henceforth Tone), to the more recent indicate that the archi-originary and the decisive are in dispute there, in what is at once the most intimate and the most foreign, in the tones and the rhythms of our voices, as what does not permit itself to be calculated or thematized, resulting in the absence of a thematic of rhythm. And if the subject can be approached only through bias and dissemination, which must be even more the case with rhythm since the subject is, for rhythm, the stabilizing interruption. We will return to this in Part 4.

25. The attention that Derrida pays to the notion of *gramophonics* in "Ulysses Gramophone" seems to signify a displacement of focus: if it is actually a matter of saying that the voice is always in some sense enregistered, inhabited by a trace or a *grammē* and never pure presence to itself, this must also be a matter of saying that it is in the same movement thus (and only thus) a living voice: this is how a notion such as that of *text* is effaced or at least not manifested.

26. " . . . (and the subject is a pause, a stance, a stabilizing stop, the thesis or rather the hypothesis *we always need*)," "'one must eat' or the calculation of the subject" (UG, 286).

27. The subject is certainly this radical transcendence that disjoins it, since that transcendence forms its heart. This is a matter, in the Derridean context, of the archi-originary *yes* that gives the voice the rhythm of the Self. It will be

necessary to return to the delicate "articulation" enabling the Self to be as much at one of these poles as at the other.

28. In the foreground of this difference between Derrida and Henry lies an affinity of two thought processes that are attached to an originary subjectivity as affection of self. It is true that Derrida speaks of "hetero-tautology" (UG, 130), while Henry, if he is made to speak in the language of Derrida, evokes a "tauto-heterology": this is a difference of accent simultaneously manifesting intimacy (doubtless misunderstood by these writers themselves, and above all by Henry, but that is immaterial here) *and* the decisive difference separating and uniting their texts.

29. Contamination has the same delicate function, within the "impossible" economy of the Self, as diachrony for Levinas: it is opposed to the latter, in that it is not the *cutting edge* of the interruption within continuity—on the contrary—but as the latter it does not bow to a simple order, be it logical, ontological, or simply chronological.

This contamination (see, for example, UG, 120) is clearest in the decisive fact that the yes is always and ineluctably repeated or redoubled in a "yes, yes": there is no pure yes that is absolutely first in its immanence; the yes is always caught in its repetition, which guarantees it to itself such that it is never outside this repetition.

In the same order of ideas, we must note that Derrida insists, in a number of texts, on the idea that it is *still* and "always a calculation that pretends to be carried beyond calculation" (as Derrida says in UG, 100). And one of the reserves that returns for Derrida regarding Levinas consists of signaling that a number of Levinas's formulations allow us to think that Levinas believes too much in the Other as such, in the "as such" of the Other, and consequently, correlatively, in the possibility of a subjectivity that is, so to speak, *purely* exposed, integrally *beyond* all calculation.

30. From this point of view, spectrality is the mode of appearance of what in other texts Derrida calls the "the quasi-transcendental"; that is, at the very least, what does not have, within Kantian transcendental difference, sovereignty over itself and, consequently, over all that appears—but that, at the very center of this fragility, remains an "it without which" nothing could be given. The archi-originary *yes* emerges from the quasi-transcendental. But in its own way the subject of the metaphysics of presence as well.

PART 4, INTRODUCTION

1. In order to lay out these implications, we must rely in a privileged way on Levinas's texts, from this exemplary point of view. But those of Derrida and Henry are also of great importance.

2. *OB*, chapter 2, 4, particularly "Speech and Subjectivity": (a) Speech in the Speech Act, and (b) Speech as Exposure to the Other.

3. Some useful reference texts: for Levinas, see *OB* chapter 5, no. 2, *b, d, e*. For Michel Henry, for whom the notion is less explicit, see, for example, PR. For Derrida, for whom the notion is increasingly an insistent—and disseminated—one, see *Monolingualism of the Other* (henceforth *MO*).

4. And this must never be forgotten if we want to account for the *nuanced* nature of Derridean thought.

5. If this is understood explicitly in Levinas's *Otherwise Than Being*, and if the problematic of the *voice* "coordinates with" *text* for Derrida (for more on this, see "Spectral Subjectivity According to Jacques Derrida," Part 3, Chapter 4), it is less obvious in the concerns of the thinker of immediacy, Michel Henry: in the following pages I will attempt to show that Henry is nonetheless not without connections to this problematic configuration, and even that he is essentially concerned with it.

6. In addition, in a coherent and rigid paradox, our attention to philosophical discourses as such, and insofar as they always occur in texts, far from distancing ourselves from testing the paradoxical givens of phenomenology for subjectivity, we must come closer to it, closer to the Word that testifies to it in the alteration of its voice—at least as close as possible. And the *textual trace* must always "be heard," as an *echo* of the Word; then inversely the Word must always be heard as being *retained* only in its *trace*, as being truly itself only in its *echo*; that is, already in a sense in its "becoming-text," out of which emerges its legitimacy and even the necessity of the philosophic text in which the Speech Act and Speech interlace, for Levinas: the philosophic text is like the ultimate echo, or at least like the most radical need for echoing this incredible test. *Diachrony*, as the radicality of an interruption reconnected beyond itself without self-contradiction, will have avoided becoming nonsense only by always maintaining itself in its *echo* or its *trace*. (For a further discussion, see *OB*, chapter 2, V, 2). "In relating the interruption of discourse, or my delight in discourse, I renew my connection with it," Levinas writes in chapter 5 of *Otherwise Than Being*.

7. This analysis has been deployed here through a framework in which *Otherwise Than Being* has been privileged, but it has also relied on *Totality and Infinity*, in particular its description of "the teaching word": the performative aspect of teaching is there described in such a way as to imply that signification is not an already-constituted prerequisite that it would then be constrained to "communicate," but rather that it emerges—that it is revealed—in the disturbance of the master in his speech acts and his *present* countenance, for which he is named. The present is certainly the time of naming, of interpellation, and interpellation is certainly the place of meaning. But it must be understood that this immediate presence of authentication and of revelation in and by the master's face

is nonetheless never *simply* a monolithic self. In fact, from the point of view of the one named, this present is traumatic: the named one is *rendered present* by having "brought help" to his words through the act of naming that, in the strictest terms, "elevates" him in his novelty since it is addressed to him from above. The present thus consists of no form of density, and above all not the continuity of Bergsonian duration: it is the "incessant *reprise* of itself" out of the originary traumatism already emanating from him.

8. One proviso: this problematic, as it is imposed on us, can only allusively raise a question whose important *requires* it to be mentioned: that of the connections between Levinas, Henry, and Derrida, on the one hand, and negative theology, on the other.

9. Éveil.

10. See "Le retour de l'exclu."

11. Rhythm is thus *tempo*, if tempo is an uncalculable rhythm, a "movement that is not defined in any absolute way." See Loraux, *Le tempo de la pensée*; and Steinmetz, *Les styles de Derrida*.

12. See *RPE*. Maldiney writes: "and just as the coherent light of the laser requires the use of impure crystals, a true rhythm is incompatible with the exact measure of its basic elements," to which he adds, "this affirmation is paradoxical, even incomprehensible, in that we persist in confusing, both near and far, rhythm with cadence" (154).

Maldiney reminds us of Benveniste's famous analysis according to which *rutmos*, despite the radical *ru* that, in Greek, means "flow," does not designate a *flux*. This autonomization of rhythm with regard to the co-penetration of its different moments does not provide for "space" or minimal articulation that would allow it to decompose—this autonomization of rhythm with regard to flux, then, does not lead to a pure explosion into discontinuity: rhythm is recognized as *form*. But it must immediately be said that this does not mean just any form, but rather that which is infused with the primordial tension of appearance that "flashes" on the edge of disappearing. Rhythm is the form that presents what is given—as appearing—and yet that threatens all continuity, since it is the event, the *eruption* of appearance. This is the tension that makes up the primordial rhythm of diastolic exploding in the very movement of systolic gathering.

Our central figures here, especially Levinas, have a tendency to accentuate the eruptive dimension (we might say the syncope) that is constitutive not only of the rhythm of their phraseology but, even more fundamentally, of the rhythm producing all phenomenality. (This remains always a question of knowing the point to which the radicality of any gesture is possible.) We might remember Jean-Luc Nancy: "the syncope *simultaneously* attaches and detaches (in Greek, for example, the suppression of a letter in a word; in music, a strong beat over silence). Of course, these two operations do not add up to anything, but neither do they cancel each other out. There remains the syncope itself, the same syncopated, that is, cut to pieces (its first meaning) and *somehow* rejoined through amputation" (*Discourse of the Syncope*, 10; henceforth *DS*).

13. If rhythm is not, for us, something we can know at a linguistic level, we think nonetheless that we can escape the reproach of "panrhythmism" if we understand by this the temptation and the risk of multiplying the various *sites* of rhythm (from the cosmic to that of the body), to the point that if *everything* is rhythm, then it is no longer anything specific. It is not a matter for us of saying that everything is rhythm but of locating the rhythm debate between Meschonic and Sauvanet, in *Rythmes et philosophie*.

14. We thus find once again, with regard to rhythm, the structuring opposition at the very core of the common preoccupation between the phenomenological "family" that might be called Merleau-Pontian (of which Garelli is a part) and the "family" being described here.

15. In complete agreement with our analysis here, it turns out that rhythm arises from the performative aspect of language. And in this context we must subscribe to Marc Richir's judgment that "rhythms are not easily detectable and demonstrable because . . . they *make* the language that is always behind language, not in its expressive power of signification (since for that, rhythm is already lost to logico-linguistic structures) but in its power, precisely, of *making sense*, as presence. There is thus no language for the rhythms of language, but there is without doubt the possibility of language itself *in eurythmy* with interperceived rhythms. An *art* of language, then—certainly not a science—an extraordinarily demanding *praxis*, that can only accompany an art of living . . . and thus a certain style" (*MP*, 109).

16. This interweaving is formulated in Levinasian terms as that between Saying and the Said; it is an interweaving who signifying of the Saying owes nothing to the constituted Said but can only resonate in it. See *OB*, 64.

PART 4, CHAPTER I

1. See Derrida's commentary, to which I owe much, on Levinas's terms, in "At This Very Moment in This Work Here I Am," in *Psyche*.

2. This good self-government through reading Levinas, I suggest, implies the short-circuiting of two ways of reading that are quite similar in their symmetrical opposition: that of discipline, this being understood as adhering without reserve to the integrated fabric of statements of a particular philosophy in the fond hope of preventing any surprises in its encounter with reality, such as a refusal or a too-radical recoiling in the face of the test imposed by the text, which thus claims to deliver it permanently from any connection with the test. Two ways of *not* reading, two denials of reading.

3. He does this only when he is to some degree forced to do so, as in an interview or a discussion. See, for example, *Les entretiens du centre Sèvres, Autrement que savoir, E. Levinas,* in particular the passage in which Jean-François Lyotard tells Levinas that he considers him a Jewish thinker, to which Levinas responds indignantly.

4. Thus the refusal to confront the fact that his discourse alternates between philosophy and religion, as has been shown.

5. In saying this, I am formulating for Levinas—taking the extreme radical position of the traditionally phenomenological!—the very objection that he makes regarding Heidegger when he recalls that Heideggerian transcendence is "deduced" from being; that being is always "presupposed" for Heidegger (see, for example, *GDT*).

6. Religious dogma that is as such always already in the sense conceptual idolatry, according to Jean-Luc Marion, if not philosophy then at least knowledge.

7. Such is the originary ambivalence through which philosophy is astonishment itself—the electrical discharge of the torpedo fish—and already knowledge, constituted Said; and that religion is the disruption of the infinite and al-ready dogma or theo*logy*, in a sense knowledge. And both the opposite of these.

8. An agreement in which its discourse, being quite radical, must venture toward its opposite, as Levinas knows and says: "It is time to denounce the abusive confusion between morality and foolishness" (*OB*, 201).

9. In a sense the Levinasian text, like the face about which he speaks, is always at "*the limit . . .* of caricature," to borrow an expression from *TI* (172).

10. The image that presents itself immediately is that of a petrified lava flow recovering—that is, masking and protecting—the magma that produced it. (This is significant: this image was used by Jacques Rolland with regard to Levinas, but also by Desanti on Granel regarding what takes place in phenomenology.)

11. I cannot take time here to go into detail; this violence perhaps first and foremost appears in Levinas's texts as syntactic twists and ruptures.

12. On this impossibility in Levinas—to be able to say to others what I *must* say, see JLC.

13. These differing modalities of connectivity to others are clearly distinguished in *Totality and Infinity*.

14. In fact, it is a return that is perpetually interrupted, that is, properly speaking, a blinking, a *clignotement*. Within this notion, as I have already indicated, is embedded the Levinasian conception of temporality as self-indicating diachrony.

15. For more on what is in play here, see the first part of this chapter.

16. "It [the disincarnation of reality through the image] springs from an ontological dimension that does not extend between us and a reality to be grasped but rather where the interaction with reality is a rhythm" ("Reality and Its Shadow,"

131; henceforth RS). On the notion of rhythm, see particularly p. 128, and to the commentary on this text in JC.

17. We can speak of "localization" of rhythm only to add quickly, in a quite phenomenological way, that Levinas does not define rhythm as a characteristic of the real in itself: "the idea of rhythm, invoked so frequently in the critique of art, while still leaving it a vague, suggestive, expansive notion, indicates the way in which the poetic order affects us rather than a law internal to this order" (RS, 128).

18. "The specific automatism of walking or dancing to the sound of music is a mode of being where nothing is unconscious, but where consciousness plays, paralyzed in its liberty, entirely absorbed in this play. To listen to music is, in this sense, to be held in dancing or walking" (RS, 129).

19. See *EE*, 109–15. The meaning of insomnia itself is "reversed" in the course of Levinas's work; see Part 3, Chapter 2.

20. Speaking rigorously, this is not a question of alterity.

21. From this point of view, rhythm is installed in the *il y a*, the "there is"; it is even in a sense its paradoxical "mode of being." (On the *il y a*, see Part 3).

22. It is almost useless to specify it, the opposition being so clear: the "negative" characterization of rhythm in Levinas, as dissolution in the *il y a*, corresponds precisely to the "positive" characterization of rhythm in Jacques Garelli, as the dephasing that at once "makes appear from" and "gathers to" primordial metastability, pre-individual and presubstantial ("proto-ontic," according to Garelli). This opposition in the status of rhythm is certainly subordinate to the passage constructed from the central opposition between Levinasian mistrust of "spectres" that do not know how to extract themselves from the anonymity of the *il y a*, on the one hand, and the Merleau-Pontian valorization of anonymous metastability hemming in the milieu of ipseized (or at least individualized) substances, on the other.

23. On the semantic network of *caricature, idol,* the *arrest* or *stopping, status,* in which art is grasped, see RS, 138–39.

The interweaving of the notions of rhythm and the *il y a*, mentioned in the previous notes, accounts for the *ambiguity* that can only astonish someone reading it for the first time, namely, art is connected by Levinas to both rhythm, on one side, and the image insofar as it is lionized (insofar as it *arrests* movement), on the other; this might seem contradictory. But what links rhythm and the image is their communality in the business of desubstantialization, of derealization; an association in which the movement of rhythm, quite paradoxically, is constructed by Levinas as, so to speak, its own result, read in the light of stasis, of suspension in the pale caricature to which it will always already have led. It is in this sense that it is incising. And what is implied is a completely specific mode of temporality that Levinas calls the *entretemps*, the *meantime*, or "the eternal duration of the interval." What is this? It is temporality suspended between life and death, knowing how neither to truly begin nor to truly finish; a shadow of temporality for a shadow of life, for what has the courage neither to be nor not to be. It is the temporality of the agony of spectres who have not known how to avoid the *il y a*. And art, like mortal skin, already a caricatural mask, stops in the shadow of the unreality of what is no longer life but still not death, achieves the paradoxical and, says Levinas, "inhuman," "monstrous" duration. To summarize the analysis of this temporality, we must say that it is not plenitude to itself of living duration as it is in Bergson, that it is still less the convenient eternity of pure presence to self of the being whose perfection does not bow to the laws of time, is not added to life through temporal ecstasies. Nor is it, or not simply, indefinite duration, sempeternality, although it approaches it in that it is a "suspended temporality." Finally, it is not destruction of time in the nothing. What is it? It is the temporality of the interval, in that it does not renounce life without having the power to bring it about—it is "aspiration to life," as Levinas says—which, considered from an inverted point of view, signifies that, entirely incapable of death, it "is" hardened in the idea of death, always paralyzed by the anguished presentiment of death as *fatum*, which prevents it from living and keeps it suspended *between* life and death.

(On the notion of *meantime*, see RS, 137).

24. I cannot fully develop here the inspiration according to—and through which—biblical prophecy plays a role in Levinas. On this theme, see Chalier, "Pour une pensée inspirée" (henceforth CC).

25. In "Jean Atlan et le tension de l'art" (henceforth JA). See also Armengaud, "Éthique et esthétique" (henceforth FA).

26. This is confirmation that, according to my initial hypothesis, we can speak of rhythm only in its strictest sense if the regularity of repetition is interrupted to the point of breaking all resemblance—or at least risking doing so.

27. This occurs in the same way as the diachrony of phenomenality's primordial rhythm, in order to be "torn" from the simultaneity and continuity of the canvas by Atlan's brush, which also—always—presupposes this space of the canvas in the gesture of disjoining.

28. On this matter, see the analysis in the first part of the previous chapter.

29. This is true for reasons into which we cannot go here and that I have described in the first part of the chapter.

30. Two remarks regarding the status of "this moderation in immoderation":

1. It cannot be completely formulated but simply indicated, since if it thematized itself clearly, it would moderate itself *too much*; it would smother the brilliance of the Infinite, of the Otherwise than being; it would erase the trace.

2. It could not exist in the search for a "just medium"—in the simplest sense, and thus not Aristotelian—between being and Otherwise than

being; that in no case would it be a matter of dulling excess down. Rather, it exists in a manner only slightly Greek, in the test of the limit, of a threshold; a test in which contrasting tensions are intensified much more than reduced.

31. I will not go further here in excavating the idea that "to think is to dance." (We could approach this idea through the importance of laughter, and to a certain extent of the dance, in Ouaknin's Talmudic practice. See *Lire aux éclats*.

One final point. My conclusion regarding Levinas's text as an invitation to dance nuances what I said at the beginning of this chapter in defining the "unassumable test." I repeat, however, that this is neither to contradict nor to diminish the preceding phase of my analysis, but to expose us to the rhythm of this text, in a commentary that itself "blinks," exposing itself to the rupture as well, but that only exposes itself *as much as possible*.

PART 4, CHAPTER 2

1. See " . . . les tautologies décisives de christianisme"; "C'est Moi la Voie, la Vérité et la Vie," (John 14:6). The identity of the four terms is: Moi = la Voie = la Vérité = la Vie," 159.

2. From this point of view—and only from this point of view—we might approach Henry's regime of philosophical writing with that of Spinoza, so long as we can put to one side the *more geometric* approach of the *Ethics*: both the one and the other are kept entirely whole in their affirmative act. As for the first type of these gestures, in order for us to exemplify it in all its radicality, we must construct the fiction of a philosophic work that would consist of a species of Hegelianism weakened, and thus reversed, in which the work of the negative would not be "raised." This would entail an impossible work that would stop on its own threshold—that, in the very radicality of its exigency would make its own failure. On this last point, see the analyses of Patrice Loraux in *Le Tempo de la pensée*.

3. Thus, to employ an easy dichotomy that is not at all obvious—we find at the level of "form" in the Henrian discourse the principal "aporias" into which he runs with his "content."

4. This is a question of proceeding such that the connection to self as self-affection does not transform itself, as inescapably, in a connection to self in which Life becomes estranged from itself, would be objectivized, and such that nonetheless the connection, the affection, as such, are described.

5. The fact that the Henrian philosophy of life is lived as the exact opposite of the apophatic is clearly marked in a text such as that one: "In other words, Being devises no word that is proper to itself; it has no name. It has no name, not because it is beyond all names but, on the contrary, because there is always a name

before it. Always before it a Word has already been spoken, which brings the appearance to which being must be, and the being with it" (PR, 132).

6. More radically still, far from being the place of aporia, the self-revelation of Life will always have lent to representation the small power of "making-see" that is its own; the Word of Life will always have been subsumed under the apophantic *logos* that nevertheless suppresses it.

7. What distinguishes revelation from representation is that revelation is always self-revelation while representation is the very medium of becoming-estranged from oneself. See, for example, "Qu'est-ce qu'une Révélation?," 51–59.

8. "This other Word differs by nature from all human words; it includes neither words [*mots*] nor significations, neither signifier nor signified; it has no referent; it does not lead a speaker to speak properly and is also not addressed to some interlocutor, to anyone, to whoever it is who might have existed before it—before it had spoken" (PR, 131). The pure appearance that is this Word is thus situated beyond (or on this side of) the word's materiality, as well as of formal, logical norms and of the logic of sense (these last controlling the connection to the referent). And the fact that this Word can be nothing but a pure "making-see" legitimizes its being named "Word" (see a more exhaustive analysis of these notions of the Word in general, and of the Word of Life in particular, in chapter 12 of *IAT*, 275–76).

It is obvious that this Word of Life is also more originary than all words constructed in the materiality of sound that are inscribed in the mundanity of an effective link between two individuals localized in space. This is, however, a matter of a Word in that if it is addressed to no one who has been born, come into the World, it nonetheless exists nowhere other than in its address to itself. Originating in itself, entirely itself in the act of being addressed to itself, it is thus Word, in the sense in which—to return to a Merleau-Pontian vocabulary toward which Henry has the greatest reticence, but that seems to be appropriate here—there is authentic word only as "speaking word." At base, this means a speaking word possessing what it specifically claims as the only authentically spoken word, in being produced as ("its") self-event.

9. See *IAT*, chapters 10 and 12, where it emerges that the heart of this ethic and this practice, in being situated this side of the objective body and the action taking place in a World, thus reveals the profound, immanent sense of the action, through *generation*, that is itself a self-revelation. Henry's understanding of the Word as pure appearance, consisting only in a self-appearance, is the truth of action and, ultimately, of all ethics and all practice. Ethics and true practice exist, for Life, in the act of being self-revealed, and the ipseity thus generated of "continuing" this self-revelation by giving evidence of it.

10. This, despite all of Henry's efforts, is not obvious, as I tried to show in Chapter 3 of the previous section. I will not return to it here since the problem of

the "articulation" of the Word of Life to the Word of Self is certainly formally homologous with that of the "articulation" of Life to the Self (or Selves) born in it.

11. Henrian thought, for its part, is certainly not it—and that "on principle"—shielded from its own caricature: seen in the double bind of having to show as simultaneous the pure immanence of Life in its immediacy and the fertile gap from which living beings result, it must implement what I am here calling a practice of excess. This practice of excess is always threatened with being redoubled in an excessive practice of excess marked by the gesture of taking refuge in the mechanical functioning of well-known figures: this is the risk, against which thought must ceaselessly be on guard, of a production of uninhabited "tautologies." For an elaboration of the "excessive practice of excess," see the previous chapter.

12. This is a little like what we find in Levinas, but in another rhythm, since there we are concerned not with an alternating flashing or blinking but with a reversal that is, so to speak, instantaneous.

13. It is also always the same fundamentally false problem, seen from different angles, that according to Henry are rooted in a misunderstanding of the mode of Life's "articulation" and of its singular constraints. On this point, and thus also that they are opposites like immanence and Ek-static transcendence, Henry and Merleau-Ponty find themselves again in their *manner of thinking*, one that consists of opposing to the problem the primordial evidence that will always have been forbidden: Merleau-Ponty says, in *The Phenomenology of Perception*, that the problem of solipsism can only be asked of one who is from the outset enclosed within the fortress of the cogito.

14. We will not take up the fundamental objection that we have had occasion to formulate in the preceding chapter with regard to the birth of subjectivity—since this is the same fundamental aporia circulating between the *content* and *form* of the text (to allow myself the facility of that dichotomy). Here I will simply signal: would there not in such a context be only an *experience* of others, if nothing resisted, if nothing is encountered? Or again, to ask the question otherwise: is there experience of *others*—do not others surge up entirely from the test, from the encounter? Is not an engagement with the economy of the traumatizing test of the face, to speak like Levinas, already to engage the economy of others? This objection could also be made to the later Husserl, who tends to "transcend" the aporia in the *Fifth Cartesian Meditation*, thanks to the Leibnizian model of monadology.

15. There is thus nothing inconsequential in saying that the Henrian work pretends to say life in its universality *and* that it is a *work*, singular as such; the work, precisely, of an *author*.

16. See in particular certain passages of *IAT* and of PR.

17. This idea is strongly inspired by Schopenhauer, whom Henry refuses to follow, however, into a legitimacy accorded to a "World as representation" in

The World as Will and Representation. For a formulation of this idea, see Henry's "Graphie de la subjectivité," 25–60 (henceforth GS).

18. For a more detailed and more elaborate analysis of this forgetting in which and through which the *I* is *I*, see *IAT,* chapter 8: "Forgetting, by humans, of their condition as Son: 'Me, I'; 'Me, Ego,'" for example: "in this way, *the forgetting by man of his condition as Son is not an argument against this but its consequence, and thus its proof.*"

19. For example: "Clearly, it is the phenomenological essence of Life that makes it the greatest Forgetting, the Immemorial to which no thought leads" (*IAT,* 290). But it is true that Henry is the first to indicate the *ambiguity* of the status of Forgetting in the essence of Life, given that the text continues thus: "Due to the Forgetting that defines its phenomenological status, life is *ambiguous* [emphasis added]." The indicating of the *ambiguity* of Life is so rare among thinkers of Life as immediacy of self-revelation, and so must be marked here. Nonetheless, this ambiguity seems, in the end, neither radical nor definitive. In fact, we cannot *not* think, within Henrian philosophy, that Life does not have immediate "self-knowledge" that saves him from being known essentially through the mediation of his Forgetting of the World: "Life is what knows itself without knowing it" (291). This self-knowledge of Life, requiring no distance, is self-revelation: when it plays out as my rediscovered knowledge of my condition as Son, as my second birth, it is called Faith.

20. Moreover, this is why the theme of Life as *Immemorial* cannot in the end, from Michel Henry's point of view, mean that Life would be in some way inseparable from its forgetting. While for Heidegger, for example, it seems that being is fundamentally contaminated by the forgetting of being, never truly sharable with it, even if we maintain its authenticity and the originarity axiomatically.

21. And yet all of Henry's effort consists of thinking simultaneously that in Life each ipseity is born in its singularity. We will not return to this here but simply remember that I pointed out a double bind, an untranscendable aporia, even if according to Henry it is thus not lived.

22. One formula repeats itself frequently in Henry's writing after *The Essence of Manifestation,* in several forms: according to this formula, inspired by Goethe and Meister Eckhart, the Eye through which I see the Absolute and the one through which the Absolute sees me are one and the same Eye—its being understood that there is, phenomenologically speaking, no Eye, no vision, no World (see PR, 141). The situation of the reader relative to the text signed by Henry allows itself integrally to describe, through this formula, who declares the situation of all ipseity associated with Life, since the first of these two situations is a redoubling and, more profoundly still, a simple variant, of the second.

23. See GS.

24. This relationship seems to be asserted in covered words by Henry when he says of von Briesen that the latter is without historical filiation, that he has "an entire consciousness of his creative solitude" (GS, 50). No doubt, the tone of von Briesen's fundamental creative existence enters into collaboration with Henry's philosophy: rejecting all historical filiation, since history is at base, from this point of view, but one of the modes of Ek-stasy, of inscription in the World, and thus of forgetting, it feels itself in atemporality, or at least the ahistoricity of Life, and in the solitude of the absolute singularity of its connection with Life, that simultaneously constitutes its solitude in the crowd of those who, in the World, forget Life. And yet at the heart of this solitude we feel, rarely, the absolutely distanceless proximity with those who have not forgotten Life, strictly speaking, "brothers" in Life, or more exactly, since we are all "brothers" in Life, brothers who do not forget, those with whom the gesture of complicity and of friendship is immediately possible. Would we not find, meditating on this sense of existence, a good characterization of Henry's relationship with "the authors of the history of philosophy" with whom he is associated (Descartes and Marx in particular)? Except that Henry lodges the same reproach against philosophers who precede him: all, at one time or another, betray Life, while the draftsman von Briesen seems to be credited by Henry with as close a proximity to Life as his own. And if it is necessary to write about him, Henry would not write *about* him (about him to make understood what Life is): if *all* the sons of Life lived outside Ek-static forgetting, with Life, then the philosophic text signed "Michel Henry" would not have been necessary.

25. Regarding Henry's thoughts on von Briesen's musical drawings, see "Musique et philosophie," 21–29.

26. In Husserlian terms von Briesen's graph is not *expression* in the sense that it is not the medium of any *signification*, and thus rises to the category of *index*, but an index that, contrary to what Husserl claims, would be radically living and would retain its expression of the radicality of immediacy in its connection to Life.

27. Henry speaks of "claw," "notch," "incision," in GS, 56.

28. This is why it is absolutely foreign to all representative structures and all calculation through which a will determines means and an end, why this gesture must be thought within the register of a force, as an intensity, a quantity of energy, etc. I should also mention, and this is decisive in the current perspective, that subjective life, at once invisible and incalculable—since the representation and calculation of the *ratio* seem interconnected—thus declares itself in the register (in part borrowed from Kandinsky) of tonality, of tone, of rhythm.

29. For Henry's interpretation of Kandinsky's work, see his *Voir l'invisible, sur Kandinsky*.

30. Henry also says, for example, that each form of a drawing by von Briesen is in fact "not even the sketch" of a form, "that it is the form of nothing and that it keeps within itself what it seemed to intend to show" (GS, 44).

31. And we should think that the parallels with von Briesen's work must be pushed to the end. The sign of Life-intuition in Henry's text is certainly not in its rigorous *composition* but rather in its "tautologies" that, as it were, flash at the horizon of the apophantic *logos* against which they stand out: this horizon is necessary to them as such, but would remain plunged in the night of inauthenticity if they had not been illuminated in their fulgurant clarity, their flashing forth, a clarity that is darkness for itself.

32. As we have shown, this is less exclusively the case for Derrida than for Levinas and Henry. And since our task here has been to prioritize the study of the marks of traumatic violence, we have privileged the works of Levinas and Henry.

CONCLUSION

1. It is in getting to the bottom of this interpretation that we have carefully distinguished this gesture from that of the apparently related thought of Jean-Luc Marion, who pretends to present the ultimate reduction giving access to pure presence.

2. Alliez, *De l'impossibilité de la phénoménologie.* Alliez concurs with the idea developed by Gérard Lebrun in his commentary on Michel Foucault according to which "the greatest teaching of phenomenology . . . would be the impossibility of phenomenology." According to Debrun, who is more nuanced than Alliez, Foucault would still be a phenomenologist in the very gesture in which he would dismiss phenomenology, being true in that to the capacity for perpetual transgression of itself through being true to the radicalism of his research into Husserlian phenomenology. But according to Lebrun, Foucault makes use of certain Husserlian gestures only in the very movement of returning them to their existentialist and thus omnitemporal illusion; Foucault is not essentialist simply because he is prepared to make use, for example, of the Husserlian notion of the a priori *historic* to determine what human beings could and must think in a given time and a given place. Thus, while he can make use of theoretical gestures linked with Husserlian gestures, Foucault interprets the Merleau-Pontian reprise of the Husserlian project as being "the destruction of phenomenology becoming irrationalism," a destruction that would thus seal "the conclusion of phenomenology's destiny as a transcendental philosophy in the Kantian tradition." In such a Foucauldian perspective, phenomenology, having proven its impossibility through self-destruction, would effectively be part of a past epoch that must be erased. See Lebrun, "Note sur la phénoménologie dans *Les mots et les choses*," 33–53.

3. This bifurcation, in which the fruitfulness of phenomenology is in play, consists of a certain manner within a certain decision according to the interpretation of the Husserlian living-present and, what is more, of Heideggerian ontological difference.

4. See Janicaud in *Chronos*, 52 (henceforth *CPI*). It is in this passage that the Desantian practice of phenomenology offers a good example of minimalist phenomenology (see also JTD).

5. It is not a matter here, in these conclusive lines, of laying out once again the differences in the manners of Henry, Levinas, and Derrida, of describing their discontinuities. However, we should remember the most significant among them:

- Levinasian diachrony signifies a pure interruption that paradoxically is itself only insofar as it resonates in its trace.
- "The chance of anachrony" (to use an expression from the final page of *Aporias*) indicates for Derrida a temporality of surprise that disjoins the continuity of the entire horizon of waiting. And it does so in a quite singular way since it is a matter of a temporality that is always a contretemps, a setback, that "gives" the event to be reported *too* early or *too* late: this coming in non-coming implies that indefinitely preparatory continuity is already changing in the echo or the trace of an encounter that will never have actually taken place.
- Michel Henry describes, under the name "transcendental Time," the pure movement of the "coming into the self" of Life. He is opposed as much to Levinas as to Derrida in claiming that this temporality is the temporality of the plenitude of presence and not temporality of the gap. But like them he describes a temporality of the event. In fact, the event can also be understood as what pierces, what makes gaps, and as what absolutely coincides with the self: and this second perspective returns to the first in that the immanence of the "now" is thus conceived as what has always destroyed the continuity of temporal linearity.
- One final, decisive difference between Henrian and Levinasian flashing forth. For Henry, the discontinuity and the alternative nature of this blinking or flashing (the term *clignotement* is not Henry's) cancels the irreversibility of time (this is particularly flagrant in Henry's description of the alternation of phases of *jouissance* and of pain in which Life gives itself to itself). For Levinas, on the other hand, as we have seen, diachrony signifies the absolute liberation of a moment of time with respect to what has preceded it: this absolute *separation* renders all reversibility impossible. An exemplary instance of this is Levinas's reading of the father/son relationship. There, "fundamentally," "transcendence of the Infinite is an *irreversible* gap relative to the present, like that of a past that can never be made present" (*OB*, 241).

6. We should remark in passing that Derrida's interpreters who make a "sophist" of him in the pejorative sense as the denigrator of truth and the admirer of seeming, are hardly reading him, since his exemplarily philosophical concern for the aporia does not signify the killing off of truth, nor even the renouncing of truth—truth thus reconsidered as the givenness of appearance, but its impossibility. What is an entirely other thing, since this impossibility of truth is thus solidarity with the impossibility of the impossibility of truth. See JR.

In the same order of ideas, the essential function of skepticism in the final pages of *Otherwise Than Being*, if it warns of a reading that would reduce Levinas to revelation and its dogmatics, certainly does not lead to a crisis of all truth but, in a more complex manner, acts within the device of diachrony, where the trace, despite everything, assures a relation with the Otherwise than being.

7. This is why these texts are works; that is, works of writers. That said, I certainly do not wish to reactivate the naïveté of an author as master of his work, but to be installed in the distinction that Roland Barthes institutes between the writing—for which the work of writing is strictly instrumental—and the writer, for whom sense is absolutely indissociable from the writing oeuvre in which it is produced, and for whom, above all, it is a matter of its very being, even in his writing work.

8. The diachronic aesthetic of reception addressed here displaces Hans Robert Jauss's claim in *Toward an Aesthetic of Reception*, at least regarding the idea "that henceforth it is impossible to understand the work in its structure and art in his history as substances, as entelechies" (268), and on the assertion that "if we define the work as resulting from the convergence of text and its reception, and thus as a dynamic structure that can only be understood in its successive historical 'concretizations,' it is not difficult to distinguish the *action* of the work, the *effect* it produces, from its *reception*" (269). The fundamental problem clearly has to do with the articulation between effect and reception.

9. See, for example, Depraz, "Phénoménologie et non-phénoménologie," 3–27.

10. It is useless to specify that such a presentation of the debate is caricatural, if the hermeneutic gesture, properly understood, far from making the text the philosopher's goal, simply notes that we are always inscribed in an "already-there" invested with a meaning, within a tradition.

It is also important to note that the texts we have read here, at least those of Derrida and, to a certain extent, those of Levinas—but certainly not those of Henry—share not so much a hermeneutic horizon as one of grammatology, to recall an opposition thematized by Jean Greisch (see *HG*). In brief, if the Gadamerian hermeneutic and Derridean grammatology share the idea that the text is not subsidiary in its access to meaning, hermeneutics aims at the Derridean sense of the text, while grammatology exhibits the text's—and writing's in general—irreducible opacity, an opacity that absolutely ruins the originary position of any meaning in favor of a constitutive delay. While it is possible to oppose grammatology and hermeneutics as much from the viewpoint of the *Stimmung* of thought as from that of method and of outcome. Following Greisch too quickly, we might oppose grammatology to hermeneutics as being the opposition of laughter to the staging of seriousness and patience, as the strategy in a dialogue, as the rupturing of mediation, as doing violence to the ecumenism of the *logos* and to illusions of neutrality.

We must agree with Greisch, however, on the fact that the Derridean method of "deconstruction" is never uniquely a transgression, a eulogy without reserve for excess; and that it is certainly not the crossing of a frontier and an installation beyond it. It is always also, as we have seen, prudence and calculation. From this viewpoint, the Levinasian valorization of the anarchic is all the more on the side of excess. Moreover, the *usage* of excess is not, for essential reasons, made explicit by Levinas (this would already be to betray the *test* of excess). And yet if it is true, as we have tried to show here, the Levinasian text can no longer consist entirely of the economy of the controlling of excess that succeeds the tour de force of control by exposing itself. Taking this governance of the text in charge redounds in the end to the reader, as the writer after the writer.

These remarks also provide the opportunity to provide nuances for Greisch's presentation of grammatology, or of deconstruction—the label is unimportant—in light of the Derridean texts that appeared subsequent to *Herméneutique et grammatologie*. We must acknowledge the generosity required by this "method" that, as the integral exposition of what is to come, is never reduced to the strategy of a calculation, and whose very immoderation thus has more in common with the overabundance of gift of the self than with "the deregulation of all meaning" of a cruel celebration. That said, this generosity is still more disquieting, in its very immoderation, than that—mastered and respectful—of the hermeneutist. In conclusion, we should insist on the performative dimension in which an *I*, born of the exposure resultant from this "method," and that finally takes him far away from strategies of interpretation of meaning. This dimension, as we have addressed it here, doubtless provides an increasingly decisive connection by Derrida in the direction of Levinas (i.e., in the direction of the problematics of address in Levinas).

11. "It is upon losing what we have to say that we speak—upon an immanent and immemorial disaster—just as we say nothing except insofar as we can convey in advance that we take it back," Blanchot writes; "where power does not reign—nor initiative, nor the cutting edge of a decision—there, dying is living. There dying is the passivity of life—of life escaped from itself and confounded with *the disaster of a time without present* [emphasis added], which we endure by waiting, by awaiting a misfortune that is not still to come but that has always

already come upon us and that cannot be present" (*The Writing of the Disaster,* 21). The "unhappy" tone of Blanchotian fragments, when juxtaposed with certain aspects of Derrida's—and especially Levinas's—work, is completely foreign to Henry's work and does not seem essential, in any case, to the idea of "disaster": there is such a thing as joyful disaster. We must also specify that the disaster takes, for Blanchot, all subjectivity for the benefit of anonymity, while in the texts read here, it tests out authentic subjectivity. This is also the place of a decisive difference between Levinas and Blanchot in terms of an explicit and required intimate proximity.

12. Except for Michel Henry, for whom transcendental naïveté is even, as it were, required. But as we have tried to show, this Henrian transcendental naïveté is always secretly operated by an uneasiness.

13. At play here is the intimate connection manifested by Derrida between the "(not) step [*pas*]" as rhythm (as when one says "y aller d'un bon pas [to take the initiative, to take the right step]") and as threshold ("le pas de la porte [the doorstep]."

Bibliography

Alliez, Eric. 1995. *De l'impossibilité de la phénoménologie. Sur la philosophie française contemporaine.* Paris: Vrin.

Armengaud, François. 1991. "Ethique et esthétique: De l'ombre à l'oblitération." In *Cahier de l'Herne Emmanuel Levinas,* 499–507. Paris: Herne.

Bachelard, Gaston. 1932. *L'intuition de l'instant.* Paris: Gonthier.

———. 2000. *The Dialectic of Duration.* Trans. Mary McAllester Jones. London: Clinamen Press.

Badiou, Alain. 2001 [1998]. *Ethics. An Essay on the Understanding of Evil.* Trans. Peter Hallward. London: Verso.

Bailhache, Gérard. 1994. *Le sujet chez E. Levinas: Fragilité et subjectivité.* Paris: PUF.

Barbaras, Renaud. 1994. *La perception.* Paris: Hatier.

Benoist, Jocelyn. 1994. *Autour de Husserl.* Paris: Vrin.

Bergson, Henri. 2007. *The Creative Mind.* Trans. Mabelle Andison. New York: The Philosophical Library.

Bernet, Rudolf. 1994. *La vie du sujet.* Paris: PUF.

Blanchot, Maurice. 1995 [1980]. *The Writing of the Disaster.* Trans. Ann Smock. Lincoln: University of Nebraska Press.

Certeau, Michel de. 1987. *L'écriture de l'histoire.* Paris: Gallimard.

Chalier, Catherine. 1991. "Pour une pensée inspirée." *Epokhè,* no. 2, 281–307.

Chrétien, Jean-Luc. 1991. "La dette et l'élection." In *Cahier de l'Herne Emmanuel Levinas,* 262–74. Paris: Herne.

Colette, Jacques. 1984. "Levinas et la phénoménologie husserlienne." In *Les cahiers de la nuit surveillée.* Lagrasse: Verdier.

———. 1987. "Musique et philosophie." *Philosophie* 4, no. 15, 21–29.

———. 1993. *L'existentialisme.* Paris: PUF.

Colléony, Jacques. 1991. "Levinas et l'art: La réalité et son ombre." *La part de l'oeil,* no. 7, 81–90.

Cugno, Alain. 1999. *Au coeur de la raison. Raison et foi.* Paris: Le Seuil.

Dastur, Françoise. 1991. "Husserl et la neutralité de l'art." *La part de l'oeil,* no. 7.

———. 1993. "Le temps et l'autre dans Husserl et Heidegger." *Alter*, no. 1.

———. 1994. "Heidegger et la théologie." *Revue de la philosophie de Louvain*, 92.

———. 1995. *Husserl: Des mathématiques à l'histoire*. Paris: PUF.

David, Alain. 1992. "Je ne résiste pas aux larmes." In *L'éthique du don*. Paris: A. M. Métailié.

Deleuze, Gilles. 2000. À quoi reconnaît-on le structuralisme?" In *Histoire de la philosophie*, ed. François Châtelet, 331. Paris: Hachette.

———. 2003 [1972]. "How Do We Recognize Structuralism?" Trans. Mike Taormina. In *Desert Islands*, 299–335. New York: Semiotext(e).

Depraz, Natalie. 1991. "La vie m'est-elle donnée?" *Etudes philosophiques*, no. 4.

———. 1993. "Naître à soi-même." In *Alter*, no. 1, n.p.

———. 1995. "Phénoménologie et non-phénoménologie." *Recherches husserliennes* 4, 3–27.

Derrida, Jacques. 1973 [1967]. *Speech and Phenomena and Other Essays on Husserl's Theory of Signs*. Trans. David B. Allison. Evanston, IL: Northwestern University Press.

———. 1978 [1967]. "Structure, Sign, and Play in the Discourse of the Human Sciences." In *Writing and Difference*, trans. Alan Bass, 278–94. Chicago: University of Chicago Press.

———. 1981. *Positions*. Trans. Alan Bass. Chicago: University of Chicago Press.

———. 1981 [1978]. *Spurs, Nietzsche's Styles*. Chicago: University of Chicago Press.

———. 1982 [1972]. *Margins of Philosophy*. Trans. Alan Bass. Chicago: University of Chicago Press.

———. 1987 [1980]. *The Post Card*. Trans. Alan Bass. Chicago: University of Chicago Press.

———. 1990. *The Problem of Genesis in Husserl's Philosophy*. Trans. Marion Hobson. Chicago: University of Chicago Press.

———. 1988. "Ulysses Gramophone: Hear Say Yes in Joyce." Trans. Shari Benstock. In *The Augmented Ninth*, ed. Bernard Benstock. Syracuse, NY: Syracuse University Press.

———. 1989 [1962]. *Edmund Husserl's Origin of Geometry: An Introduction*. Trans. John P. Leavey Jr. Lincoln, NE: Bison Books.

———. 1990 [1987]. *Glas*. Trans. John P. Leavey. Lincoln: University of Nebraska Press.

———. 1992. *"Donner la mort."* In *L'éthique du don*. Paris: A. M. Métailié.

———. 1992. "Eating Well." Trans. Peggy Kamuf. In *Points . . . : Interviews, 1974–1994*. Stanford, CA: Stanford University Press.

———. 1992. "L'ethique du don." In *Jacques Derrida et la pensée du don*, ed. Michael Wetzel and Jean-Michel Rabaté. Paris: Diffusion Seuil.

———. 1992 [1991]. *Given Time 1: Counterfeit Money.* Trans. David Wills. Chicago: University of Chicago Press.

———. 1993. *Aporias.* Trans. Thomas Dutoit. Stanford, CA: Stanford University Press.

———. 1995. *Points . . . : Interviews, 1974–1994.* Trans. Peggy Kamuf. Stanford, CA: Stanford University Press.

———. 1995 [1992]. *The Gift of Death.* Trans. David Wills. Chicago: University of Chicago Press.

———. 1997 [1967]. *Of Grammatology.* Trans. Gayatri Chakravorty Spivak. Baltimore, MD: Johns Hopkins University Press.

———. 1998 [1983]. "On a Newly Arisen Apocalyptic Tone in Philosophy." Trans. John Leavey. In *Raising the Tone of Philosophy,* ed. Peter Fenves, 117–72. Baltimore, MD: Johns Hopkins University Press.

———. 1998 [1996]. *Monolingualism of the Other: or, The Prosthesis of Origin.* Trans. Patrick Mensah. Stanford, CA: Stanford University Press.

———. 1999 [1997]. *Adieu to Emmanuel Levinas.* Stanford, CA: Stanford University Press.

———. 2004 [1990]. "Punctuations: The Time of the Thesis." In *Eyes of the University: Right to Philosophy,* trans. Jan Plug. Stanford, CA: Stanford University Press.

———. 2007 [1998]. *Psyche: Inventions of the Other, Volume 1.* Ed. Peggy Kamuf and Elizabeth Rottenberg. Stanford, CA: Stanford University Press.

Desanti, Jean-Toussaint. 1968. *Le sens du temps et de la perception chez Husserl.* Paris: Gallimard.

———. 1975. "Matérialisme et épistémologie." In *La philosophie silencieuse.* Paris: Le Seuil.

———. 1993. "Libre propos sur les *Leçons sur la conscience intime du temps*: Du temps qui s'écoule au temps qui s'écroule." *Alter,* no. 2, 417–33.

Descartes, René. 1999 [1649]. *Meditations and Other Metaphysical Writings.* Trans. Desmond M. Clarke. London: Penguin Classics.

Dreyfus, Henri-Louis, ed. 1982. *Husserl, Intentionality and Cognitive Science.* Cambridge, MA: MIT Press.

Les entretiens du centre Sèvres. 1988. *Autrement que savoir, E. Levinas.* Paris: Osiris.

Fink, Eugen. 1994. "La philosophie tardive de Husserl dans la période de Fribourg." In *Proximité et distance.* Grenoble: Millon.

Franck, D. 1992. "Le corps de la différence." *Philosophie* 19, no. 34, 70-96.

Garelli, Jacques. 1991. *Rythmes et mondes. Au revers de l'identité et de l'altérité.* Paris: Millon.

Granel, Gérard. 1968. *Le sens du temps et de la perception chez Husserl*. Paris: Gallimard.

———. 1972. *Traditionis traditio*. Paris: Gallimard.

———. 1990. *Écrits et politiques*. Paris: Gallimard.

———. 1995. *Études*. Paris: Galilée.

Greisch, Jean. 1977. *Herméneutique et grammatologie*. Paris: CNRS.

Haar, Michel. 1987. "Michel Henry entre phénoménologie et métaphysique." *Philosophie* 15, 21–29.

———. 1990. "Le jeu de Nietzsche dans Derrida." In *Revue philosophique de la France et de l'étranger*, 207–27. Paris: PUF.

Hegel, Georg Wilhelm Friedrich. 1971. "The Spirit of Christianity and Its Fate." Trans. T. M. Knox. In *Early Theological Writings*. Philadelphia, PA: Penn Press.

Heidegger, Martin. 1982. *The Basic Problems of Phenomenology*. Trans. Albert Hofstadter. Bloomington: University of Indiana Press.

———. 1982. *On the Way to Language*. San Francisco: Harpers.

———. 1985. *Schelling's Treatise on the Essence of Human Freedom*. Trans. Joan Stambaugh. Columbus: Ohio University Press.

———. 1996. *Being and Time*. Trans. Joan Stambaugh. Albany: SUNY Press.

Henry, Michel. 1973 [1963]. *The Essence of Manifestation*. Trans. Girard Etzkorn. Paris: Broché.

———. 1986. "Graphie de la subjectivité." In *Réflexions philosophiques sur l'oeuvre d'August v. Briesen*, ed. François Laruelle, 25–60. Paris: Fondation Brandenburg-Neumark.

———. 1990. *L'univers philosophique*. Paris: PUF.

———. 1992. "Parole et religion: La Parole de Dieu." In *Phénoménologie et théologie*. Paris: Criterion.

———. 1992. *Phénoménologie et théologie*. Paris: Criterion.

———. 1994. "Qu'est-ce qu'une révélation?" In *Filosophia della rivelazione*, ed. Marco M. Olivetti, 51–59. Padua: CEDAM.

———. 1995. "Phénoménologie non intentionnelle: Une tâche de la phénoménologie à venir." In *Intentionalité en question, entre phénoménologie et recherches cognitives*, ed. Dominique Janicaud. Paris: Vrin.

———. 1996. 'C'est Moi la Voie, la Vérité et la Vie' (John 14:6). The Identity of the Four Terms Is: Moi = la Voie = la Vérité = la Vie." In *C'est Moi la Vérité. Pour une philosophie du christianisme*, 159. Paris: Seuil.

———. 2002 [1998]. *I Am the Truth: Toward a Philosophy of Christianity (Cultural Memory in the Present)*. Trans. Susan Emanuel. Stanford, CA: Stanford University Press.

———. 2005 [1988]. *Voir l'invisible, sur Kandinsky.* Paris: Bourin-Julliard, collection "Quadridge."

———. 2008. *Material Phenomenology.* Trans. Scott Davidson. New York: Fordham University Press.

Husserl, Edmund. 1958. *Ideas I.* Trans. W. R. Boyce Gibson. New York: Macmillan.

———. 1959. "Phenomenological Technique." In *Cahier de Royaumont.* Paris: Minuit.

———. 1960 [1929]. *Cartesian Meditations.* Trans. Dorion Cairns. The Hague: M. Nijhof.

———. 1965 [1910]. *Phenomenology and the Crisis of Philosophy: Philosophy as a Rigorous Science, and Philosophy and the Crisis of European Man.* Trans. Quentin Lauer. New York: Harper and Row.

———. 1965 [1910]. "Philosophy as Rigorous Science." In *Phenomenology and the Crisis of Philosophy.*

———. 1970 [1954]. *The Crisis of European Sciences and Transcendental Phenomenology: An Introduction.* Trans. David Carr. Evanston, IL: Northwestern University Press.

———. 1982 [1913]. *Ideas Pertaining to a Pure Phenomenology and to a Phenomenological Philosophy—First Book: General Introduction to a Pure Phenomenology.* Trans. F. Kersten. The Hague: Nijhoff.

———. 1990 [1928]. *On the Phenomenology of the Consciousness of Internal Time (1893–1917).* Trans. J. B. Brough. Dordrecht, Netherlands: Kluwer.

———. 1990. *Philosophie première.* Vol. 1. Trans. A. L. Kelkel. Paris: PUF.

———. 2001 [1921]. *Logical Investigations 1.* Trans. J. N. Finlay. New York: Routledge.

———. 2001 [1921]. *Logical Investigations 2.* Trans. J. N. Finlay. New York: Routledge.

———. 2003 [1891]. *Philosophy of Arithmetic.* Trans. Dallas Willard. Dordrecht, Netherlands: Kluwer.

———. 2010 [1907]. *The Idea of Philosophy.* Trans. L. Hardy. London: Springer.

Janicaud, Dominique, ed. 1995. *Intentionalité en question, entre phénoménologie et recherches cognitives.* Paris: Vrin.

———. 1995. *Sixth Cartesian Meditation: The Idea of a Transcendental Theory of Method.* Trans. Ronald Bruzina. Bloomington: Indiana University Press.

———. 1997. *Chronos. Pour l'intelligence du partage temporel.* Paris: Grasset.

———. 2001. *Phenomenology and the "Theological Turn": The French Debate.* New York: Fordham University Press.

Jauss, Hans Robert. 1982 [1977]. *Toward an Aesthetic of Reception.* Trans. Timothy Bahti. Introduction by Paul de Man. Minneapolis: University of Minnesota Press.

Lapoujade, David. 1995. "Le flux intensif de la conscience chez W. James." *Philosophie*, no. 46, 55–76.

Laruelle, François. 1991. "L'appel et le phénomène." In *Revue de métaphysique et de morale*, no. 1, 27–41.

Lebrun, Gérard. 1989. "Note sur la phénoménologie dans *Les mots et les choses*." In *Michel Foucault philosophe*, 33–53. Paris: Le Seuil.

Lenger, Hans Joachim. 1995. *La différence comme non-différence, éthique et altérité chez E. Levinas*. Paris: Kimé.

Levinas, Emmanuel. 1969 [1961]. *Totality and Infinity: An Essay on Exteriority*. Pittsburgh, PA: Duquesne University Press.

———. 1985. *Ethics and Infinity*. Trans. Richard A. Cohen. Pittsburgh, PA: Duquesne University Press.

———. 1991. *Entre nous: Essais sur le penser-à-l'autre*. Paris: Grasset.

———. 1991. "Jean Atlan et la tension de l'art." In *Cahiers de l'Herne Emmanuel Levinas*, 509–10. Paris: l'Herne.

———. 1994. *Les imprévus de l'histoire*. Paris: Fata Morgana.

———. 1994. *L'intrigue de l'infini*. Paris: Flammarion.

———. 1998 [1967]. *Discovering Existence with Husserl*. Trans. Richard A. Cohen and Michael B. Smith. Evanston, IL: Northwestern University Press.

———. 1998 [1986]. *Of God Who Comes to Mind*. Trans. Bettina Bergo. Stanford, CA: Stanford University Press.

———. 1998. *Otherwise Than Being: or, Beyond Essence*. Trans. Alphonso Lingis. Pittsburgh, PA: Duquesne University Press.

———. 2000 [1993]. *Entre nous: Essays on Thinking-of-the-Other*. London: Athlone Press.

———. 2000 [1993]. *God, Death, and Time*. Trans. Bettina Bergo. Stanford, CA: Stanford University Press.

———. 2000 [1948]. "Reality and Its Shadow." Trans. Alphonso Lingis. In *The Continental Aesthetics Reader*, ed. C. Cazeaux. New York: Routledge.

———. 2001 [1947]. *Existence and Existents*. Trans. Alphonso Lingis. Pittsburgh, PA: Duquesne University Press.

———. 2003 [1998]. *On Escape: De l'évasion*. Trans. Bettina Bergo. Stanford, CA: Stanford University Press.

———. 2003. "The Trace." In *Humanism of the Other*. Urbana: University of Illinois Press.

Loraux, Nicole. 1992. "Le retour de l'exclu." In *Le passage des frontières*, ed. Marie-Louise Mallet. Paris: Galilée.

Loraux, Patrice. 1993. *Le tempo de la pensée*. Paris: Le Seuil.

Maldiney, Henri. 1994. *Regard parole espace*. Lausanne: L'age d'homme.

Marion, Jean-Luc. 1973. *The Essence of Manifestation*. Trans. J. G. Etzkorn. London: Springer.

——. 1991. "Réponses à quelques questions." *Revue de métaphysique et de morale*, no. 1, 70.

——. 1994. "Esquisse d'un concept phénoménologique du don." In *Filosofia della rivelazione*, ed. M.-M. Olivetti. Padua: CEDAM.

——. 1994. "Temporalité et affection." *Alter*, no. 2, Fontenay-aux-Roses, n.p.

——. 1995 [1982]. *God Without Being*. Trans. Thomas A. Carlson. Chicago: University of Chicago Press.

——. 1998 [1989]. *Reduction and Givenness: Investigations of Husserl, Heidegger, and Phenomenology*. Evanston, IL: Northwestern University Press.

——. 1999 [1986]. *On Descartes' Metaphysical Prism*. Trans. Jeffrey L. Kosky. Chicago: University of Chicago Press.

——. 2000 [1992]. "The Saturated Phenomenon." Trans. Thomas A. Carlson. In *Phenomenology and the "Theological Turn": The French Debate*. New York: Fordham University Press.

——. 2001. *The Idol and Distance*. New York: Fordham University Press.

——. 2002 [1997]. *Being Given: Toward a Phenomenology of Givenness*. Trans. Jeffrey Kosky. Stanford, CA: Stanford University Press.

Marion, Jean-Luc, and G. Planty-Bonjour. 1984. *Phénoménologie et métaphysique*. Paris: PUF.

Marty, François. 1991. "La hauteur et le sublime." In *Cahiers de l'Herne Emmanuel Levinas*. Paris: l'Herne.

Mauss, Marcel. 2000 [1954]. *The Gift*. Trans. W. D. Halls. New York: W. W. Norton.

Merleau-Ponty, Maurice. 1968 [1964]. *The Visible and the Invisible*. Trans. Alphonso Lingis. Evanston, IL: Northwestern University Press.

——. 2002. *The Phenomenology of Perception*. New York: Routledge.

Meschonnic, Henri. 1998. "Henri, l'enjeu du rythme pour la philosophie." In *Rythmes et philosophie*, by Pierre Sauvanet. Paris: Kimé.

Montavont, Anne. 1992. "Le phénomène de l'affection dans les *Analysen zur passiven synthesis*." *Alter*, no. 2, Fontenay-aux-Roses, 119–39.

——. 1999. *De la passivité dans la phénoménologie de Husserl*. Paris: PUF.

Morabia, Ariel. 1994. "Monadologie et trans-individuel," *Alter* no. 2, n.p.

Nancy, Jean-Luc. 2008 [1976]. *The Discourse of the Syncope*. Trans. Saul Anton. Stanford, CA: Stanford University Press.

Ouaknin, Marc-Alain. 1992. *Lire aux éclats. Eloge de la caresse*. Paris: Quai Voltaire.

Patočka, Jan. 1988 [1977]. "Le subjectivisme de la phénoménologie husserlienne et la possibilité d'une phénoménologie 'asubjective.'" In *Qu'est-ce que la phénoménologie?*, trans. E. Abrams, 189–216. Grenoble: Millon.

Poirié, François. 1987. *Emmanuel Levinas (Qui êtes-vous?)*. Lyon: La Manufacture.

Richir, Marc. 1991. "Phénomène et infini." In *Cahiers de l'Herne Emmanuel Levinas*. Paris: l'Herne.

———. 1992. *Les méditations phénoménologiques*. Paris: Millon.

Ricoeur, Paul. 1995 [1986]. *Oneself as Another*. Trans. Kathleen Blamey. Chicago: University of Chicago Press.

Rogozinski, Jacob. 1999. *"Il faut la vérité*: Notes sur la vérité de Derrida." *Rue Descartes*, no. 24 (June), n.p.

Romano, Claude. 1993. "Le possible et l'événement." *Philosophie*, no. 40 (December), 68–95.

Rosenzweig, Franz. 1985 [1921]. *The Star of Redemption*. Trans. Barbara E. Galli. Madison: University of Wisconsin Press.

Salanskis, Jean-Michel. 1997. *Heidegger*. Paris: Les Belles Lettres.

Sartre, Jean-Paul. 1962 [1936–37]. *Transcendence of the Ego*. Trans. Forrest Williams and Robert Kirkpatrick. New York: Noonday Press.

——. 2001. *Being and Nothingness: An Essay in Phenomenological Ontology*. Trans. Hazel Barnes. London: Citadel.

Sauvanet, Pierre. 1998. *Rythmes et philosophie*. Paris: Kimé.

Schürmann, Reiner. 1982. *Le principe d'anarchie*. Paris: Le Seuil.

Sebbah, François-David. 1993. "Éveil et naissance. Quelques remarques à propos de M. Henry et E. Levinas." *Alter* no. 1, Fontenay-aux-Roses, 213–39.

——. 1997. "Intentionnalité et non-donation." In *Analecta Husserliana*, 50:101–13. Dordrecht, Netherlands: Kluwer Academic Publishers.

——. 2000. "Naître à la vie, naître à soi-même. La naissance de la subjectivité chez M. Henry." In *Michel Henry, m'épreuve de la vie*, ed. A. David and J. Greisch. Paris: Le Cerf.

Souche-Dagues, Denise. 1972. *Le développement de l'intentionnalité dans la phénoménologie husserlienne*, Paris: Vrin.

Steinmetz, Rudy. 1994. *Les styles de Derrida*. Brussels: De Boeck/Wesmael.

Taminiaux, Jacques. 1977. *Le regard et l'excédent*. The Hague: Nijhoff.

Thierry, Yves. 1995. *Conscience et humanité selon Husserl*. Paris: PUF.

Tran-Duc-Thao. 1985. *Phenomenology and Dialectical Materialism*. Boston: Springer.

Wittgenstein, Ludwig. 1961. *Recherches philosophiques*. Trans. Pierre Klossowski. Paris: Gallimard.

Cultural Memory | in the Present

Erik Peterson, *Theological Tractates*, edited by Michael J. Hollerich

Feisal G. Mohamed, *Milton and the Post-Secular Present: Ethics, Politics, Terrorism*

Pierre Hadot, *The Present Alone Is Our Happiness, Second Edition: Conversations with Jeannie Carlier and Arnold I. Davidson*

Yasco Horsman, *Theaters of Justice: Judging, Staging, and Working Through in Arendt, Brecht, and Delbo*

Jacques Derrida, *Parages*, edited by John P. Leavey

Henri Atlan, *The Sparks of Randomness, Volume 1: Spermatic Knowledge*

Rebecca Comay, *Mourning Sickness: Hegel and the French Revolution*

Djelal Kadir, *Memos from the Besieged City: Lifelines for Cultural Sustainability*

Stanley Cavell, *Little Did I Know: Excerpts from Memory*

Jeffrey Mehlman, *Adventures in the French Trade: Fragments Toward a Life*

Jacob Rogozinski, *The Ego and the Flesh: An Introduction to Egoanalysis*

Marcel Hénaff, *The Price of Truth: Gift, Money, and Philosophy*

Paul Patton, *Deleuzian Concepts: Philosophy, Colonialization, Politics*

Michael Fagenblat, *A Covenant of Creatures: Levinas's Philosophy of Judaism*

Stefanos Geroulanos, *An Atheism that Is Not Humanist Emerges in French Thought*

Andrew Herscher, *Violence Taking Place: The Architecture of the Kosovo Conflict*

Hans-Jörg Rheinberger, *On Historicizing Epistemology: An Essay*

Jacob Taubes, *From Cult to Culture*, edited by Charlotte Fonrobert and Amir Engel

Peter Hitchcock, *The Long Space: Transnationalism and Postcolonial Form*

Lambert Wiesing, *Artificial Presence: Philosophical Studies in Image Theory*

Jacob Taubes, *Occidental Eschatology*

Freddie Rokem, *Philosophers and Thespians: Thinking Performance*

Roberto Esposito, *Communitas: The Origin and Destiny of Community*

Vilashini Cooppan, *Worlds Within: National Narratives and Global Connections in Postcolonial Writing*

Josef Früchtl, *The Impertinent Self: A Heroic History of Modernity*

Frank Ankersmit, Ewa Domanska, and Hans Kellner, eds., *Re-Figuring Hayden White*

Michael Rothberg, *Multidirectional Memory: Remembering the Holocaust in the Age of Decolonization*

Jean-François Lyotard, *Enthusiasm: The Kantian Critique of History*

Ernst van Alphen, Mieke Bal, and Carel Smith, eds., *The Rhetoric of Sincerity*

Stéphane Mosès, *The Angel of History: Rosenzweig, Benjamin, Scholem*

Pierre Hadot, *The Present Alone Is Our Happiness: Conversations with Jeannie Carlier and Arnold I. Davidson*

Alexandre Lefebvre, *The Image of the Law: Deleuze, Bergson, Spinoza*

Samira Haj, *Reconfiguring Islamic Tradition: Reform, Rationality, and Modernity*

Diane Perpich, *The Ethics of Emmanuel Levinas*

Marcel Detienne, *Comparing the Incomparable*

François Delaporte, *Anatomy of the Passions*

René Girard, *Mimesis and Theory: Essays on Literature and Criticism, 1959-2005*

Richard Baxstrom, *Houses in Motion: The Experience of Place and the Problem of Belief in Urban Malaysia*

Jennifer L. Culbert, *Dead Certainty: The Death Penalty and the Problem of Judgment*

Samantha Frost, *Lessons from a Materialist Thinker: Hobbesian Reflections on Ethics and Politics*

Regina Mara Schwartz, *Sacramental Poetics at the Dawn of Secularism: When God Left the World*

Gil Anidjar, *Semites: Race, Religion, Literature*

Ranjana Khanna, *Algeria Cuts: Women and Representation, 1830 to the Present*

Esther Peeren, *Intersubjectivities and Popular Culture: Bakhtin and Beyond*

Eyal Peretz, *Becoming Visionary: Brian De Palma's Cinematic Education of the Senses*

Diana Sorensen, *A Turbulent Decade Remembered: Scenes from the Latin American Sixties*

Hubert Damisch, *A Childhood Memory by Piero della Francesca*

José van Dijck, *Mediated Memories in the Digital Age*

Dana Hollander, *Exemplarity and Chosenness: Rosenzweig and Derrida on the Nation of Philosophy*

Asja Szafraniec, *Beckett, Derrida, and the Event of Literature*

Sara Guyer, *Romanticism After Auschwitz*

Alison Ross, *The Aesthetic Paths of Philosophy: Presentation in Kant, Heidegger, Lacoue-Labarthe, and Nancy*

Gerhard Richter, *Thought-Images: Frankfurt School Writers' Reflections from Damaged Life*

Bella Brodzki, *Can These Bones Live? Translation, Survival, and Cultural Memory*

Rodolphe Gasché, *The Honor of Thinking: Critique, Theory, Philosophy*

Brigitte Peucker, *The Material Image: Art and the Real in Film*

Natalie Melas, *All the Difference in the World: Postcoloniality and the Ends of Comparison*

Jonathan Culler, *The Literary in Theory*

Michael G. Levine, *The Belated Witness: Literature, Testimony, and the Question of Holocaust Survival*

Jennifer A. Jordan, *Structures of Memory: Understanding German Change in Berlin and Beyond*

Christoph Menke, *Reflections of Equality*

Marlène Zarader, *The Unthought Debt: Heidegger and the Hebraic Heritage*

Jan Assmann, *Religion and Cultural Memory: Ten Studies*

David Scott and Charles Hirschkind, *Powers of the Secular Modern: Talal Asad and His Interlocutors*

Gyanendra Pandey, *Routine Violence: Nations, Fragments, Histories*

James Siegel, *Naming the Witch*

J. M. Bernstein, *Against Voluptuous Bodies: Late Modernism and the Meaning of Painting*

Theodore W. Jennings, Jr., *Reading Derrida / Thinking Paul: On Justice*

Richard Rorty and Eduardo Mendieta, *Take Care of Freedom and Truth Will Take Care of Itself: Interviews with Richard Rorty*

Jacques Derrida, *Paper Machine*

Renaud Barbaras, *Desire and Distance: Introduction to a Phenomenology of Perception*

Jill Bennett, *Empathic Vision: Affect, Trauma, and Contemporary Art*

Ban Wang, *Illuminations from the Past: Trauma, Memory, and History in Modern China*

James Phillips, *Heidegger's* Volk: *Between National Socialism and Poetry*

Frank Ankersmit, *Sublime Historical Experience*

István Rév, *Retroactive Justice: Prehistory of Post-Communism*

Paola Marrati, *Genesis and Trace: Derrida Reading Husserl and Heidegger*

Krzysztof Ziarek, *The Force of Art*

Marie-José Mondzain, *Image, Icon, Economy: The Byzantine Origins of the Contemporary Imaginary*

Cecilia Sjöholm, *The Antigone Complex: Ethics and the Invention of Feminine Desire*

Jacques Derrida and Elisabeth Roudinesco, *For What Tomorrow . . . : A Dialogue*

Elisabeth Weber, *Questioning Judaism: Interviews by Elisabeth Weber*

Jacques Derrida and Catherine Malabou, *Counterpath: Traveling with Jacques Derrida*

Martin Seel, *Aesthetics of Appearing*

Nanette Salomon, *Shifting Priorities: Gender and Genre in Seventeenth-Century Dutch Painting*

Jacob Taubes, *The Political Theology of Paul*

Jean-Luc Marion, *The Crossing of the Visible*

Eric Michaud, *The Cult of Art in Nazi Germany*

Anne Freadman, *The Machinery of Talk: Charles Peirce and the Sign Hypothesis*

Stanley Cavell, *Emerson's Transcendental Etudes*

Stuart McLean, *The Event and Its Terrors: Ireland, Famine, Modernity*

Beate Rössler, ed., *Privacies: Philosophical Evaluations*

Bernard Faure, *Double Exposure: Cutting Across Buddhist and Western Discourses*

Alessia Ricciardi, *The Ends of Mourning: Psychoanalysis, Literature, Film*

Alain Badiou, *Saint Paul: The Foundation of Universalism*

Gil Anidjar, *The Jew, the Arab: A History of the Enemy*

Jonathan Culler and Kevin Lamb, eds., *Just Being Difficult? Academic Writing in the Public Arena*

Jean-Luc Nancy, *A Finite Thinking*, edited by Simon Sparks

Theodor W. Adorno, *Can One Live after Auschwitz? A Philosophical Reader*, edited by Rolf Tiedemann

Patricia Pisters, *The Matrix of Visual Culture: Working with Deleuze in Film Theory*

Andreas Huyssen, *Present Pasts: Urban Palimpsests and the Politics of Memory*

Talal Asad, *Formations of the Secular: Christianity, Islam, Modernity*

Dorothea von Mücke, *The Rise of the Fantastic Tale*

Marc Redfield, *The Politics of Aesthetics: Nationalism, Gender, Romanticism*

Emmanuel Levinas, *On Escape*

Dan Zahavi, *Husserl's Phenomenology*

Rodolphe Gasché, *The Idea of Form: Rethinking Kant's Aesthetics*

Michael Naas, *Taking on the Tradition: Jacques Derrida and the Legacies of Deconstruction*

Herlinde Pauer-Studer, ed., *Constructions of Practical Reason: Interviews on Moral and Political Philosophy*

Jean-Luc Marion, *Being Given That: Toward a Phenomenology of Givenness*

Theodor W. Adorno and Max Horkheimer, *Dialectic of Enlightenment*

Ian Balfour, *The Rhetoric of Romantic Prophecy*

Martin Stokhof, *World and Life as One: Ethics and Ontology in Wittgenstein's Early Thought*

Gianni Vattimo, *Nietzsche: An Introduction*

Jacques Derrida, *Negotiations: Interventions and Interviews, 1971-1998*, ed. Elizabeth Rottenberg

Brett Levinson, *The Ends of Literature: The Latin American "Boom" in the Neoliberal Marketplace*

Timothy J. Reiss, *Against Autonomy: Cultural Instruments, Mutualities, and the Fictive Imagination*

Hent de Vries and Samuel Weber, eds., *Religion and Media*

Niklas Luhmann, *Theories of Distinction: Re-Describing the Descriptions of Modernity*, ed. and introd. William Rasch

Johannes Fabian, *Anthropology with an Attitude: Critical Essays*

Michel Henry, *I Am the Truth: Toward a Philosophy of Christianity*

Gil Anidjar, *"Our Place in Al-Andalus": Kabbalah, Philosophy, Literature in Arab-Jewish Letters*

Hélène Cixous and Jacques Derrida, *Veils*

F. R. Ankersmit, *Historical Representation*

F. R. Ankersmit, *Political Representation*

Elissa Marder, *Dead Time: Temporal Disorders in the Wake of Modernity (Baudelaire and Flaubert)*

Reinhart Koselleck, *The Practice of Conceptual History: Timing History, Spacing Concepts*

Niklas Luhmann, *The Reality of the Mass Media*

Hubert Damisch, *A Theory of /Cloud/: Toward a History of Painting*

Jean-Luc Nancy, *The Speculative Remark: (One of Hegel's bon mots)*

Jean-François Lyotard, *Soundproof Room: Malraux's Anti-Aesthetics*

Jan Pato<hac>cka, *Plato and Europe*

Hubert Damisch, *Skyline: The Narcissistic City*

Isabel Hoving, *In Praise of New Travelers: Reading Caribbean Migrant Women Writers*

Richard Rand, ed., *Futures: Of Jacques Derrida*

William Rasch, *Niklas Luhmann's Modernity: The Paradoxes of Differentiation*

Jacques Derrida and Anne Dufourmantelle, *Of Hospitality*

Jean-François Lyotard, *The Confession of Augustine*

Kaja Silverman, *World Spectators*

Samuel Weber, *Institution and Interpretation: Expanded Edition*

Jeffrey S. Librett, *The Rhetoric of Cultural Dialogue: Jews and Germans in the Epoch of Emancipation*

Ulrich Baer, *Remnants of Song: Trauma and the Experience of Modernity in Charles Baudelaire and Paul Celan*

Samuel C. Wheeler III, *Deconstruction as Analytic Philosophy*

David S. Ferris, *Silent Urns: Romanticism, Hellenism, Modernity*

Rodolphe Gasché, *Of Minimal Things: Studies on the Notion of Relation*

Sarah Winter, *Freud and the Institution of Psychoanalytic Knowledge*

Samuel Weber, *The Legend of Freud: Expanded Edition*

Aris Fioretos, ed., *The Solid Letter: Readings of Friedrich Hölderlin*

J. Hillis Miller / Manuel Asensi, *Black Holes / J. Hillis Miller; or, Boustrophedonic Reading*

Miryam Sas, *Fault Lines: Cultural Memory and Japanese Surrealism*

Peter Schwenger, *Fantasm and Fiction: On Textual Envisioning*

Didier Maleuvre, *Museum Memories: History, Technology, Art*

Jacques Derrida, *Monolingualism of the Other; or, The Prosthesis of Origin*

Andrew Baruch Wachtel, *Making a Nation, Breaking a Nation: Literature and Cultural Politics in Yugoslavia*

Niklas Luhmann, *Love as Passion: The Codification of Intimacy*

Mieke Bal, ed., *The Practice of Cultural Analysis: Exposing Interdisciplinary Interpretation*

Jacques Derrida and Gianni Vattimo, eds., *Religion*